ROBERT KENNEDY
In His
Own Words

Given to Jan, on his
birthday, 5/10/89, by Lori Y.
Webster.

ROBERT KENNEDY

In His Own Words

THE UNPUBLISHED RECOLLECTIONS OF THE KENNEDY YEARS

Edited by Edwin O. Guthman
and
Jeffrey Shulman

PUBLISHED IN COOPERATION WITH
TWENTY-FIRST CENTURY BOOKS

A
BANTAM
TRADE
PAPERBACK

BANTAM BOOKS
NEW YORK · TORONTO · LONDON · SYDNEY · AUCKLAND

PHOTOGRAPHS COURTESY OF:

WHITE HOUSE PHOTOGRAPHIC COLLECTION, JOHN F. KENNEDY LIBRARY:
  insert pages 6, top and bottom; 8, top and bottom; 11, top and bottom; 12, top and bottom; 14, top and bottom.
LOOK MAGAZINE PHOTOGRAPH COLLECTION, JOHN F. KENNEDY LIBRARY:
  insert pages 1; 2, top and bottom; 4; 5; 9; 10, top and bottom; 13, bottom; 15, bottom.
OLLIE ATKINS PHOTOGRAPHIC COLLECTION, SPECIAL COLLECTION AND ARCHIVES, GEORGE MASON UNIVERSITY, FAIRFAX, VIRGINIA:
  insert pages 3; 15, top; 16.
UPI/BETTMANN NEWSPHOTOS:
  insert pages 7; 13, top.

ROBERT KENNEDY: IN HIS OWN WORDS
A Bantam Book
Bantam hardcover edition / June 1988
3 printings through June 1988
Bantam trade edition / May 1989

Cover photograph courtesy of: The Ollie Atkins Collection, Photographic Collection, Special Collections Archives, George Mason University, Fairfax, Virginia

ISBN 0-553-34661-X

Published simultaneously in the United States and Canada

PRINTED IN THE UNITED STATES OF AMERICA

FG   0 9 8 7 6 5 4 3 2 1

ACKNOWLEDGMENTS

We welcome the opportunity to thank the people who made this book possible:

First and foremost, Mrs. Robert F. Kennedy, for her generosity in donating to the Robert F. Kennedy Memorial the rights to publish these materials.

On behalf of the Robert F. Kennedy Memorial: John Douglas, Stephen Smith, John Seigenthaler, John Nolan, and Ken Ludwig.

We are especially appreciative of the generosity of Anthony Lewis, Arthur Schlesinger, and John Steward for their permission to publish their interviews. Permissions were also graciously granted by Mark and Bill Martin, the sons of the late John Bartlow Martin, to publish their father's interviews; and by Burke Marshall to publish his interview with Robert Kennedy on civil rights.

Lee Fentress
Chairman of the Board of Trustees
The Robert F. Kennedy Memorial

At the John F. Kennedy Library: Betsy Crawford, Susan D'Entremont, Megan F. Desnoyers, Allan Goodrich, Susan Lindsey, Amy Spence, Cindy Stocking. I am grateful for the efforts of Henry Gwiazda who directed the difficult task of retranscribing the oral history tapes with great professionalism and met the equally difficult task of meeting repeated requests for more material with great patience.

At Twenty-First Century Books: Mary Ahmed, Anne Craft, Darla Treat-Courtney, Martha Jones, Rosemary Orthmann, Michael Moscato, Sharon Phelps, Peter Sandler, Gretchen Super, and Ruth Thomson. Special thanks are due to John Moscato, founder of Twenty-First Century Books.

I also want to thank Rachel Spring and Sarah Courage Shulman. I hope when they are old enough to read this book, they will appreciate the life and career of the man it honors.

Jeffrey Shulman
Twenty-First Century Books

CONTENTS

THE INTERVIEWERS

ANTHONY LEWIS, twice winner of the Pulitzer Prize, is a columnist for *The New York Times*. Born in New York City on March 27, 1927, Lewis worked for the Sunday Department of the *Times* from 1948 to 1952. He joined the Washington bureau of the *Times* in 1955, covering the Supreme Court, the Justice Department, and other legal matters. He is the author of two books: *Gideon's Trumpet*, about a landmark Supreme Court case, and *Portrait of a Decade*, about the great changes in American race relations. Having taught at a number of universities, Lewis has held the James Madison Visiting Professorship at Columbia University since 1983.

JOHN BARTLOW MARTIN, 1915–1987, born in Hamilton, Ohio, a career journalist and diplomat, was professor of journalism at Northwestern University. He had been a visiting professor and fellow at Wesleyan University, Princeton University, and the City University of New York. From 1962 to 1964, Martin was Ambassador to the Dominican Republic. He worked for Robert Kennedy and, after Kennedy's death, for Hubert Humphrey in their 1968 election bids. He wrote numerous books, including *The Deep South Says Never, Overtaken By Events, The Life of Adlai Stevenson*, and *U.S. Policy in the Caribbean*. His interviews are published with the kind permission of his sons, Dan and Fred Martin.

ARTHUR M. SCHLESINGER, JR., born October 15, 1917, in Columbus, Ohio, holds the Albert Schweitzer Chair in the Humanities at the City University of New York. The recipient of two Pulitzer Prizes (in both history and biography), the Francis Parkman Prize, the Bancroft Prize, and other awards, Schlesinger is the author of numerous books, including *The Age of Jackson, A Thousand Days: John F. Kennedy in the White House, The Imperial Presidency, Robert Kennedy and His Times*, and *The Cycles of American History*. Active in the 1960 Kennedy presidential campaign, Schlesinger was a Special Assistant to the President from 1961 to 1964. He later served as a campaign adviser to Robert Kennedy in 1968.

JOHN FRANCIS STEWART, born December 15, 1932, in Bedford, Massachusetts, was chief of the Oral History Project at the John F. Kennedy Library from 1966 to 1969. From 1971 to 1976, Stewart was the Library's chief archivist, and from 1969 to 1971, and again from 1986 to 1987 he was acting director of the Kennedy Library. Currently director of education at the Library, he is also a member of the Society of American Archivists and the Oral History Association. Stewart is also active in community and political affairs. He has been twice elected to the City of Newton Board of Alderman, in 1975 and 1987.

EDITORIAL NOTE

In 1964, 1965, and 1967 as part of the oral history program of the John F. Kennedy Library, an extensive series of interviews was conducted with Robert F. Kennedy. Until 1987, only a rough transcript of these interviews existed. That transcript has been available to the public at the Library. In cooperation with this publication, the archivists at the John F. Kennedy Library have re-edited this transcript to ensure complete fidelity to the original tape recordings. These interviews are now being published for the first time.

This text is based on the verbatim transcript. The editors have not attempted, however, to reproduce the verbatim transcript in its entirety. This transcript contains, for example, some interruptions—phones ringing, dogs barking, and children singing. There are some passages, moreover, where Robert Kennedy repeats the same account of events to two different interviewers; and when the accounts are redundant, we have chosen the richer and more substantial one for inclusion. Ellipses have been used to indicate where material has not been reproduced in this publication. Brackets have been used to indicate editorial additions such as identifying notes.

We have attempted to reproduce the transcript with the same fidelity to the original recordings shown in the verbatim transcript. To do so, the editors have allowed for occasional awkwardness in style, expression, and syntax. However, where the process of interviewing obscures Robert Kennedy's meaning or impedes the flow of his answers, we have undertaken the editing needed to clarify the text and render it readable without the obtrusion of ellipses and brackets.

Edwin O. Guthman
University of Southern California

Jeffrey Shulman
Twenty-First Century Books

FOREWORD

History is filled with might-have-beens (historians more solemnly call them counterfactual propositions), and an irresistible speculation for a student of contemporary America is what would have happened if Robert Kennedy had not been assassinated in Los Angeles in 1968.

No one can tell where roads not taken might have led. Yet the probability is that Robert Kennedy would have gone on from his victory in the California primary to win the Democratic nomination for President and that he would have beaten Richard Nixon in the general election.

A Robert Kennedy presidency would have changed a number of things. It would have meant an earlier withdrawal of American troops from Vietnam, perhaps in 1969 rather than in 1972—and many Americans (and many more Vietnamese) killed in those years might be alive today. It would also have meant a culmination of the reform phase of the political cycle, consolidating and extending the achievements of John Kennedy's New Frontier and Lyndon Johnson's Great Society.

The liberal tide of the 1960s was still running strong enough in 1969 to shape even Richard Nixon's domestic program (the Environmental Protection Act, the Occupational Safety and Health Act, the Comprehensive Employment and Training Act with its CETA employment program were all enacted under Nixon); and it would have given a reform President signal opportunities. The confidence that both white and black working-class Americans had in Robert Kennedy created the possibility of continued progress toward racial justice; and his appeal to the young might have mitigated some of the under-thirty excesses of the period. And, of course, the election of Robert Kennedy in 1968 would have delivered the republic from Watergate with its attendant perversion of the Constitution and destruction of faith in government.

Might-have-been propositions are exercises in fantasy. But the existence of a political personality vital and creative enough to bear the weight of such speculation is an arresting fact. Most Americans who remember the '60s, even those (and there were many) who disliked Robert Kennedy, would very likely agree that he would have made a difference as President. He was a man of passionate conviction, carrying a message of change and, for the forlorn and dispossessed of America, a message of hope. He was also a tough and experienced party politician who knew the ways, and byways, of all three branches of the national government. And he was a compelling campaigner with the capacity to inform and inspire the electorate, or at least large sections thereof, and to rally popular support for his policies.

The Robert Kennedy who emerged as a liberal leader in the 1960s could not have been easily predicted by those who knew him in earlier years. He was born on November 20, 1925, in Brookline, Massachusetts, the seventh child in the famously spirited, closely knit, and highly competitive Kennedy family. He was the smallest of the boys, the least coordinated physically, the least articulate, the most gentle and dutiful. His father was sometimes impatient with the little boy; and the contrast with his commanding older brothers—Joseph, Jr., and John—doubtless increased feelings of inadequacy. "I was the seventh of nine children," he later recalled, "and when you come from that far down you have to struggle to survive."

He went to Milton Academy and, after wartime service in the Navy, to Harvard. School was a struggle for survival, too, and he concentrated more on sports than on scholarship. Perhaps more important for his education was the Kennedy dinner table, where the parents systematically involved the children in discussions of history and public affairs. "I can hardly remember a mealtime," Robert Kennedy once said, "when the conversation was not dominated by what Franklin D. Roosevelt was doing or what was happening in the world."

Striving to win his father's approval and love, he began to harden his personality. The inner sensitivity and vulnerability remained, but a protective covering formed over it. He became in these years the Robert Kennedy who burst on public notice in the 1950s: a cocky young fellow, opinionated, censorious, rigid, moralistic, prickly, disposed to tell people off and to get into heated arguments.

He irritated old-line Irish pols in Massachusetts when he managed his brother's successful campaign for the Senate in 1952; and he irritated liberals when he went to work for the Senate committee headed by Joseph McCarthy, already notorious for his reckless accusations of Communist infiltration in government. However, the one assignment Kennedy carried out for McCarthy—an investigation of the trade between America's NATO Allies and Communist China during the Korean War—was conducted in a factual manner and at no point implied, in the McCarthy style, that traitors were making American foreign policy. Disturbed by McCarthy's hit-and-run tactics, Kennedy resigned from the staff after six months. In 1954 he returned as counsel for the Democratic minority, in which capacity he wrote the minority report condemning McCarthy's investigation of alleged Communists in the Army. His later work as chief counsel for the Senate Rackets Committee investigating racketeering in trade unions won him the friendship of honest labor leaders like Walter Reuther of the United Auto Workers and the undying enmity of Jimmy Hoffa of the Teamsters. It also confirmed his reputation as an able but "ruthless" prosecutor.

In 1960 he was the tireless, intimidating, and coldly effective manager of John Kennedy's presidential campaign. After the election, John Kennedy persuaded his reluctant younger brother to become Attorney General in the new administration. As he had earlier revised his identity to please his father, he now subordinated his identity to serve his brother. Though nearly nine years separated them in age, the two brothers could hardly have been closer. Under John's humanizing influence, Robert began to lose his intolerance and rigidity. He grew relaxed and rueful, acquired more ironic views of life, developed his wry, self-mocking humor, and in time displayed a charm against which newspaper editors soon warned their reporters.

Yet, united by so many indestructible bonds, the two brothers were still different men. John Kennedy was urbane, objective, controlled, a man of reason; Robert was brusque, subjective, intense, a man of emotion. The older brother mistrusted passion; the younger trusted his passions. John Kennedy was, in the end, a realist disguised as a romantic; Robert, a romantic disguised as a realist.

Robert Kennedy describes his role in politics and the Kennedy administration in the interviews that follow. Oral history is an application to scholarship of interview techniques long familiar to journalism. As with any interview, much depends on the interviewer, who must sufficiently acquaint himself with his subject to know what questions to ask—and what answers to question. Even with expert interviewers, oral history can be no better than memory, and we all know there is little that is more self-serving than memory. Yet historians rarely hesitate to draw on diaries, letters, and memoirs, which are no less self-serving.

Oral history rescues, for the critical eye of the future scholar, evidence that would otherwise perish with the witness. With all its limitations, it is a powerful means of enriching the record.

After the murder of President Kennedy, Robert Kennedy saw at once the importance of gathering the recollections of those who had known and worked with his brother. A Kennedy-style campaign was organized to conduct interviews while memories were still vivid. The result is the large and valuable oral history collection at the Kennedy Library in Boston.

Having sponsored the campaign, Robert Kennedy had to set an example by submitting to interviews himself. This he did, as is observed in the introductions to the texts, with good grace but during a very difficult period in his life. He was still in shock after his brother's death—hurt, angry, distracted, abrupt, frustrated, abnormally sensitive to implied criticism of the Kennedy administration. His conversational style was always laconic; and, in these months of preoccupation and melancholy, terseness became a means of dealing with questions that in other moods he would have answered in detail. Pain robbed him of some of those flashes of self-deprecating wit that usually balanced his judgments of people and events. In the course of these long and exacting interviews he made drastic comments, especially on personalities, that he might well have modified had he had the chance to reconsider them in tranquillity. It has seemed better to let these comments stand. The reader will understand his anguish of 1964 and will set his brusque words against the totality of his life.

John Kennedy's death devastated him. For weeks and months he wandered in grief. Yet, in a paradoxical sense, it liberated him too—to become a voice and a leader in his own right. He had repressed his inner self since childhood, first to prove himself to his father, then to help his brother. In 1961 his father was hopelessly disabled by a stroke; in 1963 his brother was murdered. At last Robert Kennedy was on his own.

Two themes absorbed him in his last years. One was the quest for peace—an end to the senseless war in Vietnam and new initiatives to bring the nuclear arms race under control. The other was an agonized sense that the disparities of power and opportunity in American society were acute and becoming intolerable. Such conditions, he would say in speech after speech, were "not acceptable"—and need not be accepted, and we diminished ourselves as a moral community when we accepted them.

He never stopped learning and growing, in insight and in sympathy. He grew because he possessed to an uncommon degree what T. S. Eliot called an "experiencing nature": a capacity to perceive and respond to the turbulence of the world around him. Now, he identified himself increasingly with the desolate and injured people of America: Indians on reservations, Chicanos picking grapes in California, hungry blacks along the Mississippi delta, migrant workers in filthy camps in upstate New York, families in rat-infested tenements in New York City. "Today, in America," he said, "we are two worlds."

The climax came in 1968 when, after much vacillation, he decided to run for President. It was an uproarious campaign, filled with enthusiasm and fun. One newspaperman described it as a "huge, joyous adventure." It was also a campaign moving in its sweep and passion. Many people saw him as a divisive figure. Indeed, he embodied a rude challenge to the complacencies of American life. But Kennedy saw himself as on a journey of reconciliation, seeking to bridge the great schisms in American society—between white and nonwhite, between rich and poor, between young and old, between order and dissent. Born the son of wealth, he died a champion of outcasts of the world.

The themes of Robert Kennedy's life came to seem exotic amid the conservatism of the 1980s. Perhaps they were not obsolete—only out of fashion. American politics seems to flow in thirty-year cycles between times dominated by public purpose and times dominated by private interest. The 1980s, like the 1950s and the 1920s, were a time where private action and private enterprise were deemed the best way to meet national problems. But private-interest eras do not go on forever. Rest replenishes the national energies; problems neglected demand remedy; greed, as the point of existence, seems inadequate. After a time people begin to ask not what their country can do for them but what they can do for their country.

Soon the dam will break, as it broke at the turn of the century, again in the 1930s, again in the 1960s. Sometime around the year 1990, if the rhythm holds, we can expect a breakthrough into a new and generous epoch in American life. When this time comes, the Kennedy ideals will no longer seem exotic. And the republic will remember, too, the conviction by which Robert Kennedy lived, the conviction that infused hope into the excluded and powerless in American society—the intense conviction that an individual can make a difference to the life of his times. As Robert Kennedy said at Capetown in South Africa in 1966: "It is from numberless diverse acts of courage and belief that human history is shaped. Each time a man stands up for an ideal, or acts to improve the lot of others, or strikes out against injustice, he sends a tiny ripple of hope, and crossing each other from a million different centers of energy and daring, these ripples will build a current which can sweep down the mightiest walls of oppression and resistance."

Arthur M. Schlesinger, Jr.
January, 1988

PART I

■

STAFFING
THE
NEW FRONTIER

INTRODUCTION

For anyone who knew Robert Kennedy well—whether they worked with him or against him—there is only one way to introduce this book, and that is to say: "That's Robert Kennedy giving his recollections and his opinions while well aware he was speaking for posterity."

The interviews that follow were conducted at a difficult point in Robert Kennedy's life. Beginning on February 29, 1964, and continuing episodically through February 27, 1965, they show him at a time when he was picking up the pieces of his life, both personally and in public service, after the terrible shock and loss that he, his family, and the world sustained on November 22, 1963, when his brother, John F. Kennedy, was assassinated.

Robert Kennedy knew the impact a particular individual can have on his country and the world. The business of running the government, that public trust, "should be placed in the best possible hands," he said. In Part I of *Robert Kennedy: In His Own Words*, RFK reviews the personnel decisions that led to the formation of the Kennedy administration: the Cabinet, the selection of Lyndon Johnson as running mate, the State Department, and elsewhere. He is interviewed separately by Arthur M. Schlesinger, Jr., an eminent historian who served as Special Assistant to President Kennedy, and John Bartlow Martin, a distinguished journalist who served as JFK's Ambassador to the Dominican Republic.

It was especially difficult in those months shortly after the President's death, and even in the years that were left to him, for Robert Kennedy to talk about his brother, to talk about the trials and triumphs they shared so deeply. Nevertheless, he responded fully to the questions that were asked him. It was a time when the events that he and his brother faced were fresh in his memory.

His interviewers frequently asked Kennedy for his personal views about people in the administration and abroad, and he answered candidly, even pungently, as he was wont to do. Those characterizations are interesting in themselves and often give as much insight into aspects of his personality and method of operation as they do of the person about whom he is talking. But the far greater value of this oral history will be found in the reflections on the problems and difficulties—and complexities—of governing and finding sensible solutions to both longstanding problems and sudden emergencies.

Robert Kennedy was not yet forty years old when these interviews were conducted. Having been tested over and over in a series of uphill struggles, beginning with his brother's first race for Congress in 1946, he was an experienced administrator and an inspirational leader. It is hard to read his words and not be amazed at the responsibilities he undertook outside his duties as Attorney General. He was amazed himself: "I was involved in more things," he commented, "than I thought."

This book covers many of the principal players and the main events of the Kennedy years, as well as some nooks and crannies too often overlooked. *Robert Kennedy: In His Own Words* is important as a highly placed insider's account and as the recollections of a courageous, spirited activist who served his brother and the cause of freedom with unwavering commitment.

INTERVIEW WITH
ARTHUR M. SCHLESINGER, JR.

■

WASHINGTON, D.C., FEBRUARY 27, 1965

THE DEPARTMENT OF STATE AND FOREIGN AFFAIRS

SCHLESINGER: Let's talk about the Cabinet. Let's begin with the Secretary of State. The President had only one conversation with [Dean] Rusk before he made up his mind?

KENNEDY: That's right. Yes.

SCHLESINGER: Do you remember any of his [JFK's] reactions to that talk?

KENNEDY: I don't think it went very long, really. I think, finally, it had come down to Rusk, and he was reasonably impressed with Rusk. But I don't remember any particular reaction to Rusk. It finally had come down to where everybody else had been eliminated—and Rusk was left. Bob Lovett [a Kennedy adviser on foreign policy] had refused.

SCHLESINGER: Why was Bruce eliminated? Probably age? [David E. Bruce, Ambassador to Great Britain, was then past sixty.]

KENNEDY: I thought that. It seems to me it was age. Just the fact that he was a tired figure who was being brought back in. Nobody was very enthusiastic for him. That's what I remember: age. I don't know if there were some individuals against him, also. I think it was age.

SCHLESINGER: When did you first meet Rusk?

KENNEDY: Just when he came up for the appointment. I don't remember particularly when I met the rest of the members of the Cabinet.

SCHLESINGER: Of course, [Chester] Bowles was in as Under Secretary. That was fairly well agreed upon.

KENNEDY: Yes. It was kind of a political obligation. Bowles, of course, wanted to be Secretary of State.

SCHLESINGER: On [Adlai] Stevenson, I imagine the President had fairly well excluded him a long time before.

KENNEDY: Yes. He wasn't even considered. He was so unpleasant at the time we offered him Ambassador to the United Nations. The conversation with Stevenson at President Kennedy's home was very unpleasant. The President really disliked him. [Stevenson] was so concerned about what he was going to do and what his role was going to be and whether he'd take the position or not that the President almost withdrew it. He said he'd have to think about it for twenty-four hours. He was very unpleasant. . . .

SCHLESINGER: He wanted to know who the Secretary of State was.

KENNEDY: The President was so pleased that he hadn't taken him as Secretary of State. It confirmed all he thought about Stevenson. He was really disgusted with him.

SCHLESINGER: Do you know that for a moment he considered Stevenson for Attorney General?

KENNEDY: I think that's probably true.

SCHLESINGER: He asked me about it, and I called up Bill Blair [then Stevenson's law partner, later Ambassador to Denmark and to the Philippines]. I discouraged him. I didn't think that Stevenson would be interested in it or that he would be an appropriate man for it.

How soon did the President begin to find problems in the State Department? Was it the Bay of Pigs [the CIA-sponsored invasion of Cuba in April 1961 by anti-Castro exiles] or was it the Laos situation?

KENNEDY: The Bay of Pigs was the indication. There was an effort thereafter to organize it [the State Department]. That arose to some extent from our investigation of the Bay of Pigs and to some extent from the realization of what had occurred in the Bay of Pigs even before our investigation was finished: lack of coordination between the various departments, the failure of heads of agencies and departments to work together, the failure to discuss some of these problems together and consider all sides of them.

Right after the Bay of Pigs, for instance, we were involved with

Laos and involved in Vietnam. And I suggested we appoint a task force, and that Ros Gilpatric [Deputy Secretary of Defense] head it up, to go into Laos; and that one person be charged with responsibility for all governmental agencies and departments in a particular field, so that the President could look to one person for making sure that the plans were drawn up. The whole idea of task forces with one person having the areas of responsibility arose out of the Bay of Pigs.

SCHLESINGER: Actually, wasn't the Laos task force before the Bay of Pigs?

KENNEDY: I don't know whether there was a task force, but I mean for one person to have the responsibility—[that idea] was after the Bay of Pigs. I remember the conversation in President Kennedy's office because at that time he thought about having me do it and go out to Laos. Ros Gilpatric was appointed. I think Paul Nitze then headed up another one. That ordinarily—under the right circumstances—should be done by the Secretary of State and the Department of State. They are in a position to bring other government agencies into discussions and try to work out a program. But that was never done by Rusk. He never took that kind of initiative.

SCHLESINGER: I always felt the President was very perplexed by Rusk, because he is a nice man in many ways, an intelligent man who always knew the technical details of issues.

KENNEDY: He spoke well. I know at meetings, for instance, if you were discussing a subject and if the President would come in a half hour late, he could summarize everybody's point of view in about two and a half minutes and do it in a very articulate, bright fashion. But as far as focusing attention on what should be done himself, sticking with his guns, knowing the facts and having developed them himself in the Department of State, and being prepared—he didn't have that. He was always going to meetings, it appeared to me, without his mind completely made up—ready to listen to all kinds of arguments and discussions—and then developing his mind as to what our position might be at the meeting. He was tremendously influenced by what the President wanted to do and adjusted himself accordingly. He didn't have any strong point of view that this was the right thing to do and was then prepared to argue about that position—very, very seldom. And by the time 1963 came along he almost never did. . . . At one time he said, "I've been trying to act the position of a dumb dodo during these discussions"—which I thought was a strange way of putting it. . . .

SCHLESINGER: Whom did the President rely on most in the State Department?

KENNEDY: He used to say to me he very seldom ever received an idea from the State Department—an original idea—as to how matters should be handled. Secondly, every paper that was written by the State Department, he had to rewrite. We often used to talk about the fact that what he had in the White House was really a small State Department. They [the State Department] might do some of the mechanics, but as far as really accomplishing a great deal—coming up with any ideas as to what our policy should be, even writing notes—I mean the letters to Khrushchev and the other major communications with De Gaulle all had to be done or redone by the President or somebody over at the White House. That disgusted him.

He was, of course, very impressed with what Averell Harriman did at the time of the [nuclear] test ban treaty and his outstanding negotiations. But then he was very unhappy with Averell Harriman and his handling of the Vietnam matter and, particularly, this rather precipitous action in that famous weekend[1] where there was this letter sent to the President which he approved. We had a conversation, he and I, on Monday about what was being done, and I in the meantime talked to Maxwell Taylor [Chairman of the Joint Chiefs of Staff] and Bob McNamara [Secretary of Defense] about what was going to be done in Vietnam—the fact that nobody was behind it, nobody knew what we were going to do, nobody knew really what our policy was. It hadn't been discussed, as everything else had been discussed since the Bay of Pigs, in full detail before we did anything. Nothing like that had been done before the decision was made on Diem. And so, by Tuesday, we were trying to pull away from that policy. That's what caused the great difficulty. From then on it was felt that Averell Harriman hadn't handled that well, nor had Mike Forrestal [Presidential Assistant for Far Eastern Affairs], or some of the others. The President was not happy about that.

SCHLESINGER: Averell pushed too fast?

KENNEDY: Too fast, yes. . . .

SCHLESINGER: How about [Under Secretary of State] George Ball?

KENNEDY: The President didn't feel he had any organizational ability. That was the great problem about the State Department. He thought [Ball] was able enough but didn't have any rapport with him particularly. He wasn't really a major factor. I had so many dealings with the State Department myself after the Bay of Pigs and knew what was going on probably a good deal over there and a great number of the problems. We tried different ways of organization and sent [Assistant Attorney General] Bill Orrick over from the Department of Justice, and that didn't work out successfully. I always felt, if you had somebody who was a really good organizer, you could do something with the State Department.

The State Department really came down to four sections:

1. The Secretary of State who should deal with the major crises that were going on in the world—which during most of our time were Berlin, Vietnam, Southeast Asia, Cuba, sometimes Latin America, and the Berlin Wall. That really took full time to develop a policy and your ongoing position. Then there were all the small crises that would arise, whether it was going to be Zanzibar or whether it was going to be Peru or whatever it might be. The Secretary of State should be focusing on major matters that would be coming to his attention and the smaller crises that were always arising. And that really took a full-time Secretary of State.

2. Then you had a Secretary of State who should in some way administer the Department of State—not a difficult administrative problem, but there should be somebody who would do that.

3. Then you had a Secretary of State who should be receiving ambassadors, a hundred or so ambassadors always wanting to visit. They should have somebody who is going to talk to them, listen to them, hold their hand, listen to their problems, and do the social part, go to dinners—and do that function. That's a full-time Secretary of State.

4. And then you should have a Secretary of State who handles ninety other countries all over the world which aren't in crisis but which should receive attention to follow up on matters.

Well, if you don't have it well organized, the Secretary of State doesn't have all those functions, those four which are really full-time operations. If he doesn't have them well organized, then the whole situation is going to deteriorate. What happened, as far as the Department of State is concerned, is that Dean Rusk didn't organize it. . . .

What was needed, therefore, was a tough administrator who could just run the Department. [Under Secretary] George McGhee was over there and he was supposed to do that, but he was useless. In every conversation you had with him, you couldn't possibly understand what he was saying. I was involved with him a good deal in 1962, and it was just impossible. Finally, I talked to the President at his birthday. I guess it was '62. He said, "If you feel so strongly" —George McGhee was a good friend of Dean Rusk—"why don't you go see Dean Rusk and ask him to get rid of him?"

So I went with Brumus [RFK's dog] one Saturday morning and said I thought it was discouraging. I gave [Rusk] some examples of the fact that George McGhee didn't know what he was doing, that we needed organization on a lot of potentials. For instance—at the time this disgusted me—the Russians exploded their bomb and there was no protest around the world, and if we do anything, they are throwing bricks through our windows. I just thought there were a lot of things that we could do—things that should be thought about— about the organization of the State Department. It should be established in such a way that we could take advantage of a lot of things. George McGhee couldn't. You'd have a conversation with him, and he was just useless, worthless.

Dean Rusk said, "You don't think this is perhaps personal?"

I said no, it wasn't personal. I gave him three or four examples.

He said he would take it under consideration.

Well, finally, George McGhee was shipped off. But unless you have the control and the domination and the push at the top, it is difficult. And George Ball was not a good administrator. Averell Harriman, of course, performed the kinds of functions that he performed tremendously well, and the President was very pleased with what he did in Laos and, as I say, the test ban treaty. He thought very highly of that. He didn't think highly, really, of any other people in the State Department.

SCHLESINGER: Did he have any people in mind?

KENNEDY: I think he thought he would appoint Bob McNamara. Bob McNamara, under President Kennedy, would have been a good Secretary of State. Under Lyndon Johnson, I'm not so certain he would be a good Secretary of State. But he would have been good under President Kennedy because President Kennedy knew so much about it himself that it would be well organized and he could make the major decisions himself. As a matter of fact, McNamara was almost functioning in both roles by 1963 due to the fact that the

State Department and Rusk virtually gave up its operation, delivered himself of it and the responsibility.

SCHLESINGER: What happened in that meeting [at the White House, April 19, 1961] after Cuba with Bowles? Do you remember?

KENNEDY: You mean Chester Bowles and me?

SCHLESINGER: Yes.

KENNEDY: Chester Bowles came up to me and said, "I hope everybody knows that I was always against the Bay of Pigs." And I just said that I thought it was a helluva thing to say now that this decision had been made, and as far as this administration was concerned, he should keep his mouth shut and remember that he was *for* the Bay of Pigs.

SCHLESINGER: Bowles, I think, played a useful role in the appointments of ambassadors and so on.

KENNEDY: Very, very. He was very good at that. He put a lot of good people in. And I like Chester Bowles. I think he has that weakness that he was so interested in himself. And he pushed himself. He pushed himself in a way that was unpleasant—which is just what you shouldn't do as far as President Kennedy's people were concerned. He handled himself personally just the wrong, wrong way.

SCHLESINGER: But the reasons why he was removed were other than that? They had to do, again, with an inability to organize the Department, I gather.

KENNEDY: Yes. But I think his appointments and suggestions of ambassadors were the best that they had. He was primarily responsible for some of the good ones.

SCHLESINGER: He worked very hard at that, I think. I think he did a very good job.

KENNEDY: Yes.

SCHLESINGER: You mentioned one thing that happened after the Bay of Pigs, and that was the establishment of the task forces with one man responsible for coming up with something. The other consequence was that Maxwell Taylor came to the White House.

KENNEDY: And that made a helluva difference. We reoriented our whole strategic thinking. We had been affected tremendously by his book, *The Uncertain Trumpet*.[2]

SCHLESINGER: Had you and the President known Maxwell Taylor before?

KENNEDY: No.

SCHLESINGER: So your first close association was in the Cuba investigation?

KENNEDY: Right. I don't know if the President had ever met him. I didn't know him.

SCHLESINGER: The President had read the book through?

KENNEDY: Yes. I'd read the book too. And I really liked him. We worked closely for four months, every day for three or four months, however long it was. And we made certain recommendations, major recommendations, regarding the establishment of a group that would look to the future and prepare for the future—which would be a committee operating with the State Department, a permanent committee to deal with those crises instead of an *ad hoc* committee that would be established every time a crisis came along. It was never accepted, because the State Department didn't want it; they had visions of competition with the State Department itself.

SCHLESINGER: Would you say that the report of the Taylor group [on the Bay of Pigs failure][3] led to the counterinsurgency thing?

KENNEDY: The Counterinsurgency Committee?[4]

SCHLESINGER: Yes.

KENNEDY: Yes. That was one result of it. The second result, really, was that the Bay of Pigs and our investigation led to a reorganization. It would have evolved in any case, but the Bay of Pigs and our investigation stimulated some more clear-cut lines of authority. Everybody was going to President Kennedy directly. That was a mistake. Mac Bundy [Special Assistant to the President for National Security Affairs] should have had more primary responsibility to people reporting through him and with him. President Kennedy could still talk to these people directly.

The State Department wouldn't accept the idea of this one committee that would deal with problems continuously. So there were other task forces appointed as we went along. Out of that, for instance, came the idea of the ExComm committee [the Executive Committee of the National Security Council].[5] The National Security Council was worthless as far as dealing with any problems. I mean, you've got to make up your mind and then get the concurrence of the National Security Council. If you don't want the National Security Council trying to decide, you have to decide before you go in to the National Security Council.

The Bay of Pigs was the best thing that happened to the administration, because if it hadn't been for the Bay of Pigs, we would have sent troops into Laos.

SCHLESINGER: You think it was that close?

KENNEDY: Yes, because the military wanted to send them in. And President Kennedy, based on the Bay of Pigs, started asking questions that were not asked at the Bay of Pigs and making [the Joint Chiefs of Staff] go back. For instance, one time they wanted to send troops into two airports in Laos. We could land troops, and it would make a major difference. We could take over this part of the area.

So the President said, "How many troops?"

And they said they could land one thousand troops a day—and so that was fine.

Then [JFK] started asking questions. He said, "How many troops do the Pathet Lao [the Communist guerrillas in Laos] have?"

They said that they had five thousand.

So he said, "Now what kind of an airport is that?" And it turned out that the airports could be used only during the day. So then he said, "How long would it take to get troops overland to these strips?"

And they said, "Fifteen days or so." I don't remember the exact time.

So he said, "What happens if the Pathet Lao allow you to land troops for two days at both airports and then they bomb the airports? Then what are you going to do?"

Well, they said, they really hadn't thought about that.

SCHLESINGER: I had the impression that the President was more disappointed in the Chiefs after the Bay of Pigs than any other body.

KENNEDY: Yes, I think that's true. Certainly I was. Their advice during the spring and fall of 1961 about Laos and Vietnam and the guerrillas was not at all helpful. Maxwell Taylor made such a big difference. He had some sense. He could see the whole perspective. They just wanted to go in and drop bombs on people. Even after the Cuban missile crisis, two of the Chiefs of Staff were really mad. One of them suggested that we go and bomb them anyway on Monday, and the other one said, "We've been sold out."

SCHLESINGER: Oh, really?

KENNEDY: LeMay [Air Force Chief of Staff] and Anderson [Chief of Naval Operations]. That's really the major reason why the President got rid of Anderson.

SCHLESINGER: What was the President's feeling about [CIA Director Allen] Dulles?

KENNEDY: He liked him. Thought he was a real gentleman, handled himself well. There were, obviously, so many mistakes made at the time of the Bay of Pigs that it wasn't appropriate that he should stay on. And he always took the blame. He was a real gentleman. [JFK] thought very highly of him.

SCHLESINGER: I had the impression John McCone [Dulles's successor at the CIA] did a pretty good job.

KENNEDY: I think he probably did. He has not the loyalty that, for instance, Bob McNamara has. He is very careful of his own position. That's how he's been able to survive so many years in Washington. And that's why there was so much bitterness between Bob McNamara and John McCone in 1963. Because McCone was testifying, trying to protect his own position as to why they didn't know there were any missiles in Cuba earlier and didn't warn about what the problem was—being a real hawk. This was creating a political embarrassment for President Kennedy and [building] some kind of support for [Senator Kenneth] Keating's position.[6] McNamara, on the other hand, who went up in order to avoid the embarrassment to President Kennedy, went too far by acting as if Cuba was no problem whatsoever. He was saying it [was] not even a base for subversion of Latin America. Of course, that was disproved, and the result was that there was a conflict and a good deal of bitterness between the two of them. And President Kennedy became involved in the middle.

I had a very good personal relationship with John McCone, so we were able to keep it under control somewhat. He liked Ethel very much because, when his wife died, Ethel went over and stayed with him. So he had a good deal of feeling for us, and I think he liked the President very much. But he liked one person more—and that was John McCone.

SCHLESINGER: How much validity is there to John's feeling that he forecast the possibility of missiles in Cuba?

KENNEDY: None. I wasn't present at the meeting, but he said, evidently at some internal meeting, that he thought it was strange that the Cubans would put in SAM [surface-to-air missile] sites and that we should be alert to that. As far as ever putting anything in writing, as far as ever communicating this thought to President Kennedy or to anybody else, he didn't. And to indicate the fact that he wasn't really concerned about it himself, he went to Europe for a honeymoon for a month during that period of time. If he was so concerned and thought that something should be done, number one, he should have written and told the President; number two, he should not have gone off to Europe for a month during that critical period of time.

Now, at the end, when they were saying, "Why didn't you know there were missiles in Cuba?" then he came back and said, "Well, I had a feeling there were missiles in Cuba." Nobody pressed him sufficiently, really. That was what was picked up in newspapers, et cetera: John McCone thought there might be missiles in Cuba. If John McCone thought there must be missiles in Cuba, President Kennedy must have known what John McCone thought, and President Kennedy ignored this warning by John McCone! Therefore, Ken Keating was right.

See, that's the whole thing: John McCone then became identified with Ken Keating—warning President Kennedy, and President Kennedy wasn't doing anything about it. That's what distressed the President during this period. John McCone was not apt to say, "I didn't tell anybody." It was just sort of left as "I thought there were missiles in Cuba." And he was among friends up there because congressmen were saying, "Well, John, you thought there were missiles in Cuba. Why didn't they do something about it?"

SCHLESINGER: This sort of thing, then, he just sort of threw off in a conversation as a speculative possibility.

KENNEDY: I never even heard about it, and I used to see him all the time. It was certainly never communicated to the President. It was never communicated to anybody in any definitive form during that period of time. There was no question about that. And to show, really, his failure to feel this matter strongly himself, he was in Europe that month—and then he went off to California. You know, I like John McCone, but he created this feeling in Congress. He had a sympathetic hearing because, for political reasons, this made some sense: President Kennedy knowing; Ken Keating knowing; John McCone, you know; [news commentator] Fulton Lewis and all the others knowing; and the CIA knowing about it—and the President did nothing to dissuade the Russians. That's what frustrated Bob McNamara, because he knew to the contrary, but he couldn't be in the position of going up and attacking John McCone. We all knew that John McCone was moving around among senators and congressmen peddling this idea because it got him off the hook. Who was primarily responsible for not knowing there were missiles in Cuba earlier? The CIA. He wasn't going to have that on his back. So he got it off his back in this way.

SCHLESINGER: But no one ever asked him: "If you knew, why didn't you—?"

KENNEDY: I think it was brought out in the end, but it was all fuzzed up by that time.

SCHLESINGER: Did the Vice President play any role in foreign policy besides making occasional trips?

KENNEDY: No. No, he was never in on any of the real meetings. I heard him testify when he came up to Buffalo during the [1964 presidential] campaign. He used to speak about the ExComm at the time of the Cuban missile crisis. He said, "There were thirty-six meetings, and I was present at thirty-five of them. And I know the responsibility of putting your finger on the nuclear buttons, how vital and how important it is, because I went through thirty-five of those day-and-night meetings."

Well, he was there for the first meeting, I think. Then he went to Hawaii because they didn't want to disrupt anything, to indicate that there was a crisis on hand. He wasn't there at all when the decisions were being made. He came back on the Saturday night before the Russians withdrew their missiles from Cuba. . . .

Lyndon Johnson never made any suggestions or recommendations as to what we should do at the time of the Cuban missile crisis. He was displeased with what we were doing, although he never made it clear what *he* would do. He said he had the feeling that we were being too weak at the time of the Cuban missile crisis and that we should be stronger. We discussed it afterward. The President knew it because he was talking to some of his congressional friends. So we planned to have people call him on the telephone and say the government is acting like a war party—and then see if he changed his position.

SCHLESINGER: His people give out the story that he was very much opposed to the Vietnam policy in the dumping of Diem.

KENNEDY: Yes. I think that's true.

SCHLESINGER: Did he express that much in meetings?

KENNEDY: No, he didn't. And he didn't come up with an alternative suggestion. But it's true he was not in favor of getting rid of Diem. He was opposed to that. Now, he didn't have any alternative suggestion. I don't know if you knew about that whole business. The person who did that, really, was Henry Cabot Lodge [then Ambassador to South Vietnam]. The individual who forced our position at the time of Vietnam was Henry Cabot Lodge. In fact, Henry Cabot Lodge was being brought back—and the President discussed with me in detail how he could be fired—because he wouldn't communicate in any way with us. The President wanted to find out who was going to replace Diem and what arrangements could be made, and Henry Cabot Lodge would never work on that. He would never communicate about that. The President would send out messages, and he would never really answer them.

But it's true that [Lyndon Johnson] liked Diem, and he liked Madame Diem very much. He was very struck with Madame Diem. In fact, when we were having some communications with them, one time it was felt that the communications should come from him because they got along.

SCHLESINGER: So Lodge really got the bit between his teeth?

KENNEDY: Wouldn't communicate. It was an impossible situation during that period of time. We'd send out a message and ask a lot of questions, and he'd send back a message of one line: "Your message both concerned and amused me. Signed: Henry Cabot Lodge."

SCHLESINGER: How would you describe Mac Bundy's role [in the Cuban missile crisis]? Was it more a clarifier of issues?

KENNEDY: Yes. . . . He was for an [air] strike. He was for violent action. Then by Thursday night he was against doing anything. He said, "If you do anything in Cuba, then they'll march on Berlin. And nothing's worth losing Berlin. We should just let the missiles stay!" And then Friday morning he changed back again—and he was for a strike. . . .

SCHLESINGER: In retrospect, who looked the best in those days?

KENNEDY: Bob McNamara was very good. Tommy Thompson [then Special Adviser on Soviet Affairs to the Secretary of State] was tremendously helpful, much better, in my judgment, than Chip Bohlen [Thompson's predecessor at State, recently named Ambassador to France]. Chip Bohlen ran out on us—which always shocked me. He was there for the first day, and then he went on a boat and went to France. That wasn't necessary; he could always have postponed it. We said he could fly over, but he decided to leave this country in a crisis such as that when he had been working with all of us for such a long period of time. We didn't know Tommy Thompson, and this put Tommy Thompson in the middle of it. But Tommy Thompson was terrific—very tough—always made a good deal of sense and, really, was sort of the motivating force behind the idea of giving the Russians an opportunity to back away, giving them some out. Ted Sorensen [Special Counsel to the President] was very helpful. He made some sense: Although he wasn't as vocal as some of the others, his position was the right position. Ed Martin [Assistant Secretary of State for Inter-American Affairs] was very helpful. And Douglas Dillon [Secretary of the Treasury], although he took a different position, [he favored an air strike against Cuba] you know, always made sense.

SCHLESINGER: Of course, the business of leaving the Russians an exit must have been something which was very much in the President's mind anyway. That was characteristic of his whole approach to these matters.

KENNEDY: That's right. But just to have somebody keeping that in mind—you see, the President wasn't participating in these meetings then.

SCHLESINGER: That was a deliberate decision, to permit a freer conversation?

KENNEDY: Freer conversation, and secondly, [JFK] was campaigning. Don't forget that. And I always felt that things didn't go well when he was there. We had a fight about it at the time.

SCHLESINGER: Who chaired the meetings?

KENNEDY: Well, Rusk was supposed to be the one to chair the meetings, but, as I say, he disappeared or wouldn't. Sometimes there wouldn't really be any chairman, so we just sort of went along as best we could. But he wouldn't chair the meetings; and when he was there, he wouldn't have an agenda. We just worked it out between ourselves really. Then [former Secretary of State Dean] Acheson was called in. He was in favor of bombing, of a strike.

SCHLESINGER: What did the President think of Acheson?

KENNEDY: He liked him. No, he didn't like him—that's not correct. He respected him and found him helpful, found him irritating; and he thought his advice was worth listening to, although not accepted. On many occasions, his advice was worthless.

SCHLESINGER: In the Berlin 1961 [crisis], he played a rather continuous role at one time—and then dropped out.

KENNEDY: Yes, he did. He was in favor of increasing the number of troops there and increasing our buildup. I think that was very instrumental in turning the Russians back.

My judgment is that Khrushchev got the idea at the Vienna [summit] that he was dealing with a young fellow, that he was dealing with a rather weak figure because he didn't do what Khrushchev would have done in Cuba, in not going in and taking Cuba. And he thought, if he was so weak and so vacillating at the time of the Cuban Bay of Pigs, that he was a pushover—and all he had to do was show strength and he would back down. And that's what he tried to do at the [Berlin] Wall. He thought he'd take Berlin. And the fact that we'd built up our own armed forces, called up other troops, sent troops to Europe—all of that, I think, dissuaded him. That was what did it.

And we sent troops to Thailand.[7] There was no question that the Marines we sent to Thailand brought Khrushchev to put pressure on Laos to bring things to peace and quiet there. . . .

"HE WANTS IT!":
THE SELECTION OF LYNDON JOHNSON
AS VICE PRESIDENT

SCHLESINGER: Los Angeles, 1960: Does the Graham memorandum correspond to your own recollection?[8]

KENNEDY: I'll tell you what happened. If the indication in the Graham memorandum is what I interpreted from it—that the President had the thought of Lyndon Johnson as Vice President prior to his own nomination, other than just passing through his mind—that's not true. The idea that he'd go down and offer him the nomination in hopes that he'd take the nomination is not true. The reason he went down and offered him the nomination is because he thought he should offer him the nomination because there were enough indications from others that he wanted to be offered the nomination. But he never thought he'd take the nomination.

SCHLESINGER: He did not?

KENNEDY: No. He thought that he should offer it to him, but he never dreamt that there was a chance in the world that he would accept it. I gathered from the Graham memorandum that Phil Graham [publisher of *The Washington Post*] said to him: "If you offer him the nomination, he might take it"—and the President was very pleased. If that's what he means to imply, that's not true.

I remember [JFK] coming back up after he went down to see Lyndon Johnson. From the memorandum it sounds as if it wasn't done until later on in the morning. The first thing he did in the morning was he went to see Johnson. The first thing after he got up he went to see him. And before he did that, the President thought how terrible it was that he only had twenty-four hours to select a Vice President. He really hadn't thought about it at all. He said what a mistake it was, when it was such an important position, that you only had twenty-four hours to think about it.

SCHLESINGER: Why hadn't it been thought about?

KENNEDY: Because we wanted to just try to get the nomination. We weren't starting to worry about it. We were counting votes! We had to win on the first ballot. We only won by fifteen votes. North Dakota had the unit system—I think in North Dakota and South Dakota. We won it by half a vote. California was falling apart. If there were an indication that we were going to go for somebody else for Vice President—we had the governor of Iowa [Herschel Loveless], who was very difficult, and we couldn't possibly have kept him. We had Orville Freeman, who was having a fight with Hubert Humphrey, plus Gene McCarthy. You know, there were just about thirty-two balls up in the air.

You couldn't even think about it. Carmine De Sapio [chairman of the New York County Democratic Committee] came to me and said what we'd like to do is make a deal with you: "Thirty votes will go to Lyndon Johnson and then you'll get them all back on the second ballot."

I said, "To hell with that. We're going to win it on the first ballot!"

It was all that kind of business. There wasn't any place that was stable. We weren't even thinking about it. To keep everybody happy and to keep in contact with everybody, as you remember, it was just a helluva operation.

SCHLESINGER: Was there any meeting the Wednesday night after the nomination, discussing the Vice President?

KENNEDY: The President and I discussed it, just the fact that he was going to go offer it to Lyndon Johnson the first thing in the morning. I was up in his room when he came back.

And he said, "You just won't believe it."

I said, "What?"

And he said, "He wants it."

And I said, "Oh, my God!"

He said, "Now what do we do?"

So the thing is that we spent the rest of the day—and we both promised each other that we'd never tell what happened—but we spent the rest of the day alternating between thinking it was good and thinking that it wasn't good that he'd offered him the vice-presidency— and how could he get out of it. One of the major factors ultimately that persuaded him that he should take him was the fact that he would be so mean as Majority Leader that it was much better having him as Vice President, where you could control him, than to have him as Majority Leader. Particularly after you had offered him the job, then it would have been disastrous to have that affront and withdraw it.

Finally, we decided by about two o'clock that we'd try to get him out of there and not have him, because Jack thought it would be unpleasant with him, to be associated with him. If he could get him to withdraw and still be happy, that would be fine. Now, I think I made two trips down to see him. The first trip, I think, was just to sort of feel him out, how strongly he was in favor of it, and I think I saw [Speaker of the House] Sam Rayburn and him at that time. I haven't got a clear recollection of that, but one conversation—which was the important one—that I do remember was when I tried to get him to withdraw.

SCHLESINGER: Now was this directly with Johnson or just with Rayburn?

KENNEDY: Just Johnson and me. . . . Rayburn wasn't present. There were just the two of us. He was seated on the couch, and I was seated on his right. I remember the whole conversation.

This was about two-thirty in the afternoon. This is the famous conversation in which Phil Graham says I went down by myself and on my own. I went down to see if I could get him to withdraw. Obviously, with the close relationship between my brother and me, I wasn't going down to see if he would withdraw just as a lark on my own: "My brother's asleep, so I'll go see if I can get rid of his Vice President"—you know, that's what flabbergasted me about Phil Graham's memorandum. It was just generally accepted that I was going down there trying to get rid of the Vice President while [JFK] was up in his room.

I said, "There's going to be a lot of opposition." This was what we worked out: that I'd tell him there was going to be a lot of opposition, that it was going to be unpleasant, that we were going to have trouble with the liberals. They were going to get up and fight it, and [JFK] didn't think that he wanted to go through that kind of an unpleasant fight. But [JFK] wanted to have him play an important role, and he could run the party—the idea being that to run the party he could get a lot of his own people in, and then, if he wanted to be President in eight years or something, he would have the machinery where he could run for President or do whatever he wanted. That was the idea at the time. We didn't really know whether he'd want to go through it, and in any case [JFK] wanted to get rid of him.

So I went, and I said, "You can run the party." And in my judgment—seeing him since then—he is one of the greatest sad-looking people in the world. You know, he can turn that on. I thought he'd burst into tears. I don't know whether it was just an act or anything. But he just shook, and tears came into his eyes, and he said, "I want to be Vice President, and if the President will have me, I'll join with him in making a fight for it." It was that kind of a conversation.

I said, "Well, then, that's fine. He wants you to be Vice President if you want to be Vice President, we want you to know."

And then I went back, and Jack said, "I just got a call from Clark Clifford"—or somebody—"saying that this is disastrous. You've got to take him. I'm going to make an announcement in five minutes. You've got to get this thing done. Otherwise, you'll blow the whole business." So he went out in the hall, and ten minutes later the announcement was made. But during that whole three or four hours, we just vacillated back and forth as to whether we wanted him or didn't want him. And finally we decided not to have him, and we came upon this idea of trying to get rid of him. And it didn't work.

SCHLESINGER: Was there a real liberal revolt?

KENNEDY: No. The President just had this uneasy feeling about him. There was some opposition to him.

SCHLESINGER: The meeting with the labor leaders, for example?[9]

KENNEDY: There were some who were opposed to him, yes, generally opposed to him. Once the President made up his mind, it was all right. There was, of course, as I say, a good deal of conversation about the fact of how unpleasant he would be as Majority Leader. And the President—after [Johnson] became Vice President—was very, very pleased that he was there, rather than Majority Leader. He said he would have just been impossible. And, you know, by the time it was over, finished—by 1963—he was really irritated with him. I think [JFK] admired him—and he rather amused the President—he admired the obvious ability that he had, but [LBJ] wasn't helpful at times that he might have been helpful. He was very loyal and never spoke against the President, but he never gave any suggestions or ideas on policy. He was opposed to our policy—I mean, the two major matters: the Cuban missile crisis and the [1963] civil rights bill. He was opposed to the civil rights bill. He was opposed to sending up any legislation.

SCHLESINGER: He was? After Birmingham?[10]

KENNEDY: Yes. And, of course, he was opposed to what we were doing in the Cuban missile crisis although he never spelled out what he was for. He just said that he was opposed to it. The President always made it a point of asking him what he thought, because he said that [Johnson] is just going to say, "I was opposed to these things."

"I'm going to give him a chance at all these meetings to go on the record as to how he stands."

And he would never say how he stood on any matter! He'd never give his position on any matter. And then he groused at people afterward, you see, or complained. And that's why [Assistant Attorney General for civil rights] Burke Marshall went over and saw him about the [civil rights] legislation he was very, very strongly opposed to.

SCHLESINGER: Had it not been Johnson, was there any clear person?

KENNEDY: No. Maybe Stu [Missouri Senator Stuart Symington] . . .

SCHLESINGER: Hubert [Humphrey], of course, was out as a result of his—

KENNEDY: Behavior. Orville [Freeman] the President liked. He wouldn't do us any good.

SCHLESINGER: Did you have a confrontation with Rayburn in the course of this?

KENNEDY: No.

SCHLESINGER: I wonder where that—

KENNEDY: Oh, I know where it originated. It originated with Phil Potter [of *The Baltimore Sun*], because Phil Potter wrote the story and I never denied it. I said to Sam Rayburn the next morning that I read that story in the paper and not to say anything about it. But I didn't have any of those conversations—I mean, what he said about the son of a bitch or something like that. I never had any of those conversations. I just decided that the thing was past and we should get on to something else. And so I never denied or never discussed it with anyone.

SCHLESINGER: Once, sometime in '62 or '63, Johnson told me his account of it, which did go into this side of it but involved the President's coming down and telling him. First, it involved the night before, Sam Rayburn's calling him and saying he mustn't do it: "They're going to ask you, and you mustn't do it." The President then came down and offered it to him. And then they had a conversation. And Johnson, according to his account, stalled.

And then the President said, "Is the Speaker against it?"

And Johnson said, "Yes, he is."

And the President said, "Do you mind if I talk to the Speaker?"

And Johnson said, "No, certainly not."

And then Johnson told me that the President went and saw the Speaker and, as a consequence of that conversation—which must have taken place around ten to ten-thirty in the morning—Rayburn called Johnson and said, "I've changed my mind. I think you have to do it."

And Johnson said, "Well, you told me the opposite last night."

And Rayburn said, "I'm a wiser man today than I was last night. And we have to lick this fellow—meaning Nixon—and you have to go on the ticket."

And Johnson said this was obviously the result of the President's talk with Rayburn. Do you remember any talk?

KENNEDY: No. As I say, the only reaction that the President had after talking to Lyndon Johnson was just surprise and then concern that he would take it. He never dreamt—he never considered that he would take it. After that, there was a good deal of time spent in trying to get him off the ticket.

SCHLESINGER: But so far as you know, the President did not call on Rayburn?

KENNEDY: I have no recollection of his calling on Rayburn or making an effort to try to persuade Rayburn to have Lyndon Johnson accept it.

SCHLESINGER: That would be inconsistent with the general picture of not wanting him on the ticket?

KENNEDY: Yes. It is conceivable that Lyndon Johnson said, "You better talk to Sam Rayburn about it," and that the President said, "I'll talk to Sam Rayburn"—and then talked to Sam Rayburn about it. I think that's conceivable, because there was no excuse not to talk to Sam Rayburn. What would you say once he'd said to Lyndon: "Won't you be on the ticket?" If a part of it was "Why don't you talk to Sam Rayburn?" he might have talked to Sam Rayburn. Phil Graham—I don't think he said that the President talked to Sam Rayburn.

SCHLESINGER: No.

KENNEDY: At the time, Lady Bird [Mrs. Johnson] was not in favor of it because of Lyndon Johnson's health, and I thought some other people were opposed to it as far as Lyndon Johnson was concerned. But I don't have any recollection of him ever talking to Sam Rayburn, and if he talked to Sam Rayburn, it was not an important factor during this period. And Lyndon Johnson's account of what happened that he'd given Phil Potter and others is just false now. I don't know what he said to you then. It's wrong.

SCHLESINGER: Jim Rowe [friend and adviser to LBJ] told me that the next day, Johnson was very gloomy. He felt he had made a great mistake. But he didn't seem to vacillate as far as you and the President were aware?

KENNEDY: No, no.

SCHLESINGER: He was consistent all the way?

KENNEDY: Well, as I say, when I tried to get him off, he wouldn't go off. I'm sure he wanted it as much as anybody ever wanted anything.

Johnson is—as President Kennedy said Thursday night, November 21, [1963]—incapable of telling the truth. I mean, I had a conversation with him at the White House in 1962, at one of those dances after a dinner, at which he said he never tried to beat the President, he never ran for President, he was never interested in being President, he was just interested in helping John Kennedy—there were people he couldn't dissuade right away, but he never lifted a finger himself—and that he never heard of anybody saying anything bad about President Kennedy, that he never knew about John Connally saying anything bad.

And my experience with him since then is that he lies all the time. I'm telling you, he just lies continuously, about everything. In every conversation I have with him, he lies. As I've said, he lies even when he doesn't have to.

OTHER APPOINTMENTS AND FOREIGN STATESMEN

SCHLESINGER: In Defense, McNamara, of course, was a great success.

KENNEDY: Yes, the President liked him very much. . . .The major leak in the government was made in connection with Hanson Baldwin [of *The New York Times*], about the fact that we could tell that the Russians were not hardening their missile sites and how many missile sites they had. The only way we could obtain that information was from satellite photography. . . . It blew the most important source of information that we had. The result of that article was that the Russians then changed their missile sites.

SCHLESINGER: Oh, God.

KENNEDY: There was a great to-do about it. The security committee headed by Clark Clifford looked into it and said it was the most important classified information the Soviet Union had ever received of this order. We had a major investigation as to who gave it, with the understanding that the person who gave it was going to be fired. Everybody was interviewed by the FBI. It was a complete investigation. Hanson Baldwin, of course, was very bitter towards the President. The President finally had the owners of *The New York Times* down and gave them the paper which showed how top-secret this information was and that it should never have been revealed. . . .

SCHLESINGER: Yes. Was Paul Nitze a figure at all?

KENNEDY: The President didn't like Paul Nitze very much. He thought he was an effective fellow. He was considered as Secretary of Defense, he was considered as Under Secretary of Defense, he was considered as Under Secretary of State. But he was rather a harsh figure, and he didn't please the President very much in some of the answers he gave at the time of the Cuban missile crisis. The President wasn't very fond of him.

SCHLESINGER: Connally, I gather, was pretty good as Secretary of the Navy.

KENNEDY: I think he was, but it's kind of tough to know. At one time, you know, I liked John Connally. I don't like him now. You know, he never helped with the [John F. Kennedy Presidential] Library; he never helped when the Library exhibit went down there. Rather than not help, he really hindered it. And he has never lifted a finger since that period. He's been very ungracious. I really dislike him. . . .

SCHLESINGER: Did [JFK] have clear ideas about what he wanted from the White House staff?

KENNEDY: No.

SCHLESINGER: You were really working somewhat at recruiting for the White House.

KENNEDY: Yes.

SCHLESINGER: You recruited me, for example.

KENNEDY: Did I?

SCHLESINGER: And Fred Dutton [as Special Assistant to the President]. You were concerned over getting new people into the White House.

KENNEDY: Yes. I don't think that area interested [JFK] or that sort of thing interested him. He wanted to make sure there were able, bright people around, but what they were doing—or their work or organizational parts of things—was never worked out satisfactorily. People worked hard because they were working for him, and they put up with a lot of stuff they wouldn't put up with from other people. And it sort of evolved that there was so much being done and to do that there weren't the kind of difficulties you would have ordinarily.

But he never was clear about the chain of command, or how it was handled, or any organizational part, or who some of the people were. So I just got involved in that and, particularly after the Bay of Pigs, in the organizational part of the White House. Those were some of my responsibilities or areas of responsibility. And then it evolved with the personalities over there: People who had important positions moved and consolidated their positions, and others did not. I think Fred Dutton was pushed out of there really, in my judgment, just because others wanted to make sure that nobody was affecting their position or their role. The same thing with Dick Goodwin [Assistant Special Counsel to the President who moved to the State Department].

SCHLESINGER: Well, the President, I think, wanted Dick. Dick wanted to leave. Ted [Sorensen] wanted Dick to go. And the President wanted strength in the State Department, I think.

KENNEDY: Yes, he didn't have any friends over there. . . .

SCHLESINGER: Mennen Williams wanted HEW?

KENNEDY: Yes. The President didn't think that much of him. I think he did a damn good job as Assistant Secretary of State for Africa myself. His judgment was always good, and he made a helluva effort. And he came up with a lot of good ideas. I never saw him off base. I mean, I never heard of him botching it up. I don't think he would have, probably, at HEW, but I don't know that. But I think he did a damn good job as Assistant Secretary for Africa.

SCHLESINGER: . . . Do you remember anything about the atmosphere— the President's expectations about the Soviet Union—when he came in? Remember, there were messages from Khrushchev (Harriman had some) saying that now the slate was wiped clean, and so on. But then early in January, Khrushchev gave a very tough speech.

KENNEDY: Oh, I think it was just a continuation of what he thought during the campaign. What was revealing—the two most revealing experiences for the President—were Vienna and the buildup [of missiles in Cuba]. Vienna was very revealing: This was the first time the President had ever really come across somebody with whom he couldn't exchange ideas in a meaningful way and feel that there was some point to it. And then the Cuban missile crisis: He said the Russians and the Communists and Khrushchev were like the gangsters that both of us had dealt with, that Khrushchev's kind of action—what he did and how he acted—was how an immoral gangster would act and not as a statesman, not as a person with a sense of responsibility.

And that was due to the fact that [Khrushchev] gave him promises that he wouldn't do this, that he wouldn't put missiles in: number one, that he wouldn't put missiles in Cuba; and number two, that he wouldn't do anything prior to the [1962] election which would have any effect on the election. In fact, he promised specifically that he wouldn't come to the United Nations because that might have an effect on the election. He would wait until after the election. He wanted the President to understand that nothing would be done in September and October.

SCHLESINGER: At Vienna, what was the President's personal reaction to Khrushchev?

KENNEDY: He just thought that he was completely unreasonable—that he was tough. And he had to be as tough. And I think it was a shock to him that somebody would be as harsh and definitive, definite, as this.

SCHLESINGER: Among foreign statesmen, whom did he like? [British Prime Minister Harold] Macmillan?

KENNEDY: I think they had the closest rapport. He hated, of course, [Canadian Prime Minister John] Diefenbaker—had contempt for him.
He liked the President of Korea, admired him.[11]

SCHLESINGER: Of Korea?

KENNEDY: Yes, because he's so tough.

SCHLESINGER: He liked [Venezuelan President Romulo] Betancourt?

KENNEDY: He liked Betancourt. And I think he liked the Latin Americans. I think he liked the President of Costa Rica.[12]

SCHLESINGER: The ex-President.

KENNEDY: Yes. The one I remember him talking about was Korea.

SCHLESINGER: I was interested in David Harlech [William David Ormsby-Gore, Baron Harlech, British Ambassador to the United States] and the Cuban crisis. David, I guess, was probably as close to him as anybody, apart from you and one or two others.

KENNEDY: That's right. He was almost part of the government. [JFK] would rather have his judgment than that of almost anybody else. His judgment—David Harlech's—I would think, of everybody, including Bob McNamara or anybody in the United

States—he'd rather have his judgment, his ideas, his suggestions and recommendations than even anybody in our own government.

SCHLESINGER: Of course they met in 1958, but your family had fairly continuous relations with David since then?

KENNEDY: Yes, and you see, Kick [Kennedy's sister Kathleen Hartington] was the godmother of their oldest child. And they were married into the same family. . . . His mother's sister was Kick's mother-in-law.

SCHLESINGER: That's right, yes.

KENNEDY: And then he came over quite often. He stayed with us at Georgetown.

SCHLESINGER: David played a specific role in the test ban?

KENNEDY: Yes. I think he really was the motivating force to have the President make this a major area of interest. It was made a major area of interest because of David feeling that we really weren't doing enough. And the source of information for the speeches during the campaign—of how few people were working on this subject, of how little was being done—was David.

SCHLESINGER: You mean in the American government?

KENNEDY: Yes.

SCHLESINGER: Fascinating. Of course, David had been involved in the British negotiations.

KENNEDY: That's right. You see he was their delegate to Geneva, so he knew everything that we were doing. And he was also an instrumental figure in effecting what we should do in Laos—the fact that we were backing the wrong government and doing it in the wrong way.

SCHLESINGER: Oh, really? The President had not known Macmillan before, had he?

KENNEDY: No, he had not. Macmillan, of course, had great reservations about him.

SCHLESINGER: Oh, really? Why was that?

KENNEDY: Because of his youth, the kind of a person he was—Irish, Joe Kennedy's son: "How can I possibly get along with this boy when I had such a nice relationship with Eisenhower?"

SCHLESINGER: They hit it off immediately?

KENNEDY: Yes. I think they did. And it kept getting stronger and stronger. The President really liked Macmillan.

SCHLESINGER: I saw Macmillan when I was last in England. He talked with the greatest feeling and perception about the President. He didn't mention the other things, but he felt the separate differences in generations.

KENNEDY: The person [JFK] really disliked was Nehru. He really hated Nehru. Nehru was really rude to us when we went to India in 1951.

SCHLESINGER: Oh, really?

KENNEDY: Yes. Very, very rude. Jack went to see him, and Pat [Kennedy Lawford] and I. He was terrible. And after [JFK] saw him here, he said he'd gotten no better. He was ruder than he was then— opinionated, self-satisfied, stuffy. Everything had worsened. He really disliked him.

SCHLESINGER: De Gaulle?

KENNEDY: I think he rather admired De Gaulle and what he was trying to do, but he was making things difficult.

SCHLESINGER: [German Chancellor Konrad] Adenauer?

KENNEDY: He didn't like Adenauer very much. He thought he was always giving us an unpleasant time unnecessarily, and then he knew that Adenauer liked John Foster Dulles. Adenauer used to say to me the person he loved the most was Dulles. And Adenauer was living in sort of a different generation. He was very difficult to get along with and work with. Adenauer used to leak things to the newspapers all the time to make things unpleasant. We were always having unpleasant stories coming out of Germany.

SCHLESINGER: Among our ambassadors, were there any that the President particularly liked?

KENNEDY: Ed Gullion [Ambassador to the Republic of the Congo], he liked.

SCHLESINGER: That tie went back to Saigon, didn't it, to that trip?

KENNEDY: Yes. In 1951.

SCHLESINGER: Ken, of course—Galbraith [then Ambassador to India].

KENNEDY: Ken.

SCHLESINGER: He came to like David Bruce.

KENNEDY: I think he did. Oh, Ed Reischauer [Ambassador to Japan]—he thought was terrific. Howard Jones [Ambassador to Indonesia] —these are probably people that I had personal support for too. Thailand he didn't think was very good.[13] Pakistan was not too good. The fellow we sent—

SCHLESINGER: [Walter P.] McConnaughy. Yes.

KENNEDY: Jim Gavin [Ambassador to France], I think he liked. The State Department hated him. And they thought that the reason that we weren't getting along with De Gaulle was because we had an ambassador over there who was an amateur, and so they were cutting him continuously. Now, I don't know whether it was justi- fied. I don't see that Chip Bohlen has done a helluva lot better, and he was one of the ones who said you had to have a Foreign Service officer: "It's so bad over there. Gavin doesn't know how to handle De Gaulle. You need a Foreign Service officer." I had a lot of fights with Chip Bohlen about that.

And then we had a terrible delay about the appointment [to the USSR]. [JFK] wanted to get somebody else to go to the Soviet Union. He spoke to me. You remember when we had the long delay about the ambassador.

SCHLESINGER: Yes.

KENNEDY: He spoke to me about going to the Soviet Union.

SCHLESINGER: Were you interested?

KENNEDY: No. I didn't think it was a good idea.

INTERVIEW WITH
JOHN BARTLOW MARTIN

■

McLEAN, VIRGINIA, FEBRUARY 29, 1964

CABINET CANDIDATES

MARTIN: How do you prepare an administration? How do you pick the Cabinet members and the Assistant Secretaries and so forth? This is something you were engaged in from November 1960 until about April 1961, I think. How do you do it?

KENNEDY: I think the first important thing, really, is the fact that we came into this administration without a political obligation. Now, I don't mean that people didn't do favors for us and that we wanted to do favors for them. There weren't any promises made to anyone that they would get a job in the government. There were certainly no Cabinet positions promised. It really was a fresh slate—beginning with this question of selecting the members of the Cabinet and then, really, the jobs further down the line.

MARTIN: You started with the Cabinet?

KENNEDY: Well, really both, because what we tried to do was to get a pool of names. For instance, the Brookings Institute had done a study of the various departments and agencies and also, I think, some papers on transition. So we studied those, and they were quite helpful. But they were just a beginning and just to give us some ideas.

Second, we tried to put together the names of all the able people who would be qualified for particular positions in government. We had the list of the positions that were open, and as I remember—and I could be very wrong—it seemed to me that we had to fill three or four hundred positions by January. And then after that, we had to fill—by April or May—we had to fill another eight hundred or a thousand.

MARTIN: So, you've well over a thousand people you have to find in the space of three or four months?

KENNEDY: That's right.

MARTIN: No, two months—November and December. Where do these names come from?

KENNEDY: In the first place, I think for the first time in the history of the country it was organized. It wasn't just somebody coming in off the street and getting a job. We organized it. We broke the positions down into categories and then we broke the individual names down into categories. And the chief responsibility, I suppose, was mine—and with me, Sargent Shriver and Larry O'Brien, and then a group of people worked with them.

It was sort of a continuation of the campaign. Right after the election I went away for several weeks. When we came back, all of our time and effort was devoted to that. And a good part of my time was really spent with Jack on the question of who was going to be in the Cabinet.

MARTIN: On the Cabinet, I don't know that you want to go through every one, but I suppose we'd just take a couple of them and stick with them.

KENNEDY: Maybe I'll take McNamara first. The three important ones, obviously, were Treasury, Defense, and State. There were five or six people mentioned as far as the State Department, perhaps a slightly lower number for Defense and also for Treasury. The first person we thought of, really, was Robert Lovett.

MARTIN: This is for Defense?

KENNEDY: For Defense or State. The President asked him if he'd be interested in being Secretary of State or Secretary of Defense. He said because of his physical infirmities—the fact that he had some problems with his health—he couldn't do that. He said he'd be glad to consult with the President but that he wouldn't be able to take either one of those positions—wasn't well enough to do so.

Sarge came up with the name of Bob McNamara. He went to a lot of different people to get suggestions for the various positions, and somebody—I don't know who—suggested Bob McNamara as well as a number of other names. I mean, there were a number of other people who were considered first, but nobody appealed to the President after Lovett turned it down. And McNamara had good credentials. So finally—and this was after some period of time—the President sent Sarge out to interview Bob McNamara and, at that time, offered him the job of Secretary of the Treasury or Secretary of Defense.

MARTIN: Had the President known him?

KENNEDY: No, he had never met him. Oh, [Shriver] didn't *offer* him the job: he asked him if he might be interested *if* the President offered him the job. And he said he'd just taken a contract with Ford Motor Company and he was unsure. They talked at some length about whether it would be the Defense Department or Treasury, and he indicated that, if he came, he wanted to come to the Defense Department. But he wanted to study the situation, talk to some people, and see if he wanted to come.

MARTIN: He's a Republican, isn't he?

KENNEDY: He's nominally a Republican, but I think he backed Jack for the election. At least, that's what I've learned since then. In checking with people from Michigan, I know that we talked to [United Automobile Workers president] Walter Reuther, who was very enthusiastic about him.

MARTIN: Who else might you check on a thing like that? Governor Williams, for example?

KENNEDY: I think probably he was talked to in Michigan.

[McNamara] came back then. The President arranged for him to come back. There had been some discussion with him about the fact that we wanted Franklin Roosevelt, Jr., for Secretary of the Treasury—no, Secretary of the Navy—and Bob McNamara made it clear in the preliminary conversation, and then very clear when he met with the President, that he would not have Franklin Roosevelt as Secretary of the Navy and that, as far as any of the positions within the Defense Department, although they would be approved by the President, they also had to be approved by him. Otherwise, he wouldn't take the job.

When he saw the President, he saw the President for a few minutes alone and then the two of us met with him at his Georgetown—

MARTIN: You and Sarge?

KENNEDY: No, no, the President and I met with McNamara. He had a memorandum that he had prepared in which he set forth quite specifically what he wanted and what he didn't want to do. It was quite clear that he was going to run the Defense Department, that he was going to be in charge; and although he'd clear things with the President, that political interests or favors couldn't play a role in the operation [of] the Defense Department.

MARTIN: Is this what the President wanted?

KENNEDY: Yes. Also, he was so impressed with the fact that [McNamara] was so tough about it—and strong and stalwart. He impressed him.

At that time, there was a question of where I was going. At one time I thought of going over as Under Secretary of Defense. We discussed it shortly after this meeting and felt that the Defense Department wasn't large enough for both of our personalities. So then Bob McNamara went on and asked Ros Gilpatric to come down. There was a good deal of opposition to Ros Gilpatric [in regard to] some position that he had taken in connection with the Defense Department prior to that time, and it seems to me that the opposition came from Stuart Symington. I remember there was a good deal of feeling about him.

The other person that we were thinking about in an important position was Paul Nitze. He was considered as Under Secretary of Defense and also, I believe, the Secretary of Defense. But he was turned down also because of the fact that he had made a good number of enemies. And there were those who had worked with him who didn't feel that he had the personality to carry that job, carry the position—although he is supposed to be a very bright person. As it turned out, I don't think there's any question that that was the right decision. Some of his positions on matters were very frustrating to the President later on, particularly at the time of the second Cuba.

Mac Bundy was suggested as Secretary of State. His background rather appealed to me. But there was a definite problem about the fact that he didn't have experience, hadn't been around long enough. There were four or five people who were mentioned for Secretary of State. David Bruce was one, I remember, and I think [New York Times columnist] Arthur Krock was a great booster of his. [New York Herald Tribune correspondent] Maggie Higgins, as I remember, was pushing him.

MARTIN: Who else was mentioned?

KENNEDY: It finally came down to—in the last three or four days—to William Fulbright. The President was quite taken with having Fulbright, and I really stopped Fulbright.

MARTIN: Why?

KENNEDY: Because I thought that—with so many problems with newly developed nations and so many problems on racial difficulties—you could never get over the fact that you had selected a Senator from Arkansas to be Secretary of State, one who had signed the [Southern] Manifesto and who had been tied up in all the segregation votes.

MARTIN: Of course, Rusk was from Georgia, but he wasn't so pointedly identified with Georgia.

KENNEDY: No, not a bit, and also he hadn't been voting on these matters. Of course, Rusk came from the Rockefeller Foundation, in which he was involved with the new countries.

Let me just say further that we had a rather strong argument—the President and I—about Fulbright. [JFK] had worked with Fulbright and thought he had some brains and some sense and some judgment. He was really rather taken with him. I don't know whether my concern about the segregation problem really would have amounted to something. Even if he was all right on this problem—and everybody said that he would be, once he became Secretary of State—I thought that we'd have to spend so much of our time proving ourselves right on it that we'd even have to take positions we wouldn't otherwise take, just because he was from Arkansas and Secretary of State. In any case, that was my feeling.

MARTIN: Was the President's feeling that this didn't matter?

KENNEDY: He thought they could get by with it, and he liked Fulbright. He was the only person who was mentioned as Secretary of State whom he knew. And so he thought it was worthwhile doing.

MARTIN: I don't mean civil rights as such doesn't matter; I mean in this situation it really could have been overriden. But you thought it did?

KENNEDY: Yes. And then it was a question that time was running out. We had to get somebody. And Dean Rusk was one of the names suggested. Robert Lovett was very high on him. The President greatly, greatly valued his counsel, his advice. He was always very high on him. And a number of others—Dean Acheson—were very high on him.

MARTIN: Who else was consulted?

KENNEDY: I remember those two. And [Rusk] had a good reputation. There was some feeling that he might, I guess, emphasize the Far East too much, but that was about the only thing. So the President—he had never met him—invited him down to Florida and asked him right away. We'd gone through all the other names. It was really a question of elimination. It came down, in the last three or four days, to Fulbright and to Rusk. Fulbright was eliminated, and we had to select somebody. So Rusk was selected, not for any great enthusiasm about him as such, although people spoke highly of him.

MARTIN: Can I ask you another thing on State? A lot of people thought Stevenson was being considered.

KENNEDY: No, no.

MARTIN: Was he not considered seriously?

KENNEDY: No.

MARTIN: Do you want to say why?

KENNEDY: Well, he never got along. The President never liked him. He put up with him. . . .

MARTIN: How far back does this go, Bob?

KENNEDY: I think from the beginning, to some extent. But it got more and more pronounced. And then, of course, his behavior at the convention irritated [JFK] and frustrated all of us. They're just different types, different types and kinds of people. . . . And it really came through at the Los Angeles convention when Bill Blair was for us and Newt Minow was for us, and he then—Adlai Stevenson— went to [Chicago Mayor] Dick Daley, after Dick Daley had come out for us, and asked him to switch on the first ballot. He said, "We've got to have a favorite son. And I come from Illinois. And you've got to be with me because it would be embarrassing if I don't have Illinois." And Dick Daley almost threw him out of the office. He said Illinois had met its responsibilities to Adlai Stevenson and they had pledged to Jack Kennedy—and that's the way they were going.

And then the whole behavior in Los Angeles. It seemed to us to be the actions of an old woman. And he was petulant when he came to see the President because, I think, he thought he was going to be Secretary of State and the President asked him to go to the United Nations. He was very bad-mannered about it, and he handled himself badly.

MARTIN: Did he lay conditions down?

KENNEDY: Well, he was very ungracious about it and a bit cross. And he said that he'd have to wait for twenty-four hours and go back and think about it. The President was about to tell him that he couldn't even have that. . . .

MARTIN: This continued right on through the whole of his administration?

KENNEDY: The whole three years. The President really never enjoyed his company, never enjoyed his counsel particularly. . . . He was not really much help. He did the job at the United Nations well: I mean, the President was glad to have him up there. But he'd hate to have him around him.

MARTIN: The President did think he was effective at the United Nations?

KENNEDY: At the United Nations. Just as long as he stayed away from him. But Jack used to talk about him frequently—what a pain in the ass he was.

MARTIN: Let me ask you one thing to try to tie this down in time and place. Where were these conversations [on Cabinet appointments] taking place, physically?

KENNEDY: Oh, Jack's home in Georgetown. I don't know what the address is.

MARTIN: No, but that's what I mean. Who was normally present in the house? Was the campaign crowd?

KENNEDY: No, no, I don't think anybody was.

MARTIN: It was pretty much a one-to-one relationship?

KENNEDY: Yes. He had some of the staff people there. Pierre Salinger might have been upstairs, but there wasn't anybody else. He met with a lot of these people alone or with me—like Douglas Dillon when he asked him. Douglas Dillon's primary advocate was [journalist] Joe Alsop, who always wanted him. My father was opposed to Douglas Dillon. He felt he didn't know enough about finances. That's what slowed the President down in selecting Douglas Dillon.

MARTIN: He was in State at the time, wasn't he?

KENNEDY: Yes. If Bob McNamara had wanted it, he would have selected Bob McNamara; but once McNamara took Defense, then it was a question of who was to go over to Treasury. The other person who was mentioned was Henry Alexander [of Morgan Guaranty

Trust]. And [JFK] finally decided not to select Henry Alexander and decided to select Douglas Dillon.

And the question I raised was about the big problem for the Democrats—financial responsibility. [JFK and Dillon] didn't know each other; and all we had to do was have Douglas Dillon in there and, six months afterward, saying that this administration is, obviously, financially irresponsible, that they don't care about money—just interested in big spending—and quit in a huff. So I said that I felt we should have an understanding with him, before he took on that position, that if he left he would leave in a peaceful, happy fashion and wouldn't indicate directly or indirectly that he was disturbed about what President Kennedy and the administration was doing.

MARTIN: Was this raised with him?

KENNEDY: Yes. The President talked to him and asked him if he wanted the job, and he said that he did. Then the President called me in so that the two of us would be there.

MARTIN: You asked the hard questions?

KENNEDY: No, no. We just talked about it quite frankly and said that we needed a commitment from him. And he readily gave it—said if he left, he'd leave under peaceful circumstances. We were talking about it the other night, with Douglas Dillon, and he [still] thought it was perfectly satisfactory.

There was violent opposition within the Republican party, particularly as far as Nixon was concerned, with his taking this job. [Dillon] had rather a tough time with him. I think, initially, Eisenhower thought he should take it, but when [Dillon] decided to take it, he was not very pleasant about it. And I guess George Humphrey [Eisenhower's Secretary of the Treasury] never spoke to him—or spoke to him in a rude fashion—and Christian Herter [Secretary of State] spoke in the same way and Mrs. [Mary Pratt] Herter. But it was funny because Mrs. Herter wouldn't talk, I guess, to either one of them—and then, of course, the Herters ended up working for the President too. The situation was somewhat changed.

MARTIN: Are there other Cabinet jobs you'd like to talk about?

KENNEDY: Well, then, Agriculture: There was a major candidate for Agriculture. Well, Orville Freeman, of course, was always considered for Agriculture, but the major candidate was a fellow from Missouri,[14] who's head of the Farm Bureau or—

MARTIN: Was that Patton, Jim Patton?

KENNEDY: No, no.

MARTIN: That's Farmer's Union.

KENNEDY: [It was Fred Heinkel], a friend of Senator Symington. He came to the house, and the President had me sitting in the other room so that I could listen to the conversation to see what we thought. And [JFK] asked him about agriculture. He said, "Well, what about surpluses?"

And he said he thought that what we should do with surpluses is that we should sell them abroad.

So the President said, "Well, that's right. Now, what about the payment for the transportation abroad? And what do you do about the effect that all of these commodities coming on the market would have on the rest of the market?"

And he said, "I'd never thought of that."

So he didn't become Secretary of Agriculture. That's when Orville Freeman was called. . . .

Arthur Goldberg had always been a friend of ours, and so [his appointment] was almost understood right from the beginning. I talked to him about it, and he wanted to be a judge. He didn't want to be Secretary of Labor; he was opposed to being Secretary of Labor. So I talked to him once, and I talked to him again. He was my great friend. And finally he took it with the understanding that, if a vacancy came in the circuit court in Illinois, he would be considered for that. And I said I'd talk to the President, and the President said "Fine"—without any absolute commitment, but with the understanding that he would get that position. As I say, he was against it. And the Building Trades were against him getting the job and, in fact, protested to [AFL-CIO president] George Meany. In fact, I think that George Meany was not enthusiastic, interestingly enough. There was some opposition to him. He got a real shaft from some of his brethren. He could probably spell that out in greater detail. Ask him about the people who were opposed to him being Secretary of Labor. It was basically the Building Trades and really the same people, of course, who didn't like me—because the same ones who were opposed to him then were opposed to me being Attorney General. So we used to talk about it.

Then, let's see, I could tell you about the Postmaster General. Congressman [William L.] Dawson, I think, was mentioned. His name came up in the papers—that the President had offered him the job and that he had turned it down. This, in fact, was not true. But his name had come in the papers so prominently, and the Democratic organizations had gone out so far for him, that it became an embarrassment for him. And the President decided that he didn't want him. He didn't have—just looking into his background—the right kind of background that we wanted in the administration, and secondly, he just didn't have the capacity for this position. So we arranged at that time—I think, with Dick Daley and others—that he would come meet with the President, and then go out and say the President offered him the job but he turned it down because of his health and age.

Then Ed Day [of Prudential Insurance] was suggested by the Democrats out in California. He had a good record. We didn't have anybody particularly. It seemed like a rather good choice because he was a businessman and got away from the political aspects of it. Ed Day had supported us. He had been interested in coming back.

MARTIN: Did John Bailey want it?

KENNEDY: I don't think so. I think he was satisfied being at the Democratic National Committee. At least, I don't remember that being a major problem.

Stewart Udall supported us—there wasn't much of a problem about that [his appointment as Secretary of the Interior].

MARTIN: No, he's a natural.

KENNEDY: [Connecticut Governor] Abe Ribicoff—that was another reason why I think John Bailey wasn't mentioned, particularly, because Abe Ribicoff got appointed [Secretary of Health, Education, and Welfare]—well, the President offered [Ribicoff] the Attorney Generalship, actually, at the beginning, down in Florida. And he turned it down because he said he didn't want a Jew putting Negroes in Protestant schools in the South. He thought that would be making a mistake. He wanted to go on the Supreme Court, and he thought that, if he had to take that job, he'd build up so many enemies, create so much controversy about himself personally, that he could never get approved for Supreme Court. And so he turned the President down.

MARTIN: He wanted [Supreme Court Justice Felix] Frankfurter's seat?

KENNEDY: Yes. So, actually, I was second choice.

MARTIN: What about Secretary [of Commerce Luther] Hodges?

KENNEDY: Well, that was more of just balancing it off and having southerners come in.

Terry Sanford [Democratic gubernatorial candidate in North Carolina], whom I had become very friendly with, was a great admirer of the President. I asked him to nominate—to second—the President out in Los Angeles, and he finally agreed to do so, which was very, very important for us, because it broke the southern bloc for Lyndon Johnson. We got him, and we got [Governor] Howard Edmondson from Oklahoma; and although they didn't bring many votes with them, it made a big difference for us psychologically. Well, when [Sanford] did that, Luther Hodges was furious with him. And Terry Sanford went to Jack at that time and said, "If I ever nominate or suggest Luther Hodges for any job, throw me out of your office."

He went back [to North Carolina], and the fact that he had nominated—seconded—Jack and had been in favor of Jack and not for Lyndon Johnson was very, very damaging to him in North Carolina, because people felt that he had betrayed the southern cause. He won [the 1960 North Carolina gubernatorial race] anyway, but not nearly by as large a margin as he expected to. Luther Hodges supported Jack after the Los Angeles convention, and then, after the election, he wanted to be Secretary of Commerce. And Terry Sanford came up and saw Jack and said, "I remember the conversation I had with you in Los Angeles, and I'm here to suggest Luther Hodges." He said he wanted him out of the state of North Carolina, and this was the way to get him out! He was well regarded and had done a good job as Governor of North Carolina. So the President appointed him.

MARTIN: I notice in a couple of these [appointments], you acted as sort of a political protector for the President—that is, you thought of the political considerations that might militate against an appointment. For example, in the case of Fulbright, you had civil rights in mind as a handicap. Against Dillon, you were afraid that he might resign and charge the Democrats with fiscal irresponsibility. And so forth. Is this a role that you played very often—trying to think of the political handicaps?

KENNEDY: No, I don't think so. Not political, particularly. But I did, I suppose, during the administration, play a role of raising problems about courses of action that were suggested to the President at conferences. I mean, whether it's going to be Laos, or Cuba, or whatever it might be, it wouldn't be political so much as to raise some of the difficulties that might occur to me, looking at it from an outside point of view.

MARTIN: To try to make that a little more concrete—I know it's a digression from the present subject, but—the President, or anyone who is in a position of tremendous power, is always surrounded by a bunch of yes men, people who want to say yes always to what he wants. But you were uniquely in a position to say no—and to raise questions and ask them. Isn't that so? There are an awful lot of people who are awfully anxious to wait and see which way the cat's going to jump and then go ahead and say yes. Do you think he was free of this?

KENNEDY: Well, not free, I'm sure, but there were an awful lot of people who raised questions, particularly after the first six months in the administration. Perhaps less so at the beginning, but once they understood how [JFK] operated—I mean, Ted Sorensen did, and I think some of the other people did.

MARTIN: This is the role that Ted played?

KENNEDY: Yes, and he played it well. Kenny [O'Donnell] did and Pierre [Salinger, White House Press Secretary] did, as well as some of the others who came in. I think there was an advantage in our relationship, because my motivation really could never be questioned. There wasn't anything to be gained by me, and I wasn't running for any office, so I didn't have any political future that I was attempting to work for or help. So that, therefore, I surely think it had some advantage.

THE PRESIDENT AND HIS MEN

MARTIN: There were very few Cabinet changes during the administration. Was [JFK] happy with his Cabinet during this entire time?

KENNEDY: Well, at the end he was very frustrated with Rusk, who became rather a weak figure; and where the State Department functioned poorly; where [Rusk] was not prepared on issues to discuss them fully, or really he had never done his homework; and where all the important papers that were written—the good ones—were written by [JFK] personally or by people in the White House. And he really felt, at the end, that the ten or twelve people in the White House who worked under his direction with Mac Bundy or under Mac Bundy really performed all the functions of the State Department, except the managerial functions of being an ambassador.

From my own experience, I think that that's true. The good ideas that came out over the period of the last two years came, really, from the President or perhaps from one of his advisers. The vast majority came from Jack. The really good ideas, the original ideas and thoughts, came from him and then from people down the line. Very few suggestions of policy or position came from the State Department. And Rusk, when you'd get into any kind of a conference, had not anticipated problems that would arise and not prepared himself to answer questions—was frequently unaware of the factual basis for a position and, really, had not done his homework. A rather weak figure.

The President and I discussed on a number of occasions—particularly in the last couple of months, after the election—moving Rusk out, perhaps to the United Nations, and appointing Bob McNamara Secretary of State.

MARTIN: Why didn't the President move on this earlier? This must have become clear to him rather soon, didn't it?

KENNEDY: Well, I think more so at the end, in the last six or eight months.

MARTIN: Really?

KENNEDY: Yes. I don't think it was so bad at the beginning or that he noticed it as much. That's understandable, because Rusk speaks very well and is an awfully loyal and very nice man—though [JFK] knew that perhaps he wasn't the strong figure of McNamara. But the concentration mostly at that time was on the fact that the State Department wasn't managed correctly or properly.

MARTIN: At what time?

KENNEDY: For the first two years. And then it appeared that the problem was deeper than that and wasn't just a question of bad management but a question of lack of preparation of major issues, failure to anticipate, and then failure to do your homework—even on such important matters as Cuba or Laos.

But I've seen it even since November 22. The Secretary is not taking positions on important matters. And it's really much worse now, because Jack was his own Secretary of State.

MARTIN: This is really what it came down to, isn't it?

KENNEDY: Yes. So it was all right, really. It functioned adequately with that kind of arrangement. But with the kind of a President that you have now [LBJ], it can't function so well. But I think [JFK] didn't have much contact, speaking of the Cabinet members. I don't think he saw Luther Hodges except very occasionally.

MARTIN: Now, he saw Rusk a good deal.

KENNEDY: Yes. But we're talking about other Cabinet members, you know. McNamara, he thought the most highly of—of any Cabinet member. And we anticipated in 1968, you know, Lyndon Johnson becoming a candidate. And [JFK] thought of trying to move in the direction that would get the nomination for Bob McNamara. The President didn't really have much respect for Johnson, didn't think that he would do well. And as he said to Jackie on Thursday night, November 21 [1963, the night before the assassination], Lyndon Johnson was incapable of telling the truth. So he thought most highly of McNamara and thought—particularly after Cuba, where you can see what can happen to a country and how much depends on a particular individual—that it should be placed in the best possible hands. And we thought that McNamara was that individual.

MARTIN: McNamara was the strong man in the Cabinet whom the President would rely on?

KENNEDY: Yes. Now, he had, of course, his weaknesses like everybody else, but he was head and shoulders above everybody else. He'd done his homework; he spoke well; and he worked with the President.
I've seen him since that time, again with a different President. He's more effective and stronger almost, but that becomes more dangerous because there's not the balancing force that the President was for a very, very strong personality. [Johnson] doesn't have the background and experience that President Kennedy had, and so therefore [McNamara's] position carries. And then he gets influenced by what President Johnson wants, so that therefore he adapts himself to some extent. Where he could adapt himself to President Kennedy, he was adapting himself in the right direction, and where he adapts himself to somebody who is not quite that effective, that can be dangerous.

MARTIN: Were there others that the President was dissatisfied with, or was it a question that they really didn't make any difference?

KENNEDY: They really didn't make much difference. . . .

MARTIN: Isn't it the fact, though, Bob—and I don't want to put words in your mouth, but I just suggest this—there are only two things that really have made a difference in the last few years. One, at home, is civil rights; and the other is foreign policy. The jobs that matter in the government are the Secretary of State, Secretary of Treasury, Secretary of Defense, and Attorney General for the civil rights question?

KENNEDY: Well, I think another one that would make the difference is the head of GSA [General Services Administration] because it's where the corruption exists. There was a good deal of that in the past. We have an honest [Administrator of GSA], Bernie Boutin. The first fellow in there was from Pennsylvania,[15] a fellow who was put in on the recommendation of some of the Democratic politicians from Pennsylvania—

MARTIN: Who was that?

KENNEDY: I can't think of his name. He was a college president. Bernie Boutin was his deputy—from New Hampshire—who is a good friend of ours and a Democratic political leader. He was his deputy, so he took it over. And he's the first real . . . strong head of GSA that has existed, at least since 1950. But I think that if you're going to take jobs, the jobs I would get for control of domestic affairs would be GSA and Attorney General.

MARTIN: What about other sub-Cabinet posts: independent agencies and Assistant Secretaries?

KENNEDY: Over in the Department of Justice a high percentage of those who were selected were recommended by Byron White [Deputy Attorney General, later on the Supreme Court].

MARTIN: Was he a good friend of yours, Bob? That's how he happened to get into the thing?

KENNEDY: No, he got into the campaign because he was in PT [Patrol Torpedo boat] with the President, and then he heard Jack speak in 1958 or '59, liked him, and went to work to take the [Colorado] delegation away from the Governor, who was opposed to Jack. They didn't have a vote when they started and ended up getting the majority of the delegation in Colorado, all because of the hard work he did—plus Joe Dolan [Assistant Deputy Attorney General]. And then I asked him to be head of the citizens committee [Citizens for Kennedy–Johnson], which he agreed to do. I called him up, at the

President's request, and told him he could be either Secretary of the Army or Air Force, or Deputy Attorney General. I think those were the jobs. He said he wanted to come back and work with me in the Department of Justice.

MARTIN: You spent a lot of time on this in the first three months of the administration itself, didn't you?

KENNEDY: Yes. I think I spent most of or a good part of my time doing that, plus getting things started in the Department of Justice and becoming familiar with the work I was doing there. I had an office over at the Department of Justice for a month before I actually went to work there. They gave us office space during the transition.

MARTIN: I remember at the time there was a lot of talk or publicity about various task force reports being written, from right after the election on. Were these used much? And did they come to much or not?

KENNEDY: Yes. For instance, [*Life* magazine correspondent] Don Wilson and I got to do one on the USIA [United States Information Agency], and then he became Deputy [Director of] USIA. There were a number of others on important issues which, I think, played a role in guiding the President in steps he took after he became President.

MARTIN: The White House staff came right out of the campaign—

KENNEDY: Yes.

MARTIN: —and was almost self-surviving, wasn't it?

KENNEDY: Yes. Kenny O'Donnell became Jack's Assistant Secretary, sort of, during the campaign—general handyman—so he continued with that as the Appointments Secretary at the White House. That was rather natural.

Larry O'Brien . . . always had bad news. You know how people are always apt to see the worse side of things? Well, he was very competent, which I used to see, but I think Jack made him nervous, and so he offset that by telling him some terrible piece of news. Kenny O'Donnell always saw the bright side of things. Larry O'Brien always saw the gloomy side. Jack was not enthusiastic about him doing that [Congressional liaison work], because he didn't think he'd had any experience, and of course, as I say—

MARTIN: Well, then why did he have him?

KENNEDY: Well, I think just because I was a great booster, and Kenny thought [Larry] would do well. He wanted the job, and that was the only natural one for him—and so we sort of slid him into it.

MARTIN: I see. What about Ralph Dungan?

KENNEDY: Ralph Dungan worked in the campaign, and so, again, he sort of slid into the job [as Special Assistant to the President].

MARTIN: Arthur Schlesinger?

KENNEDY: I don't know—he's just sort of a natural. And Archie Cox. He did work in the campaign.

MARTIN: He never was with the President on the plane, or never was visible.

KENNEDY: No, but there were a lot of other people who did work in the campaign who weren't visible. The President wanted [Archibald Cox] to be Deputy Attorney General—I mean, Solicitor General. We asked him, and he agreed to take that.

MARTIN: Sorensen, of course.

KENNEDY: Yes.

MARTIN: Was there anybody else over there whom you might mention—who needs to be covered? Mike Feldman [Deputy Special Counsel to the President], of course, was in the campaign. Dick Goodwin was in the campaign. What did Dick do in the early days of the administration?

KENNEDY: He worked on the Alliance for Progress.[16] The President said [Goodwin] had two ideas. One was the Alliance for Progress, which was a pretty good idea—he had a number of ideas, but two worked out pretty well. The second was the Nobel Prize dinner, which was also his idea.[17]

MARTIN: Was that Dick Goodwin's idea?

KENNEDY: Yes. Both of them were fundamentally his ideas—which were pretty good. The President was rather high on him. And then he did some speech-writing which the President liked.

MARTIN: Then the President put him over in State under Woodward, right? [Robert F. Woodward was Assistant Secretary of State for Inter-American Affairs.]

KENNEDY: Yes, and he had such a tough time that he was about to quit government. He used to talk to me quite frequently about the difficulty, and I used to talk to the President. And finally he ended up over at the Peace Corps. He's been, as he says, up to the top and down at the bottom. I think the President appreciated him and thought he had some talent to offer.

MARTIN: Adolph Berle [Chairman of the Interdepartmental Task Force on Latin America, from January to July 1961] was in early on Latin America. What happened about that?

KENNEDY: Well, he just— he was— I don't know how he got in. I remember he was in at the Bay of Pigs, and he was in some other matters, and then he disappeared. But I was not involved in international affairs, really, up until after the Bay of Pigs. I went to a couple of Cabinet meetings, but I didn't get intimately involved except on a sporadic basis. And so some of those people who were working on some of these problems for the first three or four months, I didn't have much contact with.

MARTIN: What were you doing during the first three or four months?

KENNEDY: For the most part, seeing newspaper people.

MARTIN: Why was that?

KENNEDY: Well, I suppose because I knew so many from the campaign, from working—

MARTIN: And the President didn't have time?

KENNEDY: The President didn't have time.

MARTIN: Except at press conferences?

KENNEDY: Yes. And then I saw an awful lot of people on appointments. That was what I was doing.

MARTIN: There was another thing that was quite important very early on: this was that fight in the House over expanding the House Rules Committee.[18] Were you involved in that?

KENNEDY: Yes, I was involved with it.

MARTIN: Do you think it was important? At the time, it was considered quite important. I think it had to do with getting civil rights legislation out of the House.

KENNEDY: I got involved in it. I guess I talked to quite a few people. Larry O'Brien didn't know anybody. In fact, I suppose I spent some time on that.

MARTIN: What did you do?

KENNEDY: I called people and met with people—

MARTIN: People? You mean, Congress? ·

KENNEDY: Congress. And I also organized at least part of the fight. I don't remember who else was working on it. But, as I remember, it was right after we got in. Larry didn't know anybody—this was his first. He didn't know one Congressman from another, and I, at least, had had some experience with them—a lot with Dick Bolling [Democrat from Missouri] and Thompson[19] and some of these others from the campaign who were strongly in favor of the President. And then Bill Battle [of the U.S. Civil Rights Commission] was still around.

MARTIN: You were also, at the same time, working on sub-Cabinet level appointments. Did you use these as weapons to put pressure on the Congress to get the Rules Committee expanded?

KENNEDY: I don't think those things ever worked. No. Actually, you know, I read about those things. I don't think that they really are very effective. I think it's probably the relationship that exists, rather than blackmail or threats. I think it's just the fact that you've established a relationship; and it goes without saying that, if you want to continue the relationship and everybody wants to be friends, one person does a favor for somebody and then they in turn make sure the favor's done back. It's not done with saying, "Well, if you don't do this, we won't give you that job." But I think everybody understands that that's in the background. And there are some people for whom you can't do anything who were very, very helpful, and some people for whom you have to do a lot. Senator [Robert] Kerr was the most impossible one. He was a real bandit as far as this was concerned. He really held us up. We wouldn't get a tax bill unless he got his judge.

MARTIN: That's the way he put it?

KENNEDY: Yes. Senator [Allen] Ellender caused difficulty later on, on the farm bill, unless he got his U.S. Attorney. So there are some of those kinds of things. But our contact, at least during the Rules

Committee, was mostly in the fact that we had friends who had just been elected and who were willing to go along.

MARTIN: Was that an important move?

KENNEDY: Yes. It would have been very bad if we had lost it. Of course, Sam Rayburn was anxious to win it, you see. And it might be that we would have compromised it because Bill Battle—you know, from Virginia—was in the course of working something out. I had a lot of discussions with him on behalf of the President about this, of working something out with Howard Smith [Democratic Congressman from Virginia] so that Howard Smith would report out or would commit himself to report out the bills the President was really interested in—education and some of these others—in return for not getting into this fight. But by that time, the President, even if he had wanted to, couldn't pull out of it because Sam Rayburn wanted to win it. [Rayburn] was involved in it, and it became a bitter fight between two old men. And so even if we'd wanted to, we couldn't have gotten out of it. Once we got into it, it was important that we win it. Then, as you know, we won it by just a very small margin.

And the President always pointed to that later on when people were wondering why he couldn't get some of the bills through the House, or why he had to go slow, and why he had to deal with Congress. It was said that here we had Sam Rayburn and, therefore, the Texas delegation, that we had the maximum strength—the Democrats—and yet we only won it by a couple of votes. And how would we do on something that was far more controversial, where we didn't have a Sam Rayburn, couldn't bring along a lot of these southerners that he could in this kind of a fight? How much more difficult it was doing that. And I think it's a good lesson. *The New York Times* used to write editorials all the time that the President should use his art of persuasion and get these bills through the House, little knowing or realizing or bothering to realize that this was, then, far more difficult. We could point to this, where we won this fight—but only after that much bitterness and only with that much strength. How much more difficult it was when the odds were much higher against us!

MARTIN: The first Cabinet meeting was on the 22nd of January. Do you remember it? What happened? What was said?

KENNEDY: I think the President went around the room, as I remember. I remember he had a joke about me.

MARTIN: What was it?

KENNEDY: About calling me Attorney General. I remember we laughed about it. I think that we heard from everybody for five minutes or something. And he talked about—I think he talked about civil rights, hiring of Negroes.

MARTIN: The President really didn't use the Cabinet in the ordinary way, did he?

KENNEDY: No.

MARTIN: Why?

KENNEDY: Well, because, first, the Cabinet can't decide anything. The Secretary of Defense knows nothing about farm legislation and the growing of cotton in Georgia or the growing of wheat in Nebraska and what you should do about supporting the price of tobacco. The Secretary of Agriculture knows nothing about the situation in Saigon. The head of HEW can't advise the Attorney General about civil rights in Alabama. And the Attorney General can't advise the Postmaster General about the employees you should have in the Post Office. So, therefore, what subjects are there in common? There aren't any, except generally, I suppose, to brief the Cabinet members on what you're doing, to have them feel that they are members of an organization, and not all independent operators.

MARTIN: President Eisenhower, of course, felt differently, apparently, and did have regular, formal Cabinet meetings.

KENNEDY: With prayers.

MARTIN: Yes, I believe so.

KENNEDY: I suppose you could talk about general problems such as the economy or hiring Negroes—or those kinds of matters. Even though [JFK] had them very infrequently, I don't think that I probably attended half of the Cabinet meetings that he had.

MARTIN: He didn't have many.

KENNEDY: He didn't have many, and I didn't go to—

MARTIN: You didn't go to many that he had, I know that. Did the President tend to like small meetings and meetings that were aimed at a precise problem?

KENNEDY: And with those people whose advice he considered meaningful. And then he'd talk about the problems with them.

MARTIN: It was a more intimate give-and-take relationship?

KENNEDY: Give and take. But the most important factor was just the point that he had people whose judgment he had confidence in. So he'd have them around. He'd talk about a problem and then get their advice about it.

MARTIN: And aimed precisely at a problem?

KENNEDY: Yes.

MARTIN: Rather than general discussions at a large meeting?

KENNEDY: He might have a general discussion in a larger meeting—I can't think of any, except maybe the National Security Council—just to make sure they were on board about a particular point. But he'd have just the people who knew something about a particular point. He had always operated in that fashion, always felt he was able to rely on people who were around him, either when he was in the Senate or on the campaign.

That's really one of the basic reasons that we had the disaster at the Bay of Pigs. Because he came in there and met with the chairman of the Joint Chiefs of Staff, and the head of the CIA, and the head of the State Department and the Secretary of Defense; and he'd ask for their advice and he'd be asking them questions—factual questions—and he'd get answers; and he always had thought before, when he did any of that, that he could always rely on people. Well, it wasn't until after the Bay of Pigs that he found out that he couldn't rely on people. The mere fact that somebody was head of CIA or that General [Lyman] Lemnitzer had been in the Army thirty, forty years, didn't mean that you could rely on them to be prepared to give him a correct, factual presentation. Plus, their judgment was not infallible. He knew before what people's strengths and weaknesses were, and he just assumed rather naturally that everybody had equal strength and that he didn't have to go behind the military judgment of the Joint Chiefs of Staff or the intelligence judgment of the CIA.

And it was a major change made in the government of the United States—it was based, really, on the Bay of Pigs.

MARTIN: Just at the time of the election, [JFK] had a talk with President Eisenhower—I think on inauguration day or the night before. I've forgotten which.

KENNEDY: I think the day before. He told me of the conversation. He talked about Southeast Asia and he talked about Adenauer, about

Adenauer looking like an Asiatic—I can remember just incidental, little things. He said that Eisenhower had a very interesting description of Adenauer.

They talked about the problems of Southeast Asia and Laos. They talked about *The Longest Day* [by Cornelius Ryan],[20] and he was fascinated that Eisenhower had never read the book—and, in fact, hadn't seemed to have read anything! You know, he thought he had a rather fascinating personality and could understand, talking to him, why he was President of the United States.

He was a strong personality. I think [JFK] just felt that [Eisenhower] hadn't done his homework, that he didn't know a good deal about areas that he should know. I think he always felt that Eisenhower was unhappy with him—that he was so young and was elected President. And so—feeling Eisenhower was important and his election was so close—he always went out of his way to make sure that Eisenhower was brought in on all matters and that Eisenhower couldn't hurt the administration by going off and attacking. And that's why he made such an effort over Eisenhower—not that Eisenhower ever gave him any advice that was very helpful.

MARTIN: How did [JFK] feel about his inaugural speech and about the proceedings in the beginning?

KENNEDY: Oh, he was very happy, very pleased.

MARTIN: Do you recall that some time before the inaugural—I think it was right after the election, in fact—the President announced that he was going to ask J. Edgar Hoover [FBI] and Allen Dulles [CIA] both to stay on?

KENNEDY: And, also, the head of the Bureau of Narcotics.

MARTIN: [Harry J.] Anslinger, yes. Why?

KENNEDY: Well, he knew he was going to have Hoover. He was going to stay, he knew. He didn't have anything against Hoover. And he thought it was well that Hoover stayed, that we didn't cause any internal disruption by firing him, and that it would be well to get any speculation about that out of the way. Same thing with Allen Dulles, which was the same relative position. He'd been briefed by Allen Dulles, and I think he had respect for Allen Dulles—as he always had, even afterward. He always liked Allen Dulles. He spoke well of Allen Dulles. And I think the other one [Anslinger] was because my relationship had always been good with the Bureau of Narcotics.

MARTIN: During this spring and up to the Bay of Pigs, which was April 16 [1961], you were working in your office mainly on appointments, sub-Cabinet appointments. What were you doing about Justice?

KENNEDY: Well, I was working in Justice, and I was familiarizing myself with the operations of Justice. We were selecting our own Assistant Attorneys General. And I was just organizing that department. I also established our unit on organized crime.

MARTIN: Is that Walter Sheridan's unit?[21]

KENNEDY: No. Organized crime. There was a man by the name of Bill Hundley who had been there, and we moved him and put in a fellow by the name of Ed Silberling, from Long Island, who had had some important successes. And he turned out to be not very satisfactory— difficult to get along with and finally I removed him and put Bill Hundley back. I enlarged the unit with sixty lawyers, and then I brought in Mort Caplin as the Commissioner of Internal Revenue. He taught me down at Virginia, at the University of Virginia Law School. And I had a talk with him before he came in. The Internal Revenue Department had never done any work in organized crime, and I asked him—if he became Commissioner—if he'd be willing to devote his real major effort to that. And he agreed to that. I also, before Douglas Dillon was appointed to the Treasury Department that day, spoke to him. There had been a directive that had gone out from the Treasury Department that they couldn't do anything in this field, by a fellow by the name of [Walter R.] Schreiber. So this was going to be a real reversal for them. We had a meeting with Hoover, Caplin, Dillon, and myself on coordinating a drive on organized crime so that everybody'd get behind it. I had all the investigative agencies of government departments in and had meetings with them, and then—with the understanding that we'd pool their information— we set up this list of major underworld figures to go to work on.

Then I established the unit to deal with the Teamsters. We brought in a lot of young lawyers—

MARTIN: Is that a special unit on the Teamsters?

KENNEDY: Yes. It was headed up by Walter Sheridan.

MARTIN: This was the Sheridan group?

KENNEDY: Yes. It's made up now of about twelve or eighteen lawyers. And in the original [group], there were two or three lawyers who were working in the Department of Justice already, and they were working on the case in Sun Valley, down in Florida.[22] Ultimately, because the judge was so weak in Florida, I couldn't go ahead with the case. The judge I don't think was dishonest, but he was a very, very weak man, and I knew that if we did not get a strong judge we could never have any hope of winning the case. There was an indictment in Chicago which supplemented that.[23] I was involved in that.

As I say, most of the appointments were suggested. The major one that I worried over was the head of the Civil Rights Division. The fellow who should naturally have been appointed was Harris Wofford, who had done the work for us on civil rights during the campaign. I was reluctant to appoint him because he was so committed on civil rights emotionally, and what I wanted was a tough lawyer who could look at things objectively and give advice—and handle things properly. And that's why I finally settled on Burke Marshall.

NOTES

PART I: INTERVIEW WITH ARTHUR M. SCHLESINGER, JR., WASHINGTON, D.C., FEBRUARY 27, 1965

1) **that famous weekend.** The weekend of August 24–25, 1963. The letter (or, more properly, the cable) was drafted by Averell Harriman, Roger Hilsman, and Michael Forrestal. It authorized the Ambassador to Saigon, Henry Cabot Lodge, to suggest to a group of disaffected Vietnamese generals that the United States would not oppose a coup to unseat Ngo Dinh Diem, Prime Minister of South Vietnam.

2) *The Uncertain Trumpet* by Maxwell Taylor (New York, Harper Brothers, 1959). A landmark study of American military security needs.

3) **the Taylor group.** The Cuba Study Group, consisting of Maxwell Taylor, Robert Kennedy, Allen Dulles, and Admiral Arleigh Burke served as a board of inquiry for the Bay of Pigs failure.

4) **Counterinsurgency Committee.** In January 1962, John Kennedy created a new National Security Council committee—Special Group, Counterinsurgency or Special Group (CI)—to coordinate American efforts in this area. It was headed by Maxwell Taylor.

5) **ExComm committee.** The Executive Committee (ExComm) of the National Security Council drew its membership from the NSC but did not include all of its statutory members and was supplemented by other advisers on occasion.

6) **Keating.** A prominent critic of the Kennedy administration's Cuban policy, New York Senator Kenneth B. Keating publicly charged the administration with ignoring the existence of Soviet offensive missiles in Cuba.

7) **troops to Thailand.** In May 1962, after renewed fighting broke out in Thailand, the United States sent naval and ground forces to support anti-Communist forces.

8) **Graham memorandum.** The reference is to an account of the events surrounding Lyndon Johnson's selection as running mate prepared by Philip Graham, publisher of *The Washington Post.*

9) **meeting with the labor leaders.** Walter Reuther, Arthur Goldberg, and Alex Rose met with John F. Kennedy as representatives of the labor movement to discuss the vice-presidential nomination.

10) **Birmingham.** Birmingham, Alabama, was the scene of a series of civil rights demonstrations, police assaults, and riots from April 12 to May 10, 1963. Renewed violence occurred on May 12, 1963, and federal troops were dispatched to nearby Fort McClellan.

11) **the President of Korea.** The reference is to General Park Chung Hee, who seized power in a bloodless coup, May, 1961.

12) **the President of Costa Rica.** Mario Enchadi Jimenez.

13) **Thailand.** The reference is probably to Kenneth Todd Young.

PART I: INTERVIEW WITH JOHN BARTLOW
MARTIN, McLEAN, VIRGINIA, FEBRUARY 29, 1964

14) **the major candidate.** The reference is to Fred Heinkel.

15) **fellow ... from Pennsylvania.** The reference is to John L. Moore.

16) **Alliance for Progress.** The Alliance for Progress was a U.S.–Latin American social and economic development program inaugurated in March 1961.

17) **the Nobel Prize dinner.** The reference is to a White House dinner to honor recipients of the Nobel Prize from the Western Hemisphere.

18) **that fight in the House.** In January 1961 the House of Representatives voted to expand the Rules Committee from twelve members to fifteen.

19) **Thompson.** The reference is probably to Frank Thompson (b. 1918), who served as the Democratic Representative from New Jersey, 1955–1977.

20) **The Longest Day** by Cornelius Ryan (New York, Simon & Schuster, 1959). An in-depth account of the Allies' Normandy Invasion on June 6, 1944, considered to be the turning point of World War II.

21) **Walter Sheridan's unit.** Sheridan headed a unit on labor rackets in the Organized Crime Section of the Justice Department.

22) **the case in Sun Valley.** James R. Hoffa, president of the Teamsters Union, was indicted in 1960 for mail fraud in connection with a Florida real estate venture.

23) **indictment in Chicago.** After an investigation of the Teamsters' Central State Pension Fund in Chicago, Hoffa was charged with conspiracy to defraud the trustees of the fund. Hoffa was convicted on jury-tampering and other charges in 1964.

PART II

■

"WHATEVER IS NECESSARY"

ROBERT KENNEDY AND CIVIL RIGHTS

INTRODUCTION

Robert Kennedy served as Attorney General from January 20, 1961, to September 3, 1964, when he resigned to run for the Senate in New York. He did not seek the Attorney General's office. After John Kennedy's election he had toyed with the idea of leaving Washington and carving out an independent career. But at his father's urging and his brother's insistence, he took the post. He did so with misgivings, mainly because he believed that he would be involved in so many controversial issues, especially civil rights, that he would become an albatross around his brother's neck.

When President-elect Kennedy announced from the front steps of his home in Georgetown on a cold morning in early January 1961 that RFK would be the new Attorney General, reaction was generally negative. *The New York Times* fumed editorially about nepotism and Bob's lack of experience as a practicing lawyer. Some pundits and some politicians predicted that he would fail spectacularly.

The naysayers were wrong. Robert Kennedy recruited a group of diverse, highly motivated young lawyers for key positions in the Department of Justice. They formed, as Victor S. Navasky observed in his book *Kennedy Justice* (a less than laudatory critique of Bob's tenure as Attorney General), "the most talented top-level team on the New Frontier, certainly a rival to anything past Attorneys General, with the conceivable exception of Francis Biddle, had been able to muster." Moreover, because he was the President's brother and closest confidant, he became without question the most powerful Attorney General in the nation's history.

Kennedy was always aware, as he says in the following interviews, that if he hadn't been the President's brother, FBI Director J. Edgar Hoover and other barons of the bureaucracy "wouldn't have paid any attention to me." But he *did* make those in charge of the machinery of the Justice Department pay attention to him. He used the power of the attorney generalship, a power he describes as frighteningly subject to abuse, to bring government agencies into line for coordinated action, notably to deal with one civil rights crisis after another and to mount a sustained attack on organized crime.

Robert Kennedy was a hardworking, innovative leader, and he infused those qualities throughout the Department. Fed by a restless curiosity and a probing mind, by a need to learn and grow with every experience, he felt compelled to act whenever he saw a need. Whatever it was—a child standing forlornly outside a cabin in West Virginia, or the condition of the Washington, D.C., public schools, or organized crime's expanding influence—he had to act. More often than not, he managed to bring about badly needed changes. More often than not, he made a difference.

Those qualities are quite evident in his answers in Part II, especially to those questions concerning the Justice Department's role in civil rights. He came into office aware that civil rights would be a major issue, one that would sorely test the administration's mettle. But like most of his fellow countrymen, he only dimly perceived the true desperation of America's black population. It was as he grappled with crisis after crisis that he steadily gained understanding and sensitivity. By the time he left office, he had begun to identify closely with the dissatisfaction of blacks and the problems of other minorities.

RFK also had a hard-nosed sense of honesty that enabled him to admit freely his mistakes, to change his opinions, and to adopt new perspectives. Thus, some of the opinions he expressed here, and elsewhere in the interviews, changed in later years. Although he once felt that Governor George Wallace's "stand in the schoolhouse door" looked ridiculous and would be seen as a sham throughout the nation, he came to realize (particularly after the Governor's strong showing in the 1964 primaries) that Wallace had touched a wellspring of harsh opposition—in the North as well as in the South—to political and social equality for black Americans.

Another example was his anger at what James Baldwin and other blacks said to him during what he thought was to have been a pleasant exchange of views. Robert Kennedy had never heard an American citizen say he would not fight to defend the country. When his indignation at last subsided, he would say, "I guess if I were in his shoes, if

I had gone through what he's gone through, I might feel differently about the country." And it was not long before he was asking the Senate Judiciary Committee: "How long can we say to a Negro in Jackson, 'When war comes you will be an American citizen, but in the meantime you're a citizen of Mississippi—and we can't help you'?"

Part II of Robert Kennedy's oral history traces the Attorney General's increasing involvement in the central domestic issue of the 1960s: the struggle for racial equality. Accompanied by Burke Marshall, his Assistant Attorney General for Civil Rights, RFK is interviewed here by the Pulitzer Prize-winning journalist Anthony Lewis. Lewis questions Kennedy most extensively about the major civil rights crises and issues of the early 1960s: the Freedom Rides, James Meredith's admission to the University of Mississippi, alleged Communist involvement in the civil rights movement, the civil rights activities of the FBI, the University of Alabama, the Birmingham riots, the drafting of the 1964 Civil Rights Act, and the 1963 civil rights "March on Washington." RFK's responses portray the evolution of his and President Kennedy's roles in civil rights concerns, his relationship with the FBI and its strong-willed director, and his sense of the proper role of the federal government in an era of turbulent social change.

INTERVIEWS WITH
ANTHONY LEWIS (WITH
BURKE MARSHALL PRESENT)

■

NEW YORK CITY, DECEMBER 4, 1964;
McLEAN, VIRGINIA, DECEMBER 6 AND 22, 1964

TOWARD THE PRESIDENCY

LEWIS: I remember talking with you long ago about what interest there had been in your family, what awareness of the situation of the Negro in this country. And I remember your saying, "Well, we didn't lie awake nights worrying about it."

Can you say a little more about that—how you really came to be concerned about the issue?

KENNEDY: I don't think that it was a matter that we were extra-concerned about as we were growing up. There wasn't any great problem. I know it's the worst thing in the world to say that some of your best friends are Negroes, but as I was growing up, I suppose two out of my four best friends were Negroes. It was all sort of accepted. You know, there was never any thought about the fact that there was anything different.

What we did grow up with was the idea that there were a lot of people who were less fortunate and a lot of people who were hungry—this was during the 1930s—people who had a difficult time. White people and Negroes were all put in that same category. One had a social responsibility to try to do something about it.

But as far as separating the Negroes as having a more difficult time than the white people, that was not a particular issue in our house, just for the reason that we were looking at the overall picture of problems here in the United States—plus the problems abroad—of people having a very tough time.

LEWIS: Relating that to your brother specifically, do you recall any occasions on which race—the Negro—was an issue to him as a young man, a boy, in the family, any episode in which this came acutely to his attention?

KENNEDY: No. As I say, there was a good deal of conversation and discussion about the fact that people had problems. I remember it during the 1930s—the Depression—and thereafter, even though I was very young. So it must have been much more of a point to him.

Then we came to the war. People were being killed, so that was the problem. A lot of his friends and a lot of people who used to be around our home, my home, during that period of time were killed during the war or badly hurt during the war. So the focus of attention was on that.

Then he ran for Congress, and, I suppose, groups broke down more at that time on the basis of how they voted.

LEWIS: Was there much of a Negro population in that district?

KENNEDY: In the Eleventh Congressional District there were some. At least it was somewhat of a factor. There's not a great number of Negroes in Massachusetts, anyway. In 1952, in that election, I don't think that it was as much of an issue or much of a question. We spent some time in those areas, in those wards. But it was mostly—I think, probably, like the Democratic Party generally—looking at how many votes we would receive rather than what you were going to do afterward, particularly.

LEWIS: But no question of dealing with Negro politicians, as one would in running for President, in terms of what you'd have to promise or what was desirable to say to that group?

KENNEDY: Yes, I think, more in that way. [Negro] Democratic politicians at that time I don't think were looking for anything particular for their people. They were looking just for power or recognition for themselves. I think that was the great change during the 1960s—that that was no longer possible. But I think those running for office in the Democratic party looked to just three or four people who would then deliver the Negro vote. And you never had to say you were going to do anything on civil rights. You never had to say you were going to do anything on housing. It was mostly just recognition of them. And it was much easier if you were a Democratic politician running for office: You could receive the vote quite easily. So there was never anywhere where we'd have to get certain civil rights legislation passed or fight for them. That was never an issue in Massachusetts.

LEWIS: And, concomitantly, it was not really necessary for you and your brother to be brought face to face with what was qualitatively different about the Negro's life in this country—that it wasn't just another person who was poor, for example?

KENNEDY: No, I suppose in Massachusetts it wasn't really a problem. They were having a difficult time but there were a lot of white people who were. Where my father came from—which was all Irish originally and then became all Italian—and in the North End, where my mother came from, there was tremendous poverty. The Negroes were a relatively small population. And we weren't thinking of the Negroes in Mississippi or Alabama—what should be done for them. We were thinking of what needed to be done in Massachusetts.

LEWIS: Did this change at all during the campaign for the presidency in 1960? Or was it still more or less a kind of traditional bloc-vote affair?

KENNEDY: I might say that I went—if I get into my part—that I went down to law school at the University of Virginia, where we had a Negro in our class. I guess he was the first Negro—

LEWIS: This was about 1950 or so?

KENNEDY: Yes. I think he was the first Negro who went there. . . . I became head of the Student Legal Forum, which invited visitors in. I invited Ralph Bunche to come down. There was tremendous opposition to that in my own group and in the law school. Then, also, I said that he had to speak to a desegregated audience, so there was a split in our own group about that. Finally, I went to the president of the university, [Colgate] Darden. And he gave approval to it. It was the first time they had had a Negro speak to a desegregated audience, I guess, certainly at the law school or the college—he spoke under the aegis of the college—and, I think, in that part of Virginia.

In 1960 there wasn't really much difference as far as the Negro was concerned. We had some problem with the Negroes at that time because they didn't associate President Kennedy with the cause of the Negroes, particularly. He voted against Title III [in the Civil Rights Act of 1957]. Wasn't that it?

LEWIS: And I believe he voted in favor of the jury trial amendment. That was the key vote, I think.

KENNEDY: That was the key vote. He voted in favor of the jury trial amendment, so there were some reservations about him on that. Nixon didn't have a bad record as far as Negroes were concerned, so they were reasonably interested in him. They were traditionally Democratic; but they had reservations about Senator Kennedy and they didn't think badly of Nixon. The Negro vote in the 1960 election was to be won or lost. We could win it or we could lose it.

LEWIS: Now, a special effort was made, beginning right back at the convention. I remember the setup with Shriver and Harris Wofford—breakfast with Negro leaders at the convention.

KENNEDY: We were doing that with every group. I mean, you always have to do that.

LEWIS: It was done with every group?

KENNEDY: He always had. You'd have to do that. That's automatic.

LEWIS: But there seemed to me to be something qualitatively different about that though, because it was more issue-oriented. They [Shriver and Wofford] were people who talked to the Negroes about civil rights, not about bloc delivery of votes.

KENNEDY: Yes, but I think that would be true in any national campaign. You'd still have to do that, and you'd have to go through the motions with a lot of these people. But I'd say it was more pronounced in 1960 than it had been four years before or eight years before.

Secondly, we had an extra problem. We had to make more of an effort because they weren't tied to John F. Kennedy as they would be ordinarily to a Democratic leader: first, because, as I said, they had some feeling for Nixon; and, secondly, because they hadn't any strong feeling for John Kennedy or knew how he felt. We had to make a major effort through the traditional ways as well as the ways that were just then coming into existence.

LEWIS: Let's pick out a specific episode from the campaign because it's well known. Tell us about Dr. [Martin Luther] King—from your point of view—the two telephone calls: your brother's and yours. [In response to the arrest of Martin Luther King, Jr., in De Kalb County, Georgia, in the spring of 1960, John Kennedy called Mrs. Coretta Scott King, and Robert Kennedy phoned Judge J. Oscar Mitchell of De Kalb County Civil and Criminal Court.]

KENNEDY: I think that the stories that have appeared were, as far as his telephone call, reasonably accurate, as I remember it. I never discussed it with him that I can remember, and I'm not sure that I knew about his telephone call at the time that I made my telephone call. I was up in New York, and I don't know whether it was Griffin Bell [then chief of staff for Georgia's Governor Ernest Vandiver] or maybe Bob Troutman from Georgia—

LEWIS: What was Griffin Bell at that time? Was he helping you in your campaign?

KENNEDY: Yes, the campaign. I'm not sure now who it was, because I think Bob Troutman [Kennedy campaign director for the southern states] was against us having anything to do with Martin Luther King at the time. But someone called me from Georgia and said that the Governor would like to speak to me.

LEWIS: Who was Governor at that time? Griffin?

KENNEDY: No.

BURKE MARSHALL: Vandiver.

KENNEDY: Yes. Either I talked with the Governor or the Governor sent me a message—I think I talked with the Governor—and he said that, if I called the judge, he thought that the judge would let Martin Luther King off—and that that would be helpful.

LEWIS: In other words, the suggestion came from Governor Vandiver.

KENNEDY: Yes.

LEWIS: There's a footnote to history.

KENNEDY: Yes, I know, isn't it? It's the first time I've told it, because I thought it would destroy the Governor. Anyway, the suggestion came from him either directly or indirectly. The judge was a good friend of the Governor, and the judge said that if I called and it was a matter of importance, he'd make the arrangements. So I called. And I was out on Long Island speaking at the time. I went into a pay booth and I called the judge and said, "Will he get out on bail?" Whatever I said, he got him out.

LEWIS: He let him out on bail.

KENNEDY: I thought that it would be very helpful. And the judge said, "Bob, it's nice to talk to you. I don't have any objection about doing that." So he let him out on bail.

And the judge came to see me after I became Attorney General.

We had a very nice visit, and neither of us mentioned how I happened to call him. I've seen him once since then—the judge. I don't know if he's still a judge.

LEWIS: I thought you were going to end the story by saying that today he's on the Supreme Court.

KENNEDY: Supreme Court. No, he never asked for anything. Very interesting. That's how that happened. And our actions, my brother's and mine, were independent of one another.

LEWIS: That's an ironic twist on what happened later with Governor Vandiver, which I was going to come to. You remember all the noise there was shortly before your brother took office about whether he would appoint Governor Vandiver as Secretary of the Army or something of that kind—the objections from civil rights groups?

KENNEDY: Well, I don't think that, first, Vandiver is the brightest man in the world. Secondly, I don't know, I think that was not any strong conviction on behalf of Martin Luther King that he—

LEWIS: Loyalty to the ticket, I suppose, wasn't it?

KENNEDY: Yes.

LEWIS: Which is good enough. You don't want any more than that. What else during the campaign? Let me ask you this. These philosophical questions are probably a little hard to answer. But was there anything during the campaign that you think brought you or your brother face to face with the actual situation that you saw later, as Attorney General, of the Negro in the South?

KENNEDY: No.

LEWIS: This terrible helplessness?

KENNEDY: No. I just have to keep going back to the point that there was a good deal of feeling on the part of President Kennedy about helping those who were helpless. I think there was a general feeling that Negroes were in difficulty in the South as well as in many of the northern communities—as well as a lot of white people. A lot needed to be done.

But we just didn't sit down and wring our hands and shake our heads, and have meetings about how awful it was about the Negro in Mississippi. That didn't occur after he became President, other than saying, "Aren't they bastards!"—or something—"to be treating—"

LEWIS: Yes, but there were some rather acute incidents of killings and beatings that made it rather hard to escape.

KENNEDY: But when you asked me: "Did you ever talk about it or concentrate on it?"—well, we didn't do it. And we didn't do it after he became President and I became Attorney General, either.

LEWIS: I didn't ask you whether you talked. I asked you whether you became aware of the rather special horror of life for the Negro in the South.

KENNEDY: No.

LEWIS: During the campaign, what Negroes or civil rights leaders did you or the President talk to with any frequency? Was Louie Martin [a journalist then on the campaign staff] involved at that point?

KENNEDY: Louie Martin was the best, had the best judgment. I talked to him a lot. Harris Wofford was consulted, but he didn't have nearly the judgment that Louie Martin did. Of course, he's not Negro. And he didn't have nearly the judgment.

LEWIS: But he knew those people?

KENNEDY: He knew those people much better than any of *us* knew them. And he was helpful. But, as I say, his judgment was not nearly as good. Then up in New York, [Congressman] Adam Clayton Powell. Adam Clayton Powell always exacts a price, a monetary price, for his support. He always bids one party off against another.

LEWIS: What was the price in 1960?

KENNEDY: I don't remember what the figure was.

LEWIS: By monetary, you mean cash?

KENNEDY: Yes.

LEWIS: Cold cash on the line? Not favors?

KENNEDY: No, no. He [wants] money. Of course, he says he uses it to help his—

LEWIS: Flock?

KENNEDY: Yes. To help in the district, to bring the votes out and everything. I don't know how much ever goes to that, but that's what he's always done here in mayoralties and all the rest of the campaigns. He had a much more difficult time with us.

I think generally, basically, the person who knows the situation the best as far as the Negro effort during the campaign would be Louie Martin.

THE NEW ATTORNEY GENERAL

LEWIS: I think the next question . . . would be how you became Attorney General and whether there wasn't the consideration that the newspapers were talking about at the time: that you should not be Attorney General because of the heat that would inevitably arise about civil rights and whether it would hurt your brother to have someone so close to him associated with it.

KENNEDY: That was my strongest feeling. And what really made an impression upon me was [Attorney General] Bill Rogers hiding in the plane when he went to South Carolina.

LEWIS: Tell me about that.

KENNEDY: During the campaign he went on a tour with Nixon, and they stopped first in South Carolina. Then they went on to Texas. And while he was in South Carolina, he hid in the plane.

[South Carolina Governor] Fritz Hollings found that he had hid in that plane. And so that next week or ten days of the campaign were all on the fact that Bill Rogers, who was Nixon's closest friend, was hiding in the plane while they were in South Carolina. Then they went on to Texas. And Bill Rogers was brought out then because he had made some recommendation regarding the tidelands or something. So he was a great hero.

I thought, first, it was going to be so difficult—civil rights—and secondly, that if my brother were going to run again in 1964, to have an Attorney General who can't hide in a plane and has the same last name as the President of the United States would just be fatal. Because we'd be doing nothing but getting into fights anyway. That was, I suppose, my greatest reservation. Plus the fact that I thought I'd like to get away from him for a while. So that was a major factor which we discussed frequently.

LEWIS: How was that factor eliminated? Did your brother ever say to you—

KENNEDY: No. First my brother offered Abe Ribicoff the position of Attorney General when they were in Florida. And Abe Ribicoff, in my judgment, wanted to be a justice of the Supreme Court. And he thought he would alienate so many people on the Judiciary Committee that he could never get approved as a justice of the Supreme Court. And as he said it, he didn't think a Jew should be putting Negro children in white Protestant schools in the South—that wasn't the way to handle it—at the instruction of a Catholic. He didn't want to do it. He thought that it was too controversial. And the better place to go was HEW.

Well, my father was strongly in favor of my taking it. And I think it eventually came down to the fact that President Kennedy felt that it might be nice to have somebody around whom he could discuss things with. And there was no way of me being around—I wasn't going to work in the White House—there was no way of being around and having a position of authority unless you were a member of the Cabinet, because therefore you were equal to everybody else. But if you had any position that was lower than that, then—

LEWIS: As in the White House, you mean?

KENNEDY: I didn't want to be in the White House. I didn't want to do that. If I was going to work in the government at all, I wanted to have a position of my own responsibility, not just taking direct orders from anybody. I didn't want that. If I was going to do it, I had to have a position which had equality of responsibility and prestige, because otherwise I would be resented, and rightfully so, by anybody for whom I would be working or anybody else who had a higher position. So I had to be in the Cabinet if I was going to perform that function. And the only place I could really be in the Cabinet was as Attorney General.

That was finally what resolved the issue for my going, because I decided the night before he announced it that I wouldn't do it. We finally talked about doing this at breakfast—my doing it on this basis that I'm discussing now. For that reason I did it— not so much to become Attorney General as to be around during that time.

LEWIS: How did Bill Lawrence happen to write the story that he did, a week or so before the event? I think it was at least a week.[1]

KENNEDY: You see, this was being discussed during that period of time. The President was considering it. And I was considering it. That was the basis of it.

LEWIS: Did either you or your brother at that time have any idea what a large proportion of your time and your effort as Attorney General would be devoted to this issue?

KENNEDY: I think probably yes. I don't know if we foresaw or anticipated the great number of problems. But that was a factor that we had discussed, which I felt very strongly about, as I say: just the fact that I was going to be so much involved in it and so much needed to be done that it could create tremendous political difficulties and problems for him—not only in the '64 election but in attempting to obtain the passage of legislation in other fields.

LEWIS: Well, it did create those problems but probably no more than you anticipated.

KENNEDY: No. By '63, in my judgment, the fact that I was Attorney General caused him many more problems than if I hadn't been his brother.

LEWIS: In the South?

KENNEDY: Yes. In fact, as we said, instead of talking about Robert Kennedy, they started talking about the "Kennedy brothers"—which he used to point out to me frequently. It was no longer Robert, the Attorney General, but now they were talking about the Kennedy brothers. In fact, it became so extensive that in 1963, I discussed with him about trying to get out of there so that he—

LEWIS: At what point in 1963? How early?

KENNEDY: Oh, I suppose September or October of 1963. About getting out as Attorney General. And on what basis I could get out as Attorney General, because I thought it was such a burden to carry in the 1964 election.

LEWIS: It was very hard to do while the civil rights bill was pending.

KENNEDY: Yes. He felt that it was impossible to do because it would make it look as if we were running away from it. It became that much of a factor, that much a problem. Everything I did before then, up to '62, was focused on *me*. And *he* wasn't such a bad fellow. By 1963 it was focused on both of *us*. And that caused problems, politically, as we got ready for the election in 1964. The only basis on which I could get out was that he wanted me to manage the campaign or something, so that I'd get out at that time, but—

LEWIS: That would have been very hard for you, also.

KENNEDY: Well, that wasn't important. He didn't think it was a good idea. The way we left it was just that we would watch it and see if there was something that we should do. The important thing was that he get elected and that this was causing a lot of problems.

LEWIS: Well, he would, in any event, have been elected without the southern states—most of them, I mean. He would not have won any of the states that [1964 Republican presidential candidate, Senator Barry] Goldwater won, as it turned out, would he? Georgia, conceivably.

KENNEDY: No, he wouldn't have won any of them, and I suppose he might have lost—probably lost—Texas.

LEWIS: Oh, do you think so?

KENNEDY: I think he might very well have lost Texas, and I think he might have lost the rest of the southern states.

LEWIS: Well, then, you just would have had to lose those southern states.

KENNEDY: Yes, that's right. But we didn't know at that time who was going to be the opponent. The one he was most concerned about was [Michigan Governor George] Romney.

LEWIS: Romney? That surprises me.

KENNEDY: Because he thought that he'd be so difficult to soak, and that such an evangelist would have been more difficult to run against. He was always for God, and he was always for—

LEWIS: Mother.

KENNEDY: —and against big government and against big labor—everything that appealed. So that he would have some appeal in the South and he would have some appeal in the North, and could cause some difficulty. Barry Goldwater, [JFK] always thought, was the easiest.

LEWIS: There was no question of changing the vice-presidential candidate, was there?

KENNEDY: No, there wasn't.

LEWIS: I meant the question seriously.

KENNEDY: No. The President always felt that Johnson, on civil rights, wanted to get too far involved in it—personally—than was necessary.

LEWIS: Now what do you mean by that?

KENNEDY: At the time the matter arose, he spoke frequently on civil rights. And the President didn't think that it was necessary during that time because he felt that the burden was being carried by action and that Lyndon Johnson should, well—

LEWIS: Remain a more acceptable southern figure?

KENNEDY: Well, [speak] no more than the President was speaking— when it was necessary to speak, and where it made a difference, and where it helped. That was the thing to do. Where it didn't help, there wasn't any point in doing it.

LEWIS: I was going to get to the point of your choosing Burke [Marshall] —how that was done—the transitional period you were in, in the Justice Department. When you first moved in there, you had a little office, as I recall.

What did you learn in that opening period, if anything, about [the Justice Department's] civil rights activities? I have the impression that you were struck about their not doing enough on voting, particularly. How did you learn about that?

KENNEDY: All the southerners were very much in favor of my being Attorney General. The strongest support I received as Attorney General came from the southerners.

LEWIS: You mean, at the beginning?

KENNEDY: Yes, because I had been investigating labor unions. They didn't like labor unions much. Just as businessmen thought I was wonderful during that period of time. So, I mean, [Senators] Jim Eastland [of Mississippi], and John McClellan [of Arkansas], of course, and Sam Ervin [of North Carolina], and Olin Johnston [of South Carolina] all spoke out in favor of me.

I went and had a visit with Jim Eastland. He talked about what he thought of my predecessors. First, he talked about [Deputy Attorney General Lawrence E.] Walsh, who he thought was a fine fellow— very honest, very upright, and whom he trusted completely. And then he talked about Bill Rogers, who he said he liked very much, and he said, "You can't have the same confidence in him, of course, as you could in Walsh—as far as his integrity or his honesty was concerned." He said, "Did you know that he never brought a case in the state of Mississippi. Never brought a civil rights case in the state of Mississippi." Then he winked at me.

The whole thrust of his statement was just the fact that Bill Rogers hadn't met his responsibility and done his duty on Mississippi. And Jim Eastland felt a certain amount of contempt for him. I might say, as far as Eastland is concerned, that he never made any effort to stop us from doing anything in the state of Mississippi, to try to impede anything that we did in the state of Mississippi. Nor did he ever tie any legislation that we were interested in—whether it was crime legislation or any other legislation that we were interested in before the Judiciary Committee—tie it to anything that he wanted in Mississippi, either because of judges that he wanted appointed, or steps that we were taking, or cases that were being brought in Mississippi. He never called me to suggest I not bring a case in Mississippi, nor did he ever call me to ask me not to take any action in Mississippi that we took. I had a lot of conversations with him during all the crises that occurred in the state of Mississippi. And he has always kept his word, and he was always available, and he always told me exactly where he stood—what he could do and what he couldn't do. And he also told me who I could trust and who I shouldn't trust in the state of Mississippi, in his judgment. And his advice was very, very helpful during that three-and-a-half-year period. I found it much more pleasant to deal with him than many of the so-called liberals in the House Judiciary Committee or in other parts of Congress or the Senate.

LEWIS: We'll make sure that this entire conversation is kept out of New York politics for the next hundred and fifty years.

Here you are in the Justice Department back in 1961, January. Let's just say a word about how you came to have Burke as your assistant.

KENNEDY: I think I was influenced a good deal by Byron White.

LEWIS: You did not know Burke before this at all?

KENNEDY: No. But I knew Harris Wofford. And the person who was logical for that position was Harris Wofford, who wanted the position, and who Sargent Shriver and everybody who was associated with our fight on civil rights wanted for that job. Harris Wofford was very emotionally involved in all of these matters and was rather in some areas a slight madman. I didn't want to have someone in the Civil Rights Division who was dealing not from fact but was dealing from emotion and who wasn't going to give what was in the best interest of President Kennedy—what he was trying to accomplish for the country—but advice which the particular individual felt was in the interest of a Negro or a group of Negroes or a group of those who were interested in civil rights.

I wanted advice and ideas from somebody who had the same interests and motivation that I did.

LEWIS: That's always the hard thing to find, isn't it?

KENNEDY: Yes.

LEWIS: You were lucky.

KENNEDY: Then we found it. That was the reason I looked outside of Harris Wofford.

LEWIS: Just in all fairness, for history, to Harris, I'm going to interject two things. One is, there wasn't any question about his loyalty to President Kennedy for a long period.

KENNEDY: No.

LEWIS: And the second was that I think he, among other people, suggested Burke's name as an alternative.

KENNEDY: I remember that. That's possible. I think Harris Wofford's a fine fellow. And he did a terrific job. He did a great job for the Peace Corps and all the rest of it. I just don't think that he would have been fitted for that position. So I wanted to get a very good lawyer and somebody, also, who had some feeling about this and knew something about it. And Burke Marshall was suggested. It really came down to Burke Marshall or Harris Wofford—until I decided on Burke Marshall.

LEWIS: And you did it on the basis, primarily, of Byron [White]'s friendship with Burke? His knowledge of Burke?

KENNEDY: Well, he suggested him, and, I think, just the fact of what I wanted to have and the recommendations I heard about Burke Marshall—that he was such a good lawyer—and the rest of the qualifications. It was on that basis that he was selected.

"THE LOGICAL THING TO DO": DESEGREGATION
IN NEW ORLEANS

LEWIS: The first time, specifically, when Burke knew that you and he would get along was the time of the New Orleans school crisis. [U.S. District Judge Skelly Wright had ordered school integration against the vigorous opposition of the Louisiana legislature, which attempted to prevent the New Orleans school board from complying. In September 1961, schools were integrated in New Orleans without violence.] It was a big political issue in Louisiana, involving politicians with whom you had been dealing very regularly. The Justice Department previously had temporized on the situation. But you showed no hesitation in saying that the court orders had to be [obeyed].

MARSHALL: Yes. The Justice Department had temporized on that. Judge Wright had the New Orleans school case before him since— well, going back several years, in any event. Finally, in 1960, he decided he'd already ordered the school board to submit a plan—and they hadn't submitted a plan. There was no desegregation. They weren't paying any attention to his order. So he entered an order of his own that gave Negro children the choice, in first grade, of either going to the school closest to them or to the school that they would be assigned as Negro children, which would have involved some desegregation of some schools.

Then he got in touch with the Department of Justice, and he asked for assistance through the use of marshals in enforcing that order.

KENNEDY: Which was rather interesting because, in view of Little Rock[2] and all the rest of it, you would think that that would be almost automatic.

LEWIS: . . . Did Judge Wright renew the request when you took office?

MARSHALL: I think Judge Wright called me. In any event, the issue that came up was paying the teachers and withdrawing the funds from the desegregated schools. And it was a question of whether we would do anything about that. It was a defiance by the Governor and by the state school board. And Judge Wright wanted us to get into that. That's how the issue started: It was whether we would proceed against the Governor.

KENNEDY: And to stop them on the payments.

There were different facets than ever before, because it was a question of what we were going to do about the money and the payment of the teachers and where the money was going to come from—and then, finally, whether we were willing to put some of these people in jail. Some important public officials.

So we were involved, within two months, in a really major struggle with them.

LEWIS: The whole Department was much more intimately involved day to day than it had ever been. There was new legislation passed every day in an effort to change the school board and do everything else.

KENNEDY: That's right. We had a fight, a struggle each day in which decisions had to be made as to how far we were willing to go—and then, eventually, whether we were going to put people in jail.

LEWIS: What we ought to get at here, I think, is what you talked to your brother about on this.

KENNEDY: I don't remember discussing it with him, particularly. I must have kept him advised. But I think that it was just understood by us—which has always been understood—that I have, you know, my area of responsibility. And I'd do it. If there was a problem where he should be kept advised, then I'd let him know—or where I'd have to have his ideas of which way we wanted to proceed. But I don't remember that there was any sort of major issue as to whether we should or shouldn't do something during that period of time. I think it was always clear that we wanted to move ahead.

MARSHALL: If there was one thing I'd say you had to make a decision on, basically, it was whether or not the Department of Justice was going to accept full responsibility for the enforcement of school orders—or whether it wasn't. The fact is, it never had before then. Someone had to back down. Either they were going to back down or they were going to end up in contempt and with having to jail important public officials.

LEWIS: That's what I was trying to get at: this rather general decision as to whether the Department was going to go ahead and assume this very intimate role of responsibility. And, I gathered from you, that more or less just happened because it seemed the necessary thing to do.

KENNEDY: That's right.

LEWIS: There wasn't any grand meeting or anything of that kind?

KENNEDY: No.

LEWIS: A big Cabinet meeting?

KENNEDY: It was just logical. I mean, it was just the logical thing to do. The United States government couldn't back down.

LEWIS: That's one way of looking at it that now seems right and seemed right to many at the time. But it hadn't been the previous position, as Burke points out. It had not been.

MARSHALL: This is a specific recollection: talking about it at the time. We did talk. We did talk about those implications—I mean, you and me. And you said, "We'll have to do whatever is necessary." And that, at the time, would have involved, I think, specifically, putting Shelby Jackson [the Superintendent of the Louisiana State Board of Education] in jail.

KENNEDY: I remember that was the question. I remember that came up, about putting some of these people in jail. I'm sure I talked to [JFK], and I'm sure I kept him advised. But as far as having a decision to go ahead or not to go ahead, I think, once again, it seemed so logical what we had to do, what we should do. There wasn't a question of sitting down and deciding that. I think it was just taken for granted that the United States had to do what needed to be done.

THE ROAD TO FREEDOM: RFK AND THE FREEDOM RIDERS

LEWIS: The next crisis, so to speak, was the Freedom Riders that spring. What do you recall about that, again, as far as what was really (probably doesn't seem so now but really was) quite a novel assumption of responsibility—that is, the assumption by the Justice Department of the responsibility for the protection of interstate travelers? Am I right, Burke, in thinking that that was somewhat novel at the time?

KENNEDY: Can I just say that I think that one of the situations was, really, that we never—at least, I never—knew they were traveling down there?

LEWIS: What do you mean by that? Before they got there, you knew nothing about it?

KENNEDY: I didn't know anything about it.

MARSHALL: Before the bus was burned at Anniston.[3]

KENNEDY: Before the bus was burned at Anniston. Oh, I guess I knew about it from reading the paper the next morning.

MARSHALL: That's right.

LEWIS: You knew nothing about it that day that it happened?

KENNEDY: No.

LEWIS: And then what did you do when you read about it in the paper?

KENNEDY: I can't remember all the details, but let me just say that there were things going on that shouldn't be going on—and we had to figure out some way of becoming involved in it, or otherwise, the situation was going to get worse. So when you say that it was rather a novel approach, I think it was really based on the fact that we had to discover some new way of being of some help. That's how we got into it.

LEWIS: Do you remember talking to your brother about that on the Monday after reading it in the newspapers? That probably is something you would have talked to him about, wouldn't it be, at least on the telephone?

KENNEDY: In the first place, he probably had read about it in the paper, so he'd know about it. So there wasn't any reason to call about it. I'd call and say, "This is what I—" if I had an idea about what we should do. And I'd call and say, "This is what we're going to do." Or, if I had a problem about alternative steps, I'd call him. But I wouldn't call or talk to him just to be gabby about what was going on in the South.

LEWIS: You wouldn't have called him that morning and said, "This is a pretty rotten thing in—"

KENNEDY: No.

LEWIS: "—in Birmingham or Anniston, and Burke is trying to figure out what to do about it"?

KENNEDY: No. Because there wouldn't be any reason for calling him and telling him that. He could reach his own conclusion. He didn't have to have the Attorney General call and tell him what was bad and what was good.

LEWIS: And he wouldn't have called you?

KENNEDY: He might have called me to say—

LEWIS: "Are you doing something?"

KENNEDY: Yes.

LEWIS: He might have done that?

KENNEDY: Yes.

LEWIS: In any event, did you do anything specific during the week? What were the first steps?

MARSHALL: You sent John Seigenthaler [RFK's Administrative Assistant] down. Right away. The reason was that the buses stopped moving. All these people were in the hospital. And then we learned that there was a new group that was coming down from Nashville to take up the Freedom Riders. And no one would move the bus. So, although it was fairly—publicly—quiet, if you remember, during that week, it just kept getting, from our point of view, worse and worse and worse. He [Seigenthaler] went down there so that we'd have somebody there on the scene to tell you what was going on. That's why he went down.

KENNEDY: When did he get beaten up? Saturday?

MARSHALL: Saturday. I can give you a chronology of the week. I can remember the chronology. The bus-burning and riot in Birmingham was on Sunday, on Mother's Day, as I say. That's when [Birmingham Commissioner of Public Safety, "Bull"] Connor said that he didn't have any police because he let them all off for Mother's Day. On Monday, you sent John Seigenthaler down there to see what was going to happen. That time, the Freedom Riders hadn't decided what they were going to do. Monday afternoon they decided they were going to quit. Those were the original Freedom Riders. You talked to some of them in the hospital.

KENNEDY: Yes, I remember.

MARSHALL: I think you talked to Simeon Booker, who was down there. [Booker was Washington Bureau Chief for Johnson Publications, publishers of *Ebony* and *Jet* magazines.] I think you talked to someone else to find out what was going on. Then on Monday night or Tuesday morning, John Seigenthaler found out that this new group of students was coming down. Diane Nash [head of the central committee of the Nashville Student Movement] and Kelly Miller Smith [president of the Nashville Christian Leadership Conference] and the student group from Nashville had decided to come down and take it up. They got there on Tuesday morning or Monday night and went down to the bus station. And no one would drive the bus. There was a big crowd and mob around the bus station. Connor kept the crowd away from the bus. You talked to him or to the Mayor [Arthur Hanes] or someone down there. They said that they'd protect the bus station, but they wouldn't do anything once the bus left the station. Greyhound wouldn't get a driver for the bus.

The next day you decided that, unless the Governor [John M. Patterson], who wouldn't talk to you at that time, changed his position, the federal government would have to do something in order to correct the situation. Because the situation was that the buses were not moving between Birmingham and Montgomery. There were mobs every day around the bus station.

And so, then, you explained it to [JFK] in some detail and told him what the political developments were. And the immediate thing that he decided was that he should try to get in touch with the Governor himself, and make sure that the state wouldn't take this on. And he did try.

KENNEDY: And then the Governor was out fishing or something.

MARSHALL: The Governor wouldn't respond to him. And then, finally, the Governor agreed to meet with a representative.

KENNEDY: The Governor called at about three o'clock one afternoon, I remember, when we were out. Wasn't that it? And then the President said that he would have John Seigenthaler, who was going to be his representative as well as my Administrative Assistant, talk to him. Isn't that right?

MARSHALL: Yes.

KENNEDY: And the Governor met with John Seigenthaler. Then Friday night—

MARSHALL: I interrupted you at dinner.

KENNEDY: Yes. I talked to John around ten o'clock at night, and he was with the Governor. I went through it then with John—what the Governor had agreed to. And the Governor had agreed to give protection to the buses and make sure that nothing—

MARSHALL: The bus did go: that's when you had this conversation about a driver. [Robert Kennedy phoned George E. Cruit, superintendent of the Birmingham Greyhound terminal, to insist that a driver be found for the Freedom Riders' trip from Birmingham to Montgomery. "I think," Kennedy said, "you had better get in touch with Mr. Greyhound."] But the bus did go.

LEWIS: Saturday morning?

MARSHALL: Saturday morning. And there was a riot in Montgomery. And after the riot in Montgomery, we sent the marshals in.

KENNEDY: John got beaten up then.[4]

MARSHALL: Yes.

LEWIS: Got beaten up in that riot?

MARSHALL: You sent a telegram to the Governor which sets forth—I think, in his exact words—the responsibility that he had undertaken.

LEWIS: This conversation took place Friday evening?

KENNEDY: I talked to him Friday evening, from this dinner, from the Mayflower Hotel, in a phone booth.

LEWIS: Governor Patterson said—what I think was reported in the papers—that he didn't need any marshals, that that was none of your business, that they could take care of it?

KENNEDY: That's right. John Seigenthaler was in the room with him, and I talked to John Seigenthaler. John Seigenthaler would repeat to me what the Governor was saying—the assurance of the Governor. So that we didn't have to worry. They didn't want any marshals and didn't need any other help. That was Friday night.

LEWIS: How did you hear about John Seigenthaler being beaten up the next day?

KENNEDY: I think Byron [White] called me. Byron had the idea of getting marshals ready, anyway.

LEWIS: Before Saturday morning?

KENNEDY: Yes. He wanted to make sure that we had some marshals who were going to be available in case they were needed—and who were *trained* marshals. So during that period of the week, we worked on that, didn't we?

MARSHALL: After the meeting with the President, I think, we started to collect them and, plus, put them on alert.

KENNEDY: So they'd be available in case they were needed. It was a very important step.

I talked to John Seigenthaler in the hospital and said that I thought it was very helpful for the Negro vote, and that I appreciated what he had done, and that maybe he could run for office himself. I don't know whether he laughed or not. I can't remember.

LEWIS: Did you talk to Governor Patterson after that and tell him what you thought of his assurances?

MARSHALL: He sent the telegram to Governor Patterson.

KENNEDY: I sent the telegram. And then—what did we do with the marshals?

MARSHALL: We sent them down.

KENNEDY: I must have talked to the President that morning.

LEWIS: The essence of the telegram to Patterson was that deeds, not words, would be appreciated.

KENNEDY: Yes. I think we set forth the fact that John had been beaten up, the personal representative of the President.

MARSHALL: And was left lying in the street for twenty-five minutes, unconscious.

LEWIS: When you talked to the President that morning, before sending the marshals, there was never any question about the necessity—

KENNEDY: No.

LEWIS: —or the duty of sending in marshals?

KENNEDY: No, there was never any. There was never. And the reason that we sent marshals—it seems more natural now—but the reason we sent marshals was to avoid the idea of sending troops. We thought that marshals would be much more accepted in the South and that you could get away from the idea of military occupation. We had to do something.

LEWIS: The President, during the 1960 campaign, rather specifically said he would not use troops, if at all possible—that troops were a bad idea.

KENNEDY: I think so.

LEWIS: So that must have weighed heavily.

KENNEDY: No, I don't think so, really. I mean, he never gave absolute assurances that, under those circumstances, he wouldn't use troops. What he did say is that he thought that these things, as much as possible, should be headed off before a showdown—so that wouldn't be necessary. It was the idea—I think it was really Byron's good idea—that we try to concentrate on marshals, who were civilians, rather than troops.

MARSHALL: There were troops on the alert on that weekend.

LEWIS: How long after this first dispatch of marshals?

KENNEDY: Do you remember how many?

MARSHALL: I can't remember the numbers, but they, at one point, were in the planes on Sunday in Birmingham.

KENNEDY: Sitting in the planes. They were doing that almost every crisis we had.

MARSHALL: That's right. But this was the first one. This was the first one.

LEWIS: That's just what I was coming to. Was Sunday night the episode at the church in Montgomery?[5] How soon after the Saturday thing did the Montgomery [episode] come? Was it the next day?

MARSHALL: Sunday night.

LEWIS: The following night, when Dr. King and his band were in the church and the crowd was outside, they were talking to you on the telephone, weren't they?

KENNEDY: Yes, yes.

LEWIS: What can you tell us about that?

KENNEDY: I talked to Martin Luther King, I guess, several times. And I talked to Governor Patterson.

LEWIS: Sunday night?

KENNEDY: Sunday night. And Martin Luther King was concerned about whether he was going to live. I was concerned about whether the place was going to be burned down. He kept getting these reports that the crowds were moving in and that they were going to burn the church down and shoot the Negroes as they ran out of the church.

MARSHALL: They did burn a car right in front of the church.

LEWIS: What was Governor Patterson saying on the phone?

KENNEDY: Well, first, on Martin Luther King: I said that our people were down there. And that as long as he was in church, he might say a prayer for us. He didn't think that that was very humorous. He rather berated me for what was happening to him at the time. And I said to him that I didn't think that he'd be alive if it wasn't for us, and that we were going to keep him alive, and that the marshals would keep the church from burning down.

LEWIS: Berated you for what? I don't quite understand.

KENNEDY: Well, I don't remember why he was so mad at me. He was exercised, anyway, about whether he was going to live, I guess.

MARSHALL: Yes, at first. It was, I thought, a rather dramatic conversation. You told him that the marshals were coming. I don't know what you knew, but you couldn't have known more than I knew; and all we did know, really, was that they were on their way from Maxwell Field. Whether they'd get there in time or not was—
    Byron was at Maxwell Field, and he had some radio contact with them. But not even he knew. Well, they did arrive just as you said that—almost as you said that. They got there in between the church and the crowd. I don't think he berated you then. But then, later in the night, they had to stay in the church for some time, right up until four or five in the morning. And it was at some point along there that he started complaining.

LEWIS: About having to stay in the church so long?

MARSHALL: Yes, yes. And why wasn't there law and order in the United States or something like that. And you remarked at that time that he would have been dead as Kelsey's nuts.

LEWIS: What's that? Since I don't understand that, perhaps you should explain this for the historians.

MARSHALL: It's Irish. I can't explain that.

KENNEDY: Well, I remember when he was saying about the fact that—I guess that was it; it was later on in the evening—he wanted to get out. And I said that we were doing the best that we could and that he'd be as dead as Kelsey's nuts if it hadn't been for the marshals and the efforts that we'd made. Have you ever heard that expression?

LEWIS: Never have. Who's Kelsey?

KENNEDY: I don't know who Kelsey was.

LEWIS: Somebody long dead, I take it.

KENNEDY: Yes. I don't know what he said to that. I should have recorded all those conversations.

And then I talked to the Governor, and the Governor was furious. I talked to him for about forty-five minutes.

LEWIS: Why was he so furious?

MARSHALL: I remember a comment you made to the Governor. You said, "You're making political speeches at me, John. You don't have to make political speeches at me over the telephone." Do you remember saying that?

KENNEDY: Yes.

LEWIS: Why was he furious? Would he rather have had some people killed?

KENNEDY: No. I think just the idea that the marshals had come in there—come into his city and come into the state—and what we were doing there. The fact the marshals were there had aroused the crowd. Wasn't that the whole thrust of his conversation?

And then, as I say, he just made a speech. He was in a frenzy about it and, I thought, almost irrational in his conversation with me and what this meant. And, of course, John Patterson had been a friend of mine. John Patterson and Alabama had come out for President Kennedy. John Patterson became friendly with President Kennedy because of me, because I had gone down there and spoken in 1959. I'd spoken on the work of the [Rackets] Committee, and he'd come to the speech. He asked me to come to speak to the Alabama legislature the following day because he was so impressed. He wanted to introduce me to the Alabama legislature. He just thought that the Kennedys were fantastic. So then he came up, and he met President Kennedy, and thought that *he* was fantastic. That got him very enthusiastic.

It was all based on this relationship that he had with me. During the campaign he worked with me. And out at the Los Angeles convention we were very closely involved. We only got three votes of the Alabama delegation on the first ballot, but that was arranged because I didn't want to get any more votes from Alabama at that moment, just because it would be damaging in the rest of the country. And he understood that. And that's why it was kept down to three when we could have gotten more, but with the understanding that on the second ballot, if we needed it, he'd come back with nine or ten.

I had this long relationship with John Patterson. He was our great pal in the South. So he was doubly exercised at me—who was his friend and his pal—to have involved him with suddenly surrounding this church with marshals and having marshals descend with no authority, he felt, on his cities. And so he went into a long tirade, which, as I said to him on the phone, sounded like a political speech. That was the background. He couldn't understand why the Kennedys were doing this to him.

LEWIS: In fact, you speak of him as your ally in the South. I recall the civil rights groups being suspicious of John F. Kennedy because of that [relationship] with Patterson.

What about Floyd Mann [Alabama State Public Safety Director] at this period?

KENNEDY: Is there anything more about that night? Because it was a rather dramatic night.

LEWIS: Well, that night—I'm asking, didn't Floyd Mann say to you on the phone, separately, that he could not protect it and that he had to have marshals, in disagreement with Governor Patterson, at some point? Floyd Mann welcomed the marshals, unlike Governor Patterson. Wasn't that right?

MARSHALL: Yes, I'm sure that is right. I think, even going back to earlier that week: You know, when Governor Patterson finally said that he had the means and the will and the desire to protect everyone in Alabama; then we worked out details with Floyd Mann—and Floyd Mann was very cooperative.

The highway patrol, I guess on the Governor's orders, peeled away from the bus when it went into Montgomery. When it went into the bus station, the cops just stood by and let the riot take place.

LEWIS: Continuing with the Freedom Riders, what about the conversations with the bus companies during that week? Did you talk with the ownership in New York or—

KENNEDY: There was conversation. Was it—on what morning?

MARSHALL: I think the conversation they recorded—that got all the publicity in the South afterwards—with the bus company was recorded on Friday morning.

KENNEDY: What we had been trying to do was to get the Riders on their way and out of Alabama. And finally we arranged with the authorities in Alabama that they'd give them protection. We arranged with the Freedom Riders that they'd get on the bus. You know, those were the two major steps. Then the great problem was that the bus company provided the bus, but they couldn't get a driver to drive the bus. So then my struggle was to try to get a driver who would drive the bus to Montgomery. That's what the Attorney General of the United States was trying to do: get a bus driver!

LEWIS: Well, you were often doing things like that, weren't you?

KENNEDY: Yes.

LEWIS: Raising bail for people and that sort of thing?

KENNEDY: Yes. So anyway, I struggled. And finally I called up the head of Greyhound.

MARSHALL: The person you talked to, who recorded the conversation, was the manager of Greyhound in Birmingham. He took it all down. Then, after it was all over, MacDonald Gallion [Attorney General of Alabama] and John Patterson used that conversation in a way that made everyone in Alabama believe—and I think they believe to this day—that the whole Freedom Ride was your idea.

KENNEDY: Because I was saying to them—

LEWIS: You were insisting on getting a driver.

KENNEDY: Which looked like I was insisting on making sure that these Freedom Riders had the right, had the ability to drive throughout Alabama. So, just taken out of context, that's what it appeared to be: that this whole thing was a conspiracy on my part so that the Freedom Riders could ride through Alabama, when, in fact, I was getting the bus to drive them so they'd get out of Birmingham, in accordance with my agreement with the Freedom Riders and my agreement with the state authorities that they'd give them protection, trying to get protection for them and then to get the Freedom Riders to move—because they couldn't move.

It was an explosive situation each hour that went by. We finally arranged with everybody that they'd move and that the state would give them protection. And then suddenly it bogged down. We got the bus, and they got in the bus, and nobody would drive them. So I told the Greyhound, Mr. Greyhound, that he should get a bus driver. What, didn't I call him "Mr. Greyhound"?

MARSHALL: You called him Mr. Greyhound. The sentence that you said that was so misconstrued afterwards was "We've gone to a lot of trouble to make it possible for these people to move, and now it's all falling down because you don't have a driver." The troubles you were referring to were the efforts, that weren't very large, to get the state to accept responsibility after the riots in Birmingham. But they took that to mean that you had gone to the trouble of getting CORE [Congress of Racial Equality] to put on the Freedom Rides.

KENNEDY: I never recovered from it. That was damaging—just like waking the newspapermen up.

MARSHALL: It was used over and over again in the next two years. Over and over again.

LEWIS: You've touched on something just there that you haven't really described, and that is: in fact you were not encouraging more Freedom Riders to go in. But as I recall, you were criticized by some civil rights groups for trying to stop the Freedom Rides at that point. And you just touched on some agreement you had with the Freedom Riders to get out and not to continue coming in. What was that about?

KENNEDY: The agreement was that they'd get out of Birmingham and get out of the state of Alabama. You see, they were just sitting in Birmingham as a festering sore. And what were we going to do with them? They were going to go on; and if I could have them go on with the agreement from the Governor that he'd protect them, protect the highway, and see that nothing happened to them, then we avoided a problem.

LEWIS: With whom did you have that agreement? Some CORE official?

KENNEDY: Well, no. We had a lot of conversations with the ones who were on the bus.

LEWIS: With the particular Freedom Riders who were in Birmingham?

KENNEDY: Yes.

MARSHALL: With the particular group.

LEWIS: The Nashville students?

MARSHALL: Diane Nash and Kelly Miller Smith and—

KENNEDY: All they said they had to do was to get on the bus and keep going. So that was important for us. I got the Governor to agree that he'd not protect them but protect the highways, as I understand it. So everything was done, in other words—

LEWIS: In order to close the episode out.

KENNEDY: And have it be done without participation by the federal government. I was doing it in that way so that we wouldn't have to send marshals or troops or any other federal presence. And it would be behind us.

LEWIS: How close did you come to using troops? We touched on that a little bit. Burke?

MARSHALL: Well, it was very close at one point on that Sunday night. The troops were on an alert in the planes. I don't know how many, but a substantial number of planes at Fort Benning, which was very close. My recollection is that you had really almost decided to get the planes airborne and had called the Army and then decided to wait a few minutes to see if things got better at the church. And they did.

LEWIS: Was this after the marshals arrived or just before?

MARSHALL: It was after the marshals arrived.

LEWIS: And there was some question about whether they could successfully hold the—

KENNEDY: It was a very serious question.

MARSHALL: It was a very serious question whether they could, because for one thing, although many of them—as many as we could get— had had training in that, riot training, some of them hadn't. They hadn't worked together. And it was the first time anything like this had ever been done.

And Byron was in charge of it. It wasn't like having someone in charge of it who had a group of men that he had been in command of for some period of time. And he didn't know! I remember that he said that it was going to be very close. And at one point, it really looked as if the mob might overcome the marshals and get in there. And the consequences, of them burning that church, for the next day or the next few hours would have been so calamitous.

LEWIS: More than for the next few hours.

KENNEDY: Yes, but I mean it was that close. I remember now that it was that close. And you didn't know how the marshals were going to react. Nobody knew whether they were going to be able to stand. They'd never been subjected to this kind of a test before. There was a big crowd—all mad and angry.

LEWIS: Of course, I suppose a great many of these marshals had never seen each other before. They hadn't seen anybody. They were just called in from various points, I suppose.

MARSHALL: The deputy marshals themselves, I think, had had that training in South Carolina, or wherever it was. But there were also members of the Alcohol and Tobacco Tax Unit and prison guards and border patrol. The border patrol are very good at that kind of thing, but the others hadn't really been subjected to that kind of thing at all.

KENNEDY: The border patrol had some of the cars and the communication, and they were very good. But the prison guards were not terribly good. And then the alcohol tax group didn't like it.

MARSHALL: No. They were never used again.

KENNEDY: No. And in fact, some of them were from Mississippi, I guess, weren't they? Jim Eastland had a lot of reports of how opposed they were. They were on the side of the people who were on the other side—

LEWIS: Did he warn you of that?

KENNEDY: Yes. He said that you can't use them. He said it not so much in warning—I suppose it was partially warning—but just to tell me that he knew that we had a good deal of opposition to what we were doing.

LEWIS: One thing Burke said when we discussed this earlier was that the President had been kept rather regularly informed by telephone calls during the week and perhaps even during that night. Do you recall that? Talking to him during that difficult night? Sunday night?

KENNEDY: Yes. I just kept him advised as to what was going on. I don't remember where he was. But, again, there wasn't anything for him to do. There wasn't any decision that he could make at that moment, at that time. I don't think the night was over until—what?—about six o'clock in the morning. I remember going home.

LEWIS: Now, the immediate aftermath of this thing was the application to the Interstate Commerce Commission—

KENNEDY: No. Then they were going on to Mississippi. And then we had a lot of conversations with them.

LEWIS: Oh, now, I don't know about that.

KENNEDY: They were going, after they left there, to go on to Mississippi. So we had a lot of conversations during this week and afterward about what was going to happen in Mississippi. Then I had, I suppose, sixty conversations with Jim Eastland.

LEWIS: Sixty?

KENNEDY: Maybe that's an exaggeration. Maybe. But more than thirty or forty. I talked to him, probably seven or eight or twelve times each day, about what was going to happen when they got to Mississippi and what needed to be done. What was finally decided was that there wouldn't be any violence: as they came over the border, they'd lock them all up.

LEWIS: Those were the arrests in Jackson?[6]

KENNEDY: Yes.

LEWIS: Which are only now reaching the Supreme Court and which will all be reversed, eventually.

KENNEDY: And as you remember, as they came across the border, you got all those pictures of all those troops picking them up and guarding them, making sure they were protected, and then they were all arrested.

MARSHALL: Not federal troops.

KENNEDY: No. I guess they weren't. What were they? Troopers?

MARSHALL: They were highway patrol.

LEWIS: They were arrested when they got to Jackson, is that right?

MARSHALL: Yes.

LEWIS: And McComb? Were there some that went to McComb?

MARSHALL: That was later.

KENNEDY: [Eastland] told us that they'd all be arrested. I said to him my primary interest was that they weren't beaten up. So I, in fact, I suppose, concurred with the fact that they were going to be arrested—although I didn't have any control over it.

MARSHALL: We had a great deal of advice that they could be killed in Mississippi. You had to make that decision whether or not to trust Governor [Ross] Barnett, really, and Senator Eastland.

KENNEDY: Yes.

LEWIS: Advice from whom?

MARSHALL: I remember specifically, though this was just one of many conversations, talking to J. P. Coleman [Barnett's predecessor as Governor of Mississippi]. And he told me they'd never reach Jackson. They'd never reach Jackson. He said you couldn't trust Barnett and that the Riders would never reach Jackson. They'd be killed. That's what he said.

LEWIS: The former Governor?

MARSHALL: Yes.

LEWIS: He was generally right about not trusting Barnett, but in that particular instance, it seems to have worked out.

KENNEDY: I think Jim Eastland really took responsibility for it. This wasn't just Barnett. But [Eastland] took a major part of the responsibility himself. And what I trusted mostly was him, I think, basically. I mean, the assurances that he gave me that this was what was going to happen: that they'd get there, they'd be protected, and then they'd be locked up.

LEWIS: Now, you had a lot of criticism, of course, because they were arrested and because what had been protected was the peace but not the right to travel freely in interstate commerce. What was your response to that criticism?

KENNEDY: I put out a statement, which was criticized, about the fact that I thought that these Freedom Riders should slow down.

LEWIS: They'd made their point?

KENNEDY: Yes. And that was criticized. But I didn't think that it was very helpful, and I thought that people were going to get killed. And they had made their point. What was the purpose of continuing with it? I don't know what day I put that out.

MARSHALL: I think that it was the Monday after the riot at the church. I think it was the day that Bill Coffin [social activist Reverend William Sloane Coffin, Jr.] went down to Montgomery.

KENNEDY: Everybody, then, was trying to get into the act for publicity and attention, and I thought that they should stay out of there and stay home.

My response to that was that I was interested in preserving the peace, not having somebody killed. And then we tried to deal substantively with the problem. We then had a lot of conversations with the ICC [Interstate Commerce Commission] to see what could be done, to destroy the color bars that existed in interstate commerce. Burke worked on a solution to it, and we talked to the newly appointed member from Massachusetts.

MARSHALL: Bill Tucker.

LEWIS: The response is interesting because it really is a preview of the response which resulted in the Civil Rights Act of 1964, which is to deal with the substantive problem and not with the violent manifestations of it.

KENNEDY: I suppose it comes down, fundamentally, to what authority you have. That's the conflict between us and some of the civil rights groups—their feeling that we had more authority than we exercised.

We did everything that could be done under the circumstances.

LEWIS: Did you or the President face up at that time to what is still a great issue of disagreement with the civil rights groups, and was particularly last summer: that is, the capability and the authority of the federal government to act as a police force in a place like Mississippi? They certainly wanted you, as I recall it, to provide protection for the Freedom Riders and not to allow them to be arrested in Mississippi. Was there much discussion then about the limitations?

KENNEDY: Well, [JFK] was very concerned about what could be done, what steps we could take. He wanted, obviously, to know what authority he had or what authority we had to deal with the problem. And then he would make a decision as to what should be done under that authority. Our authority was limited in my judgment, and in Burke's judgment; and having had conversations with Byron White and [Assistant Attorney General] Nick Katzenbach, there wasn't really any disagreement within the Department of Justice as to how far our authority would go. What we did was to outline what our authority was, and we went to the maximum of what we felt we could do constitutionally.

If I had said to [JFK] that I thought we could do something beyond that or give protection, then he would have had to make the decision as to whether we really wanted to do that. But my conversations with him [concerned] the fact that, really, we didn't have the authority to do that. The only authority we had was what I had outlined for him, and we used that authority to the maximum.

LEWIS: Let me break in with another of these mystical philosophical questions here and ask you, just in retrospect, how you feel now about the wisdom of our federal system of government, which you've so often had to cite under the most difficult circumstances. I remember your explaining it to the parents of the two of the three people killed, the boys killed in Philadelphia, Mississippi:[7] that we have a system in which the primary responsibility for law enforcement is at the state and local level. Would you change that if you had it to do all over again—

KENNEDY: No.

LEWIS: —in this country?

KENNEDY: No.

LEWIS: The Constitutional Convention? You still think it's wise?

KENNEDY: I still think it's wise. I think that for periods of time it's very, very difficult. I'm just looking at it from over a period of a hundred years or fifty years or even a shorter period of time: I think it's a wise way to proceed. Because I just wouldn't want that much authority, much more authority, in the hands of—whether it's the Federal Bureau of Investigation or the Department of Justice or the President of the United States. And I think that it's well that it's not centered, all of that great power is not centered in Washington with the federal government. I think it causes great difficulty.

LEWIS: Abroad as well as at home?

KENNEDY: Abroad as well as at home. In my judgment, you would have accomplished much more if you had had a dictatorship during the period of time that President Kennedy was President, because you would have gotten federal aid to education, you would have gotten medical assistance for the elderly, you would have gotten all kinds of domestic legislation, you would have been able to protect our open spaces, you would have been able to do something about congestion in the cities, and you would have been able to do something about the slums—all of these things you would have been able to accomplish if you had a dictatorship.

Therefore, you could argue, during that period of time it would have been much better to not have this system of government—you know, not to have a democracy. I think, at any time, you can say that it would be much better if we could have sent people—large numbers, perhaps—down to Mississippi and been able to protect that group down there. But I think that it comes back to haunt you at a later time. I think that these matters should be decided over a long range of history, not on a temporary basis or under the stress of a particular crisis.

In my judgment, Mississippi is going to work itself out, and Alabama is. Now, maybe it's going to take a decade and maybe a lot of people are going to be killed in the meantime. And that's unfortunate. But in the long run I think it's for the health of the country and the stability of the system. It's the best way to proceed.

LEWIS: It's also part of the assumption, just fitting in with what you said, that it's well, in the long run, to have the consent of the governed. Things work better not only in the civil rights situation, but in aid to education or to open spaces or anything else that you mentioned. It's better not to impose things from above because people resent it.

Are we through with the Freedom Rider episode now?

KENNEDY: Well, you've described our conversation with the ICC and then, of course, the struggle that they had within the ICC and the slowness.

MARSHALL: What they did—our petition[8]—is all a matter of public record. Of course, what occurs to me is that, after the ICC acted, we had sort of a repeat on this at McComb. Do you remember? At McComb there was disobedience with the ICC regulations. We brought a lawsuit and got a court order. And then the Freedom Riders came to McComb, and we had a mob scene on the question of who was going to enforce the law there. And the Mayor [C. H. Douglas] was finally persuaded that he should do it.

That would have been in late 1961. It was another one of these pretty close things. We had some marshals in Louisiana we'd collected to send to McComb if we needed to. We had them in a motel right across the Mississippi border. And the first people—Freedom Riders or whatever you want to call them—the mixed, racially mixed group that went to McComb got beaten in the bus station in McComb. And they announced they'd come back. And of course all the press was there. The question was who was going to maintain order. We had long conversations—at least I did—with the Mayor of McComb. And you did too.

KENNEDY: Yes.

MARSHALL: I can't remember his name, but he was about a seventy-one- or seventy-two-year-old man. He finally issued a statement saying that "I didn't make this law, but it's the law—and I'm going to enforce it." And he deputized some additional people and put them on the police force. And they controlled a mob of, I would say, well over a thousand people while a group came over from Baton Rouge and went into the bus station and sat down in the white waiting room, I guess for five minutes or something.

KENNEDY: And we got through another crisis.

LEWIS: As a last thought on that, do you recall—a general catchall question—any expression of the President's impatience with the ICC?

KENNEDY: No. I think he was fed up with John Patterson. He was fed up with the way they had handled it in Alabama. He was fed up with the Freedom Riders who went down there afterwards when it didn't do any good to go down there.

LEWIS: What about the political reaction? It doesn't seem to me that you got an awful lot of credit in the North to balance off against the discredit in the South.

KENNEDY: Yes. I think you could play it more a demagogic way. If you were looking at it from a political point of view, you probably wouldn't put a statement out against the Freedom Riders going down there. It's clear that, if what you're doing—even though it might not be the primary motivation—is to obtain political credit for some of these matters, then I would expect you to handle it in a different way. That, I might say, is not always easy, because while you're doing that for the North, you're not accomplishing a great deal in the South. But you know, that never entered in the conversations during any of these periods of time, at least between me and my brother. I think, in any of the decisions that were being made, that I wasn't very heroic at all, in the slightest. It was just the idea that it was so obvious, really, what needed to be done and what you could do and what, therefore, should be done. There were immediate decisions that had to be made on specific things, but there wasn't any great shaking of heads and grand meetings about deciding whether we should do what we did.

LEWIS: I just wondered whether the President ever expressed any resentment, even lighthearted resentment, about the fact that you did take this beating in Alabama and the South and got relatively little credit in the North—even for the move to the ICC, which was something that you didn't have to do and that was a fairly groundbreaking thing to do.

KENNEDY: No, there wasn't any. As I think I said earlier, most of the focus of attention and resentment at that time, in any case, was on me rather than on the President. It hadn't become a major political problem by that time.

OPENING THE DOOR:
THE RIGHT TO VOTE

LEWIS: I think we should turn now to the question of voting. I remember Burke saying, in the understated way that Burke says things, that very soon after he came into that office, it was evident that not very much had been done. I think it was Burke who said to me that, you know, they just hadn't really been trying on this. No suits had been brought in Mississippi, as you pointed out. Now, how did you react to this?

KENNEDY: I thought a good deal more needed to be done. I felt that of course this was the area in which we had the greatest authority; and if we were going to do anything on civil rights, we should do it in that field where we had the authority. And number two: I felt strongly that this was where the most good could be accomplished. I suppose that's coming out of a political background, but I felt that the vote really makes a major difference. From the vote, from participation in the elections, flow all other rights far, far more easily. A great deal could be accomplished internally within a state if the Negroes participated in elections and voted.

I look at—just coming out of the election of 1960—the amount of power that the Negro had, the amount of power he had in the state of New York, where twenty percent of the population is Negro. And so many decisions are made to insure that they are satisfied, and they are always consulted about matters. I could see it all over the country. And here you had almost fifty percent of the population in the state of Mississippi who were Negro, forty percent of the state of Alabama, and a large percentage in Georgia: if they registered and participated in elections—even if a half of them or even if a third of them, if you get it up over fifteen percent of the whole voting population [being] Negro—they could have a major influence.

Now, during the Freedom Rides, I had a number of meetings with these various civil rights groups, and I said that it wasn't as dramatic and perhaps there wasn't going to be as much publicity about it and as much attention on it—going down and registering people to vote—but I thought that's where they should go and that's what they should do. I had some conversations with Martin Luther King along those lines.

I think that they rather resented it. That's not what they wanted to do, and that's not where they were going to focus their attention. In fact, Martin Luther King and I didn't see eye to eye on some of these matters, nor did I with a good number of these other groups.

I explained two reasons. Number one: that this was the area where we had the authority. We didn't have the authority to give protection or to move in some of these other fields. But we did have authority in voting, and we could do something about that. Secondly, I thought it could make a major difference and be far more help than anything else that they could do, if they just focused attention and registered a hundred people a day. In some of these communities it could make a big difference. And that was the key to opening the door to all of what they wanted to accomplish in education, in housing, in jobs, and public accommodations. All rested in having the vote and being able to change the situation internally.

LEWIS: Now, Dr. King and some of the others, as you've suggested, were rather unresponsive to that at first, as I understand it, perhaps because it was not very dramatic. But they did seem to come around to take a greater interest in the vote later on. What was responsible for that?

KENNEDY: I think that they perhaps just realized that they could accomplish a great deal more. I don't know if they came around.

LEWIS: They got a lot of money from private foundations.

KENNEDY: We worked on that too.

MARSHALL: Yes. Every time they came in to see you, you talked to them about voter registration. And finally out of that—I think it was your suggestion, originally, that they could get some money—they could get some money and put a big effort into this. And then we did take it up with Stephen Currier of the Taconic Foundation. I went to those meetings where they set up the Voter Education Project.[9] He put in a good deal of money, and some other foundations put in a lesser amount of money. There was that effort which involved money, and which they therefore worked on in order to participate in the funds.

KENNEDY: I think I suggested that they set up an outside organization and that the money that could be given to it would be tax free.

MARSHALL: That's right. And it was.

KENNEDY: I was able to work out with Mort Caplin for them to receive a tax [exemption].

MARSHALL: That's right.

LEWIS: That, again, was probably something that was a little different. One thing that struck me was the generality about the Department of Justice during those three years. Your willingness—and Burke's and others'—to go outside the normal official actions and talk to private foundations, talk to the Greyhound Bus Company, talk to insurance companies about bail for people—that sort of thing. Don't you think that it made a great deal of difference to you in that regard that you were the President's brother? That you never had to have any concern about, really—

KENNEDY: Yes. About what he would think?

LEWIS: —what he would think about going outside the regular channels.

KENNEDY: Yes. I never would have to call him. You know, it wasn't necessary on something that was as important as this and was as significant as this to have to call the President of the United States every time you did something or be concerned that he'd think it was the wrong thing to do.

LEWIS: Because you knew pretty much what he'd think would be the right thing to do?

KENNEDY: So there was never a problem. I wouldn't have to bother him with it, nor would he have to think about it. If somebody calls you up and says, "Should I do this?" then that means a decision that the President has to make. He has to consider the pros and cons. And that's frequently difficult. But I could look at that from my own position much better than he could, and I'd know, once I looked at it, if it was clear that it was the thing that should be done. Now, where it became more difficult was where what I was going to do would have implications for him which might be adverse and which were of a more major nature. Obviously, then we'd talk. Or where I'd have a question about it.

LEWIS: What sort of thing? Give me an example.

KENNEDY: I think the whole question of the University of Alabama[10] when you're going to nationalize the guard, what troops you're going to call up—

LEWIS: Or Mississippi before that—Oxford?[11]

KENNEDY: Yes. Yes, a lot of the details of those arrangements at the University of Mississippi were really made by us. But I can think more of Alabama because I was confused, myself, as to when we should call up the National Guard and how many should be called up— because that was so difficult, wasn't that, really? Because we were playing such a cat-and-mouse game at that time. At least the University of Mississippi, in some ways, was slightly easier because we were talking to the Governor and knew what he was going to do.

LEWIS: You thought you did.

KENNEDY: I mean, the decision that we were going to work with him—that's the decision that you had to make at the University of Mississippi. Then the course of events, once we made that decision, was clearer than at the University of Alabama, where we didn't know what [Governor George C. Wallace] was going to do.

LEWIS: Let me bring you back to voting and ask this question: Did you ever discuss with the President the political implications, the long-run political implications—and I don't mean this in an invidious way at all—of an increase of Negro voting in the South? The obvious possibility of a transformation of the Democratic party into a more liberal, multiracial party in the South?

KENNEDY: No, I didn't. I thought, politically—which I said to Burke at the time—that if I were a Republican, that's the area that I would emphasize. And I'd be a moderate in the South if I were a Republican. Because I thought that the Democratic leadership in the South was traditionally opposed to civil rights and the Negro. The wave of the future through our efforts and eventually, I felt, the efforts of civil rights groups would be that the Negroes would be registered. Negroes would be voting in an election. And if they had associated themselves in a moderate way with the Negroes, that they would win all the elections—just because I think the Negro could be the swing vote. And that if I were a Republican, a Republican party political figure nationally, or even in the South, I would associate myself with that effort. Not with the idea that I would win in the '62 election or the '64 election or maybe even the '68 election, but in the '72 election, I'd win. Or the '70 election.

LEWIS: You didn't anticipate the way it has actually turned out—at least, as of 1964—with the Republican party becoming a racist, white party in the South.

KENNEDY: No, I didn't. No, I would have gone the opposite direction. You see, we lost some of those communities in the South because of the Negro vote in 1960, because the Negro vote frequently was a Republican vote.

LEWIS: Yes. Yes, I know.

KENNEDY: Georgia. Tennessee. I mean, it was Barry Goldwater. But I would have capitalized on that, on not being an extreme figure for the Negro. I'm just looking at it coldly, politically. I would have done it differently than the Republican party obviously did.

LEWIS: Let me correct you. I don't think it was only Barry Goldwater. Of course, Barry Goldwater so engulfs everything else that you can't tell. But I think it did make a difference, what you had done.

KENNEDY: Now, as far as discussing it with President Kennedy, he knew that we were making the effort on registration. And I think, perhaps in passing, we might have discussed the vote. But I don't know that we thought that it would make that much of a difference in his election in 1964, compared to the fact that we were alienating so many people. I think that he probably felt, although I really didn't go into it with him, that where it was going to make a difference was maybe eight years or twelve or sixteen or twenty years from now. But it wouldn't help in 1964.

I might say that a third factor in it is that I felt that nobody really could oppose voting.

LEWIS: It was easier to accomplish for that reason.

KENNEDY: Yes. How could anybody, really, get very mad because you're making an effort to make sure that everybody votes? I mean, they can. But they can't come out as openly as they can on schools: "We don't want our little blond daughter going to school with a Negro."

LEWIS: That's why the Civil Rights Act of 1957 passed—because it was very hard even for Senator [Richard] Russell [of Georgia] to stand up and say that people shouldn't vote.

KENNEDY: Yes. So for those three reasons, we made the effort. Number one, because we had more authority. Number two, because it would accomplish the greatest amount of good, and a great deal could be accomplished internally in the state. Number three, because there would be less internal struggle and strife within the country as a whole by the Department of Justice or the federal government coming down into southern states and telling them what they should do. They could do it themselves. And the fourth factor: because there could be less opposition to it.

JUDICIAL APPOINTMENTS

LEWIS: Some of the greatest difficulties you had in this field were with judges who would not do the job . . . Judge [William H.] Cox, I'm sure, is on the head of the list.

KENNEDY: And that fellow from Georgia?

LEWIS: [J. Robert] Elliot, from Georgia.

MARSHALL: [E. Gordon] West.

LEWIS: West, from Louisiana. And I imagine Judge [Walter] Gewin is a tough one, who came with strong recommendations.

KENNEDY: Is Griffin Bell considered good?

MARSHALL: I think he's a good judge. The civil rights people don't think he's a good judge, but I think he's a good judge. And I think he's fair on civil rights.

LEWIS: I think he's been down the middle, pretty much, on civil rights. He's not as much of an enthusiast as Judge [Elbert P.] Tuttle.

MARSHALL: Well, he's concerned about the court of appeals doing everything. He wants to stick it on the district judges. You know, he's right about that. He's right about that.

KENNEDY: He's an awful good fellow, Griffin Bell. A very decent fellow. I haven't followed his individual decisions, but I saw him linked in a paper with Gewin and—

MARSHALL: Well, I think it's not fair. Judge Gewin is not a good judge.

LEWIS: No?

MARSHALL: He's not a good judge.

KENNEDY: Yes, that's the hesitation we had about Judge Gewin: that he wouldn't make a good judge, anyway.

LEWIS: Somebody said to me that on paper he looked good.

KENNEDY: We had our hesitations about him. The hesitation about Gewin, I remember— Wasn't he a judge, a local judge, or something before?

MARSHALL: No, you're thinking about [Clarence W.] Allgood, I think, Bob, aren't you? In Birmingham? He was a master in bankruptcy.

KENNEDY: Oh, that was it. Yes. How has he turned out?

MARSHALL: Well, he's not like Judge Cox at all. And in fact, the Negroes were for his appointment—Allgood's appointment. There was a question whether he'd be any good as a judge. Well, he has been limited in the cases that he's handled. Judge [Seybourn H.] Lynne really limited him to, mainly, the criminal docket, I think. I don't know whether he'll develop or not. He's a very political fellow still. But on civil rights, now they're all against him, you know—and it's all your fault. But the fact is that there was a question of his qualifications: I think the ABA [American Bar Association] said that he was unqualified. And the Negroes supported him at the time in Alabama.

LEWIS: Now, what about Judge Cox? I think that Judge Cox came up to the Department, that you interviewed him, and he said that he would support the Constitution.

KENNEDY: Yes. We sat on my couch in my own office, and I talked to him. And I said that the great reservation that I had was whether he'd enforce the law and whether he'd live up to the Constitution, and the laws, and the interpretation of the Constitution by the Supreme Court. It's the law of the land. He assured me that he would. He was really, I think, the only judge whom I've had that kind of conversation with. He was very gracious. He said that there wouldn't be any problem about that, that he felt he could accomplish a great deal, and that this would not be a problem to him.

LEWIS: And then, soon after he was appointed, he began writing letters of what kind? I recall one that you mentioned to me: that he wrote to some defendant registrars in some suit, describing your activities in bringing the suit as political—something of that kind.

MARSHALL: I remember that. You saw that letter. He suggested that the reason for the voting suits in Mississippi was to gain political capital in the North.

LEWIS: What about Senator Eastland during this thing? Of course, Judge Cox was Senator Eastland's candidate, his friend, and so forth. Did you ever discuss with him, candidly, whether Cox could be relied on to do his duty in these areas?

KENNEDY: No, I don't think I ever had any conversations. [Eastland] was anxious for him to be appointed—I think he urged me to appoint him—but I don't think he ever gave any assurances that he would meet his responsibility. And after I appointed him, [Eastland] emphasized very heavily what a good friend he was, that he talked to him frequently, and how nice it was.

LEWIS: Let's just go back a minute before talking about another specific judge and ask: What is the problem on this? Why does this happen, in essence? It's the relationship with the Senators or—

KENNEDY: Basically, it's grown up as a senatorial appointment with the advice and consent of the President. That's really what it is. That's the tradition, and so they're making that kind of an effort. Now, what we're trying to do in giving that kind of advice and consent, which is the responsibility of the Department of Justice, is to try to obtain the best possible judges, the judges who are going to be honest and who are going to uphold the law. And in that, there are tremendous struggles, because a United States Senator will have an interest which frequently is contrary to our interests. This is where the struggle takes place.

The President of the United States is attempting to obtain the passage of important legislation in many, many fields, and the appointment of a judge who is recommended by the chairman of a committee or a key figure on a committee can make the whole difference on his legislative program. I'll give you an example. We were opposed to the appointment of the judge [Luther L. Bohanon] who was suggested by Senator Kerr [of Oklahoma], and I struggled and fought about that. . . . The one friend we had to obtain the passage of all bills dealing with finance and taxes was Kerr. Because [Senator Harry F.] Byrd was chairman of that committee [Finance Committee] and he was going to oppose any legislation that was suggested by President Kennedy. And if this judge was not appointed and the marshal whom [Kerr] wanted was not appointed, then we wouldn't obtain the passage of any legislation dealing with taxes. Now, that was important not only for Oklahoma, but important for the country. So you really have to balance it off.

It sounds terrible. And you know, you should stand fast on principle. You stand fast on principle: Kerr doesn't get his judge and you don't get any tax legislation. And they play it as tough and as mean as that. He played it as tough and as mean as that.

You consider, for instance, John McClellan. We never appointed his judge in Arkansas, and I had been so closely associated with John McClellan that that made it much more difficult. He still hasn't been appointed. And I don't think there's any question that the continued harassment of the administration on the TFX and other matters was due to the fact that we hadn't appointed this judge.[12] But we could take that, accept that.

LEWIS: Because he really wasn't for you on legislation most of the time, anyway.

KENNEDY: He wasn't going to be—and he's not going to be—a key figure who was going to affect the general good of the country. Now, Kerr was somebody who was going to affect the general good of the country. Eastland, on that matter—that wasn't a basis for appointment. It was different from Kerr. It wasn't that we were trying to get legislation out, because he, as I said before, never connected the passage of certain legislation and the appointment of his judge. He sent up his judge and he wanted him appointed—but that was all. And we'd either appoint him or just not have a judge there.

We looked into these judges and examined them and appointed them in good conscience.

LEWIS: The Mississippi situation was special simply because there aren't very many lawyers in Mississippi, if any, who are decent on the civil rights issue.

KENNEDY: That's right.

LEWIS: Were there many Senators quite as ruthless and unyielding on these matters as Senator Kerr?

KENNEDY: No. I think he was the toughest. And, you know, I think he was the judge I felt the strongest about. [Kerr] was really so blatant about it that I really disliked it. I might say that President Kennedy rather liked him.

LEWIS: Bob Kerr?

KENNEDY: Yes.

LEWIS: The roguish quality about him? The absolute blatancy of his corruption?

KENNEDY: He was so effective—I mean, the way he operated. I think he just rather admired the fact that he did it so blatantly. Not just for the judges, but the whole relationship. He was a strong figure. And he liked the President, and through his efforts we were able to obtain the passage of a good number of bills that would never get by. Douglas Dillon got along with him well because he made a major difference in that committee. He did a lot of work. He knew his stuff, and he could handle—the only person who could handle— Byrd. And, of course, they liked that. [But] the idea of holding up all this major legislation because we wouldn't appoint some judge in Oklahoma . . . didn't really make a great deal of sense.

LEWIS: You've seen, I think, something you did not realize—correct me if I'm wrong—when you first became Attorney General: what a long-run effect—bad effect—a lifetime judge can have. You can't do anything.

KENNEDY: I'll tell you one problem that existed in the last few months as far as judges were concerned. The judge that we were going to appoint in Arkansas had some questionable background. So we didn't want to appoint him. And that was—

LEWIS: McClellan's candidate?

KENNEDY: Yes. Then, when he wasn't appointed for three years, Oren Harris [Democratic Congressman from Arkansas] came to see me, and he said, "As long as you're not going to appoint him, I'd like to be appointed." Now, Oren Harris would be all right as a judge. The problem is that the next man in line for that committee [Interstate and Foreign Commerce Committee]—

LEWIS: [Congressman] John Bell Williams of Mississippi.

KENNEDY: —is John Bell Williams. Therefore, you have the choice—and that's another one of those difficult dilemmas: if you appoint Oren Harris, you get John Bell Williams as chairman of that committee. Now, is it better to have a judge who is questionable in character or have John Bell Williams chairman of that important committee in the Congress of the United States? That's the kind of decision. These things that have to be decided are frequently very, very difficult and cause many more problems than, perhaps, the editorial writer at *The New York Times* understands, on occasion.

Now let me say, again, that was not the problem on the civil rights judges generally. Just on the question of Mississippi. It was a question of us being convinced that [Cox] would be all right. I had a conversation with him. I was convinced he was honest with me and he wasn't.

MARSHALL: There was nothing specific against [Cox], either. I mean, he hadn't done anything. He wasn't associated with the White Citizens Council. He wasn't a member of the Citizens Council. Most lawyers in Mississippi were members of the Citizens Council. There were no public positions on it, no background—nothing specific to go on. And the ABA rated him exceptionally well qualified. There was nothing you could really say that was specific as to why he shouldn't be appointed. Even now I can't think of anything that could have been said then.

LEWIS: Have you ever taxed Bernie Segal [of the ABA] with that?

KENNEDY: No, but you know, some of the judges—for instance, the judge in Oklahoma we were so concerned about—have turned out very good.

LEWIS: Kerr's appointee?

KENNEDY: Yes. He's turned out fine.

LEWIS: What about Judge Elliot in Georgia, whom we've mentioned? Do you recall who recommended him?

KENNEDY: Well, yes, I think it was—

MARSHALL: [Senator Herman] Talmadge.

KENNEDY: Talmadge, yes. I remember there was a delay on it, but—

MARSHALL: Well, you were very concerned about that appointment because [Elliot] had been a leader in the Georgia legislature. At the time, they'd passed some legislation dealing with the county unit system, which really, I think, preserved the county unit system.

KENNEDY: And he made some statements about Negroes.

LEWIS: Right.

MARSHALL: And I remember quite clearly what finally decided it was your talking to Judge Tuttle. And Judge Tuttle had gone over it with Judge [William A.] Bootle and some lawyers he knew in that area. Judge Tuttle didn't know Elliot himself. And Judge Tuttle finally told you that he thought he'd be all right. In addition, Senator Talmadge got some of the Negro political leaders down there to call.

KENNEDY: Yes. Now, who were they? Didn't I talk to that old man?

MARSHALL: Colonel Waldon. A. T. Waldon.

KENNEDY: I remember he was in favor. I don't know who was opposed to it. The Negro leadership of the South, or the leadership of the Democratic Negroes, was in favor of it. And then Griffin Bell got into it.

MARSHALL: Yes.

KENNEDY: And he thought he'd work.

LEWIS: So, again, it was a question of everybody's judgment just turning out to be wrong. Now, in Louisiana, the little that I know about it suggests to me that the situation was different, and that the appointments there, of [Frank B.] Ellis and West and Ainsworth, were—at least, in considerable measure—a result of Senator Ellender's views and that you had been warned that West was no good.

MARSHALL: No.

LEWIS: You had not?

MARSHALL: No.

KENNEDY: Well, Ainsworth we thought very highly of. I think he's turned out all right. Frank Ellis was a great help to us in many of these civil rights problems, so we never felt that there would be a civil rights difficulty. . . .

LEWIS: Now, what about Judge West? Was he an Ellender [appointment]?

MARSHALL: Russell Long [Senator from Louisiana].

LEWIS: Russell Long! So I was all wrong on that, wasn't I?

MARSHALL: Well, once again, Judge West turned out this way. But there was just no basis, really, for believing he would, because Senator Long isn't that kind of a person himself. And the lawyers, everyone we talked to down there—he didn't have any history—they all thought he'd be all right.

LEWIS: Now, we are talking about judges, and I think we should say a word about the two Supreme Court appointments that were made. Perhaps, just before we do that, I should ask you, generally, how large a part the President, if any, played in the judicial appointments, aside from the Supreme Court. He left that pretty much to you, didn't he?

KENNEDY: Yes, except where we wouldn't appoint somebody and the Senator or Congressman wanted him appointed and they raised a fuss about it. Then he got into it. Otherwise, he didn't get into it.

LEWIS: Do you recall any of those episodes in which he did? For example, do you recall anything about his dealings with Senator Kerr on that matter?

KENNEDY: No, just that he was in favor of that—and I had been opposed to it.

LEWIS: I'm sorry, I didn't understand.

KENNEDY: He was in favor of it, and I was opposed to it.

LEWIS: You were opposed to making the concession to Senator Kerr?

KENNEDY: I was opposed to appointing this fellow. And then finally, you know, I said that if I were in his position, I'd probably appoint him. But I was against appointing him.

LEWIS: How did you end up feeling in general? Did you end up thinking that the appointing of judges was a more important part of your job than you had anticipated?

KENNEDY: I think I probably did.

LEWIS: Particularly because they went on for life.

KENNEDY: And then I saw some good ones—and I saw some bad ones.

LEWIS: What about the Supreme Court, the two Supreme Court appointments?

KENNEDY: Well, there were a number of people at first. There wasn't anybody considered, really, other than Arthur Goldberg for the second one. There were a number of people who were considered for the first one. [Harvard Law School Professor] Paul Freund was considered. I think some of those names appeared in the papers. In fact, I think there were ten or twelve people who were considered.

My first recommendation was [Judge William H.] Hastie. We looked into Hastie, and I went up and saw [Chief Justice Earl] Warren about Hastie. He was violently opposed to having Hastie on the Court.

LEWIS: The Chief Justice was? Why?

KENNEDY: Because, he said, "He's not a liberal, and he'll be opposed to all the measures that we are interested in, and he just would be completely unsatisfactory."

LEWIS: That's an absolute surprise to me. I mean, I'm surprised that anyone would think that about Hastie particularly. I don't know that he's identified as a liberal or a nonliberal.

MARSHALL: He's a pretty conservative judge.

LEWIS: Is he?

MARSHALL: He's got a conservative background. Of course, he's a Republican.

KENNEDY: Well, anyway, that's what [Warren] thought.

MARSHALL: He's a good judge.

KENNEDY: I think I asked him about Paul Freund too. And I think he was opposed to Paul Freund.

LEWIS: In retrospect, do you think it was appropriate to ask the Chief Justice about appointments to the Court?

KENNEDY: Yes. Yes. I think I asked [Associate Justice] Bill Douglas too.

LEWIS: And?

KENNEDY: And I think he was opposed to both of them, as I remember.

LEWIS: Hastie was the one who was most seriously considered?

KENNEDY: Hastie was very seriously considered. I thought that that would be helpful here. He was a good judge, I didn't know when another vacancy would come, and I thought that it would mean so much overseas and abroad that we had a Negro on the Supreme Court. It could do all kinds of good for the country, as well as the fact that he was qualified and people thought well of him. So I had his decisions analyzed by somebody—I don't remember who. We came that close. And then finally there was a conflict. . . . I think a lot of people in the White House were opposed to having a Negro.

LEWIS: A little too obvious?

KENNEDY: Well, I didn't think that that was it, because he was a good judge. I didn't think that the basis should be on that—it was obvious. I think that he was a good judge and that it was an appropriate time. If you were going to appoint a Negro, there wasn't any other Negro who was coming along that you could ever appoint. Here was the vacancy, and he was a good judge; and if you were going to consider the five or six best judges of the circuit court, you'd put him up there. So that wasn't the basis of it.

The President—there was a conflict back and forth—came up with the suggestion of Byron White. I didn't think there was much of a chance of his being appointed. Obviously, as far as my personal preference was concerned, he would be the person I would be most interested in. I had a conversation with Byron as to whether he'd be interested. I called him up—he was out in Denver at the time—to find out whether he really wanted to do it. And he was not very enthusiastic about it, really. I don't remember specifically his words, but they were rather interesting: I don't think he liked to retire from the active life so quickly. But I talked to him on the basis of the fact that who knew what was going to happen in the future? If you knew definitely that he could be around for five years and then be appointed in 1967, then that was fine. But you never knew that. The time to do it was at the time you could. It was really on that basis that he accepted the appointment.

LEWIS: Truly, I probably am a little naïve, but I was just quite surprised that the Chief Justice would have expressed any view on appointments to the Court. That's sort of back to the days of Chief Justice [William Howard] Taft managing appointments to the Court.

KENNEDY: Well, we didn't do that. He wasn't consulted on it. We finally just decided what we wanted to do.

LEWIS: And the other one, as you say, that really had been promised?

KENNEDY: No, it hadn't.

LEWIS: The Goldberg appointment?

KENNEDY: No, he sure hadn't. What he did want to do, what he said to me—I played a role in his being appointed as Secretary of Labor; I conducted the discussions with him—he wanted eventually to go on the circuit court. And so, without any definite commitment on that, we indicated to him that, if a vacancy came up at the appropriate time, there wouldn't be any problem about an appointment to the circuit court.

LEWIS: In Washington?

KENNEDY: No. Illinois. But there was never any discussion about the Supreme Court.

LEWIS: So, how did it develop that—

KENNEDY: I think the President just thought he'd want to appoint him. [Associate Justice Felix] Frankfurter resigned, and he just settled on [Goldberg]. There were a lot of other people who could be considered. What I think was a factor, I might say, is the fact that all these other people who also had some ability had not been actively involved in the administration. Paul Freund, for instance, was asked to come down and be Solicitor General—and he turned it down. And that was a factor, obviously: When President Kennedy wanted him, he didn't want to do it. Why appoint him when Archie Cox had done very well? I mean, the logical person, if you're going to appoint him, would be to appoint Archie Cox. And some of these other people we didn't know. We did know that Byron White had ability and that Arthur Goldberg had ability. We'd worked with them; they'd worked with us. So why not appoint them rather than somebody that someone else said was good but we didn't—neither my brother nor I—know? That was the basis of it. . . .

LEWIS: And are you surprised at the kind of judge Arthur Goldberg is turning out to be?

KENNEDY: Yes, I am. I wouldn't have— Byron White says that he would have known that, but I wouldn't have known it myself.

LEWIS: Byron White wasn't around to advise you.

KENNEDY: No, no, that's right. But I wouldn't have known that. I knew him very well—not from a legal point of view, other than in labor matters. And he was so broad-minded. And understanding.

LEWIS: Undoctrinaire.

KENNEDY: Undoctrinaire and understanding. I would not have anticipated that he would have turned out to be the kind of judge that he did. I think Arthur Goldberg is very conscious of his public image or picture, particularly with certain groups. And I think that he's very conscious of how *The Washington Post* and liberal groups think of him. I would have always thought that. But he's also a man of integrity and courage.

LEWIS: There isn't any question about that. It's just that he's been more doctrinaire a judge than anyone would have thought.

KENNEDY: Yes.

LEWIS: Just for conversation, not for the historians, I think the White appointment will go down as a very good one, a very important one.

KENNEDY: He's done well, I guess, hasn't he?

LEWIS: Yes. He's doing better all the time. It's great.

KENNEDY: Have you given your oral history of how you opposed Nick Katzenbach being appointed as General Counsel—

LEWIS: What? General Counsel of what?

KENNEDY: And how you're against Ed Guthman [Special Assistant for Public Information, Department of Justice] being appointed to the Department of Justice?

LEWIS: Wrong!

KENNEDY: See, look at that. Hell, you did! You opposed them. . . .

LEWIS: Oh, what a black episode that is.

KENNEDY: Yes.

LEWIS: Are you bringing me back to that?

KENNEDY: See? If you'd just remember these things. Don't you remember that you didn't want Nick Katzenbach?

LEWIS: I was never against Nick Katzenbach.

KENNEDY: Well, you were.

LEWIS: I was strongly for Phil Elman [of the Federal Trade Commission]. I didn't know Nick Katzenbach.

KENNEDY: I'm just saying—

LEWIS: I did know him slightly.

KENNEDY: It's lucky—

LEWIS: It's lucky for everybody that he was appointed. I'm gracious enough to say that.

KENNEDY: All right, I'm sorry. Historians, I'm sorry to bring in these weaknesses.

LEWIS: I do remember storming at Ed Guthman the first day you were there, about some terrible order that nobody should talk to the press.

KENNEDY: Gosh, you were slightly suspicious of the new administration, weren't you? The Department of Justice?

LEWIS: A tiny bit.

RFK AND THE FBI

LEWIS: Why don't we talk now about the relationship with the FBI? You had known Mr. Hoover and the FBI previously yourself, because you at least had some contact with him in the Department, had you not?

KENNEDY: Yes.

LEWIS: Had you known him personally? Had your family known him?

KENNEDY: Yes, my family. My father was a good friend of his. They used to see each other, and he used to keep in touch with my father. So that was one relationship. The second was that, while I was counsel for various congressional committees, I met him. I had a rather major dispute with the FBI when I was with the McCarthy committee in 1954,[13] particularly with Lou Nichols, because they lied to me about some documents that they made available to the committee. They were making information available to the committee, and they were telling me they weren't.

LEWIS: Well, how could they tell you that when you were working for the committee?

KENNEDY: Because I was minority counsel. By that time I was having a dispute with them.

LEWIS: I see. And you didn't know everything—

KENNEDY: I think it was—oh, I'll tell you when it was. It was when that Annie Lee Moss came up, during that period of time, which must have been that February or March of 1954.[14] But anyway, it was a mean business because they weren't supposed to be making this information available. And I could tell that they were making it available and that they were saying that they weren't. So I had a fight with them.

Then I worked closely with the FBI when I was counsel for the Senate Rackets Committee. At that time, Courtney Evans, who was an Assistant Director of the FBI, was sent up as our liaison. And they were very helpful to us. They didn't know anything about organized crime. That I knew. Because after the meeting [of organized-crime leaders, in 1957] at Apalachin [New York], which seventy people attended, I asked for files from them on each of the seventy, and they didn't have any information, I think, on forty out of the seventy. Not even the slightest piece of information. Perhaps some newspaper clippings, but nothing beyond that. I sent the same request to the Bureau of Narcotics, and they had something on every one of them.

I knew from my experience with both of them that the Bureau of Narcotics had much more information—and much more accurate information, much more thorough information, much more complete information—on organized crime in the United States than the FBI did. The FBI didn't know anything, really, about these people who were the major gangsters in the United States. That was rather a shock to me. And then, of course, they took a different position on organized crime. They took the position there wasn't any such thing as organized crime in the United States. The Bureau of Narcotics said that there was.

LEWIS: Why don't we just address ourselves first—this is a large subject—to that point: how you changed, or what part you played in the change of, the view which the FBI evidently had on that subject. Because they now do think that there's such a thing as organized crime.

KENNEDY: First, I think the work on the [Rackets] Committee and, I suppose, the information that we developed had an influence. It stimulated their working on it. Then, when I became Attorney General, I proceeded on the basis that there was such a thing as organized crime. And they started investigating it. Before that, they had—up here in the city of New York—ten people working on what we call "crime." I mean, crime in contrast to bank robberies and things like that: organized crime, where you're in crime as a business. And they went to work on it here. They had ten people up here before 1960; and by 1962 and '63, they had a hundred and forty people. That was the second biggest unit after Communists and Espionage.

LEWIS: In the New York area?

KENNEDY: Yes. And then out in Chicago they had six men; and by the time I left, I think they had sixty or eighty men working there. They just put a great number of people on it all over the country. They started to work on it, and they started to get informants. I asked them to go into it like they went into the Communist party. They began to get informants, and they had other sources of information.

And then the Bureau of Narcotics turned over to them Valachi.[15] And they were able—with what he said, together with the other material they had accumulated—to put it together in a pattern.

So by the end of 1962 they reached the conclusion there *was* organized crime in the United States and that there was a commission made up of about a dozen people across the country who ran it. And they were able to get the names of the commission members. Then they were able to break it down into exactly how it operated: who were the heads of families, and what areas they controlled, and who controlled them, and what kind of orders and instructions they took. They were able to put together—with what Valachi said, plus other informants, plus people they had within—how the Cosa Nostra worked.[16]

Now, it was of some embarrassment to them. And this is how the Valachi thing came out to some extent: J. Edgar Hoover, who had always taken a different position, agreed to write an article for

Reader's Digest. In the course of the article, he talked about Cosa Nostra right in the middle of the article and about the Valachi thing—what he'd uncovered about the Valachi business. Then they sent this up for our approval, and Ed Guthman went over it and saw that they had brought out all these things that really were damned interesting. And it was just sort of passed over. Now, it was in [Hoover's] interest to pass it over, because the best investigative agency in the world shouldn't suddenly find out that there was a Cosa Nostra—when it had been in existence for a long period of time—and that organized crime existed.

What he was trying to do in the *Reader's Digest* article was to write an article about crime and then pass over in the middle of the article that Cosa Nostra—getting it out in public—that it existed.

LEWIS: As if he'd known it all along?

KENNEDY: As if it had been always known. So we talked about it, and said that, if it was going to come out, it should come out in a more organized fashion. That's when we started to think about what would happen as far as Valachi. During that period of time, I'd had some requests from the congressional committee about Valachi. And that's why he eventually appeared before them. Then there was an article by Peter Maas in *Look* magazine that developed the whole idea of organized crime.*

And those correspondents and reporters who covered the Department of Justice, who were so interested in many matters, were never very interested in organized crime.

LEWIS: That's right.

KENNEDY: So that they never stipulated that anything be done about that. Because, I suppose, of their own ignorance.

LEWIS: Well, now, at the beginning of your term as Attorney General, was there, again, any occasion in which you sat down with Mr. Hoover—

KENNEDY: Yes, I sat down with him on this matter.

LEWIS: —and said, "Look, Edgar, we're going to have to look into this."

KENNEDY: Yes. See, what happened was the Treasury Department had always taken the position that they couldn't investigate organized crime, basically. In the first place, all the agents work on the basis of how many cases they handle; and if you just handle a case of Frank

* The article in question actually appeared in the *Saturday Evening Post.*

Costello, it takes twenty agents five years.[17] And wouldn't it be better to have a hundred cases in five years?

LEWIS: Little cases.

KENNEDY: Yes. So the result was that they were focusing attention on some dentist who hadn't paid all his bills or a taxicab driver who hadn't reported his tips or something.

LEWIS: Could you change that?

KENNEDY: Yes. And then there was a memo written by the legal counsel of the Treasury Department that they shouldn't go into this, that they couldn't: Agents of the Treasury Department couldn't be used to investigate organized crime unless there was a particular violation of the law or something. The result was they weren't doing anything in organized crime. I brought together Douglas Dillon, prior to the time that he was sworn in, and J. Edgar Hoover, and Mort Caplin, prior to the time that he was sworn in. And I said that this was something that I knew President Kennedy was interested in—this was the advantage of being the President's brother—and that I was interested in, and I thought that we should understand that we were going to go into it. So there was an understanding prior to the time of January 1961. And then I got the Bureau of Narcotics [involved].

LEWIS: And Hoover made no objection at that time?

KENNEDY: No. I said, "This is what we're going to concentrate on; this is what we're going to do. And I want it done." He agreed to do it.

There was a unit in the Department of Justice which wasn't very active or very effective in organized crime. We reorganized that, with the understanding that these other people would become actively involved in it—the other agencies. And that's what happened. I met with all the investigative representatives of these other agencies. They brought them in from all over the country, and I discussed our program with them and what we wanted done. Now, a lot of them opposed it for the first six months of the year.

LEWIS: A lot of whom?

KENNEDY: The people at the local level because they couldn't understand why we were getting [Treasury] into it. A lot of them were opposed to it because they thought they'd lose money by it. They wouldn't collect as much money, and it would be embarrassing for them to go to Congress. As it's turned out, they've collected more money making these investigations than they would have otherwise. So not only has it paid off in convictions and in intelligence information, but it's also paid off financially. And they've done a helluva good job at the Treasury Department.

The FBI was reluctant to get into it. In the first place, they never shared information with any other investigative agency; and I said if we were going to all work together, they had to give the information to the other investigative agencies. That's where Courtney Evans played a role, because if there was ever any complaint about the fact that they weren't getting any information, he'd make sure that the other investigative agencies obtained the information.

LEWIS: And that did work all right?

KENNEDY: It all worked.

LEWIS: You think that that will last?

KENNEDY: Yes. In some areas it was more successful than others. By the end of three years, it was reasonably successful everywhere.

But there's no question that I could do it because of my relationship. They wouldn't have paid any attention to me otherwise. If they could have gone over my head to the President, I couldn't have gotten the Treasury Department to do it. I couldn't have gotten them to reverse their position, because a lot of them in the hierarchy were opposed to it. They hated the idea. And of course J. Edgar Hoover didn't want to get in. We then obtained the passage of legislation to broaden their jurisdiction. Maybe we're getting off the—

LEWIS: Well, no. I wanted to come back to Hoover and the FBI. You just said that otherwise he'd have gone over your head to the President. To what extent did Mr. Hoover deal directly with President Kennedy and not with you?

KENNEDY: None. At the beginning he was very close to Bill Rogers. When I came in, I remember the conversation—the first conversation I had with him—he went into a dissertation about how awful Bill Rogers was. And I knew [Rogers] had been the Attorney General that [Hoover] had always been the closest to.

LEWIS: That doesn't make you feel too good.

KENNEDY: No. But I really deferred to him. I made a real effort because I recognized the fact I was young and coming in there and all the rest of the business, and I was making so many changes—not only in organized crime but what we wanted to do in civil rights. So, you know, I'd always go to his office; I'd never ask him to come to my office. And then I had a special phone put in so that we would have direct contact: I'd just have to pick up the receiver and talk to him. I don't know how much he liked that, either. In any case, we got all these things accomplished and done. They're a helluva good investigative agency.

Because I knew that he had that feeling about me—

LEWIS: What feeling?

KENNEDY: Just the idea that I was coming in and making changes of the things that had existed for a long period of time. I made arrangements with my brother to call him every two or three months and then arrange to have J. Edgar Hoover over, just by himself, for lunch. So the President used to meet with him.

LEWIS: But that was for purposes of social, not really strategic—

KENNEDY: Well, social, but he was also helpful. He had some good ideas about reorganizing some of the departments, getting some things done on CIA, and other organizational ideas on the Central Intelligence Agency and the White House operation, and the whole business of checking people. He had some very good ideas. And the President always [was informed about] whatever interesting cases were going along in espionage—and we had some interesting ones at that time: what the Russians were doing up here in New York at the United Nations, their increased activity.

He had a good deal of information and a good number of thoughts which were very helpful, so that the President enjoyed the luncheons. He talks a helluva lot—J. Edgar Hoover—but I think that the President always felt that they were worthwhile. And Hoover—it's what kept Hoover happy for three years, because he had the idea that he had direct contact with [JFK]. And he used to tell me that every month, I guess, Franklin Roosevelt used to have him over for lunch. And I guess he saw Eisenhower frequently. They all used to consult with him. Well, there wasn't the same need now, but we did it for the reason of keeping him happy and making sure that we were making progress. It was important, as far as we were concerned, that he remain happy and that he remain in his position. Because he was a symbol—and the President had won by such a narrow margin. And it was a helluva investigative body, and he got a lot of things done; and it was much better, if we wanted to do what we wanted to do in the South, what we wanted to do in organized crime, and what we wanted to do in a lot of other areas, that we had him on our side.

LEWIS: Do you think, in fact, he would have remained in his position after January 1965?

KENNEDY: No. The relationship that we had was not difficult. I mean, it wasn't an impossible relationship. But President Kennedy would have gotten a replacement before he left office.

LEWIS: Before President Kennedy left office?

KENNEDY: Yes.

LEWIS: He might not have extended—

KENNEDY: He might have extended—

LEWIS: Waived the retirement?

KENNEDY: Yes.

LEWIS: Or waived it briefly.

KENNEDY: Yes, briefly.

LEWIS: Perhaps this is just hindsight, but—at least now, the end of 1964—there's talk of there having been friction between you and Mr. Hoover. Perhaps it was not all as smooth as you suggest.

KENNEDY: No, I think, on the surface, for both of our interests, it was smooth. I don't think he liked— I knew that he didn't like me much.

LEWIS: How did you know that he didn't like you?

KENNEDY: Well, I mean, Courtney Evans used to say he was disturbed at me. I knew. It wouldn't be his way of operating [the Bureau]. Obviously, it made it difficult for him. For the first time since he had been Director of the FBI, he had to take instructions or orders from the Attorney General of the United States—and couldn't go over his head. It doesn't make any sense that he would. We made so many changes in the FBI and their procedures, where they concentrated, and all the rest of it.

LEWIS: Speaking particularly of organized crime and civil rights?

KENNEDY: And civil rights. Therefore, he couldn't like it. Why would he like it? He hadn't made any changes himself for twenty years. I knew that. So there was all the basis of his dislike. What happened was, during that period of time that I had control over the situation,

I made an effort with him which was in my interest and in the interest of the government.

But after November 22, 1963, he no longer had to hide his feelings. He didn't have to hide his feelings, and he no longer had to pay any attention to me. And it was in the interest, evidently, of the President of the United States—President Johnson—to have that kind of a relationship and arrangement.

LEWIS: A direct, personal relationship with Hoover?

KENNEDY: Yes.

LEWIS: Now, let's be concrete: Tell me some of the specific things, if you can face it, that happened with Mr. Hoover after November 22, within hours or days, that made it evident that he was not going to pay any attention to you anymore.

KENNEDY: First, his conversations with me on November 22 were so unpleasant. I can't go into all the details of that. Just that the tone of voice and the information and what he was giving me was— I mean, it wasn't the way, under the circumstances, I would have thought an individual would talk. That was one thing. Then I knew that, within a few days, he was over at the White House giving dossiers on everybody that President Kennedy had appointed—in the White House particularly.

LEWIS: In the White House staff?

KENNEDY: Yes. People who had some problems with their family or some personal problem, with the idea that President Kennedy had appointed a lot of people who were rather questionable figures. After that, he would never deal directly with me or through me. All of the announcements that were made after November 22 when the Department of Justice was supposed to do something, it was always: "Lyndon Johnson's requested the FBI" to do something. Now, during that period of time, I talked to Johnson about it. I said I thought it was a major mistake because I thought that [the Department of Justice] should have some control over the FBI, and that I thought that it would get into difficulty.

LEWIS: What was his response to that?

KENNEDY: His response mostly was the fact that it wasn't going on. He wanted me to control the Department of Justice. I said that wasn't important because I knew what was going on, he knew what was going on, and that under ordinary circumstances I wouldn't stay on as Attorney General. I mean, if I had just been appointed Attorney General, I would resign as Attorney General—because I wouldn't accept this relationship. I thought that if you're going to be in charge of the Department of Justice, you should be in proper charge of the Department of Justice. But that if I got out of there under those circumstances—during that difficult period of time between the two of us—it would be considered that I was getting out for a different reason. That wouldn't do any good. I was going to accept that relationship through the year—and then I would get out.

But I thought that it was a mistake. I thought that it was an intolerable situation for any other Attorney General. And I hoped that he would change it.

Well, he always said that he would. Or that that wasn't, really, the situation that existed—that J. Edgar Hoover never came to him directly. But that wasn't the truth.

I suppose there were a half-dozen different things that occurred during that period of time.

THE DANGEROUS MR. HOOVER

LEWIS: Speaking of Mr. Hoover, did you ever have the feeling, in dealing with Mr. Hoover, that he knew a very great deal about you personally? I mean, did he ever make this evident? This is, at least by way of story, of legend, something he's supposed to do?

KENNEDY: I suppose every month or so he'd send somebody around to give information on somebody I knew or a member of my family or allegations in connection with myself. So that it would be clear—whether it was right or wrong—that he was on top of all of these things and received all of this information. He would do this also, I think, to find out what my reaction to it would be.

LEWIS: What do you mean by that?

KENNEDY: I suppose that, if there were an allegation regarding a friend or something, whether I would ask to have it investigated. If it were an allegation regarding me, what I would do. I remember on one occasion that he said that my brother and I had a group of girls on the twelfth floor—he didn't say it; but Senators, somebody—a group of girls on the twelfth floor of the LaSalle Hotel and that, I think, the President used to go over there once a week and have the place surrounded by Secret Service people, and then go up and have assignations on the twelfth floor of the LaSalle. I suppose the idea was whether you'd have it investigated or what you'd do about it.

LEWIS: Did you ever do anything?

KENNEDY: Yes, I always used to have them go over and find out what was going on, on the twelfth floor or whatever it might be. There was something else going on in the Georgetown Inn or something. A lot of it was so far-fetched that, even on the face of it, it didn't make any sense. I mean, if you were going to do that kind of thing, you wouldn't go on over to the LaSalle Hotel with the Secret Service surrounding the place. It was ridiculous on the face of it. But I think that the idea was just so that you would know that they [the FBI] were continuously getting this information.

Then, people that you knew: a report that somebody had been out drinking or something; you know, so-and-so's father is a member of the Communist party; or so-and-so's brother was picked up for strange activities or something like that. You'd have that kind of information so that it was quite clear that all of this kind of information was available to him and to the FBI.

At the time of the Bobby Baker case and that German girl who was deported—

LEWIS: Ellie Rometsch. [Bobby Baker was charged with "influence peddling" in the so-called Capital Vending suit. Baker resigned his post as Secretary to the Senate Majority Leader in October 1963 amid rumors about his other business activities. A subsequent investigation by the Senate Rules Committee in 1964–1965 revealed "gross improprieties." Republicans accused Democrats of overlooking Baker's alleged use of "party girls" for political and business purposes. Ellie Rometsch was one of the so-called party girls involved in the Bobby Baker scandal.]

KENNEDY: Ellie Rometsch. Clark Mollenhoff [of Cowles Publications] wrote an article that she had been tied up with people at the White House, which was, in fact, incorrect. But in doing that I had looked into the files, what she had said—and she *had* been tied up with a lot of people at the Capitol!

LEWIS: You looked into the FBI files?

KENNEDY: I got all the information she had. It was found out that she was associated with a number of other girls, all of whom had run operations up on Capitol Hill. This is a little bit off the point, but it's rather an interesting sidelight. In any case, I put together the information regarding all the girls and then the members of Congress and the Senate who had been associated with the girls—and it got to be large numbers on both ways.

LEWIS: "Both ways" meaning girls and Congressmen?

KENNEDY: Yes. Also, all political parties.

LEWIS: Oh, yes?

KENNEDY: They [the FBI] were started down that road at that time. I went to see the President, and I said that I thought that it was very damaging to the reputation of the United States. I spoke to the President about it—and it didn't involve anybody at the White House—but I thought that it would just destroy the confidence that people in the United States had in their government and really make us a laughingstock around the world. I suggested that maybe Hoover should meet with [Senate Majority Leader] Mike Mansfield and [Senate Minority Leader Everett] Dirksen and explain what was in the files and what information they had. So that was arranged at Mike Mansfield's apartment one noon for lunch. I guess it was a shock to both of them.

LEWIS: Were you present?

KENNEDY: No. The President talked to them afterwards. From then on, there was less attention, up until the last week, on that aspect of the investigation. Some of the Senators had Negro girlfriends and all kinds of things which were not very helpful.

LEWIS: You were convinced of the accuracy of the stuff?

KENNEDY: Well, a lot of that stuff, a lot of that material was accurate. Some of it wasn't accurate. Some of the girls just obviously told lies about it, which was brought out. Some of it I had to look into further to determine the truth or the falsehood of it. And some of it was all lies.

But in any case, going back to your point, he has all of that information and that material. But we had it under control. At that time we weren't using it for any purpose. I would say the idea, really, now, is that you can use that information and that material.

LEWIS: Why?

KENNEDY: I saw it during the time of the Walter Jenkins case. [On October 7, 1964, Walter Jenkins was arrested in Washington, D.C., on a morals charge. He resigned his post as White House Special Assistant on October 14.] Lyndon Johnson was up here during the Walter Jenkins case, and I talked to him about the case. His response on the Walter Jenkins thing was to try to develop information on Republican Senators and to develop information regarding Barry Goldwater . . . being involved in something—that Barry Goldwater was closely identified with Walter Jenkins. He gave me some information about certain Senators and Congressmen that [he thought] he should bring out, and I knew it had come from the FBI because it was the same material that I had had a year or fourteen months ago. I said that I didn't think that he should do that. My advice to him at that time was that he should answer Walter Jenkins by talking about foreign policy, that he should have a meeting of the National Security Council, that he should go on television and talk about the explosion in China—and not try to answer these things. He had prepared a statement that he was going to give—which he showed me in the car driving out—which hit, sort of indirectly, at Barry Goldwater because Barry Goldwater knew Walter Jenkins.

LEWIS: He was his commanding officer.

KENNEDY: Yes. That was all going to be done on that basis. Every time I have any conversation in which there's any attack on Bobby Baker, the response always is: "We should bring this out about such-and-such a Senator." The night before he was up here, he told me, he had spent all night sitting up and reading the files of the FBI on all of these people. And Lyndon talks about that information and material so freely.

LEWIS: You think it's bound to—?

KENNEDY: It's going to get out. Bob McNamara, who's having his problems with him now, is convinced that he tried to put a tap on his telephone because he's opposed to him.

LEWIS: You mean because the President thinks McNamara is opposed to him?

KENNEDY: No, because Hoover feels that McNamara is opposed to him.

LEWIS: That Hoover put the tap on?

KENNEDY: Hoover. To get information, because he thinks that there's a conspiracy by McNamara and me to get rid of Hoover.

LEWIS: That was another question I was generally going to ask you—whether you felt that there was any wiretapping done of officials by the FBI.

KENNEDY: I just don't know. I don't have any evidence of it myself.

LEWIS: You never saw any indication of your own private conversations appearing elsewhere?

KENNEDY: No, I didn't. McNamara had a lot of this information that I had before, which had come from the FBI reports. His conversations with Lyndon Johnson were such that he thinks that the material that Lyndon Johnson had came from wiretaps of, perhaps, public officials.

LEWIS: Recent conversations?

KENNEDY: Yes. It was a matter of great concern to him. He told Lyndon Johnson the day before yesterday that he had to get rid of J. Edgar Hoover because he was such a menace.

LEWIS: And the reaction to that was?

KENNEDY: [Johnson] says he thinks he understands that, but he doesn't know how to do it. [McNamara] used to tell me that Hoover used to send over all this material on me and that Lyndon Johnson would read it to him. Now, Lyndon Johnson told me that he never received an adverse report from J. Edgar Hoover about me.

One time McNamara had a dinner at Nick Katzenbach's house to talk about their children taking a bicycle ride through Cape Cod.

LEWIS: Martha's Vineyard?

KENNEDY: Yes. Hoover sent a report in to Lyndon Johnson that there was a meeting—I think I was supposed to have been there—at this house in which we were discussing the overthrow of Lyndon Johnson, to take the nomination away from him. [McNamara] says he was sending reports every few days about me and people that I'd meet with. Abba Schwartz [of the State Department] was reported to have said at some party: "We've got to get rid of Lyndon Johnson so that Robert Kennedy can become President." This was all during that period of time. And Lyndon Johnson, of course, says that he never received such a report. The whole situation was so unhealthy during that period of time.

I had one conversation, which was interesting, with both of them. After Hoover had been down to Mississippi, they had the riots in Harlem. [Hoover] was going to come up to Harlem. He called me up and said that Lyndon Johnson told him to go to Harlem. I said that I thought that that was a bad, bad mistake for several reasons.

I thought, first, if he went into Harlem, that every time they had a riot any place in the country they were going to say, "Why don't you come here?" And if he didn't come, they'd say, "Well, it was because the President doesn't think it's important enough." Secondly, it's going to indicate that it's a federal responsibility, not a local responsibility. And thirdly, that will be used during the course of the campaign and you're going right into a political campaign.

"I don't think it makes any sense. You've got people up there. Why can't they give you a report? And then you can decide what you should do."

He said, "That's what I told the President. I didn't think I should go. But he insists that I go."

I said, "I'm going to call him up and tell him that I don't think you should go." So I called up Lyndon Johnson and said that I didn't think he should go for these reasons—that it was a mistake.

And he said, "I didn't think he should go either. But he insisted that he wanted to go."

So I said, "That's a funny thing. He just told me that you insisted that you wanted him to go."

That was the end of the conversation. He didn't go.

LEWIS: The liaison with Ellie Rometsch, and what have you . . . How is it possible for an investigative organization to have that kind of material in its files—there must be even more than you saw or were aware of—without having tremendous effect on the conduct of Senators? Blackmail, suggestion—

KENNEDY: I think it's very tough. I agree that it's very tough. The fact is that a lot of this material hasn't appeared, you know, on various people. He hasn't really used it as a wide-scale blackmail operation outside—and he's got all that material; he's got all that information. I think that there's the good side to it too.

LEWIS: Well, that's good that it hasn't come out.

KENNEDY: The information has to be there, I suppose. You have to accumulate it.

LEWIS: You spoke of that lunch with Hoover and Mike Mansfield and Dirksen. As a result of that lunch, the heat was taken off. It means, obviously, that Mansfield and Dirksen passed the word that the heat better be taken off—in their own self-interest. And, if at no previous time, members of the House and Senate must have become acutely aware of the fact that this information existed.

KENNEDY: I don't think that anybody ever knew that the luncheon took place.

LEWIS: Oh? Didn't Mansfield and Dirksen sort of pass the word?

KENNEDY: I wouldn't think they'd have done it on that basis.

LEWIS: Oh, I see.

KENNEDY: They'd never say that. I don't think they'd have done it on the basis that they had had the meeting. But I think that, when the decision was going to be made as to what areas they were going to go into, Dirksen with his Republican colleagues and Mansfield with his Democratic colleagues would indicate that that's not what they should be doing.

LEWIS: I didn't mean that they indicated about the luncheon but that they would suggest to their colleagues that such an inquiry might rebound against them or something.

KENNEDY: I don't know how they handled it. But in any case they handled it.

LEWIS: I see. What was your brother's view, in general, on Mr. Hoover? I suppose everything you've said really reflects his views, doesn't it?

KENNEDY: Yes. He felt that he could really talk. He's an effective operator.
Hoover was really of no particular importance to him.

LEWIS: Did he think—or do you now think—that Mr. Hoover is a dangerous person? Or just nasty?

KENNEDY: No, I think he's dangerous.

LEWIS: You think he is dangerous?

KENNEDY: Yes. But it was a danger that we could control, that we were on top of, that we could deal with at the appropriate time. That's the way we looked at it. In the interests of the administration and in the interests of the country, it was well that we had control over it. There wasn't anything that he could do. We were giving him direction. And there wasn't anybody he could go to or anything he could do with the information or the material. So it was fine. He served our interests.

LEWIS: Yes. That's probably what every President has thought.

KENNEDY: Yes.

LEWIS: That's his secret. I mean, that's his technique. He's useful to each President.

KENNEDY: Yes. I think there was more recognition about what the situation was at that moment. Maybe it's just because it's us, rather than some other President, but I think that what we were doing was in the interests of what was good for the country at that moment.

LEWIS: As a practical matter, is there any way that any President can allow Mr. Hoover or encourage Mr. Hoover to retire, without having the potential threat of Mr. Hoover out of office, talking about the things that he didn't talk about when he was in office?

KENNEDY: I suppose that's always difficult.

When I came in, the FBI had to clear all of their press releases and the speeches that came out of the FBI with me.

LEWIS: That was new?

KENNEDY: Yes. Through my agent, Ed Guthman. That had never been done before. Secondly, all the press releases that went out had to go out from the Department of Justice, not from the FBI. That was new. They all had to be approved, and that was new. That was never a major problem. The *Reader's Digest* article was somewhat of a problem on the Valachi [episode], which I discussed. But it was never a major problem until after November 22, [1963], when it began to be a problem. For instance, at the time of the arrest of those Ku Klux Klan members for the shooting of the colonel in Georgia.

LEWIS: Penn. Yes.

KENNEDY: Well, the press release had been approved: "The Department of Justice" or "The Attorney General announces the arrest" and then "J. Edgar Hoover says such and such and such and such." That's the way we'd proceed. They brought that [press release] up, and it was approved by Ed Guthman or Jack Rosenthal [Assistant Director of Public Information, Justice Department]. When the release finally appeared, when the statement finally appeared, it was just "The FBI." So I asked Ed Guthman what had happened to "The Department of Justice." He checked with the reporters. And [Cartha] DeLoach or somebody in that office [Crime Records Division, FBI] had called them down, given them the press release without the

Department of Justice's name in it—with the understanding that, after they had read the press release, they'd hand it back so that there wouldn't be any evidence that they had struck out the name Department of Justice. That was one example.

Then we had a major conflict about a speech that [Hoover] was going to give, which we wouldn't clear. He did change it, finally, because I said to him that I wouldn't clear it and that he'd have to take it to Lyndon Johnson.

LEWIS: In that speech, as I recall, he was attributing Communist connections to the civil rights movement.

KENNEDY: Yes, I guess that was it. So, eventually, he changed that.

LEWIS: . . . There was [another] speech in which he spoke of zealots and pressure groups lying and so forth. And the only change that Nick requested was the removal of the word *lying*—which he did not remove. He ad-libbed at that point in the speech—something about "under the leadership of Communists and moral degenerates."

KENNEDY: Yes. Bob McNamara always wanted to proceed through the Department of Justice. He understood what was happening, so he would never deal directly with the FBI. When the FBI was searching for the bodies [of murdered civil rights workers Andrew Goodman, Michael Schwerner, and James Chaney], they had to work with the Defense Department. [McNamara] would not take any requests from the FBI unless they had cleared them either through me or through Nick. That made [Hoover] furious because he wanted some divers to go down there, and Bob McNamara said that he wouldn't send the divers down unless he got clearance from Nick. That made [Hoover] mad. Then he wanted to fly over Mississippi and take pictures, and McNamara refused to do that until he got clearance. And I wouldn't do it. Finally, J. Edgar Hoover, after all this—about four or five months of really irritating work—called me to complain about Bob McNamara and said what he was doing. He gave me those two instances, and then there was a third, something about moving some more sailors in or something. I said I thought that he should proceed in that way and that I didn't want them to be flying over the state of Mississippi. We'd flown over Alabama and gotten into difficulty. I thought that we should make sure that the Governor had approved of it, and I thought that this was the correct way of proceeding.

"Was there any difficulty in locating either Nick or me?"

He grunted, "No."

And I said, "Well, I think that that's the way to proceed."

Later on, I had a conversation with him where I said that I wasn't going to stay very long and that I thought, in the interests of the Department of Justice and in both of our interests, we should make some kind of an effort to try to work these things out, that we'd worked it out beforehand, and I thought that we could work it out for the few months that I was going to remain there. But it never worked out very satisfactorily.

LEWIS: Did he have any other reason for disliking McNamara? Was the thing with Adam Yarmolinsky a factor in it at all? [Adam Yarmolinsky was Special Assistant to the Secretary of Defense, from January 1961 to September 1965. Major General Edwin A. Walker charged Yarmolinsky with alleged Communist connections in testimony before the Special Senate Preparedness Subcommittee.]

KENNEDY: That might have been. [McNamara] had a very tough time with him lately about the investigation of some "degenerates" over at the Defense Department, that McNamara had called and asked him to investigate, and which he had agreed to do. Then he called off the investigation without telling McNamara. So McNamara went to the President. Then Hoover went to the President and said that McNamara was part of a conspiracy, led by me, to get rid of J. Edgar Hoover. It's been very unpleasant.

LEWIS: To say the least. Can we focus a little bit on civil rights before we leave the subject of the FBI specifically, because that's a topic of great interest? What about the question of Negro agents? Did you do something about that?

KENNEDY: I spoke to him about trying to get more Negro agents. He was going to make a major drive to obtain Negro agents. And he gave me some statistics or figures about where he tried and that they hadn't been able to get people who passed the tests. That was basically it.

MARSHALL: He got some, though. He never really had any before.

KENNEDY: And I wanted some Negro agents sent into the South.

MARSHALL: He's never done that.

LEWIS: What about the question of infiltration of white supremacist groups in the South, like the Ku Klux Klan, similar to the infiltration of organized crime? Was that another objective?

KENNEDY: Yes. I asked him to do that, and I think that they made a real effort to do that. President Kennedy spoke to him about that, to try to do it on the same basis. I spoke to Lyndon Johnson and said that I thought that, really, they should do that in Mississippi—send a lot more agents into Mississippi and just be everywhere in Mississippi. If we were going to try to avoid the use of troops in Mississippi, we had to take some really major steps. One step was just to have so many people around there that they wouldn't violate the law, just because they thought that there was an FBI agent around at the time. That was done: They increased the size of the FBI there by fivefold.

LEWIS: As to the investigation of civil rights matters, Burke, was Mr. Hoover reluctant to get into this area?

MARSHALL: Well, we changed some procedures, again, in that area, about when they would investigate. They never would investigate bombings beforehand. They wouldn't really get into it for me. So I had to take that to you [RFK], you remember, the first time. Well, they do that all the time now. It isn't a problem now. But it was a problem at first, and to some extent, there were the same kinds of problems on investigations that involved local police. They really didn't have enough people down there. That generally was increased continuously over a period. And they did, I think, an increasingly better job.

LEWIS: Are there questions with Mr. Hoover's reluctance on that front? For example, was that a result of any personal lack of belief in the program? I mean, is he essentially opposed to civil rights measures? Or was it just a change in the established way of doing things?

KENNEDY: He's basically very conservative. I don't think that he's got a great sympathy for this. I think that he also recognizes where the power is and what he has to do; and once he reaches that decision, that is paramount. He reached the decision that we were going to do things in civil rights and that that's the way it was going to be done by the Department of Justice and the Attorney General of the United States—and it was going to be backed up by the President of the United States. Either you had to do it or you'd have to get out. He wouldn't want it to come even close to that kind of conflict. So any time I'd call and ask him to do something, which wasn't very frequent, where I'd have to put it on him directly, he was the most enthusiastic person you ever talked to. So he handled that well. And when they did things, frequently they did them damned well. At least, before November [22, 1963].

LEWIS: Well, they've done well in Mississippi since.

KENNEDY: I don't mean even in those things. Even after November, they'd do those things well. You know I've had a more difficult time with him personally, [but] I don't agree with this sort of general criticism that's been made that the FBI doesn't do anything in civil rights. I don't think that's the problem. I think the problem is deeper than that. I think that it's civilian control. As the Pentagon has civilian control of the military, this is civilian control of an investigative body.

LEWIS: How far down in the FBI does this problem, which you've stated very well, this central problem—civilian control of the activities of a force with such a tremendous amount of damaging information—how far down does that problem exist below Mr. Hoover? What about at the heads there: DeLoach and all those other people?

KENNEDY: They're loyal to J. Edgar Hoover. Nobody else. They play it very smoothly. They're all very smooth operators, aren't they?

MARSHALL: Yes, I agree. I think that probably, to say the least, he has no personal convictions about it. And he's probably not sympathetic to the civil rights groups for all sorts of reasons, including the fact that Communists are always hanging around them and that he never found it productive, from his point of view, before, to get in conflict with the political systems in the southern states. It wasn't productive in Congress, and it wasn't productive in his relationships with the people locally there. So he didn't do it. But that was true of the government as a whole, I would say, and the Bureau just shared in that. As it was changed—as the emphasis and the amount of energy and the degree of determination to do something about those problems became decided inside the administration and in the country and in Congress and everywhere—he became determined that the Bureau was increasingly effective. To the extent you can say that they weren't effective in the past, you can say that about almost every branch of the government . . .

I think that Mr. Hoover never would have changed by himself, you know. But once he had the Attorney General and the President, he would change with the course of history. It's like Mississippi would never change from inside itself. That's probably true all over. There'd be a time lag there. And there was a time lag. . . .

LEWIS: For purposes of concrete illustration, before we conclude on the FBI and Mr. Hoover, let's—if you would, Bob—say a word about the current (December 1964) episode with Martin Luther King and Mr. Hoover. At this point, Dr. King had just been in for a meeting with Mr. Hoover after Mr. Hoover called him "the most notorious liar in the country." The public impression is that Dr. King requested the meeting and they talked things out, that things are rather less tense and covered over. They're old, good friends now. What are the facts of the situation?

KENNEDY: I wasn't present at the meeting. Martin Luther King was in a very vulnerable position, first, because of his association with members of the Communist party, about whom he had been warned and which we can go into a little bit more deeply later. . . .

I might say that in 1961, to protect ourselves, when I heard that he was tied up, perhaps, with some Communists, I asked [the FBI] to make an intensive investigation of him, to see who his companions were and also to see what other activities he was involved in. I think there were rumors about him before that. They made that intensive investigation, and I gave them also permission to put a tap on his telephone [in October 1963]. So this information developed, and they followed up on him.

In any case, when [King] came in to see Hoover, from what I understand from Hoover's account that he's given to the FBI offices around the country, [Hoover] told him that he was a Marxist . . . and [Reverend Ralph] Abernathy said, "You can't say that!"

LEWIS: Hoover said these things to King as the meeting started?

KENNEDY: In the course of the meeting, [Hoover] said that he wasn't going to take any lip or any opposition from anybody like that— who's had this kind of a background in these kinds of activities. Evidently, Abernathy spoke up, and [Hoover] said, "You were involved, too." . . .

He went into considerable detail and gave him a lecture for an hour about the fact that he was not in a position to be finding fault with the Federal Bureau of Investigation or J. Edgar Hoover, based on his own record. I believe that was the reason why Martin Luther King was so mild when he left the meeting. And [King] eventually had some kind of a communication or made a telephone call in which he expressed great concern and great amazement that Hoover had so much information regarding his activities.

LEWIS: To whom did he make the call?

KENNEDY: I don't know whom he made the call to.

LEWIS: Mr. Hoover knows.

KENNEDY: Yes, Mr. Hoover knows.

LEWIS: Since we've mentioned that, we might as well go on with it for a moment. You say you did know, while you were Attorney General, that there were some Communists close to Dr. King?

KENNEDY: Yes.

LEWIS: And what did you do about it? Was this at an early enough point so that Harris Wofford was in the country, for example?

MARSHALL: The very first time that we brought it to the attention of Dr. King, Harris was here. That was in 1961. That was before you asked for an investigation or any continued watch over it by the Bureau. The information concerned Stanley Levison.[18]

LEWIS: He's someone who's active in the Southern Christian Leadership Conference?

MARSHALL: No, he's not. But he's been an adviser of Dr. King's for some time. The Bureau's information was that he was a secret member of the Communist party.

KENNEDY: A high official.

MARSHALL: Well, at that time, all that I knew was that he was a secret member.

KENNEDY: Later on, he became a member of the Executive Board.

MARSHALL: Made a member of the Executive Committee, secretly, of the Communist party.

KENNEDY: So he was quite a big figure.

MARSHALL: He was a very important figure in the Communist party. Now, that information was very highly classified. But the first warning of Dr. King was your instruction to me to have him warned. And I did it through Harris. I didn't know Dr. King well at the time. So I told Harris to talk to him about this problem. We could not say that Levison was a Communist at the time because of the security of the information and because we didn't want to accuse people. We didn't know how serious the problem was. Harris talked to him about it, and King said that he didn't believe that Levison was a Communist. He didn't do anything about it. That was the first time. Then I spoke to Dr. King about it more explicitly, once more at your direction.

KENNEDY: Because he kept up his contacts.

MARSHALL: He kept up his contacts, and I spoke to him about it more directly.

LEWIS: When you knew more, also?

MARSHALL: Yes, we knew more. I could not say that he was a member of the Executive Committee in the Communist party. We could say that my best belief was that he was a secret Communist. And I told King that. Once again, although he temporarily stopped it, he did not.

LEWIS: Temporarily stopped seeing Levison?

MARSHALL: Yes.

LEWIS: Relying on him?

MARSHALL: Yes. But he, even at that, resumed it. . . . The Attorney General discussed that with the President in June of 1963. Whether you'd discussed it with the President before or on what occasions, I don't know. But in June 1963, after the Birmingham demonstrations, at the time that the President decided to send the [1963 civil rights] bill down to Congress, he'd had a series of meetings. He met with the civil rights leaders, and he asked that King be warned again and even more explicitly. We discussed that with the Bureau.

I talked to [King] first, and then you talked to him.

LEWIS: You talked to King, yourself, Bob?

KENNEDY: Yes. And then the President talked to him.

LEWIS: My God! And what was King's reaction? Has he done anything since then or is he still—?

KENNEDY: The President was very firm and strong with him, as Burke was—as we all were. . . . He [Levison]* helped write some

---

*Levison testified before a 1962 executive session of the Senate Internal Security Subcommittee that "I am not now and never have been a member of the Communist party." Based on FBI claims later shown to be unfounded, it is certain that Robert Kennedy believed that Communist efforts to influence the civil rights movement could greatly damage the movement itself. Until his death, he also believed that the national security aspects of the FBI claims prevented him from divulging the details of Hoover's allegations against Levison.

speeches, a speech or some articles or something. During that period of time he was doing a lot of the writing.

So when Hoover turned to King and said, "You're a Marxist," that's part of the basis for it.

LEWIS: I see. Do you think, yourself, that King is just unaware of the dangers of dealing with Communists in this respect? What is his reason for doing this after advice from people whom he must respect?

KENNEDY: He's just got some other side to him. He sort of laughs about a lot of these things, makes fun of it. . . .

My only point is when you say, "Did he pay any attention to this?" he just—he used to talk about whether *he* was a Communist or a Marxist or something—just always dismissing the whole idea.

LEWIS: Well, that's quite understandable. Those conceptions may not be terribly relevant to somebody in Dr. King's situation. I mean, they might not seem relevant to him. But they are relevant.

MARSHALL: I think that, first, he may not have believed it about Levison. When the Attorney General spoke to him, when the President spoke to him, he must have believed it. Then I think that he was just probably weak about it.

KENNEDY: I might say that this is also—what we discussed about Martin Luther King—the reason that President Kennedy and I, and the Department of Justice, were so reserved about him during this period of time, which I'm sure he felt. . . . We never wanted to get very close to him just because of these contacts and connections that he had, which we felt were damaging to the civil rights movement. And because we were so intimately involved in the struggle for civil rights, it also damaged us. It damaged what we were trying to do. There was more than one individual who was involved. That was what was of such concern to us. When we were sending the legislation up or when we were so involved in the struggles of Birmingham, Alabama, if it also came out what he was doing, not only would it damage him but it would also damage all of our efforts and damage any possible chance of the passage of legislation.

I might say that I did send, in 1964, Burke and Courtney Evans up to see [Senator] Dick Russell.

LEWIS: During the debate on the legislation?

KENNEDY: Yes.

LEWIS: In connection with that? For what purpose did you send them up?

KENNEDY: Because I wanted them to understand all the facts that were involved. I had written a letter to Senator [Michael] Monroney [of Oklahoma] that there were not Communists behind the civil rights movement. I don't know what my exact words were.

MARSHALL: You said that none of the major civil rights leaders were Communists or Communist-controlled and that included Dr. King— and that there were, of course, efforts by Communists to infiltrate it. You also sent me to Senator Monroney. That was in 1963, when you wrote the letter.

KENNEDY: Yes. I sent Burke up to see Senator Monroney to give him this information.

LEWIS: But you were aware, despite the letter, of this connection?

KENNEDY: The letter was accurate. I didn't put down all the information that we had, for obvious reasons, because it was so classified. But the letter was accurate. I don't remember what brought it on, exactly.

MARSHALL: Senator Russell had written a letter. And it had gotten lost or delayed in answer.

KENNEDY: Oh, yes. To me. He wrote me a very snotty letter that I hadn't answered. I had never gotten the first letter, so I called him up and apologized. I was answering the letter, which was about Communists, about Martin Luther King. I said, "I'd like to send up Courtney Evans, Assistant Director of the FBI, and Burke Marshall." Or was it Nick?

MARSHALL: Nick went up, I think.

KENNEDY: And they explained the Communist part to Dick Russell and all we'd done. Dick Russell said that he wasn't interested in that in any case. He said that he felt that Martin Luther King wasn't a Communist. He was too smart to be a Communist. And he wasn't going to go into it himself. He didn't believe that it should be gone into.

Let me come back, also, to the book that was sent by J. Edgar Hoover on Martin Luther King, what happened about that. You know, the summary of his Communist—

MARSHALL: Oh, yes . . . Mr. Hoover prepared a memorandum, classified as top secret, which was an attack on Dr. King. It went into this business about Levison. It also went into other connections with Communists or former Communists that were less dangerous than the Levison thing, which was undoubtedly a real effort to get some control over Dr. King. . . . He sent a copy to the President, and he sent a copy to the Attorney General, and I think he sent a copy to me.

KENNEDY: And he sent a copy to Navy Intelligence, Army Intelligence, the Air Force Intelligence, the Secretary of Defense—

MARSHALL: It was a very explosive document in the sense that it was at the time that the bill was before Congress.

LEWIS: Why do you think that he sent it to the military? In the hope that somehow it would leak out?

KENNEDY: Just because they had to furnish information on top Communists in the government or top Communists in the United States—and here was one. It was a rather unfair report because it gave just one side of it. Within all of this material that we had on the tie with Levison, there was offsetting material of conversations which Martin Luther King might have had which indicated that he didn't want to have anything to do with the Communists. He wanted to make sure that the Communists stayed out of the March on Washington. There were things that gave a different side of Martin Luther King.

LEWIS: The memorandum gave only one?

KENNEDY: One side. So the memorandum was very, very unfair. I mean, if you wanted to get a picture of Martin Luther King, this was not a fair way of doing it. Wouldn't you say that that was correct?

MARSHALL: Yes, that's right. That's absolutely right. It ought to be clear that, although there was this Levison thing, we had no indications that King went to Communist meetings or was otherwise involved with Communists.

LEWIS: Was there any indication, realistically in your opinion, that King was under any real influence of Levison?

KENNEDY: Yes. Levison influenced him.

MARSHALL: Levison influenced him, all right. Whether he influenced him in a Communist—
    He had, no doubt, influenced him.

KENNEDY: Their goals were identical, really, I suppose.

LEWIS: What is so difficult in this situation is what a memorandum of that kind probably could not reflect: and that is that the situation of the Negro in Birmingham at the time of that march, for example, was such that it was a little hard to distinguish between a Communist objective and what would be the normal objective.

KENNEDY: But in any case it's very unhealthy to have an association with a person who is elected to the Executive Board of the Communist party.

LEWIS: Needless to say.

KENNEDY: Yes.

MARSHALL: And to continue it after warning.

KENNEDY: Continuing it. That in itself was bad. But [Hoover] wrote this memorandum up in an unfair way. He started out by saying that Martin Luther King is a Marxist or something.

MARSHALL: That he was a Marxist and, I think, that he was under control of a secret Communist—or something like that.

LEWIS: What did you do about this? This was September or October '63, I think.

KENNEDY: I called up Hoover and had a conversation with him about it. I pointed these things out. I said that, of course, we had the legislation up. I said that I was as concerned about this matter as he was or anybody was, but that we wanted to obtain the passage of legislation. And we didn't want to lose, to fail in the passage of legislation by a document which gave only one side.
    He said, "I think it should be recalled."
    So I said, "Fine."

LEWIS: He said?

KENNEDY: Yes. Then I had another conversation with him, and he said,

"Now, I want you always to remember: I was the one who had this document recalled and that you didn't suggest it."

So I said, "Fine."

He had them all withdrawn, including mine. He called up and asked whether to withdraw mine, and I said, "I think you ought to withdraw them all—now. If you're going to take any of them, you shouldn't just have it from the military." That night, he sent over to all the military. One of them was locked up in a safe, so they couldn't get it until the next day. But they were all withdrawn. Now, during that period of time, some people over at the Pentagon had read it. They were, of course, shocked to death.

But, fortunately, Courtney Evans was there and involved in it. He knew about all of this. His information is very important in connection with civil rights. In the whole thing with Martin Luther King, he was important, wasn't he? What you could tell Martin Luther King—

MARSHALL: That's right. . . .

LEWIS: I can just add a very small footnote to this. At the time that Hoover had his interview with the women correspondents two weeks ago—the one in which this current episode with Dr. King began, in which he called Dr. King a liar—a portion of that interview was off the record, a very small portion. In that portion of the interview, he said that Dr. King—I don't know the exact phraseology—was under the influence of Communist connections, or Communists were in control of him, or something like that.

CIVIL RIGHTS ACTIVITIES, 1961–1962

LEWIS: I'd like to turn back to civil rights. Two things during the year 1961: the preparation that was done during the summer of 1961 for the desegregation of schools in new districts that fall, which involved the President expressing some interest in getting prepared for that ahead of time; then, that was followed up in the fall of 1961 with a number of discussions about possible legislation—whether legislation was a wise or necessary idea, perhaps tied to, also, a reference to the employment orders. Let's take one at a time and begin with the school situation.

MARSHALL: We wanted to do it in advance and did it during the summer.

KENNEDY: [Assistant Attorney General] Ramsey Clark went around. Burke went around—

MARSHALL: John Seigenthaler went around.

KENNEDY: So that we would be prepared in each one of the districts and were ready in the ones where we thought there was going to be some difficulty. We'd know what their problems were, and we'd be able to tell them whom they should consult with—who had good ideas and who had bad ideas, and what they'd done in Dallas and what they'd done in Atlanta—to give them the benefit of some of those suggestions. The women down there said that they'd tried to correspond with women in other places about what the problems might be. In some places, they were successful. And they were willing to continue to help. So we just continued that.

I think that the result was that we didn't have the difficulties that people had anticipated we would.

LEWIS: Burke mentioned a meeting at Hyannis Port on Thanksgiving Day, or the Thanksgiving weekend of 1961, at which the topics of discussion—

MARSHALL: The housing order.

LEWIS: Two things that you said were [discussed were] the housing order and possible legislation. There was a great deal of kidding, you said, on the President's part, about who had written the speech saying that the President could end housing discrimination with the stroke of a pen.[19] The President kept muttering, " 'Stroke of the pen!' Who said, 'Stroke of the pen'?"

There was a feeling—and we might just ask this question generally— the strong feeling then of everybody was that legislation was hopeless, that legislation could not pass of any significance, that it was a waste of time.

KENNEDY: Absolutely. I don't think we really seriously considered sending any legislation up. There was so much unfinished business that needed to be done. And there was so much that could be done in the field of civil rights without legislation at that time, so much action that the executive branch of the government could take. What was needed at that moment was that kind of activity. Secondly, there were so many other problems around the world that all of us were concentrating on then: '61 was Cuba, the Bay of Pigs; then the fall of '61 was the Berlin crisis. Plus the economic problems; plus housing; plus the education fight; plus the fight for Medicare. All of these other things were going on simultaneously.

I never even thought or suggested or even ever had a very serious conversation—or any conversation that I can remember—about sending another civil rights legislation up. And there wasn't anybody who was calling for civil rights legislation that could really give any leadership in getting it through.

LEWIS: How about *The New York Times*?

KENNEDY: I mean anybody we paid any attention to. *The New York Times* served as an irritant. Once every four days there was a voice on the other end of the phone: "Did you read what those pricks said today?" We'd all know who "they" were: *The New York Times* editorial writers. Not that the President of the United States used that kind of language.

There wasn't any real discussion. In 1962 we wanted to do something on voting. We thought that, again, the emphasis should be on getting people to register and participate in elections. So we sent up that legislation. I went up and testified. Nobody paid the slightest bit of attention to me. We got noplace with that. Nobody paid any attention. There wasn't any public outcry for it. We went through a filibuster then, which lasted two weeks, which was very desultory and ineffective. We tried to have cloture and didn't get fifty percent of the vote—and it died.

Everybody says, since then, that President Kennedy never recognized the problem of civil rights until the Birmingham crisis. And then he realized that it was a moral issue. And then he made the speech. That was just a lot of hogwash. There wasn't anything he could do then. He didn't believe in just going through the motions about things. If giving some leadership would have accomplished something, then even if it was going to fail, he might have done it. But this wasn't going to accomplish anything. He tried to do something on civil rights in '62. And nobody was ready. And we were getting a lot done just through administrative action. I think that's really what people failed to recognize.

I think that's very important for historical reasons, because I keep reading—and this is something that's generally accepted—that President Kennedy never realized that there was a civil rights problem until Birmingham in 1963. What he realized in Birmingham in 1963, what he was bright enough to realize was that—then—you could obtain the passage of certain legislation which could never have been obtained prior to that time. There wasn't anything accomplished by sending it up [before]. It wasn't because you were going to alienate the southerners by sending up the legislation. They didn't care. They could fight the legislation. It wasn't going to alienate them by sending it up, but it wasn't going to accomplish anything, either. Our emphasis wasn't on that. Our emphasis was on what had to be done around the board, what we could do in civil rights through the Department of Justice and through other governmental agencies, and the administrative action and leadership that the President could take.

THE PRESIDENT'S COMMITTEE ON EQUAL EMPLOYMENT OPPORTUNITY

KENNEDY: We should, I suppose, also talk about our struggle in equal employment.

LEWIS: I was just coming to that because, of course, that was a notable example of executive action. I don't know what you're smiling about, gentlemen. I imagine it might have something to do with the Vice President. But I think we have to talk about it. So let's begin.

MARSHALL: President Kennedy revised the employment committee, the President's Committee on Employment, early in '61. The order that he signed was a much more effective order, a much more broad order. The committee was headed by the Vice President. The Attorney General was a member of the committee. There were policy issues that came up in the committee all the time. One of the major policy issues was on the Plans for Progress and the suggestion that that implied just voluntary action and no compulsory action.[20] Actually, the Plans for Progress was an educational program, among other things, that, I think, probably had a real effect among the leaders of industry. Bobby Troutman put a good deal of effort into it.

LEWIS: Civil rights groups were skeptical about it.

MARSHALL: They were skeptical about it. There was a question, which became an issue at some of the committee meetings, as to whether or not there was any follow-up, whether you could tell whether they were doing anything, whether their reports and statistics were properly kept.

KENNEDY: The committee was not very well run or operated. So there was continued dispute about what the committee was doing. Arthur Goldberg got into that struggle, and then he went on to the Supreme Court. Bill Wirtz [Goldberg's successor as Secretary of Labor] got into it. There was great dissatisfaction—first by Arthur Goldberg, then by Bill Wirtz—about the operations of the committee.

MARSHALL: And by some of the members of the committee too.

KENNEDY: Yes.

LEWIS: Just to say a word for the historians. It was, organizationally, a very difficult beast to manage. Is this correct?

KENNEDY: No, it could have been [managed]. It could have been. There wasn't any problem about making it an effective organization, an effective operation. It wasn't because of the built-in problems of a split in authority between the Vice President and the Secretary of Labor. That wasn't the problem.

LEWIS: How could it have been?

KENNEDY: Just if the Vice President gave it some direction. It was mostly a public relations operation. I mean, it accomplished a good deal more than it had accomplished under Nixon. But a lot of it was public relations. Secondly, there wasn't any adequate follow-up. Thirdly, the head of the staff, whatever his name is— What's his name?

MARSHALL: Hobart.

KENNEDY: Hobart Taylor was an Uncle Tom.

MARSHALL: The first two points (the last was a matter of, you know, personnel) were the main topic of discussion of a lot of the committee meetings and a main point of disagreement, I think, between the Vice President and Arthur Goldberg, first, and Bill Wirtz, second: whether or not the Plans for Progress and the emphasis on it and the signing ceremonies and so forth were just public relations. Secondly, whether there should be any effort at following up and seeing what those companies were really doing. Then the Attorney General got into it.

KENNEDY: We had some rather— The sharpest disputes I had with Vice President Johnson, I suppose, were at one committee meeting.

LEWIS: Describe that one.

KENNEDY: What concerned me was that Bill Wirtz got a questionnaire of all the companies which had contracts with the government—there were thirty-five thousand or something—and how many employed Negroes. Now, this was after we had gotten a good deal of publicity and attention, just as you said. A lot was being accomplished. And we found out that, I think, twenty-five thousand didn't employ a Negro. There were just pages of companies with zero.

A lot of them were small companies, but there were quite a few large companies that never employed Negroes. We had gotten a good deal of attention on this. There was a great deal of dissatisfaction among staff members over the fact that it was a public relations gimmick. And in the last analysis it was not going to be Vice President Johnson's committee: it was going to be President Kennedy's committee. The signings had taken place in the White House. And I could just see going into the election of 1964, and eventually these statistics or figures would get out. There would just be a public scandal.

So I went to a couple of these meetings in which everybody would give sort of generalized statements as to what they were doing. The labor leaders would get up and say, "Well, we've gotten in touch with all the labor unions and told them to employ Negroes."

And then I'd raise the question: "How many said that they are?" We followed up to find out if any of them are. "And why hasn't somebody followed it up? What companies have you actually gotten in touch with? Is anybody going to see any of the companies? Has anybody asked to see them?"

Some of this came out of the Birmingham business when we were talking so much about government employing Negroes—and we found out that the government had employed no Negroes in Birmingham. In the whole city, there were just a handful of Negroes employed. So I said that what you have to do—my feeling was just as we did with the government—is we pulled them together and told them that you have to go out and look for these people. I thought that should be the policy and that we should push it and emphasize it.

What it did was bring me into direct conflict with Johnson, because he was chairman of the committee—and this was a reflection on his leadership and also on his man Hobart Taylor, whom I have contempt for because I thought that he was ineffective and also, in my judgment, he was an Uncle Tom. And I made this clear at these meetings—I was a very big shot during that period of time. I think most of the committee members, like Walter Reuther and Francis Sayre [of Washington National Cathedral] and everybody, agreed with this.

MARSHALL: Yes, they did. There was also a great deal of dissatisfaction among the public members of the committee because the committee meetings were, until this came up, simply showpieces—

KENNEDY: See, they put out press releases. They never participated and they never took an active role. Then I'd start to raise a fuss. We'd get these statistics together. And the President saw the statistics. Oh, he almost had a fit.

We got into a conversation about it, and he said, "That man can't run this committee. Can you think of anything more deplorable than him trying to run the United States? That's why he can't ever be President of the United States."

That was one of the reasons he shouldn't be President of the United States—because he couldn't run that. And then, of course, the space committee wasn't being run well. He tried to do things in space and give some leadership. The result was there wasn't any. They were awarding these contracts badly, and they were getting in the wrong hands. It looked like that was going to get out of hand. . . . They were spending so much money. And this fellow who had been head of the Institute of Space was—whatever his name is— What's his name?

MARSHALL: Webb.

LEWIS: James E. Webb.

KENNEDY: Webb was Lyndon's man, of course, the head of the space committee.

LEWIS: How did the President deal with the Vice President on these matters, if at all?

KENNEDY: Well, you see, it really came to a head in September and October [1963], didn't it?

LEWIS: And was there any resolution?

KENNEDY: Well, then November came.

LEWIS: But nothing had happened before that?

KENNEDY: No.

MARSHALL: Nothing had happened. [JFK] did point out to the Vice President that it would reflect adversely on the Vice President if there were continued emphasis on all that had been done and then statistics came out and showed that it was really all speeches.

KENNEDY: Yes. [Johnson] wouldn't speak to Bill Wirtz, I guess, because Bill Wirtz put these statistics together and showed them to the President and showed them to me. That's what made it, after November, very difficult with Bill Wirtz.

LEWIS: Although, now, they're supposed to be famous.

KENNEDY: Yes. But for four months, it was very, very difficult. Bill Wirtz said that he was going to have a showdown with [Johnson], that he was not going to accept this any longer. It got to be rather unpleasant.

I was involved in the middle, mostly in the middle, not just because I was so worked up about the Negroes getting jobs, but because I could just visualize this coming out in 1964—after all this conversation. That's what concerned me.

"WITH A STROKE OF THE PEN": THE HOUSING ISSUE

LEWIS: What about the housing order? We've now discussed employment. The other executive action thing, this housing order, has proved, of course, to be the most intractable problem.

KENNEDY: [JFK] just delayed it. It was an unpleasant part and a most difficult part, and he didn't want to do it. It was so difficult. I suppose that's basically it. When we were considering doing it in 1962, a good number of the liberal Congressmen—I remember, from Michigan, for instance—were opposed to issuing it before the election because they thought it would be damaging.

LEWIS: Damaging where? In Congress? To passing legislation?

KENNEDY: No, just in their districts, where they were running. . . .

LEWIS: But do you think that, if the housing order had been tackled in a much more vigorous way— It was done reluctantly, quite obviously; it was done not as broadly as it might have been. Suppose that it had been done with a great flair of publicity and action and appointment of the highest-level people—not Governor [David] Lawrence [of Pennsylvania], who clearly wasn't going to be interested or do a great deal. Suppose it had been done in a very big way and pressed hard. Do you think that the country could have been moved on that issue at all?

KENNEDY: No.

LEWIS: That judgment, essentially, was behind the way it was done, then?

KENNEDY: It was a legal question of what was going to be included—

MARSHALL: I still feel, myself, that the President would have been overreaching, certainly at that time.

KENNEDY: Basically, how far we went was a legal question.

LEWIS: You had very grave doubts that the President had the power through executive action to use the rather tenuous connection of federal deposit insurance to require all the loans of that bank to be conditioned [on nondiscrimination]?

MARSHALL: Also, there is a very serious question of the presidential control over the FDIC [Federal Deposit Insurance Corporation], anyway.

LEWIS: How about the difference between legislation and executive action? Of course, if Congress were to do it, then there wouldn't be the FDIC question.

MARSHALL: Congress clearly didn't intend to, though.

LEWIS: No, I'm saying that that would make a difference, too, that it was an executive order rather than legislation.

MARSHALL: Yes.

KENNEDY: Then, didn't we add up how many votes we had on the FDIC and that there would be a vacancy?

MARSHALL: Yes.

KENNEDY: And whether we'd wait until a vacancy came and then appoint somebody who would support us. I think it was split down the middle.

MARSHALL: At that time it was quite clear that the FDIC would have taken the position that they were not subject to the direction of the President on this issue and would have refused it. You would have had a major struggle.

KENNEDY: This was all seriously considered. We thought we'd appoint somebody. Then we thought that there would be so much attention on it at that time that Congress would go into the viewpoint of the person who was appointed to the FDIC, as to how he would vote on this issue. That was an unpleasant part of it. Douglas Dillon and the rest of them were also opposed to going beyond. No question: The delay was based on just the basic concern about the implications of it and how we wanted to move and the time that we wanted to move.

LEWIS: Concern about the very deep antagonism among the white people in the North on this issue?

KENNEDY: And the effect it would have in the South. On the question of Governor Lawrence: Maybe he's not a great appointment, but I don't know if there would have been a lot of other people much more helpful.

But there's no question that we waited until after the election because of the political implications.

LEWIS: Oh, yes. That was made clear. Burke, would your answer be the same to the question I asked: that this is such a deep-seated feeling on the part of white people, the housing issue? That more publicity, a bigger effort, a more dramatic effort would not have had any impact? I think this is a serious question because *The New York Times* would say that more leadership was required to change the mind of the country on this issue.

MARSHALL: My judgment would be the same, clearly.

KENNEDY: I think it's borne out by problems that we've had in all the northern communities after that. What's the concern there? The concern has basically been, in all of these communities, a question of housing. Now, I think that's going to get better. But certainly, to try to force it in 1962—well, we've had a lot of problems since then—you would have had a lot of difficulty.

MARSHALL: The argument in favor of the broad coverage of the order was so that no housing would escape it. Well, if you accept the conclusion that he couldn't have done that at that time, that [JFK] couldn't cover more than twenty to twenty-five percent of the housing starts anyway—and only new housing starts at that—I just don't see what a big effort would have involved except to scare everybody to death, really.

LEWIS: In fact, following that, are you saying that if it had not been for the "stroke of the pen" discussion in the campaign, it might have been wiser not to issue any housing order?

MARSHALL: The housing order has not been very meaningful.

LEWIS: That is a fact. And it may have just frightened people more than anything else.

MARSHALL: I think that it's inherent in the legal situation and the presidential power and the attitudes of the people. It's not correctable in that way. It sounded so easy. That's the thing: It sounded so easy. . . .

THE CIVIL RIGHTS COMMISSION AND THE PROBLEMS OF THE NORTH

LEWIS: What is there that you could say about the relationship of the Civil Rights Commission? Were things a little difficult at times?

KENNEDY: Basically, they were difficult. I didn't have any great feeling that they were accomplishing anything of a positive nature. I thought it was almost like the House Un-American Activities Committee investigating Communism. They were investigating violations of civil rights in areas in which we were making investigations. I thought that they could do more in the North. I thought that there were matters that they could investigate, subjects that they could go into which perhaps would be helpful. I thought that what they were doing was not helpful. They were going over old ground, and they were doing what we were really doing: voting.

Secondly, I thought that their staff work was deplorable. I thought that they were not objective investigations. I didn't think that it was the kind of work that should be done and should be required of those conducting investigations or studies of such a difficult field.

I had no confidence in them. I think the chief counsel is a good fellow. But I think that a lot of the staff work was very inaccurate and not based on fact—and so, therefore, a menace.

LEWIS: It certainly served a function at the beginning, in alerting people—

KENNEDY: I think they did at the beginning. But we were willing to do the job. That's why it's so like the House Un-American Activities Committee.

LEWIS: You said just now that they could have devoted more attention to the North. I remember your saying quite early in your term as Attorney General that in the long run the problem would be worse in the North, or as bad in the North. Why did you say that? What made you say that after such a short time as Attorney General?

KENNEDY: Just because I think that the ills that people suffer are so hard to escape from in a northern community. It's basically poverty. I suppose you just have to exist to know that there's a ghetto system, and that the education's not as good, and that people can't get jobs as easily if they're Negro as if they're white people. All you have to do is walk down the street between Seventieth and Thirtieth and see how many Negroes you see in the city of New York. It's the same in every community.

I just thought that things needed to be done for Negroes in education and employment and housing. And particularly for young people. Like the work that we did with the juvenile delinquency committee [President's Committee on Juvenile Delinquency]. I think that that would have been very helpful. Seeing what has to be done for preschool education for Negroes, for instance, in major cities. The fact is that fifty percent of all your basic intelligence—your I.Q.—is determined before you reach the age of five. Well, if a Negro child is born in a home which is broken—and the mother doesn't read or write—it's pretty tough for the child ever to be developed or prepared to go to first grade, be prepared to go to school. I think they [should have] made a study of that, what could have been done to deal with that.

The problems in the North are not easily susceptible to passage of legislation for solution. You could pass a law to permit a Negro to eat at a Howard Johnson's restaurant or stay at the Hilton Hotel. But you can't pass a law that gives him enough money to permit him to eat at that restaurant or stay at that hotel. I think that's basically the problem of the Negro in the North, and that's why I think it's more difficult to be dealt with. That's what the Civil Rights Commission could have focused attention on, because I don't think that people realized the depth of the problem and the fact that the solution was not easy and required the attention of the community and the state as well as the federal government.

LEWIS: It's also true, in all fairness to the Commission, that very few people saw that problem in 1960 or '61 or '62. The tension was focused on the legal, official discrimination in the South, to a large degree.

KENNEDY: Yes, but I couldn't see how you couldn't see it if you were in this business at all. It was beyond me. And I said it to them.

LEWIS: You did?

KENNEDY: Yes.

LEWIS: You did have some meetings with the commissioners?

KENNEDY: I said it to their staff people.

LEWIS: What about the President? Do you know of any particular relations he had with the Commission?

KENNEDY: He just didn't think much of them, because they were just not doing any good. He never liked anybody who was sort of in existence and not accomplishing something.

CRISIS AT OXFORD: OCTOBER 1962

LEWIS: Let's go on now to the important subject of Oxford, Mississippi. One question that I might begin by asking is that it seems to me that I've been told that you attempted vigorously to discourage James Meredith from seeking to enter the University of Mississippi or seeking to enforce his right to entry. What can you say about that?

KENNEDY: No.

LEWIS: Not true?

KENNEDY: I never had any conversations with him.

LEWIS: I don't mean Meredith personally. But you may have said to the NAACP or others that it was unwise.

KENNEDY: No.

MARSHALL: The only thing I know that would be anything like that would be that I talked to Thurgood Marshall [of the NAACP] before he was appointed [to the U.S. Court of Appeals], back in 1961, about where we were going to have problems. He mentioned the Meredith case and how he had tried to discourage it.

LEWIS: Would the Meredith case have gone back as far as '61?

MARSHALL: Yes.

LEWIS: I'd forgotten that.

MARSHALL: He applied in January of '61 for the university, but I didn't have any conversation with Meredith until it was done. I mean, there wasn't any choice.

LEWIS: . . . What was your general impression of [Mississippi Governor Ross] Barnett in the course of the various phone conversations that you and the President had?

KENNEDY: I think he was an agreeable rogue. Weak.

LEWIS: Sane or not?

KENNEDY: Yes, I suppose I thought he must have been sane. I thought, after we got into it a bit, that it was in his interest [to permit Meredith to register]. I'm influenced a lot by whether what a person does or says he's going to do is in his interest in doing it. Although it wasn't necessarily in his interest to do it in the beginning, or particularly in his interest to have conversations with us about what he was going to do, once he'd started down that road and when we finally came to the last day and the conversation I had with him on Sunday— where I said that the President was going to go on television and expose him for a fraud—I thought that it was in his interest to keep law and order and to permit James Meredith on the campus.

MARSHALL: Which he agreed to do.

LEWIS: Burke made clear to me that the thing that was most effective was the threat that you would expose his whole sham battle plan.

KENNEDY: Yes.

LEWIS: That moved him.

KENNEDY: Yes, that moved him. I think that did it.

LEWIS: Perhaps you can tell us if the President had any thoughts on this: that your real fear, and it was a very real fear, was that there would come a point at which United States troops would be facing Mississippi troops in the form of sheriffs and police and other Mississippi law enforcement officers shooting at each other.

KENNEDY: Yes. What I was trying to avoid basically was having to send troops and trying to avoid having a federal presence in Mississippi. In my judgment, what [Barnett] was trying to accomplish was the avoidance of integration at the University of Mississippi, number one. And if he couldn't do that, then to be forced to do it by our heavy hand—and his preference was with troops. Because he wanted to be an agreeable fellow, he continued to have these conversations with me, where he got deeper and deeper, where he was trying to satisfy and please me and trying to talk me out of sending—or James Meredith coming—to the University of Mississippi. While he was doing that, he got more and more involved himself, in rather foolish ways. I don't know of any other sort of explanation. He had people pulling and pushing at him from so many different directions that, I think, he just got himself into a bigger and bigger box. He eventually pulled me in with him.

LEWIS: Did the President ever muse about these things in historic terms? Was he that self-conscious? You know, like Fort Sumter, here we are: the federal system; it's the United States against Mississippi; we're back a hundred years; we're paying for the end of Reconstruction?

KENNEDY: He did say that he never would believe a book on the Reconstruction again.

LEWIS: Meaning what?

KENNEDY: After they wrote up what the marshals had done at Oxford.

LEWIS: Oh! He'd never believe the terrible tales of the northern scalawag troops, eh?

KENNEDY: Yes.

LEWIS: That's interesting.

KENNEDY: The Reconstruction. He said that they can say these things about what the marshals did and what we were doing at this period of time—and believe it. They must have been doing the same thing a hundred years ago.

Again, I go back to the same idea: There was never any doubt or question about what had to be accomplished. There was never any discussion between us as perhaps in prior years or former years—between former Presidents and former Attorneys General—because there was never any doubt. There might have been doubt as to how you do it. But once I started down the road of having conversations with Barnett, it made some sense in my judgment, so I never really went into it in great detail with him. I kept him advised, as it got to a critical point, of what we were doing. We thought that it had been accomplished that Sunday night. It hadn't.

LEWIS: Then you had a telephone call from Nick [Katzenbach]?

KENNEDY: Yes, we had a telephone call from Nick. That was a terrible evening, because people were being shot. And of course it was right on me because I had been responsible for it.

LEWIS: For the choice of using marshals?

KENNEDY: Marshals. Also, the fact that the troops didn't arrive there—it was really my responsibility. I might say that therefore it was a nervous time for the President, because he was torn between an Attorney General who had botched things up and the fact that the Attorney General was his brother. You could just see people getting killed. I remember Nick calling up and saying, "Is it all right for the marshals to fire on them?"

LEWIS: With live ammunition, you mean?

KENNEDY: Two people had been killed, and we had all sorts of [rumors].

MARSHALL: We had rumors that they were into the dormitory to get Meredith.

LEWIS: Nick said that he had never given any order permitting any marshal to fire live ammunition at any time, except a conditional order to the people personally guarding Meredith—that they could do so to save his life.

KENNEDY: I said that that was possible. But he did call up and ask if they could use live ammunition because people were getting so close. They were coming in. President Kennedy, who heard my conversation, said that they weren't to fire under any—

LEWIS: They were not to fire?

KENNEDY: They were not to fire under any conditions.

LEWIS: That's something that I had not known before. They were not to fire even if they were being overwhelmed?

KENNEDY: Yes.

LEWIS: That's a tough order to carry out, isn't it?

KENNEDY: Of course, with the exception of James Meredith. They could fire to protect his life. That was understood. The ones who were protecting him—they could. The ones who were just protecting themselves couldn't. Let me say that that might have been subject to change, depending on whether the situation had deteriorated and if they'd gotten inside. But it wasn't as of that moment.

LEWIS: The troops, of course, did arrive shortly after that?

KENNEDY: No. Not for a couple of hours. That was, of course, a terrible evening because they didn't come as they were expected to come. President Kennedy had one of the worst and harshest conversations with Cy Vance [then Secretary of the Army] and with the general that I think I've ever heard.

LEWIS: About the failure of the troops to arrive?

KENNEDY: Cy Vance kept giving wrong and misleading advice to the President.

LEWIS: Apparently, he was getting it by phone. Cy Vance kept saying, "According to our schedule, the troops are there." The President would then talk to Nick, and the troops weren't there.

KENNEDY: Well, no; Nick didn't know. I would then call—

LEWIS: The airport?

KENNEDY: Yes. Then he would say, "They're five minutes from land-ing. They're in the helicopters. And they're going to start arriving in ten minutes." I'd call the base from where they were leaving. I think [Assistant Attorney General] Lou Oberdorfer was there, wasn't he?

MARSHALL: Not anymore. But we talked to General [Creighton] Abrams. General Abrams was still down in Memphis.

KENNEDY: He said that they hadn't left yet.

MARSHALL: Hadn't left yet—when the report to the President from Cy Vance was that they were five minutes away.

KENNEDY: But that didn't happen *once*.

MARSHALL: Over and over again.

KENNEDY: I mean, that happened six, eight, ten times during the course of the evening.

"They're leaving in twenty minutes." We'd call twenty minutes later, and they hadn't even arrived to get ready to leave.

"They're ready to go now." And they hadn't been called out of their barracks to get into the helicopters yet.

"They're in the helicopters now." They were just forming up.

"The first helicopter's leaving and will be there in forty minutes." The first helicopter went in the air and then circled and waited for the rest of the helicopters.

You know, all that kind of business. Then the way they got into the city: They were all waiting for other helicopters to arrive, and we had to get them in the buses and get them moving.

LEWIS: And the tear gas equipment was not with them when they first arrived, Nick said.

KENNEDY: That part wasn't so bad, because just the fact that they were there changed the whole complex. But they told me, you see, when they'd be able to arrive. They said they'd get there in two hours if I gave them the notice—and they didn't arrive for four hours. In the meantime, our marshals were being overwhelmed. See, two people were killed right at the beginning, so we had visions of them getting in and killing Meredith.

The Governor was calling: "Let us take Meredith off the campus." I knew that if we took him off campus, we'd never get him back on the campus. But how are you going to get him? I mean, I think I'd even have done that, but I didn't even see how we could have gotten him off campus. Where were you going to get him where he was safer? There were people who were mad.

And it was so frustrating for the Army to continuously give false, wrong, inaccurate information.

LEWIS: The result of that, as I understand it, was—and you can expound on this—that the President, quite apart from the civil rights issue, was very disturbed about the mobile capacity of the Army and the accuracy of its planning and its reporting. What was done about that?

KENNEDY: He had an investigation conducted. We had a meeting with [Army Chief of Staff Earle G.] Wheeler and some of the others [to inform them] that there was an investigation to be conducted on what had happened to them, to tighten up. They did that. I never saw the report of what the results of the investigation were. I don't know that they did a helluva lot about it other than the fact that they then started to put people on alert continuously. They had a special room over at the Pentagon, under Bob McNamara, where people were on the alert and were ready to jump off and could go into these things under very short notice.

You know, it was a great shock. We'd been through Laos, [the incident] in which the general had said, "If you sent troops into Laos, forty-five percent of them are going to catch a particular disease and be broke and be incapacitated within thirty days." We looked into it and found that they didn't even have that kind of a disease in Laos. On another occasion, we were talking about sending troops into Laos again, and they said that you could land at these two airports—there are only two airports you can use—you could land a thousand troops a day. They recommended doing that.

And the President said, "How many troops are around this airport, of the enemy?"

They said, "Five thousand."

And he said, "Well, what if they knock the airport out in three days? You'll have landed three thousand troops. Then what will you do? How long will it take to get reinforcements to them?"

"Well, it will take thirty days."

So he said, "What do they do?" Well, they hadn't thought about that. By this time, we came to Oxford, Mississippi.

LEWIS: You've omitted one other little episode.

KENNEDY: Bay of Pigs?

LEWIS: That's right. Burke said to me that Sunday night, as the President began to speak, or during that period, [JFK] was thinking of the Bay of Pigs. Now, I don't know what Burke meant by that. Did [JFK] make some remark about the Bay of Pigs?

KENNEDY: I suppose, the idea that we could have another disaster. How was he going to explain it?

LEWIS: He didn't make any such remark to you?

KENNEDY: No. But I knew that he was very concerned about how we were going to possibly explain this whole thing because it looked like it was one of the big botches. I mean, if more people had been killed—
I think we were lucky to get out of it.

LEWIS: You were lucky. Very lucky.

KENNEDY: Public relations–wise as well, I mean. Two people were killed, but there could have been a lot more people killed. The planning wasn't that bad, but the execution was disastrous. That would have been on him and particularly on me. I'm so close to him that it would have been even more difficult for him because we couldn't say, "Well, the Army said they'd be there, but they weren't there." Nobody could explain that.
The idea that we got through the evening without the marshals being killed and without Meredith being killed was a miracle.

MARSHALL: Yes. I would say that except for the troops being late, though, I don't know what else you could have done.

KENNEDY: There wasn't much else. I'm just saying, what if more people had been killed, or some of those marshals had been wiped out, or some of those marshals had fired and killed six students in the dormitory or something? The only way to deal with that kind of operation is to have overwhelming force. And that's what we would have had if the troops had arrived. But I didn't want to have the troops any closer or alerted, because that would have destroyed the whole idea of the marshals.

LEWIS: Your purpose was not to have troops in Mississippi, as Nick explained it. So the closest they could be was Memphis.

KENNEDY: Right.

LEWIS: That's understandable, although you were criticized by people afterward who had been critical of the use of troops previously and now were critical because you hadn't used troops.

MARSHALL: Of course, what would he have said if the President had sent the Army in without any riot or anything having happened and with Governor Barnett having given assurances that he would preserve the peace?

KENNEDY: That would have been much worse. The feeling would have been much worse. The Governor said that he would preserve the peace. There was no indication of a violation of law and order. If we had sent the troops in and then they had a riot, that would have been disastrous. I think what we did was right. And the procedure that we followed was right.

The execution was wrong. And the person who had been responsible for the execution was me. I don't think there's any question. I was the Attorney General. The fact that I said that the troops would arrive and they didn't arrive was my fault. But therefore, it made it particularly difficult for President Kennedy, because I had worked it all out. This was my area of responsibility.

Now, it turned out as well as could have been expected under the circumstances. I don't know how we could have done anything different, once you take the philosophy that you shouldn't be sending troops into all the states unless absolutely essential. But that was the great difficulty and that's what [JFK] was torn with that night. I mean, we could just visualize another great disaster, like the Bay of Pigs, and a lot of marshals being killed or James Meredith being strung up. How would we explain that? I don't care what excuses you have; the troops didn't arrive.

LEWIS: No, there are no excuses for those things in something like that.

What about the [JFK] speech, which, as it turned out, was a nice speech but which was irrelevant as it was being delivered—because it was an appeal to the good sense of the students of the University of Mississippi and the southern tradition of [nineteenth-century Mississippi Senator Lucius] Lamar and all that. Was that a Ted Sorensen speech?

KENNEDY: Ted Sorensen. But I contributed a lot.

LEWIS: You did?

KENNEDY: Yes. At seven o'clock it looked like they had gotten [Meredith] on the campus. You know, we'd been kept advised all day, and it looked like he was getting on the campus. The speech was worked out at that time on the basis that, when I came over to the White House an hour before, he was on the campus and the situation was under control. In that sixty minutes the situation deteriorated. In fact, in twenty minutes it did.

LEWIS: But you couldn't stop the speech? Or you didn't have enough information?

KENNEDY: We couldn't stop it. We didn't know how it was going to turn out. Really, the riot had just started five minutes before [JFK] went [on the air]. I don't even know if he knew it.

MARSHALL: I don't think he knew that.

KENNEDY: He didn't even know that there was even an exchange at the time he went on because the exchange took place while [JFK] was on the air.

MARSHALL: Tear gas.

KENNEDY: It was building up before that. But we didn't know that it was going to get so serious. I remember Kenny O'Donnell saying to me that I should be Mandrake the Magician because we had gotten [Meredith] on the campus.

LEWIS: You were happy about that.

KENNEDY: We'd done well. I knew that the evening wasn't over and we still had problems. The situation looked under control at that time. I thought that, if it got out of control, we had enough people there who would be able to handle it. And we had the troops on alert.

I think that the question of the evening would have been quite different if the troops had gotten there at the time that they were supposed to have gotten there. The Army had botched it up.

But we didn't have an exercise with the Army in which they didn't screw up.

LEWIS: At any time?

KENNEDY: I don't think so. The one thing where I got good advice— and I think that was because the general [Creighton Abrams] knew the head of the Alabama National Guard—was when he said that we should march them down to the university [of Alabama]. I was concerned. He was insistent on that. And I think he knew that, if they marched down, they would be all right. That was good advice.

LEWIS: What about at Oxford, in the use of the Mississippi National Guard? Nick made a point of saying that [a company of] Mississippi Guard under the command of [William] Faulkner's nephew or cousin or somebody of that kind had been good. He came through with a broken arm, marching through the riot and all. Did the President ever make any comment on that? Or was there discussion about it that evening? It was rather a tribute to their system that they did perform as they did.

KENNEDY: Yes. The idea, of course, was to use the National Guard. That was the great struggle: how we could get the troops in there quickly enough, the National Guardsmen. I think that we were very pleased that they did so well.

LEWIS: I wonder if the President reflected on this. For all its terror, it was a tremendously important thing. Did the President ever philosophize on these subjects. Did he remark later on the episode in any way that you recall?

KENNEDY: No. The only time where there was some of that was at the time of Cuba. We used to discuss *The Guns of August*[21]—you know, the book—and how they drifted into that war with all those tremendous casualties—and that he wasn't going to have that legacy left while he was President. [There was] the exchange between the two leaders of Germany, where one said to the other: "Oh, how did it happen?" And the other one responded, "Oh, if we ever knew. Oh, if we could ever tell." The second thing was when U-2 pilot Major [Rudolph] Anderson was killed, where he said that the worst thing about war is that it's always the good people who get killed.[22]

[JFK] stayed up until five or six o'clock in the morning and then went to bed. He was furious at the Army, furious at Cy Vance, furious at the Army general. He asked to talk to the Army general when he arrived, because he was so mad at him. I think he was as mad at Cy Vance and the information that Cy Vance was giving him as I've seen him during the course of the administration. He asked for an investigation to be conducted.

MARSHALL: Lou [Oberdorfer] was down there in charge of the marshals. He went down with the marshals on Saturday and was planning to have them go in on Monday. At that time, those were the plans: to go in on Monday.

KENNEDY: That's right.

MARSHALL: Then, after you talked with Barnett, he backed down. We changed it very, very suddenly from the point of view of the marshals and Lou, and had to give them instructions to call the marshals as if they were going on a dry run. Lou did, I think, a remarkable job of getting that organized so that it could be done. It was important that it get done on Sunday afternoon—once he [Barnett] gave up—because it was clear that there was going to be an immense crowd there on Monday.

LEWIS: Nick and the others came down later?

MARSHALL: They left from Washington on Sunday.

KENNEDY: That was rushed. And I remember about the plane. They said that they couldn't land the plane. They wouldn't have arrived there in time unless they could land the plane.

MARSHALL: That's right. The runway was twelve hundred yards short or something like that.

KENNEDY: I said that I wasn't going to be on the plane, so therefore, I thought they should land.

Then they said, "Well, we can't take the plane off."

I said, "You can take the plane apart and put it in a truck and take it to a new airport and reassemble it—but land them there!"

They had the brilliant idea of just bringing the gas in. You see, I think it was a question of landing there and also being able to take off. They wouldn't have had enough fuel or something like that.

LEWIS: They jettisoned the fuel, Nick told me.

He described how Harold Reis [of the Justice Department] wandered into the office [in Washington], and the next thing he knew he was on a Jet Star.

MARSHALL: That's right: "Are you ready to go, Harold?"

KENNEDY: He said he was ready to go. He thought he was going downtown or something. He didn't know until he was in the car that he was going to Mississippi.

LEWIS: He didn't? That I didn't know.

MARSHALL: He said, "The next time, I'll ask, 'Go where?' "

"BULL CONNOR'S BILL": BIRMINGHAM AND THE 1963 CIVIL RIGHTS BILL

LEWIS: Let's go on to Alabama—Birmingham in the spring of 1963. Again, I have to begin with a general question of when you became aware that there was something more here than just a routine demonstration of the kind that had been happening in many places over the South, that this was something new that was really tearing the whole city apart, and it was going to lead to very serious disorder—at which point you sent Burke down.

MARSHALL: That was May, the middle of May.

LEWIS: Perhaps this would be the place to begin. While Burke was in Birmingham, there was a four-hour meeting at the White House on what could legally be done about the situation there. That is, I take it, in the form of lawsuits.

KENNEDY: Yes, I'm sure I was there.

LEWIS: The result was, nothing could be done. Burke says that during this week that he had in Birmingham, in which he was talking to the two sides and discovering the lack of communication, it was a very unpleasant week for President Kennedy. Hundreds of Negroes were arrested, the dogs were biting people, their pictures were in the paper, the fire hoses were being used, feelings in virtually all the people in this country and around the world were being stirred, and the feelings were being directed at the President: "Why didn't he do something?" Then, Burke says, the President called three or four big businessmen in Birmingham and brought Cabinet members into the process of calling people.

KENNEDY: I was in touch with Burke, and one of the points was to try to bring the people together. We started making some of these telephone calls to businessmen: Harllee [Branch, president of The Southern Company] and others. I got ahold of Douglas Dillon to make some calls to bankers and steel companies. We had meetings with some of the department store owners and officials to see if they could do. something about desegregating some of these department stores, making them available to Negroes.

LEWIS: What about the sense of pressure that Burke felt, with everybody looking to the President?

KENNEDY: Yes, I think that was true. We wanted to see if we could have some solution to it. I think [JFK] understood that there wasn't anything very much, legally, that we could do. But he wanted to find out. A lot turned on the success of Burke's efforts. I kept telling him that I didn't see that we could do anything more legally. So we were involved in it in just trying to find some solution through mediation.

LEWIS: How real in your mind was this question of the possible Communist influence on Dr. King at that time?

KENNEDY: Well, what do you mean? I don't think that was a factor.

LEWIS: I should be more specific. Was there ever any feeling on your part, as a result of Burke's reports to you, that there were people on Dr. King's side who really didn't want to settle the issue?

KENNEDY: No.

LEWIS: There was not?

KENNEDY: No. There was a lot of feeling that the Negroes didn't know exactly what they wanted and that they were not very well led in certain cases. There were a lot of responsible ones and there were some irresponsible ones.

MARSHALL: As far as I know, the Communists who had some influence with King had nothing at all to do with that, weren't even in communication with him.

LEWIS: They were not?

MARSHALL: Not as far as I know.

LEWIS: And Dr. King's leadership on the whole was quite effective in the end, wasn't it?

KENNEDY: Yes. It was constructive, I think.

LEWIS: This is the point we talked about that you're rather sensitive about—the impression given by editorials in *The New York Times* that the President never had any sensation about civil rights until he was put to it by this. Did he ever articulate what this was doing to the climate of opinion in the country? I'm going to come in a moment to when you thought the possibilities of legislation—and Burke has said very strongly that it was *you*, and John Doar [the Deputy Assistant Attorney General for Civil Rights] said the same thing—could get to the substantive thing underlying this. Was there ever any discussion between you and your brother about what this was doing to the climate of opinion in the country on race relations and people's general feelings about the mistreatment of Negroes: dogs and fire hoses and all that sort of thing?

KENNEDY: No. As President Kennedy said to the Negroes and to others—and, I think, quite accurately—the civil rights legislation should be called "Bull Connor's Bill," which summarizes the idea that what Bull Connor did down there, with the dogs and the hoses and the pictures with the Negroes, is what created a feeling in the United States that more needed to be done. Until that time people were not worked up about it or concerned about it.

Perhaps because we were brothers, or whatever it might be, we didn't make speeches to each other or even discuss the fact which was obvious—I mean, the conclusion that legislation was necessary— any more than I did, really, with Burke: "What are we going to do?" or "What can we do?" You have to figure out what you can do to deal with the problem. And what you could do to deal with the problem was [mediation]. Burke went down there. There was mediation.

We had to follow up on it so that we wouldn't be in the same position again. And [legislation] would be more acceptable. People were worked up about it and were concerned about it. What kind of legislation could we get by? What kind of legislation would deal with this kind of a problem? What kind of legislation could we associate with this difficulty? That's the basis of the legislation that we sent up.

LEWIS: Burke says that after he returned from Birmingham with what was at least a tentative—and turned out to be a good—success in mediation, everybody's mind was on the future. The President wanted to know what could be done about the general problem—this [civil rights] explosion. Burke was not in Washington, but he says that the President must have asked you whether there was not a legal solution, a legislative solution. The President had to act to get the country to face the problem. Soon after you came back from wherever you went to at that point, [Burke] flew to North Carolina with you. You were going to make a speech or something in North Carolina. On that flight, he said, the two of you really settled that there should be legislation on public accommodations and that it should be based on the Commerce Clause.[23]

KENNEDY: Right.

LEWIS: Now, what do you recall about that? What instructions did you have from the President, if any, on that? I mean, what was in the background?

KENNEDY: I didn't have any instructions from him. I think that what we wanted to do was to deal with the problem. There were two ways of dealing with it: either to protect people, which is what had been generally suggested, or to deal with the substantive problem that caused these difficulties.

We didn't feel that the protection of the people was feasible or acceptable under our constitutional system. So therefore, what was acceptable was to try to get to the heart of the problem. For the first time, people were concerned enough about it—and there was enough demand about it—that we could get to the heart of the problem and have some chance of success.

LEWIS: You say now that those were the two alternatives. And it now seems obvious what they were. Actually, it's a fairly sophisticated concept. I think that it wasn't clear to most people at the time that those were the two alternatives.

KENNEDY: Even now I don't think that it is clear.

LEWIS: Not to everybody, no. But certainly *then* it was clear to very few people. Had you specifically discussed this with the President?

KENNEDY: Not so much that there were two alternatives. We were looking for solutions. We abandoned the solution, really, of trying to give people protection. We ran through that a dozen times over the period of a thousand days because there were always things arising where people would say, "Why don't you furnish protection? Why don't you send marshals? Why don't you send the troops in?" We were resisting that all of the time, except when we had some legal basis for it or felt that we had some legal basis and the situation warranted it. We were always struggling with that. Now, we had to do something to deal with this kind of a problem. The country wanted something done and would support action being taken. That's why we moved in the direction that we did.

LEWIS: In other words, there was really only one alternative.

KENNEDY: There were two things you had to consider. One, as I say, was protection, and the other was to try to go to the substance of it. The protection had all kinds of difficulties that I've described, and going to the substance of the problem made so much more sense. When you say that that's a difficult concept for many people to understand or accept, I agree with you. And it was one of the major points when I appeared before legislative committees. They kept coming back to that: "Why aren't you doing the protection part of that?" Even now, I think.

LEWIS: Of course, even now. All the time. What about the legal discussion on the basis of the preferability of the Commerce Clause?

KENNEDY: That was really Burke, pretty much. President Kennedy raised the question. We had quite a number of conversations about that. I think we discussed that and spent more time on that than any other aspect.

LEWIS: With the President?

KENNEDY: Yes.

LEWIS: Why was he interested in that?

KENNEDY: Because there was a conflict. When we said that it might be under the Commerce Clause, there were all kinds of articles that were written and statements that were written. [New York Congressman] John Lindsay, I think, and even Ted Sorensen and others in the White House were opposed to this position of putting it under the Commerce Clause rather than the Fourteenth Amendment. I don't know whether I'm right about Ted Sorensen, but that was my recollection.

MARSHALL: And the Republicans generally?

KENNEDY: Were all opposed. And there were articles that were being written. So the President was unsure. His focus of attention, really, was on Title Two.[24] What we were doing, putting it under the Commerce Clause, created a great deal of opposition at the beginning. The fight for having that maintained in that form was really conducted by Burke Marshall.

I think it was the right thing to do. But I don't think that it was ever clear, particularly, to President Kennedy or to me that it was. I mean, it made sense—what he said—so we were convinced by it. And a good deal because we had confidence in him.

LEWIS: Burke?

KENNEDY: Yes. That really was the basis of it. We spent a great deal of time on that. . . .

LEWIS: The legislation was not framed in terms of Congress using some unexpended power within the Fourteenth Amendment. The only reference to the Fourteenth Amendment was a kind of a legislative adoption of Supreme Court opinion, so that it was circular and couldn't really get you anywhere.

MARSHALL: The final bill was in the form of a Fourteenth Amendment section that was really a restatement, as you say, of Supreme Court decisions.

LEWIS: Right. . . . Let me explain it this way: There might have been two ways of bringing the Fourteenth Amendment into the legislation. One would have been to say, in effect, "We hereby—Congress—exert any power we have under the Fourteenth Amendment to base this legislation on. We think we have independent power under the Fourteenth Amendment to reach private enterprises. And we're doing it." The other was to do what they actually did and say, "The Supreme Court has said that if there's any element of state action in an enterprise, we can control it under the Fourteenth Amendment. We adopt what the Supreme Court says. Whenever there's an element of state action, we hereby invoke the Fourteenth Amendment." So that it was circular. And in order to apply the act under the Fourteenth Amendment to any enterprise, you have to show an element of state action. There wasn't any showing of an element of state action in these cases. So you didn't get anywhere, I think. Am I right?

MARSHALL: Yes.

LEWIS: The President never doubted the Public Accommodations Title or the need for it? That was accepted as a necessary part of the legislation?

KENNEDY: Yes, that's right. We used to discuss between the two of us the whole concept of sending up legislation. Frequently, when legislation caused so much difficulty and there was so much tension, there was opposition to sending legislation up within the White House.

LEWIS: Now, that we haven't come to. I'd be very interested in that.

MARSHALL: One of the things we didn't cover particularly was the Vice President, for example.

LEWIS: That's right. I think that that could be very important.

MARSHALL: And I think there were others.

KENNEDY: Yes, there were others who were opposed. First, there were those who were opposed to President Kennedy's speech—you know, the speech that he gave.

LEWIS: Yes. June 11.

KENNEDY: Yes. Kenny O'Donnell and Larry O'Brien and really, I think, generally everybody in the White House was opposed to that.

MARSHALL: I think that Ted was opposed to it.

LEWIS: Why were they opposed to it?

KENNEDY: They just didn't think that he should get involved this much in civil rights.

LEWIS: Personally? It was a terribly personal speech.

KENNEDY: No, no. Because they didn't know anything about what was going to be in the speech. This wasn't the draft of the speech. The draft of the speech didn't come until two minutes before he went on.

LEWIS: And Burke said half of it wasn't even there then. Who drafted the speech?

KENNEDY: The President dictated. We gave our views to the President. And then he gave his views with us there to Ted Sorensen. That's who put it together. Ted Sorensen put it together.

LEWIS: Was this just a few minutes or within an hour or something?

KENNEDY: The whole thing took place over a period of forty-five, fifty minutes. The President and I sat, and he made notes because he was going to do it extemporaneously. He wrote down all those notes. And just as he was leaving the room, Ted Sorensen came in with the draft. I suggested that he at least do what he had and do part of it extemporaneously. That's why he did the part at the end extemporaneously.

Opposed to that speech and opposed to the whole idea of being so involved were certainly Kenny, and I guess Larry, and, I don't know, Ted Sorensen perhaps—from sort of a political point of view, offending the southern members of Congress and the Senators certainly by giving that speech during that period of time. I was strongly in favor of giving the speech, and I was supported, I think, by everybody [at Justice]—Burke and Nick.

So he made the speech [a major civil rights speech nationally televised on June 11, 1963], and he sent up the legislation. He always felt that maybe that was going to be his political swan song. We used to discuss whether what had been done was the right thing to do, just the fact that I'd gotten him into so much difficulty. We used to talk about it about every three days, because there was so much attention focused on it at that time in an unpleasant way.

LEWIS: Tension?

KENNEDY: Just the whole civil rights problem. The fact that the legislation had been sent up and he kept getting reports that it was going to affect all the other legislation.

LEWIS: When you came to the speech, you were saying that there was opposition, not only to the speech but also to the legislation, within the White House. Now, can you expand on that a bit?

KENNEDY: It's just that these people were—

LEWIS: The same people were against the legislation?

KENNEDY: Basically, the idea of legislation. Kenny and Larry never got into the details of any of it. Just sort of the idea that legislation was not going to be very helpful for what they were trying to do.

LEWIS: Ted, I should think, was not against it, was he?

KENNEDY: I don't think that he was against the legislation. I don't know. I can't remember.

MARSHALL: He was against the speech, at least at that time. I'm sure my recollection is correct.

KENNEDY: They were all opposed, except me, to the speech. I don't know whether they felt that the speech should be given later on. Lyndon Johnson was opposed to sending up [the legislation]. We had originally intended to send the legislation up shortly afterward. [Johnson] read the legislation and felt that that was a mistake. [He felt] we should do some work in Congress before the legislation was sent up. And that was a very wise suggestion. We went around and saw all the Congressmen and Senators and that delayed sending the legislation up about ten days. Remember the delay?

LEWIS: Yes. Although some of the outlines of it were already publicly known.

KENNEDY: I mean, that was the reason for that. As I understand it, the position that [Johnson] took was basically against sending legislation up.

MARSHALL: That's what he told me. I was asked to go to discuss it with the Vice President, I guess, by the President or by you [RFK]. In any event, the President must have known about it. I discussed for about three quarters of an hour with the Vice President what we should do. And what he thought should be done was simply to stick to the economic aspect of it, not civil rights legislation as such.

LEWIS: It was really a poverty program?

MARSHALL: Yes, well, he went back to his own experiences—his Youth whatever-it-was, in the '30s.

LEWIS: National Youth Administration?

MARSHALL: Yes. And about how they'd created so many jobs in such a short amount of time, that that was the only answer, and that the kind of legislation that was being suggested and which was sent up wouldn't get passed and was impossible and would cause a lot of trouble and was the wrong thing to do. That's essentially what he said. I discussed that with the Attorney General.

KENNEDY: The President was rather irritated with him at the time because he was opposed to these things—this and a good number of other measures—but did not come up with alternative suggestions.

MARSHALL: [Johnson] also sent Hobart [Taylor] over to see me. Hobart came over to see me and said that you couldn't do anything without more education. The Negroes had to be educated.

LEWIS: Nick suggested that—perhaps in contrast and supplement to what you said about the Vice President—that he was helpful on the strategy. Once it was decided to send the legislation up, he did not play dog in the manger and undercut it in any way.

KENNEDY: That's what I said. He was helpful on the idea of going around and seeing these people.

LEWIS: But, I mean, he didn't resist once it was sent up. He didn't knife it at all but was trying to help it get passed with whatever suggestions he had.

KENNEDY: Yes. I don't know that during that period of time—July '63 to November '63—that made much of a difference in the Senate of the United States. He didn't have anything in the House.

LEWIS: No. Although I think that Nick said that one of his suggestions was to get hearings before the Commerce Committee in the Senate, so that there would be a record of some kind. I've forgotten whether he attributed that to Johnson.

KENNEDY: That might very well have been. But it was a difficult time in the relationship, just as a footnote, between the President and the Vice President.

LEWIS: Well, those other matters were coming to a head, that you spoke of.

I think that the one thing that did not come through clearly, probably because it was not verbalized at the time, was the really great importance of the decision, however casually taken, to ask for legislation of this character. Because, at least as far as outsiders were concerned, I remember very little, if any, speculation on the part of civil rights groups, the Civil Rights Commission, or anybody else that there would be or could be a federal law against discrimination in public accommodations until the time when you decided it and it began leaking out. But it was not something that had been demanded of you, that was being called for by groups. And to me, at least, it was a helluva long step. What about that?

KENNEDY: I think that there was a good deal of soul searching that went into the decision about sending up the legislation. It seemed to me that there were certain factors that were present that almost made that decision inevitable.

Number one: I think that we needed to do something about the situation. That was always true. But the added factors were acceptance by the public and the support of the public about doing something. Then it was a question of what you could do. And I think we really had two ways to proceed. You could either go into what caused the problem or try to give protection to people. That's why we moved into the direction of the public accommodations.

LEWIS: Of course. What I was suggesting by my question was that if some other administration had been in office, there might have been the third choice of not doing anything.

KENNEDY: I know you're suggesting that. And I'd like to say how brave it was of us to do it, but it was just clear to me. And I agree with you that there were people who were opposed to it. Burke said, as I knew, Lyndon Johnson was opposed to it. And a number of people over at the White House were opposed to it. I mean, even the President himself was not always rejoicing in the fact that we were doing it. As I said, he would ask me every four days, "Do you think we did the right thing by sending the legislation up? Look at the trouble it's got us in." But always in a semi-jocular way.

It always seemed to me quite clear that that was what we needed to do. I suppose some administration could have gotten by without doing anything. I think that in the long run the difficulties would have been much greater than by doing the thing that we did. That I always felt strongly about.

LEWIS: I should make clear that I meant "nothing" in the way of legislation—that you could have gone on saying, "Well, we've rescued the situation in Birmingham." You could have made some speeches about the need for law and order, and respect, and so forth—and just gotten along. Burke, what do you think about this point that he just made?

MARSHALL: I think that it was clear that the legislation would make any other legislation impossible until it was passed. The President wanted a tax cut. Apart from that, he realized that the rest of his program would just be in hopeless trouble until the civil rights thing was out of the way, as far as Congress was concerned. That would take at least the rest of that year.

LEWIS: But you also felt that legislation was simply an inevitable necessity?

MARSHALL: There were meetings that the Attorney General had at that time with businessmen, which later developed into meetings at the White House—

LEWIS: I was going to come to that.

MARSHALL: At those meetings the point was made over and over and over again that this problem faced all of us and was going to get worse during the summer—as it did in a lot of cities—in place after place, and in place of business after place of business. It really, I think, had to be faced up to. But it is certainly possible that some-body that didn't like to face up to things wouldn't have faced up to it.

KENNEDY: Yes, I don't think there's any question that you could have avoided it. In my judgment, if you had avoided it, I think that the difficulties you would have had to face a year from now would have been much greater. Not only was it the correct thing to do, in my judgment, but it was also the wise thing to do, to take that step. As I say, there were people who disagreed. There was a good number of people who disagreed with the emphasis that we were putting on civil rights.

For instance, at that period of time the President went out to make a speech to the mayors out in Hawaii [at the U.S. Conference of Mayors, June 1963]. I had been strongly in favor of him hitting that group and talking to the mayors. I think that they had spoken to me about coming earlier or something. In any case, I wanted him to talk to the mayors. Almost everybody at the White House was opposed to his going down to talk to the mayors. Kenny O'Donnell was violently against it. But he finally decided that he'd go. And I think that it was well worthwhile.

Then we had those meetings at the White House. There were a lot of people who were opposed to having those meetings at the White House because it involved the President too much in civil rights.

LEWIS: Let's just identify the meetings and how they started, first of all.

MARSHALL: They started with the meetings with the Attorney General which he called, himself—some in New York and some in Washington—which were with businessmen who were most directly concerned with the problem. You [RFK] wanted to have them, and you asked Lou [Oberdorfer] and Ralph Dungan [Special Assistant to the President] and I don't know who else to prepare lists of the businessmen who would be appropriate. It started with the ones who were most directly involved, which were the chain [store] owners. The first meeting was at the Waldorf-Astoria in New York, just after I got back from Birmingham, which would have been around the 22nd of May. I think it was the 22nd of May. That was with about fifteen or twenty owners of department store chains that had lunch counters in them.

KENNEDY: Some of them hid downstairs, didn't they?

MARSHALL: They hid. At that first meeting, they were very, very nervous about getting into a meeting on this subject with the Attorney General that had any publicity. That was one reason it was in New York.

LEWIS: Hid where?

KENNEDY: I guess they hid downstairs. And they sent one of their members up to find out whether I had television cameras with me or something.

MARSHALL: That's right. Some of them held back coming to the meeting on the theory that it was all a publicity plot by—

KENNEDY: Me.

MARSHALL: The Attorney General.

KENNEDY: I guess they thought that the devil incarnate had arrived in New York, and they were asked to meet with him. They were very concerned about what was going to happen to them and what the result of the meeting was going to be.

MARSHALL: Yes. I would say that, about a year later, we had a meeting with the same group in the Attorney General's office, and there was just no hesitation and nothing like that at all about it. They got over it in the course of about a month. But the first group that met thought they were going to be put on the rack or—

LEWIS: The screw?

MARSHALL: Or somehow mistreated by the Attorney General.

LEWIS: How did these develop then into the White House meetings? Again, there was some difference of opinion between you and, perhaps, Kenny and some other people as to whether the President should meet with these groups. And it took place, as I recall, almost immediately after—or was it even before?—the formal submission of the legislation.

MARSHALL: I think that the first White House meeting was before the formal submission of the legislation, but after the—

LEWIS: The June 11 speech?

MARSHALL: The June 11 speech. The formal submission to Congress, the message to Congress, was June 19. I would say that the first meeting was somewhere around June 13, or something like that.

KENNEDY: The idea, really, was to show the leadership of the White House, of the President, the active involvement of the President, the active involvement of the administration in trying to find some solutions to these problems. From our own experience, we could see that these demonstrations were going to continue. They were going to spread. There was going to be more violence. There were going to be more people involved, because students were getting out of school for the summer. They were the ones who were going to be actively involved in them. If we could get businessmen and community leaders to take action to desegregate their communities—namely, the public facilities—then the chance for these kinds of disorders or violence would be greatly lessened.

The fact was that many of these areas were going to do it after disorders took place and after the focus of attention had been on a particular community. Wasn't it better to do it voluntarily and do it prior to this time? That's what we urged upon these various business leaders. We went through the situation, discussed Birmingham, discussed what they could do in their local communities.

LEWIS: Discussed what had actually happened in Birmingham?

KENNEDY: Yes. We also discussed what had happened in the other communities where they had voluntarily desegregated and how much easier it was there than it was in some of the communities where violence had occurred. We had some examples, showed the communities—with a map—where desegregation had taken place and communities where there was still segregation of hotels, of theaters, of restaurant workers. We asked them to get together, four or five various groups, and talk with one another and try to work out the problems in each local community: a theater owner in New York to start focusing attention on what his theaters were doing in Mississippi or Alabama or Texas.

LEWIS: A quick question. You had people who were both the chain owners in the North and local managers or from the South as well?

KENNEDY: Right.

LEWIS: Even from some of these communities that were not desegregated, the most resistant ones?

KENNEDY: Yes. Then we had the clergy. We had people from colleges. Lawyers.

LEWIS: How did the most southern react to this message? Was there ever any bitterness in the meetings, any "Leave us alone!"?

KENNEDY: No. They disagreed, some of them. But they were all amicable and accomplished a great deal, in my judgment. Out of that came the Committee on the Clergy—they got together—and a women's committee was formed. We also expressed concern about what was going to happen in the North, that the northern communities also had to take action. That's why we had some of the college professors and—

LEWIS: The Lawyers' Committee, don't forget that.

KENNEDY: The Lawyers' Committee. The Lawyers' Committee we wanted particularly to act as a catalyst in these various communities, to bring the groups together as Burke Marshall had done in Birmingham, to try to set up their own operation down there.

The President spoke, Vice President Johnson spoke, and I spoke on occasion. Bill Wirtz spoke, too, I think.

MARSHALL: And Dean Rusk spoke to the Business Council.

KENNEDY: We had about twenty meetings at the White House. Were there that many?

MARSHALL: There was a total of between sixteen and seventeen hundred people, and I would say that there were about fifteen meetings.

LEWIS: All in how short a period of time?

MARSHALL: A month.

KENNEDY: The clergy was, I think, the most effective, really, as far as the passage of legislation. With the rest of the businessmen, a great deal was accomplished. It will be shown in the memos that Lou Oberdorfer has how many places desegregated and what actually was accomplished.

LEWIS: There's one thing that we ought to clarify because I'm not clear on it. The purpose of these meetings, really, was twofold. One was to urge individual action, quite apart from reliance on legislation. It was to get people to do things in their own communities by themselves. The other was to help in the passage of the legislation?

KENNEDY: No.

LEWIS: Or was that secondary?

KENNEDY: That was really secondary. We explained the legislation to some of the groups. But some of the groups were violently opposed to legislation. The idea, really, was to give some leadership in the local communities to deal with this problem. That was the basic purpose behind it. Then the clergy group formed itself into an active organization on behalf of the legislation, as did the women's group. But the basic purpose was, really, to try to focus people's attention on their own responsibility—what they needed to do, what could be done, and why it was in their interest to do something rather than to wait until violence occurred.

MARSHALL: They had a choice. I mean, they didn't have to just sit back and wait for a lot of street riots or demonstrations. They had a choice—personally, each of them—for the most part, I should think.

LEWIS: Did you happen to read the piece, either of you, in *The Washington Post* today, December 6, 1964? A long piece by a Negro who has just traveled through the South with his wife.

KENNEDY: Is that the same couple who had the articles in the *Herald Tribune*?

LEWIS: It well may be. I didn't see the earlier articles. These, on the whole, were very encouraging. I'd say that they were served graciously, readily, in about fifty percent of the places they went; another twenty-five percent, ungraciously; and twenty-five percent, not at all. But that's pretty good.

KENNEDY: Yes.

LEWIS: In such a short time. And they went everywhere.

KENNEDY: Especially when [Alabama Governor George C.] Wallace said, "You're going to have to bring the troops back from Berlin if you pass that law."

AT THE SCHOOLHOUSE DOOR:
THE UNIVERSITY OF ALABAMA

LEWIS: All these things came in such a very close sequence. There was Birmingham, Burke came back, the legislation, and at the same time, the situation at the University of Alabama.

MARSHALL: Which had been anticipated, of course. Bob Kennedy went down to Alabama to see the Governor. There was a great deal of effort devoted, directed at Alabama and the businessmen in Alabama and people who should be community leaders, to prevent any sort of a showdown at the university.

LEWIS: The first question should be about that conversation with Wallace which was recorded.[25] It was unhelpful, I take it.

KENNEDY: Yes, it was unhelpful. It was interesting. We really didn't get very far.

MARSHALL: It was so clearly going to be unproductive. The state capital was full of Highway Patrols, as if you were a foreign dignitary—but a somewhat suspicious one.

KENNEDY: They had the biggest state troopers you ever saw, all guarding the way in. And they all had big sticks. There wasn't anybody around there who was going to hurt me. They were all very friendly, the people. I shook hands with everybody. They were all very nice. But they had all of these state troopers. As they would stand—at least, on one occasion—one of them took his stick and put it into my stomach, like that, you know, and belted me with the stick.

LEWIS: For laughs?

KENNEDY: No.

LEWIS: Not for laughs?

KENNEDY: Oh, no. Not for laughs at all. They were the most unfriendly, for the most part—the state troopers.

LEWIS: They were under the command of— What's this man's name, again?

MARSHALL: Al Lingo [then Alabama State Public Safety Director]?

LEWIS: Al Lingo. That's right.

KENNEDY: They were unfriendly. It was completely unnecessary, but the point was to try to show that my life was in danger in coming to Alabama because people hated me so much. I think they almost had the Capitol ringed with state troopers, didn't they?

MARSHALL: Oh, yes. I think there were six hundred state troopers.

KENNEDY: I had a press conference, and I was asked whether I was a member of the Communist party.

LEWIS: By whom?

KENNEDY: By one of the reporters.

LEWIS: One of the captive newspapermen? Well, that sets the scene all right.

KENNEDY: I'm glad that you asked me that.

LEWIS: I think we have the general picture of the productivity of the meeting.

KENNEDY: We had that other awful man there who was [Wallace's] assistant?

MARSHALL: Trammel. Seymore Trammel.

KENNEDY: Impossible figure.

MARSHALL: The meeting with the Governor was bound to be unproductive because the first thing that he said when Bob came in the room was: "I'm going to tape this whole proceeding"—and he switched on the tape recorder. It was all speeches and speeches.

KENNEDY: It was necessary, then, for both of us to say things to each other on the basis that it was going to be played on the local radio station. At least for me, I couldn't let anything he'd say go by as if it had been unanswered. It made it difficult.

LEWIS: Of course it's obvious, even from the outside, that it was an unproductive meeting. But my key question is whether you got any sense then of whether he would resort to force or whether it would just be a game.

KENNEDY: No, but I had a lot of conversations thereafter for months with Dr. [Frank A.] Rose, who is president of the University of Alabama, a friend of mine I've known over a period of the last ten years. Together with Fritz Hollings, we had received the Ten Most Outstanding [Young] Men of the Year Award in 1954, I think, or '55. So I knew him, and we corresponded and talked. His assistant, Jeff Bennett, is a very good fellow.

They wanted to work it out, and we had a lot of meetings with him, talking about the University of Alabama.

MARSHALL: Dr. Rose came up here very early to see you about the university. I think it was before you went down to see the Governor, even.

KENNEDY: Yes.

MARSHALL: He came up, and he said that the university had these applications and that he thought the Governor was going to give them a good deal of trouble. But he thought that he could get the support of the majority of the directors on the board of trustees of the university to comply with the court order. That was essentially what he said. He said that he wanted to keep in touch with the Attorney General throughout, to cooperate with him. He did have this problem with the Governor, and he had to do it in such a way that the Governor didn't destroy the university in the process, by closing it or taking some other action. The Governor was the *ex officio* president of the board of trustees. . . .

KENNEDY: And gave him a difficult time. He was on our side, Dr. Rose. At least, as he talked to us, he was on our side. He was anxious to keep the university open. He was anxious to make arrangements for these Negro students to be permitted to go to the university.[26] And he was anxious to cooperate with us. But he wanted the latter factor to remain unknown in the state of Alabama, obviously, and certainly unknown to the Governor. Thereafter, we had a lot of conversations. He wouldn't talk to us on the phone, really, but he'd come out of the state, come up and talk.

LEWIS: Could I ask a question here generally about this and about the Mississippi episode and perhaps others? How closely did you, Burke, work with Jack Greenberg and the NAACP Defense Fund lawyers who were pressing these cases, in terms of the timing of them? You really were taking over the practical judgments of how to get [the black students] in, physically. So there must have been some relationship with the lawyers.

MARSHALL: They resented us. They ended up by resenting us in both Mississippi and Alabama—for one thing because we weren't in a position to tell them what we were doing. We took action and made decisions without full consultation, because of time factors and because of not being able to tell them what we were doing. . . .

Then we had entirely different responsibilities. They wanted to send in the Army. They were concerned about their clients. They weren't concerned, really, with the position of the President, with the long-range effect that hasty action, or action that didn't appear on the face of it to be justified, would have on the nation as a whole and the divisiveness it would have between the North and the South. So I would say that although they were always friendly, they always ended up by resenting us and thinking we weren't consulting them enough.

We just had to do things without telling them what we were doing. So that what we were doing appeared— I think that it was right, in general, but it sometimes didn't appear to be right to someone on the outside.

LEWIS: When was the President first brought into the Alabama situation? You knew about it for a long time before it became a great public issue. Do you remember?

KENNEDY: I don't remember. Probably, I told him sometime in the spring that we were going to have these students going to attend the University of Alabama. I think I first heard about these students at the University of Alabama from Dr. Rose. He said he had these applications, and he was going to permit them to attend. One of the questions was whether they were going to start in June or wait until September. The other question was whether they were going to attend the major university or whether they were going to attend—

LEWIS: The Huntsville branch?

KENNEDY: The Huntsville branch. These negotiations and discussions took place over a couple of months: how we should proceed; what was the best way to go; whether we should let them go into Huntsville at the same time as the university at Tuscaloosa and, therefore, make it difficult for the Governor to be in both places. In the end, we took different positions. By the last day, the relationship with

Dr. Rose was not as close. The general feeling was that Rose . . . was under tremendous pressure. It was a difficult situation for him. . . .

MARSHALL: One thing that was very irritating to Nick [Katzenbach] was that the university [drew] chalk lines where the Governor could stand in the doorway in order to get his best picture on television.

KENNEDY: [The university] made it easier so that there wouldn't be a conflict with the Governor being in two places at one time. If he wanted to go to the Huntsville branch, there would be enough time for him to get up to Huntsville.

LEWIS: Registration took place at different times?

KENNEDY: Yes.

MARSHALL: At one point, we wanted to have registration at more than one place at the same time.

KENNEDY: So they couldn't be at both places. So, at least, there would be one student entered in the university. And the Governor couldn't put on a show. No matter what he did in one place, he couldn't get to the second place at the same time. At least, there would be a student registered and going to the university. We thought that that would get us over the hump. That was at least considered. By the end, we understood that . . . what the university was doing was leaning over backwards to cooperate with the Governor and to achieve for the Governor everything that he wanted to accomplish.

LEWIS: Which was publicity?

KENNEDY: Yes.

LEWIS: A show.

KENNEDY: I didn't mind the show so much. The problem really was what the show was going to consist of, what it was going to lead to. That was the great problem for us because the Governor of Alabama—I guess, learning from what had happened to the Governor of Mississippi—wouldn't talk to me or to us. I made an effort to talk to him. . . .

The trustees were opposed to the Governor. So they would relate what the Governor said at the trustees' meeting and what his position was going to be. But this gave us great concern, because they always reported that he was crazy, that he was scared. Inevitably they'd say he was scared; inevitably they'd report that he was out of his mind; inevitably they'd report that he was acting like a raving maniac.

The result was that when you're trying to make plans as to what you should do—should you make plans on the basis of what a reasonable man would do if he were the Governor of the state of Alabama? You couldn't do that. The great question for us was not having to arrest the Governor, not having to charge him with contempt, and not having to send troops into the state of Alabama—and yet getting the students into the university. That was our problem.

LEWIS: Did you feel that he did want to be charged with contempt? He did want to be arrested and charged?

KENNEDY: I think we changed our minds a number of times about it. I don't think he wanted to go to jail, and there were some tough federal judges in Alabama who might have sent him to jail. I don't think he'd have minded going to jail for five days or a week or ten days; but I think the idea that he'd have to go to jail for six months or a year or two years didn't fit into his plans, either. What we were doing, really, was having a very difficult operation with him. We didn't want to call up the troops because then he'd say that we were trying to intimidate him. He helped us a good deal by—

MARSHALL: He had some [National] Guard units called into active service and put them on duty in Tuscaloosa, which made them immediately available when the President nationalized it—which saved several hours.

KENNEDY: Otherwise, we would have had to use federal troops. That would have delayed us. What we wanted to do, if we had to use troops at all, was to use the National Guard and use as small a group as possible. The other major question for us, if he was going to stand in the door, was how many troops did we need? We didn't want to go through the same thing we went through at the University of Mississippi. If you start having violence and you only have three hundred troops and the police weren't going to help, how many troops did you need, and under what circumstances and in what period of time?

Once again, we took a gamble at Alabama.

LEWIS: You've been using the word *troops*. No consideration was given to the use of marshals in light of the experience in Oxford?

KENNEDY: There wasn't anything to be gained particularly by the use of marshals. And Dr. Rose made it quite clear that [Wallace] wouldn't step aside. Wasn't that it?

MARSHALL: Yes.

LEWIS: For marshals?

KENNEDY: For marshals. We had to have troops to get him to step aside. We had to get him to step aside.

The final plans for the University of Alabama were really not made until that morning.

The President was consulted continuously. One of the major questions was again, as I say, when we'd call out the troops; how long it would take if we called out the National Guard; and if the National Guard wasn't enough, how long it would take to get troops there. These battle plans were made with the Army and General Abrams, who was on the scene down there.

MARSHALL: As far as going to jail was concerned, we obtained an order against the Governor. It was signed by Judge Seybourn H. Lynne, who's the Chief Judge of the Northern District of Alabama. I went down for the hearing that resulted in that order. After the hearing, we had a conference with Judge Lynne. First I did, and then he called in the lawyers for the Governor. He told them that he was going to issue an order against the Governor, and he told them that if the Governor violated the order in a substantial way, the punishment that he intended to put on the Governor would not be token. He talked in terms of at least six months—a substantial jail sentence at that time—to the lawyers. I think that it had quite an effect on the lawyers. And I'm sure that they reported it to the Governor. I imagine that affected his actions somewhat in how quickly he got out of the way once he had a show of force that he could use for his political purposes.

LEWIS: In fact, he was probably technically in contempt even at that, because you shouldn't have to have troops to enforce a court order, I suppose.

KENNEDY: We wanted to serve a specific purpose. We wanted to get the students in. We didn't want to have to charge him with contempt. And we certainly didn't want to arrest him. If we had charged him with contempt, we'd have inevitably had to arrest him. Then we'd have to occupy Alabama. These are the factors in dealing with this whole difficult problem that, I think, are harder for people to understand. Why was it so difficult? What were the elements that we were considering?

Really, the elements that we were considering were getting the students in and not having to charge the Governor with contempt. All the southerners think that we want to send troops into all these southern states. Of course, all our struggle during this period of time, and at the University of Mississippi, was to try to avoid sending the troops into either of these places. That's why it was so difficult. I think the plan that we ultimately came up with was the best one, but I remember having a conversation with President Kennedy on that morning. We'd decided the day before that maybe we ought not to call up the Guard. I called him that morning. It looked worrisome.

And I said, "Well, maybe we'll call up the Guard now." That was before the first confrontation, so the first step would have been taken by us rather than by him.

The President said, "Let's wait. We won't do it now. We decided that we wouldn't do it. Let's wait on it." That was the correct thing, as it turned out. But twenty-four hours prior to that time, when we met in the President's office, all of us virtually decided on another course of action. What made it so difficult was not really knowing exactly what the Governor was going to do. If it had collapsed or if there were violence—if we couldn't control the violence—you could never explain why you didn't do more. That's what made it so difficult.

LEWIS: . . . What about the two Senators from Alabama, [Lister] Hill and [John J.] Sparkman? Were there conversations with them on the part of the President or you during this thing?

KENNEDY: I talked to both of them. They deplored what was going on, but they weren't of any help.

LEWIS: They couldn't say anything. Wallace had them over the barrel.

KENNEDY: Then we came up with the idea of having Nick go in without the students and ask him to step aside. That permitted the Governor to refuse entrance, but it also permitted us not to charge him with contempt, because the students weren't there yet.

MARSHALL: And we didn't have the public indignity of having him face these students. That was the occasion when we acted without consulting the university officials.

KENNEDY: So that was important. The second part that was important, really, was keeping the students on the campus. When they came on the campus, they were not confronted on television, worldwide, by the Governor stopping them from going in. The only picture that was ever taken was Nick.

They never turned back the Negro students. The second thing is that when they came on the campus with Nick, they had to be there in case [Wallace] said, "Come on in." Which was unlikely.

He didn't say that. So they went into their dormitories.

LEWIS: I remember that.

KENNEDY: The university didn't know, nor did anybody else know, that we were going to keep them on the campus.

MARSHALL: We got the key to their dormitory rooms from the university on the theory that we wanted it for security purposes, to check the rooms for bombs or anything like that. That's how Nick got the key, by telling them that.

KENNEDY: So they stayed on the campus.

As I say, it was a difficult matter to struggle with. It appears a little more obvious and simple now as you look back on it. But at the time it was damned difficult.

MARSHALL: Yes, it was.

KENNEDY: And we were torn so many ways. Number one: just not knowing what he was going to do. Number two: having gone through the University of Mississippi and not being able to avoid violence there, and not knowing whether the Alabamians who were members of the National Guard would perform their duties. We had to make decisions based on some unknown quantities.

LEWIS: Did you not have a little more time and more opportunity to observe whether large numbers of out-of-town rednecks were coming into Tuscaloosa—which had happened rather suddenly in Oxford, where you weren't really prepared for that. Were you able to do that in Tuscaloosa?

MARSHALL: At both Oxford and Tuscaloosa, the [FBI] was instructed to watch the roads for people coming in from the outside. In Tuscaloosa, of course, an added factor was that you couldn't tell what effect the Governor's standing in the doorway would have on the people in Alabama. That was just something you had to gauge. Tuscaloosa happened to be the headquarters for the Ku Klux Klan. There always had been a lot of Klan out around there.

KENNEDY: They had some pretty good public officials in Tuscaloosa. And a good newspaper.

MARSHALL: Very fine.

KENNEDY: I think that all the work we did with the business community for three months preceding—all over Alabama—had a big effect. We wrote down in a book the name of every company with more than a hundred employees, I think, in the whole state of Alabama. All those names were distributed at a Cabinet meeting, to all the members of the Cabinet. Then we got in touch with the heads of all the other departments and agencies in the government. A Cabinet member or somebody called, I guess, every one of them.

MARSHALL: That was during the three weeks or so before this.

LEWIS: That's terrific.

KENNEDY: So they would understand the importance, understand what we were trying to do, understand their own responsibility. The trustees themselves and some of these other businessmen down there did a lot of work in following up with these same groups to get support. We built up a reaction to what Wallace was doing.

Wallace really didn't know what he was going to do, I'm convinced, up until at least a couple of days before and maybe a few hours before. If he had received great popular support in the state of Alabama for standing in the door, for continuing to stand in the door, I think that's what he would have done. But he was trying to get off the hook. He said in the campaign: "I'm going to stand in the schoolhouse door." So he had to stand in the door. He was in that embarrassing position. But he didn't have the support of that element within the state of Alabama.

LEWIS: He was feeling some heat from these businessmen?

KENNEDY: Yes.

MARSHALL: A great deal, a great deal.

KENNEDY: Some of the people who worked in our campaign were close to him, whom I also knew.

MARSHALL: Wallace was getting fifteen or twenty phone calls every day from business people. He'd have to guarantee them that there wouldn't be any repeat of the Oxford incident, that there wouldn't be any violence. And what could Wallace say? He couldn't say, "I'm going to commit violence." He had that kind of pressure put on him from a great many business people throughout the state.

KENNEDY: Then he finally gave the word, as I remember, to the Ku Klux Klan. He made an agreement with them, I guess. Wasn't that it? He made an agreement with them that he'd stand in the door, but that they wouldn't have violence at the time.

MARSHALL: They'd leave it up to him.

KENNEDY: Because of this pressure that was put on him by all of these elements in Alabama, he couldn't afford to have violence. So that they should rely on him, or what he would do in connection with this matter, and not bomb, themselves, or use violence themselves.

LEWIS: I must say, just as an observation, that considering the futility of his position, as it developed, it's very hard for me to understand why he was not a laughingstock in Alabama and why he went on to such a powerful political position, which he obtained in the year following.

KENNEDY: I think that his prestige was somewhat lowered temporarily, but I think that he regained it by his trips around the country and the attention that he gained in—

LEWIS: The primaries.

KENNEDY: And I might say that involved in all of these matters—those last seventy-two hours preceding what we were going to do at the University of Alabama—was the President, intimately involved in all of these decisions.

The next day the student was admitted at Huntsville without any problem.

LEWIS: There's something else that just occurred to me that has nothing to do with this. Did the President ever talk to James Meredith, on the phone or otherwise?

KENNEDY: No.

LEWIS: A character, eh?

KENNEDY: Oh, a real character.

MARSHALL: The gold Thunderbird. That was one of the great crises of the administration.

LEWIS: He wanted a gold Thunderbird?

KENNEDY: He bought one.

MARSHALL: He bought one. That shows what kind of training you need to be Attorney General. You have to deal with problems like that.

KENNEDY: Didn't you know that?

LEWIS: No. I'm awfully glad that I mentioned James Meredith's name. That's nice. And you succeeded, evidently, because I don't remember reading about it.

KENNEDY: Yes. Burke talked to— Who was it down there?

MARSHALL: I think, [Louisiana Congressman Edwin E.] Willis. I think I even got Dick Gregory [the black entertainer and activist] to talk to him about that. Dick Gregory is somewhat nutty, but he's not that nutty.

LEWIS: He got that message?

MARSHALL: Yes.

KENNEDY: Boy, that's all we needed was to have him arrive on the campus with a gold Thunderbird.

LEWIS: That would have been wonderful!

KENNEDY: These are momentous matters for the Attorney General.

LEWIS: . . . It's funny: Meredith also got into difficulty with the NAACP for his remarks. Do you remember that?

KENNEDY: Yes.

LEWIS: . . . Are there Negro students at the University of Mississippi today?

MARSHALL: Two.

KENNEDY: Any at the law school?

MARSHALL: One at the law school.

KENNEDY: Are they pretty good people?

MARSHALL: I don't know the one at the law school. The one at the university is all right. The one at the law school is Mrs. Robert Moses, the wife of [civil rights activist] Bob Moses.

KENNEDY: Oh, really?

LEWIS: Who may, therefore, not be among your fans, conceivably. . . .

MARSHALL: Bob Moses is a very radical and embittered young man.

LEWIS: Yes, that's what I mean.

KENNEDY: Is he now?

MARSHALL: Yes.

KENNEDY: He always was?

MARSHALL: He's gotten more so.

KENNEDY: Is he bitter against us?

MARSHALL: He's bitter against the government. It isn't personal. With a lot of them, it gets to be personal. They think you did this or I did this. He's too smart to attribute it to that. He's very bitter against this system, the mistreatment of Negroes that he sees in Mississippi.

LEWIS: Although that's changing for the better every day, isn't it?

MARSHALL: Well, it's changing.

KENNEDY: Very slowly.

MARSHALL: It is better. But the poverty and the ignorance—he's seeing that it's not just a question of going into hotels. The standard of living of the Negroes in Mississippi is what he really looks at now. You take voter registration. Seventy percent of the Negro adults are illiterate in Mississippi. He sees the problem in all of its depth.

LEWIS: Seventy percent?

MARSHALL: Yes, just about. Functionally illiterate.

LEWIS: What a testament to the state! That may lead to another one of these philosophical questions. Did you ever think or talk to the President or among yourselves about the tremendous question of what kind of leadership the Negroes in Mississippi would eventually have? Whether it would be a revolutionary leadership or whether it was still possible to provide a middle-class political leadership of the more traditional kind?

KENNEDY: Yes. We talked about that problem—not just for Mississippi, but for the country. And going back to the earlier question of my basis for sponsoring legislation: My basis for having the meetings, my basis for that whole effort in 1963 and 1964, was really not only the passage of legislation, but what in my judgment was even more important—to retain the confidence of the Negro population in their government and in the white majority. I thought that there was a great danger of losing that unless we took a very significant step such as the passage of legislation. To answer that question, I don't think that it was just confined to what was going to happen to the Negro leadership in Mississippi. It was far broader than that. Al-

though the legislation itself wouldn't affect the Negro in the North, I
think that it was important to pass the legislation just to show the
Negro in the North that the white population was going to do
something about this problem.

LEWIS: And that there was the hope of a traditional, middle-class (as I
call it) solution, rather than revolt?

KENNEDY: Yes. I don't like the word *middle-class*.

LEWIS: Well, I didn't mean—

KENNEDY: I don't mean in a snooty way. But I don't know where the
Negro is going to come from who's going to give the leadership or
direction. There's obviously a revolution within a revolution in the
Negro leadership. We could see the direction going away from
Martin Luther King to some of these younger people, who had no
belief or confidence in the system of government that we have here
and thought, as that meeting[27] indicated up in the apartment in New
York City—

LEWIS: We haven't talked about that, either.

KENNEDY: —that the way to deal with the problem is to start arming
the young Negroes and sending them into the streets—which I didn't
think was a very satisfactory solution, because, as I explained to
them, there are more white people than Negroes. And although it
might be bloody, I thought that the white people would do better.

"AS OLD AS THE SCRIPTURES, AS CLEAR AS THE CONSTITUTION": THE PRESIDENT'S JUNE 11 ADDRESS AND THE 1963 CIVIL RIGHTS BILL

LEWIS: When did it first occur to all of you—and how did it occur—to
use the resolution of the difficulties at the University of Alabama as
the peg, the occasion, for an important speech to the nation on the
moral issues of racial discrimination?

KENNEDY: After the problems in Birmingham, there was a feeling by
some of us that the President should go on television to discuss this
problem. Then it was a question of timing: not only what was going
to be said, but a question of when he'd say it. When we knew that
the problem at the University of Alabama was coming, we didn't

know how it was going to be resolved. We didn't know whether in the end, like the University of Mississippi, the President would have to go on and announce the use of troops or explain the fact that there had been violence—or what we had to do: the occupation of Tuscaloosa or the arrest of the Governor.

It would have been premature to go on television and talk about civil rights at the end of May, when we knew that the University of Alabama was coming up and we might have more problems and troubles. It was felt that, if he was going to go on at all, we should wait and find out what was going to occur there. There was some talk about his going on television the night before the University of Alabama, just to explain what the situation was and what steps we were taking. He eventually said that he wouldn't do that.

There was a basic conflict, as I mentioned to you, as to whether he should go on television at all, really.

MARSHALL: I remember that it was discussed particularly at one of the meetings at the White House. It was about the tactics to be used at the University of Alabama and whether he should do it—whether he should do it then or whether he should do it at all. I think that you were the only one who urged him to do it.

KENNEDY: Yes.

LEWIS: To make any speech? Who were the other people present?

MARSHALL: Kenny [O'Donnell], Larry O'Brien.

KENNEDY: Ted Sorensen. You [Marshall] were there.

LEWIS: The Vice President was not there?

KENNEDY: The Vice President was not there.

The President raised the question of what he would say. And we just talked. I thought that we were going to send up this legislation and also that there was this great problem in the country. We were going to send up the legislation, and he could talk about what we needed to accomplish, what would be done. I think he pretty much made up his mind, after that conference, that he would speak—but not finally.

He just decided that day. Called me up on the phone and said that he was going to go that night.

LEWIS: That was after the confrontation with Wallace?

KENNEDY: Yes. He and I talked almost all of that day about what was happening at the University of Alabama.

I called him about the fact that the Governor had stepped aside and let Nick come in, which is really—to look back over that period of time—a pleasant moment, after working so hard. As I say, we didn't know how it was going to turn out—the fact that he stepped aside. Nobody was certain until the time that he did. It was then, really, that [JFK] decided to go on television. He went on television that night. Burke and I went over there. I think Ted had prepared a speech.

MARSHALL: Well, there was an—

KENNEDY: Unsatisfactory draft.

MARSHALL: Yes. The time was so short. It occurred to me at the time: "How could he possibly do that?"

LEWIS: He delivered it when—at eight o'clock? I remember hearing it at a dinner party, arriving and immediately turning on the television set. It must have been around eight.

KENNEDY: It seems to me that it was around eight. It seems to me that we arrived about seven. We talked to the President—

MARSHALL: That's right. At that point, he didn't have a draft. But he'd talked to Ted. Ted had had what we sent over, and Ted was working on it.

KENNEDY: Then, [Sorensen] came back in, and the four of us met in the Cabinet Room. We gave our views, and Ted took notes. And then he went back into his office. The President and I stayed there for about twenty minutes. He thought that he was going to have to do it extemporaneously. So the two of us talked about what he'd say in the speech. He made notes.

LEWIS: On cards?

KENNEDY: On the back of an envelope or something, outlining and organizing. We sat at the end of the table and just talked for about twenty minutes. A couple of times I walked in [on Sorensen]. Ted Sorensen was still working about four or five minutes of eight. (I think that it was eight o'clock.) In any case, about four or five minutes before the hour, Ted Sorensen walked in. [JFK] looked it over in the next three minutes—what he wanted. I suggested that he do some of it extemporaneously.

Then, he went on.

LEWIS: And the end was extemporaneous.

KENNEDY: Yes. The speech was good. I think that probably, if he had given it extemporaneously, it would have been as good or better.

LEWIS: What reaction was there to the speech? Do you recall? It was a very unusual speech. I just wondered how he felt about it afterward. What did he say to you?

KENNEDY: We always used to laugh a little about the fact that I'd gotten him into so much trouble. I used to say that it was Burke Marshall who had gotten both of us in trouble.

MARSHALL: I thought it was great. He put the problem very well.

LEWIS: No funny phone calls about *The New York Times* editorial? I hope we were for that speech.

KENNEDY: I doubt it.

LEWIS: I think that it really was new, because no President had ever made a speech exactly like that. In the message with the legislation, he had used the words about the moral issues. He had said before that we have to do it because it's right and so forth. But somehow that kind of direct speech had a very different effect.

Trace how it came about that you proposed the February [1963] legislation,[28] dealing mainly with voting, prior to the whole Birmingham episode.

KENNEDY: I think that we had done a great deal, made a major effort on voting. I felt strongly about the fact that voting was at the heart of the problem. If enough Negroes registered, they could obtain redress of their grievances internally, without the federal government being involved in it at all. We had found inadequacies in the law in areas where we felt that the law could be improved. Perhaps—because it was voting, and it was such an elementary, basic right—we could obtain acceptance by Congress.

LEWIS: Did you have any serious thoughts that Congress, in the mood that it then was—which was, of course, before Birmingham—would take the trouble or pain that was necessary to pass any civil rights legislation?

KENNEDY: We thought that they might. It was so basic. At least I thought that there was a chance.

MARSHALL: Yes. It was a pretty limited proposal. It really would have affected just Mississippi, Alabama, and Louisiana—just three states. Some of the other southern Senators had come to the conclusion that the Negro vote was a good thing—Senator Talmadge, Senator Long, certainly. I think that we thought that they might make a show, but not really tear the Senate apart to defeat it, as I remember.

KENNEDY: Yes. We thought that it was very difficult, but that it was such a basic right—that we had so much on our side—that we might be able to get it through.

LEWIS: What about the President? Did he really think that there was a chance?

KENNEDY: I don't think that we ever discussed it, particularly.

LEWIS: It wasn't a big thing to him? It wasn't like the labor legislation?

KENNEDY: No. He reached the conclusion that we should send up some civil rights legislation. The motivation behind it was that there were inadequacies in the law, and we thought that we could really do something which would obtain the registration of a large number of Negroes.

LEWIS: I remember Burke telling me that Senator Mansfield, at the time of the proposing of the June legislation, just thought that it had no chance at all, that he was very gloomy.

KENNEDY: That's right. Let me say that the basic reason that the other legislation wasn't passed—or one of the basic reasons—is the fact that there wasn't any interest in it. There was no public demand for it. There was no demand by the newspapers or radio or television. There was no interest by people coming to watch the hearings or watch what took place or follow the filibuster later on.

LEWIS: That had been demonstrated the previous year in the literacy bill, which just sort of flopped.[29]

KENNEDY: That's the one I'm thinking of. Nobody came. Nobody paid any attention.

The point is continuously raised that President Kennedy only realized that there was a civil rights crisis the night after Birmingham in 1963, or otherwise he would have tried to obtain the passage of legislation in '61 or '62 or '63. That's ludicrous, really, on the basis of the facts. Number one: Nobody would have paid the slightest attention to him. If he had sent up a more comprehensive bill, it would never have gone very far in any case—as seen by the civil rights bill that we did send up, where nobody rose to great support. When the filibuster took place, we didn't even get fifty percent of the vote.

LEWIS: The previous year you did not, no.

KENNEDY: That's the previous year. Then, in 1963, it is true that Mike Mansfield basically didn't think that there was any chance of getting it passed. Do you think?

MARSHALL: No, I'm sure he didn't. I remember his saying, after the '62 legislation, that a Democratic administration could never pass a civil rights bill of any kind. I think that's what he thought in '63. I'm sure it was. I think he said so to you, I remember.

KENNEDY: The President actually talked in those terms—not so pessimistically—on the basis that a Republican had much more of a chance to obtain the passage of civil rights legislation because a Democrat couldn't get the Republican votes.

LEWIS: Now, in that connection, Burke said that, very early, the President saw Dirksen as a key figure in this. What did he say about that? Why did he disagree with Mansfield? Whose advice did he have?

KENNEDY: We thought that the feeling of the country was behind the steps that were being taken, and it was up to the President of the United States to give some leadership and devise the course of action that should be followed.

There were, I suppose, a number of alternatives. We could either make more of an effort to give protection to individuals who sat in and caused these demonstrations or, carrying that one step further, take steps to—at least, threaten to—possibly actually occupy Mississippi to be sure that all Negroes and all those participating in civil rights were protected. The other alternative was to devise some way to get to the heart of the problem. That was through the kind of legislation that was actually suggested. But the President felt that for the country, at that time, a course of action had to be developed.

Lyndon Johnson suggested that we talk to members of the House and the Senate. We would have sent the legislation up earlier if it hadn't been for that suggestion. He was not in on the drawing up of the bill and what was included in the bill. Burke went and talked to him. He felt that we should make sure that the members of Congress knew more about it—which is what took place.

LEWIS: Do you recall any conversations with the President at this time, which was particularly a time, I think, of excruciating frustration about liberalism and the fact that the "liberal" position was one that was obstructive in this situation, as you saw it?

KENNEDY: Yes. Without our getting in and discussing it in great detail, it served to prove what we had always thought.

LEWIS: Which was?

KENNEDY: What my father said about businessmen applies to liberals.

LEWIS: Will the historians remember what your father said about businessmen?

KENNEDY: They're sons of bitches. The people who are selfish are interested in their own singular course of action and do not take into consideration the needs or requirements of others or what can ultimately be accomplished. They're not very helpful, I don't think.

LEWIS: Surely, all those people involved in that negotiation—I mean, some of the civil rights people—weren't narrow in the sense of political advantage. Some of them, at least, thought that they were doing the right thing on the merits for civil rights. There's no doubt about that, is there, Burke? Or am I too kind?

MARSHALL: I think, probably, you can make a distinction between some of the civil rights groups that really didn't know what they were doing—I mean, didn't understand the function of Congress— and some of the Congressmen who did understand it and, I would say, were pretty cynical about it.

LEWIS: Well, now, [Wisconsin Congressman Robert W.] Kastenmeier, for example. What was his motivation?

MARSHALL: I would say that . . . his motivation was to make a point. And his point, really, is that he's going to be right; he's going to prove that everybody else is wrong by having the whole thing fail.

KENNEDY: I think they said on a number of occasions—some of these people—that "we'd rather lose the whole bill and lose the legislation than make the kind of effort that [the Kennedy administration] wished"—the course of action that we wished to follow. I thought that an awful lot of them, as I said at the time, were in love with death.

LEWIS: I hadn't remembered that phrase until you just said it. There is often a feeling that people would rather lose.

KENNEDY: Especially this group, I think. It's why they like Adlai Stevenson. For an awful lot of them in this kind of group, in my judgment, action or success makes them suspicious, and they almost lose interest. That's why so many of them think that Adlai Stevenson is the "Second Coming." He never quite arrives there; he never quite accomplishes anything. That's a terrible way of putting it, but I think that they like it much better to have a cause than to have a course of action that's been successful.

LEWIS: What did your brother think about that? About the same?

KENNEDY: Yes.

LEWIS: About Stevenson?

KENNEDY: He didn't like Adlai Stevenson.

LEWIS: . . . Did the President have, in this period, any personal contact with people on the liberal civil rights side, to try to show them why they were wrong? I'm thinking of Joe Rauh [of the ADA] or of Martin Luther King or—of course not Clarence Mitchell [of the NAACP] because that would have been hopeless?

MARSHALL: After he'd met with most of the other groups, you remember he had a meeting with the civil rights leaders in June—late June. He talked to them and tried to explain the difficulties that this bill was going to have in getting through Congress. They went right through the House Judiciary Committee and what they needed in the House and in the Senate. He stressed the fact that he needed the full support of Senator Dirksen. Senator Dirksen at that time had already announced that he was against part of the bill. [JFK] was very realistic and practical in explaining that. He said to them: "You've got to remember"—he was trying to make the point that he wasn't at odds with them, trying to explain these practicalities, what he wanted to be done and how he was going about it—"you have to remember that I'm in this, too, right up to my neck now."

KENNEDY: All of this wasn't a great surprise to him—the fact that he had this kind of opposition. Some of the individuals who were involved he had contempt for—people who were in opposition—on the basis that it didn't really make a great deal of sense (we were all trying to accomplish something) and that they therefore were [not well] motivated. Some of them. Others, as you point out, were well motivated, and those—well, they just disagreed. But some, who were motivated or interested only in their own political futures, their own positions, he really had contempt for. The fact was that they ostensibly were in favor of doing something in this field and, through their actions, were destroying the opportunity or chance of accomplishing it.

LEWIS: Who was useful on the liberal side as the thing came down to the climax in the House committee? Was Walter Reuther useful, helpful? Who was helpful with getting those last few votes that you needed in the end?

MARSHALL: I think that it was just the President by himself, really.

KENNEDY: Yes, so do I.

MARSHALL: I don't think that he got any help from any one of those people. Even Walter Reuther.

KENNEDY: I don't think he got any help. All the negotiations, really, with all of this group were conducted by Burke and Nick. The only reason that the liberals came along, in the last analysis, was the fact that the President got [Indiana Congressman and House Minority Leader Charles H.] Halleck and [Ohio Congressman William M.] McCulloch [both Republicans].

LEWIS: In a word, how did the President get Halleck? What was the clue? Why did Halleck do it?

KENNEDY: I can tell you that after the President talked to Halleck, he could never understand why [Halleck] did it.

LEWIS: What did the President say?

KENNEDY: He just couldn't understand why [Halleck] would cooperate with him.

MARSHALL: I understand there was a real fight within the Republican leadership in the House at that time. They couldn't understand it, either. Some of them. I don't understand it now. I think that it must have been something personal with Bill McCulloch—that he just did it for Bill McCulloch.

KENNEDY: It was a strange thing. But I wasn't present at the meeting.

LEWIS: McCulloch is on the merits. We should say that for history.

KENNEDY: Yes.

LEWIS: I mean, McCulloch wanted to have a good bill.

KENNEDY: Yes.

MARSHALL: Yes. As a man of conscience. I've always thought that he just did it out of honesty and integrity.

LEWIS: Yes. Your suggestion is that Halleck did it for McCulloch. I don't know Halleck, but nobody seems to think that he had any personal interest in civil rights as an issue.

KENNEDY: No.

LEWIS: Or belief in it.

KENNEDY: No, no. And he never would do anything for the President.
   There was a struggle within the Republicans afterwards about why he had done it. I don't know whether he just was convinced at that meeting, whether the President got carried away with it, and finally [Halleck] nodded his head in assent and had given his word, so he didn't want to go back on his word. But the President could never understand why.

LEWIS: Which meeting are you talking about now?

MARSHALL: The meeting at the White House in October after the complete confusion and fiasco of the subcommittee and the bill which the subcommittee reported out.[30] There were then efforts to put that together again. It came down that the President could get the liberals to support a compromise bill only if Halleck would support it. It came down to that. The President met with Halleck to get that assurance. He met with Halleck, and Bill McCulloch, and [Illinois Congressman Leslie C.] Arends, I guess.

KENNEDY: It was very tough as far as getting the liberals to go along with it. Even after that, some of them ran out on it.

LEWIS: Yes. But this meeting was the publicized meeting, at the end of which pictures were taken, and so on. I mean, this was a known meeting. The public knew about it right afterwards. This meeting must have then followed Nick's telephone conversation with McCulloch, in the course of which McCulloch made certain undertakings of what Halleck would support.

MARSHALL: That's right. McCulloch always told Nick and he always told me: "Charlie Halleck is for this." He made that as a commitment when we talked to McCulloch about what Halleck would support, as well as what *he* would support. Neither Nick nor I had talked to Halleck. It was just when he came over there and talked to the President. That was the first time that anyone—

LEWIS: Firsthand.

MARSHALL: Yes. Really knew. Even at that, as you know, there was some question about the employment title.

LEWIS: It's very odd. Nick remembered that, in his telephone conversation with McCulloch, McCulloch made a commitment on the employment title. But Nick's notes show that McCulloch said quite the contrary, that Halleck made no commitment on the employment title. After the meeting, Halleck was talking on the Hill to reporters about not having made any commitment on the employment title.

MARSHALL: Somehow or other [Halleck] got into the White House and in with the President—and he came out committed on this. At least, committed enough so that he could never get away from it.

LEWIS: He never did. That's true. I wanted to know why.

KENNEDY: I might just say as a sidelight to history that one of those who was supposed to go along was [Illinois Congressman Roland V.] Libonati on the liberal side. And [Chicago Mayor] Dick Daley gave the word to the President that he was very difficult. As you remember, the vote looked like it was going to be very close. Libonati was a key figure. The President talked to Dick Daley, and Kenny O'Donnell did, three or four times. I kept reporting back that I thought that Libonati might run out. Finally he gave definite word that he would stick. When, of course, the meeting finally took place, he ran out. Kenny then called up—I was with the President— Kenny called up Dick Daley to tell him that he had run out. [Daley] reported back that Libonati wouldn't be running for Congress anymore. And Libonati then retired from Congress, and they put a new man in. Kenny said that Daley said that he had broken his word, so the organization was going to get rid of him—because of the civil rights vote. Whether that was true or whether he just wanted to retire—

LEWIS: Well, that would have been a good reason, but there were a number of other reasons for not wanting Mr. Libonati in Congress.

KENNEDY: Oh, there are many reasons; but it's rather interesting.

LEWIS: [Teamsters leader James R.] Hoffa, among others. Yes, that is interesting. I wondered whether you talked to the President before when you went up and made your crucial appearance before the full committee in that session, in which you argued against the subcommittee bill. Did you discuss that with him?

KENNEDY: We were talking about this problem all along.

LEWIS: How was it decided that you would go?

MARSHALL: I can't remember for sure whether it was before or after your appearance, but I do remember your discussing with the President on some occasion right around that time, whether or not we had enough of a chance to try to patch it together—whether we should do that or whether we should just accept the fact that we were going to lose the bill and have the President, therefore, just get on the Democratic side of it and accept the liberals' position and throw the bill away. That was discussed. You and the President discussed that briefly at one point, because the President was himself so doubtful that we could ever get Halleck and Republican support for any bill that contained what he wanted in it. But he decided, I think, he decided to try to get a consensus. That's what he decided to try to do.

KENNEDY: Yes, I remember we talked. And I remember discussing with both Burke and Nick the idea of following the course of the liberals and *The New York Times*: making an effort to try to amend the bill on the floor of the House of Representatives. That's, of course, what many of the liberal groups were saying was the strongest bill possible; and then you could amend it on the floor. Out of that bill with the amendment, you could come up with a very good bill. Now, Burke and Nick felt that was a very grave thing, because once you start amending and didn't have any support from the leadership of the Republican party, it could destroy the whole bill. That was a real struggle. But it's awfully tough to convince anyone in that kind of an argument, because they're saying, "Our strategy's better. Maybe there are imperfections in the bill. But if we go ahead on this basis, we can amend the bill, and we can get a good bill. We can get John Lindsay, and we've got the other liberal Republicans, and they'll join with us. We can come up with a very strong and good bill. Then, when we go over to the Senate of the United States, we'll have a strong bill. And we can amend it further there, straighten the bill out, all of it." Our strategy was that we wanted to get the Republicans and the Democrats to agree on a bill right from the House committee, agree on it on the floor, and have that agreement made prior to the time it ever came to the floor.

The President was involved in all of those kinds of discussions. I think, based on his meeting with Halleck and McCulloch and Nick, he decided on the strategy that we followed. I don't remember my discussing my testimony with him. Again, I think that it was just on that basis that we decided between us the course of action. We just worked out what was the best way to proceed.

LEWIS: On November 22 [1963], the bill was out of the Judiciary Committee and still in the Rules Committee, as I recall. Do you remember how your brother felt the prospects were then? After the narrow victory in the Judiciary Committee and the agreement with Halleck, was he then persuaded that there was, in fact, going to be a piece of civil rights legislation?

KENNEDY: Yes. He didn't have any problem about its being passed in the House.

LEWIS: No, I meant altogether. The Senate?

KENNEDY: Let me just take it one at a time. He didn't have it hard getting it by the Rules Committee, because that was part of the agreement—that it would not only be out of the [Judiciary] Committee, not only supported on the floor of the House, but also the Rules Committee was a part of that. In the Senate of the United States, we still felt that it was very difficult. There was much more of a chance if it came through the House on that basis, because there was going to be much more pressure on Dirksen and the Republican leadership to support that kind of legislation. I felt that ultimately we could obtain the passage of the bill, but [JFK] kept asking where we were going to get the votes—just as Lyndon Johnson, in January and February, said, "Where are we going to get the votes?" They both were concerned about it. Then, when we had these conversations with Mansfield, you see, and even Hubert [Humphrey], they were all basically in favor of having a vote on cloture in March and April [1964]. And if it didn't win, we'd go to the people to show, at least, what the vote was.

LEWIS: You mean they were just so discouraged?

KENNEDY: Discouraged. And also the strategy was that "Well, we'll have a vote on cloture then, and then we'll have another vote on cloture later—and we've done everything that people can do."

MARSHALL: Hubert Humphrey thought that they should have a vote on cloture. They'd lose it substantially, and then they'd give away the employment title and try again. That's what he thought early in 1964.

LEWIS: How was it decided not to do that? What was the process?

KENNEDY: We just made such a fuss about it.

LEWIS: The Justice Department?

KENNEDY: Yes.

LEWIS: President Johnson did not take an active part in this matter?

KENNEDY: No. I had some conversations with him.

I felt not only did I want to get a civil rights bill by, but I wanted to get it by for personal reasons, you know, because I thought that it was so important for President Kennedy. So I said that we were just going to stay there. We could stay there for five years until they got the bill by.

LEWIS: Your position was that there should not be any cloture vote until you were assured of the vote?

KENNEDY: That's right.

MARSHALL: President Johnson told Mansfield and told Humphrey and told people down at the Senate that they couldn't do anything that didn't have Bob's approval.

LEWIS: Oh, he did?

KENNEDY: Yes.

LEWIS: Oh, that was very good, wasn't it?

KENNEDY: In January, he said that "I'll do on the bill just what you think is best to do on the bill. We'll follow what you say we should do on the bill. We won't do anything that you don't want to do on the legislation. And I'll do everything you want me to do in order to obtain the passage of the legislation." So we just said that we didn't want to have a vote. We said that we wanted to wait. These were the meetings that we held in January, February, and March with Mansfield, Humphrey, and sometimes I got [California Senator Thomas H.] Kuchel in.

LEWIS: That's rather extraordinary, what you just said. I never knew that [Johnson] had said it in quite those explicit terms. Why did he do that, in your opinion?

MARSHALL: He didn't think we'd get the bill.

KENNEDY: He didn't think, number one, that we'd get the bill. I don't want to be unfair about it, but secondly, I think that if we were not going to obtain the passage of the bill, he didn't want to be the reason, to have the sole responsibility. If I worked out the strategy, if he did what the Department of Justice recommended, suggested— and particularly me—then, if he didn't obtain the passage of the bill, he could always say that he did what we suggested and didn't go off on his own.

He had a particular problem, being a southerner. If we decided that he should follow a particular line of strategy and then it didn't work, it could be very, very damaging to him. I think that for political reasons it made a great deal of sense. Secondly, our relationship was so sensitive at the time that I think that he probably did it to pacify me. It was the best way to proceed.

LEWIS: It was really best for him in either event, because when the strategy did work and the bill was passed, he still got ample credit and identification.

KENNEDY: That's right.

LEWIS: But I see that it was a more sensitive thing than I had thought. Even though there may have been political motivations, it still was the right thing to do.

KENNEDY: Yes.

MARSHALL: I shouldn't say that [Johnson] didn't think that we'd get a bill. He didn't see *how* we'd get a bill.

KENNEDY: Yes. I can understand that. It was damned difficult, anyway, where we were going to get the votes for it. If he said, "Where are you going to get the votes?"—President Kennedy used to say the same thing: "Where are you going to get the votes?"—you couldn't tell him where you were going to get the votes. The person whom you're going to get the votes from, really, in the last analysis, was Everett Dirksen. We all knew that. If we could get Everett Dirksen.

Everett Dirksen was very fond of President Kennedy. Everett Dirksen liked President Kennedy a great deal and much, much, much more than he liked Lyndon Johnson. And I think that he made an effort—at least, part of his motivation, in the last analysis, was because of President Kennedy.

LEWIS: That's very interesting.

KENNEDY: He really liked the President, and he did a great deal for him. I mean, unlike the House—and Halleck—when it really became difficult or there was a real problem, when it was important legislation for the country, the President talked to [Dirksen]—and he did it.

LEWIS: The test ban treaty?

KENNEDY: That's an example. But there were a lot of other examples. They had a very good relationship, where they could really work things out between the two of them. President Kennedy appreciated what Dirksen did, and Dirksen genuinely liked the President. On various occasions the President did things for Dirksen. There were a number of appointments to regulatory commissions and judges—for example, the judge out in Illinois was appointed over Dick Daley's protest. [JFK] appointed him because Dirksen wanted him.

LEWIS: And the President was, at least, not a very vigorous campaigner in the Yates-Dirksen race. [Illinois Congressman Sidney R. Yates ran, on the Democratic ticket, for the Senate, against incumbent Dirksen, in 1962.]

KENNEDY: That's right. He could work with him. The other Republican that he liked a lot, of course, was Senator Kuchel. But he could work with Dirksen; and, as I say, on matters of considerable importance to the country, Dirksen—unlike Halleck, who wouldn't think of those matters at all—he and Dirksen would work it out.

LEWIS: What you're saying is that the answer to the question "Where are the votes going to come from?" just turned out to be Dirksen.

KENNEDY: Yes. We knew back in September and October of 1963 that McCulloch or Halleck had to deliver something and that the important strategy, really, was to have them deliver, so that it became their bill. It wasn't just the Democratic administration's bill or President Kennedy's bill or, later, President Johnson's bill. It couldn't be that, because that didn't make any sense for them. The important thing, really, was to focus attention, first, on Congressman McCulloch. *He* did it. Nobody made any effort to take any credit for it in the Democratic administration—nobody in the Department of Justice or in the administration generally. Congressman McCulloch had done it. All the statements were made focusing attention on the fact that Congressman McCulloch did it. And [New York] Congressman [Emanuel] Celler. That gave them some pride in it. The fact that it should be followed through gave them some pride. And we made certain commitments to them.

When we got over into the Senate, then it became Senator Dirksen— nobody else. He was the one who was important. [Iowa Republican] Senator [Bourke] Hickenlooper was against it and walked out of the meetings we had. Senator Dirksen made every effort, and he came in with a lot of amendments and ideas. When you'd have a conversation with him—unlike, again, some of the "liberals"—you could talk about some of these matters in a rational way, discussing both sides of it and then work it out with him. That was what made such a difference. He'd come in with strong ideas in a certain direction, and then you'd explain it to him and talk with him about it. Then he'd work it out. And it was interesting, for instance, that there wasn't really one liberal Republican who attended any of those meetings.

LEWIS: Not Kuchel?

KENNEDY: No.

MARSHALL: I think that when we talked about Title Seven,[31] [New Jersey] Senator [Clifford] Case was there, as I remember.

KENNEDY: Yes, he came in. [Pennsylvania Democratic Senator] Joe Clark was present. Joe Clark was nothing but trouble when we were having these meetings with Dirksen. Nothing but trouble. He just made it impossible.
    Senator Case was very helpful.

MARSHALL: Yes.

KENNEDY: He's a good fellow. Joe Clark was impossible. Hubert Humphrey was damn helpful.

MARSHALL: Yes.

KENNEDY: He was very good.

MARSHALL: Senator [George D.] Aiken [Republican of Vermont]; [Massachusetts Republican] Senator [Leverett] Saltonstall. They were both very helpful.

KENNEDY: Aiken was very good. Awfully good. But Dirksen was really terrific, very reasonable and rational and very understanding. Unlike Hickenlooper. If we had ever had to work it out with Hickenlooper, we'd never have worked it out. It would have been impossible. But, as I say, the focus of attention was on [Dirksen]. We had made certain agreements. The byplay was interesting because we had made certain agreements with McCulloch regarding investigations of voting fraud. We were against that in the Department of Justice. What it was aimed at, really, was—

LEWIS: Chicago?

KENNEDY: Yes. And the Democrats. That was part of the agreement. And part of the agreement with him also—with McCulloch—was that we wouldn't agree to any changes without his approval. So we went over to the Senate, and we started meeting with them. And Dirksen was against that. Of course, I was against it. We were all against it because it didn't belong in the bill. But we ended up—and I ended up—arguing in favor of it because Congressman McCulloch was in favor of it. Senator Dirksen wanted it out. And although I had wanted it out, he said that it was part of the agreement. We couldn't agree to take it out unless Congressman McCulloch wanted it out.

LEWIS: And in the end it stayed in, didn't it?

MARSHALL: Oh, yes. It's still in there. Robert Kennedy, though, is the lawyer for Bill McCulloch. That's essentially what happened.

LEWIS: Do you think that, if President Kennedy had lived, the result would have been any different in the bill?

KENNEDY: No, it wouldn't have been any different. I think that a lot of this legislation would have perhaps come later. I don't know if it would have come much later. It would have been passed in the House, I would think, a month later, maybe. I think they passed it in the House—because of November—quicker than they would have otherwise. Both those bills would have been passed, but they would have come later—the legislation and the tax bills—than they did.

I might say, just apropos to what I read in the paper about the role of Senator Humphrey as the Vice President, the fact that Hubert's going to be used a lot in legislation and that President Kennedy didn't really use Lyndon Johnson in connection with legislation in the area that he really knew: The fact is that after [Johnson] became Vice President, he used to talk to the President frequently about the fact that they resented him in the Senate. And, frequently, the President used to say that [Johnson] would not do anything in the Senate or up on Capitol Hill in connection with any of this legislation. The President asked him on virtually every occasion of a major bill, and it was exasperating to President Kennedy that Lyndon Johnson wouldn't do more or make more of an effort in connection with a lot of the legislation. His ideas about how to proceed were helpful on occasion—for instance, on the civil rights bill—but as far as making any personal effort, with even Texas Congressmen or in the Senate, he almost invariably refused to do so.

LEWIS: Of course, he may have been right—that it would have been resented and would have been unhelpful.

KENNEDY: I just wanted to make sure that we covered all aspects of it.

MARSHALL: I don't know whether the point got across, but I think that the crucial, personal involvement of President Kennedy—other than proposing the legislation, aside from making that decision—was what he did in October with the House Judiciary Committee. That could not have been put together except by him. I think it's clear. He had all the liberal Democrats over to the White House in the Cabinet Room. He talked to them one by one, individually, and asked them to vote against the subcommittee bill, which was a very difficult thing for someone who is identified as a liberal to do. Some of them didn't do it, but there were three or four who changed their vote and voted in favor of this compromise bill only at the personal urging of President Kennedy.

KENNEDY: I might say that we had an argument about having that meeting, too, because Larry O'Brien and the White House staff was against the President meeting with the liberal Democrats.

LEWIS: On what grounds?

MARSHALL: They thought that, in the first place, it would be public, you see—and the President's personal prestige would be so much on the line if it didn't work. That was the thing: They didn't think that it would work. Because I don't think Larry or Kenny—I think it's true of both of them, and it's probably true of Ted Sorensen too— they never thought that Halleck would buy the bill or stick by the commitment. Therefore, they were worried that the President would do this and personally urge these people (whom they didn't like anyway, some of them) to change their vote on this important thing—and then fail. You see, then it would have been President Kennedy's failure if it had gone that way. And they simply didn't want to take the chance.

KENNEDY: And I think that they also mistrusted people like Kastenmeier going out and talking to the press and putting the meeting in the worst possible light.

LEWIS: What was their alternative proposal?

KENNEDY: Just go down with it. And it wouldn't obtain the legislation. That's why we felt strongly that we had to have the bill and that it was worth the effort. If you didn't do it, at least you've done everything possible. If you weren't successful, at least you've done everything possible. This was so important that it was worthwhile for the President to do it. Have you gone into how we arrived at this position about the fact that we were trying to get the liberals and the Republicans to agree to a compromise? How one side said they'd do it, and the other side said they'd do it?

MARSHALL: I think the critical thing about all the detail is that the subcommittee of the House Judiciary Committee ran away and closed out this impossible bill and Congressman Celler was chairman of that subcommittee. So then there was the question of what to do; that was the first time that that question came up. You could just take this and try to go through—and save what you can and amend. McCulloch said that it would be recommitted, that it would never even get through the House. That was his advice to Nick and to me. Or do you try to put it together again? To try to put it together again, you have to have Celler change his position for the first time. So you had Celler over in your office. And that was a rather unpleasant meeting with Congressman Celler.

KENNEDY: I guess he was mad about the meeting.

MARSHALL: Yes. He thought that he was being scolded. And he *was* being scolded. He did resent it at the time. But then, I think, he finally came around and accepted it. I don't believe there was any problem about his relations with the President finally, but right at that time, he was—

KENNEDY: It was unpleasant.

MARSHALL: —very resentful. And it was unpleasant. And there was a serious question of what he'd do.

LEWIS: Without him you couldn't have gotten anywhere.

KENNEDY: No. But you see, we'd lost him. The problem was, it wasn't just a gratuitous lecture. We'd lost him, and he wasn't giving any leadership. He'd indicated that he'd come along with us—and then hadn't. It was a question whether he ever was. The reason that I was as strong as I was, was that he was no good to us with his present posture at that time. He liked me, and I liked him—but we'd lost the bill. So I just put the facts on the table: that the bill was going to go down the drain and we needed some leadership from him. He'd said that he'd give it to us and give the bill that kind of direction—and hadn't done it. So that the whole chance and opportunity of obtaining the passage of legislation was being jeopardized by his actions. He didn't like it, but what he did do was that he came around in that direction afterward.

MARSHALL: Right away.

KENNEDY: Yes.

MARSHALL: I mean, really, within the next few hours. He was very mad when he left the office. So he arranged to have Bill McCulloch come in. And Nick and I went down and met Bill McCulloch and Celler and started on the path of those two trying to put it together again. So that's how it went. Then we worked on the bill with McCulloch, to get a bill that he could sell to Halleck, that would be defended by both parties—well, by Celler and McCulloch and Halleck—on the floor of the House.

LEWIS: Have we made it clear that in order to get the liberal Democratic votes you had to produce a signed, sealed, engraved agreement with Halleck?

KENNEDY: To get both of them, you see. That was it.

LEWIS: You'd have to promise each that you'd get the other side.

MARSHALL: But, see, Bill McCulloch had been burned. He had been burned by having Libonati run out on him, he'd been burned in the subcommittee, and then was burned again by Libonati in a vote that they took in the full Judiciary Committee. Libonati was supposed to make a motion to amend Title One; that was the agreement. Libonati ran out on him. McCulloch was in the position, even if he trusted the Department of Justice, of having the liberal Democrats stab him in the back at this point. So he was very distrustful of the liberal Democrats, he felt, for good reasons, and the liberal Democrats were completely distrustful of Halleck.

LEWIS: With good reason.

KENNEDY: And also the liberal Democrats were running with the ball on a piece of legislation which they thought was helpful to them. So they weren't interested. Then we had John Lindsay and the liberal Republicans, who were—

MARSHALL: Just as difficult.

KENNEDY: Oh, impossible.

LEWIS: Well, [Lindsay] wasn't as bad as a couple of others, was he?

KENNEDY: Oh, just terrible. At the beginning.

MARSHALL: At the beginning. But then he came around.

KENNEDY: But in the beginning he was no help at all.

MARSHALL: He came around, and he was helpful.

KENNEDY: At the end. After the agreement.

MARSHALL: Yes. After.

LEWIS: Well, he really *did* want a bill.

KENNEDY: Yes. Except at the beginning, where he could have been helpful. He wasn't until Congressman McCulloch came around.

THE CASE OF APPORTIONMENT

LEWIS: I'd like to turn to an entirely different subject, one that interests me and that you said would be of interest historically. That is, how the Department of Justice came to take the position it took in the reapportionment cases . . .[32]

MARSHALL: On the question of whether the Court should take jurisdiction of the problem, the disagreement within the Department came over what substantive rule of constitutional law should be applied— whether it should be "one man, one vote" or whether it should be something considerably short of that.

LEWIS: That's what I was referring to. And the Solicitor General was very reluctant about "one man, one vote"?

MARSHALL: It came up in my division. So I discussed it with Archie Cox at length. I had that discussion over and over again with him. That and the sit-in cases. Those were the big constitutional issues that were very important. I'd gone into it in great detail with Archie. Archie was firmly of the view that the "one man, one vote" position was wrong. He was also of the view that his function was to protect the Court from itself. Therefore, he should not only urge that position on it, but really urge the opposite. I thought that the matter was of such importance—and I was really in disagreement with him on it, anyway—that the Attorney General ought to be informed on it. So I informed the Attorney General, and we had a meeting.

KENNEDY: Prior to that, a year before that, when these cases were coming up, I thought that it was a very difficult matter. What I suggested was that we write a letter to various law schools around the country, various eminent lawyers and constitutional experts, and have their views and ideas about what they thought, how this matter should be approached, what position the Department of Justice should take. Because it *was* difficult and very complicated. I asked Archie Cox to do that. He obtained answers. I don't think that he was overly enthusiastic about this. I don't know, really, how much he did do about it. I guess he did some because I asked him for an answer.

MARSHALL: He didn't want to do it really.

KENNEDY: He didn't want to do it very much. I think he just had some fixed ideas about it and really didn't want to have them disrupted. Burke spoke to me about the fact that he was taking this position, and I think that I sent a memorandum over to the President about it.

MARSHALL: Yes, you did.

KENNEDY: I asked for everybody's point of view. In addition to the professors, I asked for the point of view of Larry O'Brien and a number of political leaders.

LEWIS: This would have been some period before you actually had to write the brief in this group of cases?

MARSHALL: It wasn't before we had to *think* about writing the brief. . . .

KENNEDY: We could anticipate that this was going to come up. We discussed this long before that. I was concerned about Archie's position, and I think a number of other people were concerned. I discussed it briefly with the President.

LEWIS: Tell me what the President's reaction was. He had had a position long before he was President. He had written an article for *The New York Times Magazine* about the evil of "malapportionment." What was his gut reaction to it? That it should be "one man, one vote"?

KENNEDY: I stated some of the problems to him without really asking what his position was on it. We just discussed it with him, just informed him. I thought this was the way to proceed legally.

MARSHALL: We were at least in agreement that if we did not actively support the "one man, one vote" position in the Colorado brief, the brief should not be negative on it. The brief that was being prepared by Archie, which was changed in the draft, . . . explicitly told the Court not to do this. That was Archie's position. Archie felt very strongly about it.

KENNEDY: I had had two or three conversations with Archie, just in passing, about it. I said that I was concerned about it. I didn't think that it was an easy matter, but I wanted it moved into the direction of "one man, one vote." We couldn't do it immediately, but that's the direction I thought we should go in. I thought, probably, that it was a mistake to take any position now, but that we should keep the Court moving in that direction.

MARSHALL: Was the District Court in the Colorado [legislative malapportionment] case upheld?

LEWIS: The District Court in the Colorado case, by a vote of two to one, held the disputed apportionment valid and rejected the complaint.

MARSHALL: Archie wanted to support that. He felt very strongly about it. I did take it up with the Attorney General. It wasn't the first time that it came up, but it was the first time it came up in the context of that case. And it was very important. So we discussed it with Ted and, I guess, with Bruce Terris [then Assistant to the Solicitor General].

KENNEDY: Wasn't Larry there?

MARSHALL: And Larry. That's right. We had a meeting with Archie. And Sarge [Shriver] was there at that meeting.

KENNEDY: Oh, I sent for Sarge.

LEWIS: What was Sarge doing?

KENNEDY: I just wanted to get the viewpoint of a lot of different people about it because I thought it was very important. Because it was not just a legal matter. It was also a political matter—what the political effect would be in a state or an area of the country. I wanted to get the viewpoints of people other than just those who were looking at it from a strictly legal viewpoint.

MARSHALL: After I talked to the Attorney General about it, he told the Solicitor General [Cox] that he wanted to have a meeting on it. Between those two times, I went to the Solicitor General and told him that the Attorney General was in disagreement with him on this. He ought to think about whether he couldn't come out with a position that he could support personally in the Court, but would still not throw away, at least, the position that the Constitution required: the "one man, one vote" criterion. So Archie, before we had the meeting, had done some thinking about that and had really decided that he could support reversing the Colorado decision.

LEWIS: As I recall, it came down, to be specific, to a couple of narrow points. One was that the percentage of people in Colorado that could elect a majority under this system was somewhat lower than he had first thought. It was thirty percent instead of forty, or a few percentage points. Secondly, there was some question about whether the referendum had really been a fair referendum on that specific issue. Those two rather small points were enough. Is that right?

MARSHALL: Yes, that's right. Then it was a question of what [Cox] said in the brief.

KENNEDY: In the brief, you see. There were about three paragraphs in the brief. The brief was satisfactory except, as I remember, for about three paragraphs. It might not even have been that many.

MARSHALL: They were very important.

KENNEDY: It was a question of working out language which would satisfy his own conscience and yet cover what I felt should be the position of the United States government. He was able to, based on that conversation and other conversations I had had with him prior to that time—and the fact that he is a very decent person. He could develop and work this out in a way that was satisfactory to him. He didn't violate his own conscience.

MARSHALL: He also agreed with you that if he was asked about this in Court, he would not say anything that was in opposition to the Court's adopting "one man, one vote."

KENNEDY: That was very important. It wasn't just a question of what was in the brief, but we went into what he would say in his oral argument. It didn't really do any good if he indicated in his oral argument a position that was contrary to the position that we wanted in the Department of Justice. So we went over the language, and he agreed what his oral position would be.

MARSHALL: He wrote out, in fact, what he'd say if he were asked that question. . . .

ENCOUNTER WITH JAMES BALDWIN

LEWIS: I thought that we might turn next to a happy topic. That is, the meeting you had in New York with James Baldwin and all those people. How did that come about? I remember you had Baldwin here [Hickory Hill, Virginia] for breakfast.

KENNEDY: Oh, yes. His plane was late. We had a very nice meeting, but I had to take a plane at nine-thirty. I had a meeting at nine-thirty, and he didn't get here until nine o'clock. And I had to leave. So we only saw each other for a half hour. I said that I was going to New York the next day—would he like to meet again? We'd have a little more of a chance to talk.

I don't know who wanted me to see him—Arthur Schlesinger or Dick Goodwin. I kept getting messages that he wanted to see me.

MARSHALL: I think I arranged for him to come out to your house that morning. I can't remember who told me he wanted to see you. I think it was Dick Gregory.

KENNEDY: Anyway, he came out. His plane was delayed, so I only got a chance to see him for a short period of time. Then I said that I was coming into New York. We talked about meeting up there, and I said I'd meet him for a drink. If he had some friends, maybe we could meet, and we could talk some more. So he said, "Fine."

MARSHALL: There was also a subject matter—I mean, what he talked about was the problems of the urban centers in the North. The idea was that he was going to have some people who understood those problems and would have some suggestions as to what role the federal government could take. That, as I understand it, was a rather clear topic of conversation.

LEWIS: But it didn't work out that way. How did the meeting begin? With an assault on you, as I recall.

KENNEDY: Why doesn't Burke go into it?

MARSHALL: It's not really worth the time.

KENNEDY: No.

LEWIS: It isn't? Well, all right. There was a lot of publicity about it.

KENNEDY: I know. Well, maybe you could give it two minutes.

MARSHALL: They had a young fellow there who had been involved in a freedom ride in 1961.

LEWIS: What was his name?

MARSHALL: His name is Jerome Smith [of CORE], I think.

LEWIS: A Negro?

MARSHALL: Yes. He started out by attacking the Attorney General very bitterly. He talked in terms of himself—that he could give the word and then all the Negroes would come out with their guns into the street and kill the whites. That's the way it started, I think—with him. Then they all started sort of competing with each other in attacking us, the President, the federal government, and the whole system of government in addition to the United States. They said that Negroes wouldn't fight for the United States anymore, that we ought to recognize that. They thought the President should have sent the Army into Birmingham. They wouldn't listen to any rational discussion of what it would do there or what the problem was in Birmingham.

KENNEDY: We'd discuss how we worked some of these matters out with Martin Luther King in Birmingham. They'd laugh at that and say, "That's not true." Of course, [King's] lawyer or his associate was there—Jones?

MARSHALL: Clarence Jones.

KENNEDY: Clarence Jones was there, so he knew the truth of it. Afterward, we asked him about why he didn't speak up. What was his answer?

MARSHALL: He said he couldn't or he didn't dare.

KENNEDY: He didn't dare. Who else was there? Harry—

MARSHALL: Harry Belafonte.

KENNEDY: —Belafonte. And I asked him—because there were some matters that he had been involved in for me and also with Martin Luther King. There was the fact that we got bail to these people. There were these other matters. Some of the statements that were made were completely untrue, and he knew they were untrue. I asked him [why he didn't speak up] and he said, "I'd lose my position with these people if I spoke up and defended you."

It was not only the young fellow, Smith, saying the fact that they were going to start killing white people on the street. What was her name?

MARSHALL: Lorraine Hansberry.

KENNEDY: Lorraine Hansberry said that they were going to go down and get guns, and they were going to give the guns to people on the street, and they were going to start to kill white people. They kept talking about—let's see—the white people were castrating the Negroes. You know, it was all that kind of conversation—in poetical terms—about the position of the Negro: The white people are worried about the fact that the Negro man is more virile, so that they think, "You're trying to castrate us."

You know, it was all in those kinds of terms—the speeches. And then people got madder and madder when they thought about the treatment of the Negro. A number of them . . . I think, have complexes about the fact that they've been successful. I mean, that they've done so well and this poor boy had been beaten by the police. Others had been beaten, and they hadn't been beaten.

MARSHALL: Like [author and psychologist Professor] Kenneth Clark.

KENNEDY: Just the idea that they really hadn't done their best. They hadn't done what they should have done for the Negro. So the way to show that they hadn't forgotten where they came from was to berate me and berate the United States government that had made this position a condition. They didn't really know, with a few exceptions, any of the facts. James Baldwin couldn't discuss any legislation, for instance, on housing or any of these matters. He didn't know anything about them. Harry Belafonte said afterward— and he was right—said that it was a mistake having them because they didn't know anything. . . .

MARSHALL: They just didn't know anything about government. They never came close to having a suggestion about what could be done.

KENNEDY: But it obtained a lot of publicity for him, see. So, he played it—James Baldwin—put him in the center of things and gave him a position of leadership. Then he put out all these statements and was interviewed about it. Kenneth Clark and all the rest of them—they gave their versions of the meeting and how I didn't understand the problems that the Negroes were facing throughout the country. There was nothing I could do or say about that. It was just a mistake.

LEWIS: Did you ever run into any of these people in the course of the Senate campaign?

KENNEDY: I guess James Baldwin's name was put out for Keating. Then, I think, [Baldwin] withdrew and said that he wasn't for me, but that he wasn't for Keating. Lorraine Hansberry's friends sent me a telegram a couple of weeks ago. Her last play is a failure, so they asked me to help save her play. I sent a telegram to help save her play. They ran the telegram as an ad in *The New York Times*.

LEWIS: But you haven't seen Baldwin since then?

KENNEDY: No, I haven't.

THE MARCH

LEWIS: Let's talk about the March on Washington and the President's part in making that a picnic instead of what some people were afraid it would be: terroristic activities. How did that come up? How did you first hear about it? What was your concern? Were you concerned?

MARSHALL: They started talking about it in June, right after Birmingham. A. Philip Randolph [black labor leader, organizer of the March]. As soon as they started talking about it, everyone started getting panicky. I'm sure the President got a good deal of advice that he ought to oppose it—stop it. People down on the Hill, particularly, thought it was going to be terrible.

It came up at the meeting that he had in June with the civil rights leaders. They said that they were going to have it. As of that meeting the President knew that they were going to have it. That's what they said, and they weren't going to be called off. So he issued a statement— against a good deal of advice, I think—that he accepted the fact that they were going to have it. He gave that early in the summer.

KENNEDY: That was in a [July 17, 1963] press conference.

MARSHALL: Press conference.

KENNEDY: We discussed it before, and we discussed it afterwards.

MARSHALL: It made a great deal of difference. I mean, the fact that he took that attitude rather than the attitude that almost everyone in the Senate and the Congress were taking—most of the government officials, most white people.

LEWIS: You mean it made a difference in the character of the March?

MARSHALL: Yes.

LEWIS: Because if he had opposed it and had the government opposed it, it would have been more of a James Baldwin–type march?

MARSHALL: If he had taken the attitude which, as I say, was very widespread—that you can't possibly have several thousand or a hundred thousand Negroes without having a riot—if he viewed it that way, talked about these people that way, I would think the character of it would have been terribly different. I mean, there would have been hostility towards him and towards the government.

KENNEDY: There would have been a protest against the government, in addition, instead of what it turned out to be. So it would not only have done harm: There might have been violence and it would have been very damaging throughout the world.

LEWIS: In the course of the succeeding couple of months, as the March came to fruition, you must have been keeping in very close touch— for example, through the FBI and other things—on the character of the March. Maybe I'm too suspicious, but I just have the feeling that you must have been very concerned about it.

MARSHALL: As it developed, it was clear that it was awfully disorganized at the beginning of the summer. The President had publicly endorsed it, more or less. So the Attorney General wanted to make sure that it was a success and that it was organized right. Therefore, he put his mind to organizing it right.

I would say that Bayard Rustin [civil rights activist and co-organizer of the March] and A. Philip Randolph have taken a good deal of credit—and they should. But the person who organized it, as a matter of fact, was the Attorney General, who assigned it to [Assistant Attorney General] John Douglas. [Douglas] spent, I would say, almost full time for at least four weeks, making sure that there were enough toilets around, that there was food, that the character of people who were coming was in close touch with the police. He had meetings with these people. And so I think that that made a lot of difference—all that work.

KENNEDY: We had a number of people who just spent all their time. It was very, very badly organized.

LEWIS: And what about the question I asked? About the character of the leadership of the March and your watching that?

KENNEDY: It was just that we kept track of the people who were Communists and who might get involved in it around the country—whether they were being included or excluded—I think, mostly through the head of the NAACP.

LEWIS: Roy Wilkins?

MARSHALL: Roy Wilkins.

KENNEDY: There were many groups of Communists that were trying to get in. We knew from the reports of the Communist party that they couldn't get into it. They were expressing concern about the fact that they couldn't play a bigger role. They wanted to play a big role, and they weren't being permitted to play a big role. There were a number of Communists who came down, but [the civil rights leaders] made a conscientious effort to keep them out. We worked closely with them to make sure that they stayed out, and we kept close contact with the Communist party as an organization to find out what they were trying to do in connection with the March. They made a major effort which was unsuccessful.

LEWIS: As I recall—as I say, from a distance—there was something at the end of the main ceremony, where Martin Luther King made his speech about the dream, in which John Lewis of SNCC was supposed to talk and somehow got cut out or something.

MARSHALL: Well, he had a speech written which was a very inflammatory speech. Archbishop [of Washington, Patrick A.] O'Boyle read this speech (this was the day before the March) and said that—

LEWIS: How did he get to read it?

MARSHALL: They had an agreement that they would tell each other. I talked to the Archbishop, and the Archbishop was adamant that night, the night before.

KENNEDY: Adamant that he wouldn't go.

LEWIS: He wouldn't go if [Lewis's] speech were delivered.

MARSHALL: Then I talked to you, and you suggested that I go to Walter Reuther. I got hold of Walter Reuther. That night Walter Reuther first went over and saw the Archbishop. The Archbishop was adamant. So then he got together with [CORE director James] Farmer and King and got the other leaders of the March together and explained the situation. They all went to Lewis and made Lewis agree to let them edit the speech. And I don't know how I got hold of the edited speech, but somehow or other I ended up with it and delivered it down to the Lincoln Memorial—right through all the marchers—in the sidecar of a police motorcycle. I got it down there, and then he gave the edited speech. The Archbishop had agreed that if Lewis would change the speech in this way, that he would speak. He'd agreed to that with Walter Reuther—and he did speak. I thought at the time, and you thought at the time, that it would have been very bad if the Catholic Church— I mean, the Archbishop pulling out really would have pulled the whole Catholic Church out of the civil rights movement. I think it would have looked that way. So that's what happened.

LEWIS: Besides it being a bad speech?

KENNEDY: It was a bad speech—both reasons.

LEWIS: Who had written the speech? Do you have any idea?

MARSHALL: Lewis, I suppose, and Jim Forman [of SNCC]. You know, they're a very radical bunch. And this was a very radical speech. It was a very inflammatory speech—

KENNEDY: There was an attack on the country. It attacked the President.

LEWIS: In the end, it got no publicity at all. As I recall, nobody would hardly have known that John Lewis was at the—

KENNEDY: No. But if he had made the speech—

MARSHALL: It was a close thing. . . .

KENNEDY: The President met with all of the leaders afterwards. He watched a good part of the March on television and saw Martin Luther King speak. Boy, he made a helluva speech.

LEWIS: That was kind of the high point of the era of good feeling, wasn't it—which ended rather shortly thereafter? It seems to me that quite shortly after the March we got into the most difficult phase of demonstrations in the North: the Triborough Bridge and stall-ins and all that. The backlash moved in very shortly after the March on Washington.

MARSHALL: Of course, shortly after the March on Washington, Wallace put those state troopers and National Guardsmen around the schools in Alabama—and those four little girls were killed in a bombing. . . .[33]

KENNEDY: The responsibility for the bombing might have been those two Klansmen.[34] But in the last analysis—like in Mississippi for the

killing of those three Freedom Riders[35]—I think it's Governor Barnett and Jim Eastland and [Mississippi Senator] John Stennis and the
business community. And in Alabama it's George Wallace and political and business leaders and newspapers. They can all deplore it. In
the last analysis, I think they're the ones who created the climate that
made those kinds of actions possible. Otherwise, they would never
have occurred.

It's just an editorial comment. But I think that all the smiles and
all the graciousness of Dick Russell and Herman Talmadge and Jim
Eastland and [Florida Senators] George Smathers and [Spessard]
Holland—in fact, none of them really made any effort to counter
this. And they're the ones, really, who have the major responsibility,
rather than these rather stupid figures who think that they become
national heroes by taking on these tasks. They are to blame, obviously. Greater blame, in my judgment . . .

LEWIS: I want to ask one last concluding question about civil rights.
That is, I had the impression, from what Burke said, that the
President tended to think of these racial matters not in terms of law,
as some of us do. In fact, he may have been impatient with the
limitations of the law. "Why were these things allowed to happen in
Albany, Georgia? Why were people so cruel?" and so on. How did
he think of it? Did he think of it in terms of children? In terms of the
future? Where did he think we were going? Did he philosophize a
bit?

KENNEDY: No, no.

LEWIS: Is that too vague? That's too vague.

KENNEDY: I just think that injustice, inequality, lack of opportunity,
meanness, unfairness shocked him. So that therefore he wanted to do
something about it—all of these matters, whether it was with children
in West Virginia who didn't have enough to eat or the Negro child in
Mississippi who was being deprived of his birthright. I don't think
that it was just in the context of civil rights. All these matters he
wanted to do something about.

NOTES

1) **the story.** On November 19, 1960, Lawrence reported in *The New York Times* that Robert Kennedy was being seriously considered for the position of U.S. Attorney General.

2) **Little Rock.** On September 23, 1957, federal officers, in compliance with court orders, escorted nine black students to Central High School in Little Rock, Arkansas. An angry white mob gathered outside the building and forced the removal of the students after only three hours. The following day, President Eisenhower nationalized the Arkansas National Guard and sent federal troops to Little Rock to enforce court orders requiring desegregation of the public schools.

3) **Anniston.** On May 14, 1961, thirteen Freedom Riders left Atlanta on a Greyhound bus with Birmingham as their destination. An angry mob attacked the bus at the Anniston, Alabama, bus depot and later attacked and burned it a few miles outside Anniston.

4) **John got beaten up.** John Seigenthaler was knocked unconscious when Freedom Riders were attacked at the Montgomery, Alabama, bus terminal.

5) **Montgomery.** On May 22, 1961, Martin Luther King, Jr., addressed a mass rally at Ralph Abernathy's First Baptist Church in Montgomery while an angry mob surrounded the church and threatened those inside in a violent confrontation.

6) **the arrests in Jackson.** On May 24, 1961, when the Freedom Riders arrived in Jackson, Mississippi, they were arrested without violence.

7) **the boys killed in Philadelphia, Mississippi.** On June 21, 1964, three young civil rights workers—Andrew Goodman, James Chaney, and Michael

Schwerner—were reported missing. Their bodies were found on August 4, 1964, after an extensive and prolonged search.

8) **petition.** On September 22, 1961, in response to a petition from the U.S. Attorney General, the Interstate Commerce Commission issued regulations prohibiting segregation in interstate bus terminals.

9) **Voter Education Project.** The Voter Education Project was a voter registration effort in which several major civil rights organizations, including SNCC (Student Nonviolent Coordinating Committee) and CORE (Congress of Racial Equality), participated.

10) **University of Alabama.** On June 11, 1963, two black students enrolled at the University of Alabama over the protests of Governor George C. Wallace.

11) **before that—Oxford?** On October 1, 1962, James Meredith became the first black student to enroll at the University of Mississippi, located in Oxford.

12) **TFX.** In 1963 a Senate investigatory committee scrutinized the Defense Department's awarding of the new TFX (Tactical Fighter Experimental) aircraft contract.

13) **McCarthy committee in 1954.** Robert Kennedy was minority counsel to Joseph McCarthy's Permanent Subcommittee on Investigations of the Senate Government Operations Committee. Louis B. (Lou) Nichols was Assistant to the Director of the FBI. The confrontation concerned access to FBI files on Annie Lee Moss.

14) **Annie Lee Moss.** Annie Lee Moss was a black teletype operator in the Signal Corps who was examined by Joseph McCarthy and Roy Cohn before the Senate Investigations Subcomittee about alleged Communist associations.

15) **Valachi.** Joseph M. Valachi was a member of the Genovese organized crime family who testified before the Senate Rackets Committee.

16) **Cosa Nostra.** Literally "our thing"—the Mafia. *Cosa Nostra* was a term introduced by Joseph Valachi in his testimony before the Rackets Committee.

17) **Frank Costello.** An organized crime figure investigated for racketeering, Costello was indicted for federal income tax evasion in 1953 and served a five-year prison term; he was deprived of U.S. citizenship in 1961.

18) **Stanley Levison.** Stanley D. Levison, a New York lawyer, adviser to Martin Luther King, Jr., was described by Coretta Scott King as one of her husband's "most devoted and trusted friends."

19) **stroke of a pen.** One of John Kennedy's campaign assurances was that he could remedy discrimination in housing through executive action, by "a stroke of the pen."

20) **Plans for Progress.** Plans for Progress was a program developed by the President's Committee on Equal Employment to provide training and employment for blacks.

21) *The Guns of August.* (New York: Macmillan, 1962.) A study of the political, military, and diplomatic background of World War I by Barbara Tuchman.

22) **Major Anderson.** U-2 pilot Major Rudolph Anderson, Jr., was reported missing and presumed shot down during a reconnaissance flight over Cuba during the missile crisis. Major Anderson was the first to have photographed missile installations in Cuba.

23) **the Commerce Clause.** Prior to passage of the Civil Rights Act of 1964, the federal government relied primarily on the Commerce Clause—the constitutional stipulation giving primacy to the federal government in matters concerning interstate commerce—to protect individual civil rights.

24) **Title Two.** In matters concerning public accommodations, Title Two of the Civil Rights Act of 1964 made discrimination on the basis of race, color, creed, or national origin a federal offense.

25) **that conversation.** On April 25, 1963, Robert Kennedy, along with Burke Marshall, met with Governor George C. Wallace. At the Governor's request, the conversation was taped.

26) **these Negro students.** Vivian Malone and James A. Hood were the first black students to enroll at the University of Alabama.

27) **that meeting ... in New York City.** The stormy May 24, 1963, meeting with James Baldwin and other black activists and leaders is discussed later.

28) **the February [1963] legislation.** The February 1963 proposals called for, among other items, reforms in existing voting legislation. The June civil rights bill included proposals for equal accommodations in public facilities, fair employment programs, the establishment of the Community Relations Service, authority for the Justice Department to initiate school desegregation suits, and a provision enabling the federal government to withhold funds from discriminatory programs and activities.

29) **the literacy bill.** In the spring of 1962 a southern filibuster killed an administration bill exempting voters with a sixth-grade education from literacy tests.

30) **bill which the subcommittee reported out.** A subcommittee of the House Judiciary Committee reported out a liberal version of the administration's proposed civil rights bill, a version that won the support both of civil rights groups who favored stronger legislation, and southern Congressmen who hoped to defeat civil rights legislation altogether. The President worked out a compromise with the House leaders in late October 1963.

31) **Title Seven.** Title Seven of the Civil Rights Act of 1964 made discrimination in employment illegal for public agencies and institutions—federal, state, and local—and for all employers engaged in interstate commerce.

32) **reapportionment cases.** In a number of notable cases, including *Baker* v. *Carr,* the Supreme Court adopted the position that representation in state legislatures was a justiciable issue and that the courts could provide relief.

33) **four little girls were killed in a bombing.** On September 15, 1963, a bomb destroyed the Sixteenth Street Baptist Church in Birmingham, Alabama, killing four young black girls: Cynthia Wesley, Denise McNair, Carol Robertson, and Addie Mae Collins.

34) **those two Klansmen.** After a dramatic announcement from Governor George C. Wallace's office that "state investigators expect to break the Birmingham Church case within a few hours," police arrested three men, two of whom had strong Klan ties, and charged them only with possession of dynamite without a permit, a misdemeanor punishable by six months in jail and a $100 fine.

35) **those three Freedom Riders.** The reference is apparently to the three murdered civil rights workers Andrew Goodman, James Chaney, and Michael Schwerner.

PART III

■

THE
THOUSAND-DAY
CRISIS

INTRODUCTION

I n the first of his authoritative accounts of how Americans choose their Presidents, Theodore H. White observed that from the outset of the 1960 presidential campaign John F. Kennedy repeatedly declared that "the Presidency is the key office."

"Yet to him," White wrote, "as to any other man, the Presidency could come in 1961 only as an entirely new experience. For there is no apprenticeship a man can serve for the Presidency, no book nor any guide to the creative powers of the individual who leads the greatest of the world's free people, no instructive analysis of an office bound and defined not so much by law as by the nature of men and the pressures of history."[1]

The remorseless force of events occurring around the world—from the Caribbean to Vietnam—that bore down on President Kennedy, and his own actions and responses to world events, dominate Part III. Of all the interviews Robert Kennedy gave for his oral history, these, conducted by John Bartlow Martin, were the most difficult, for they began on March 1, 1964, barely three months after the President's death. It was a somber time for Robert Kennedy. He was coping painfully with the loss of his brother, and, shorn of the power he'd held and the pivotal role he'd played, he was grappling with what he would do next—whether to withdraw into private life or remain somehow in the public arena.

Part III deals largely with the foreign crises that occupied so much of JFK's time in the White House. Although there are interesting diversions into events at home, most notably in Robert Kennedy's accounts of Edward M. Kennedy's election to the Senate in 1962 and of the steel crisis that same year, here we see Robert Kennedy not in his role as the country's chief law enforcement officer but as the President's closest foreign policy adviser.

From the outset Robert Kennedy was his brother's adjutant, but he did not get deeply involved in foreign policy until after the Bay of Pigs. Here he speaks feelingly about the lessons learned and about how President Kennedy overhauled his foreign policy decision-making process. Out of that painful, tragic blunder the Kennedy administration emerged wiser, more questioning, and more deliberate—and Robert Kennedy's own wry judgments stand as guideposts for any occupant of the Oval Office.

(There is a noticeable gap in questions about the Cuban missile crisis. Fortunately, however, Robert Kennedy provided a detailed account of the decisions made and the actions taken during those perilous days in his posthumously published book, *Thirteen Days*, which he had almost completed writing before he was assassinated in Los Angeles.[2])

For the most part, Kennedy's tone is that of a man recalling matter-of-factly the momentous occurrences in which he had been a vital participant. There are, however, particularly poignant sections in which he gives voice to his deep feelings about his brother and his presidency, to all the hopes and aspirations they had shared. It is something he rarely could do in speaking to persons outside his immediate circle of family and friends.

We leave him speaking irritably about his antagonism toward President Johnson—about the deterioration of their tenuous relationship—and ruminating rather wistfully about what the immediate future might hold for him. (He would resolve both predicaments in the months ahead, before being interviewed by Schlesinger and Lewis.) The final section of Part III, "On His Own," gives us a picture of a man struggling with events, with the meaning of his brother's death for the future of the country and for himself.

There is, through all these interviews but particularly in Part III, a decidedly current thread woven into the fabric of his answers: The problems that JFK faced—nuclear testing, getting Allied concurrence on policies, how to respond to Soviet superiority in conventional military forces, and whether it matters what kind of government another country has as long as it's anti-Communist—all these and many more have confronted President Ronald Reagan and will be there waiting for Mr. Reagan's successor.

The Kennedy brothers enjoy a stroll behind the nation's Capitol in June 1957.

JFK and RFK enjoy a quiet meal at Hickory Hill in 1957.

JFK, RFK, and Jacqueline relax on the *Victoria* on the water at Hyannisport, Massachusetts, in August 1959.

RFK and JFK confer in Jack's Senate office in May 1959.

RFK, JFK, and Ted Kennedy enjoy the sea at Palm Beach, Florida in April 1957.

Cabinet members and their families assemble for the January 21, 1961 swearing-in ceremony at the White House.

The new members of the Cabinet take their oaths in the presence of Jacqueline and John F. Kennedy on January 21, 1961.

RFK confers with Senator John F. Kennedy at the Rackets Committee hearing on
August 8, 1959.

Joseph P. Kennedy, Sr. celebrates his birthday with his family on September 8, 1962. [*Standing, left to right:* Ethel and Ted Kennedy, Jean Smith, President Kennedy, Eunice Shriver. *Sitting, left to right:* Steve Smith, Jacqueline Kennedy holding John, Joseph Sr., Pat Lawford, Robert and Rose Kennedy, Kathleen and Joan Kennedy. *In front, clockwise:* Joe and Caroline Kennedy, Stevie Smith, Teddy Jr. and David Kennedy, Maria Shriver, Courtney, Bobby, and Kerry Kennedy, Bobby and Timothy Shriver]

Members of the Kennedy family break into song in celebration of Joseph P. Kennedy, Sr.'s birthday in September 1962. [*From left:* Joan Kennedy, Eunice Shriver, Ethel Kennedy, Jean Smith, Robert and President Kennedy, and Steve Smith]

Joseph P. Kennedy, Sr. poses with some of his children and their spouses. [*From left:* Jacqueline, Ted, President Kennedy, Ethel, Joseph, and Robert Kennedy, Eunice Shriver, Steve and Jean Smith]

RFK talks with miners before the West Virginia primary in May 1960.

RFK campaigns in West Virginia before the May 1960 primary.

JFK and LBJ watch the liftoff of astronaut John Glenn into space on February 20, 1962.

On October 29, 1962, LBJ and RFK studiously work during a meeting of the ExComm (Executive Committee of the National Security Council).

JFK addresses recipients of the "Young Americans for Bravery" medals at the White House award ceremony on May 7, 1963. RFK and J. Edgar Hoover observe the proceedings.

Robert and Ethel arrive in Bangkok, Thailand, in February 1962.

After a month-long, round-the-world
goodwill tour, RFK confers with JFK
and LBJ at the White House on
February 28, 1962.

RFK greets his brother's children,
John and Caroline, at the White House in
October 1963.

The Kennedys arrive in Hyannisport for a weekend visit on August 3, 1963. RFK poses with his son David in the foreground.

RFK poses with his children in Hyannisport. [*From left:* David, Kerry, Michael, Courtney, and Bobby]

RFK addresses a civil rights rally outside the Department of Justice in June 1963.

RFK takes a break during the 1960 West Virginia primary campaign.

INTERVIEWS WITH
JOHN BARTLOW MARTIN

■

MARCH 1, 1964, McLEAN, VIRGINIA, APRIL 13, APRIL 30, AND MAY 14, 1964, NEW YORK

INITIATION BY FIRE:
THE BAY OF PIGS AND ITS AFTERMATH

MARTIN: I propose we cover the period roughly from the middle of April to the 4th of July, 1961. This includes the Bay of Pigs, the Khrushchev summit meeting, and the beginning of the civil rights conflict in the South.

KENNEDY: Just before the Berlin crisis?

MARTIN: That's right. The Berlin crisis was in the summer. The [Berlin] Wall went up in August. Let's start with the Bay of Pigs. When did you first get involved in it?

KENNEDY: In January [1961] I went to a briefing by [General Lyman] Lemnitzer at the State Department, which Dean Rusk attended, in which there was a discussion about the possible vulnerabilities in Cuba. I remember there was a discussion of the Isle of Pines— whether a landing could take place on the Isle of Pines or whether you could foment a revolution in the Isle of Pines.[3] I think it was a Saturday morning and lasted for a couple of hours. That was my only contact with it. I don't know quite how I got into that, but I attended that meeting.

MARTIN: That was in January. At that time, did you know there were Cubans being trained by the United States, in the United States and in Central America? Was this discussed? Or do you recall?

KENNEDY: I don't recall, but I must have known it. I don't know when I learned it but I suppose I must have known of it.

MARTIN: When did you get involved in the thing?

KENNEDY: About a week before the Bay of Pigs, the President called and said, "I want to have somebody from CIA brief you on a matter." Then Dick Bissell [the CIA's Deputy Director of Plans] called me and said, "The President wants me to come over to see you." He came over one afternoon.

MARTIN: This was about a week before the actual invasion?

KENNEDY: Yes.

MARTIN: The invasion took place on April 15. During the time before that, the thing was beginning to leak in the newspapers, if you recall. Castro issued a call to arms on April 7. What did Bissell tell you?

KENNEDY: He told me about the fact that they were thinking of an invasion—or they were planning an invasion—and the invasion was scheduled to take place the following week. He outlined it to me and thought that there was a great chance of success and that they should go ahead with it. He was enthusiastic about it. He said—this was a very important factor in my mind and, I think, in the President's—he said it really can't be a failure, because once they land on the beach, even if as a military force they don't win, they can always stay in Cuba and be guerrillas. They'll cause Castro so much difficulty. It'll be a very important factor in bringing about his downfall. [Bissell] said this was guerrilla territory and that they'd all been trained for guerrilla action. This was a natural place to have a landing. Obviously, there was a chance they'd be overcome by the military forces of Castro; but even if that happened as a military action, they could easily become guerrillas and fight in that area and also take to the mountains. These [men] were very well trained, and that would be a very important factor.

MARTIN: Was he talking about the Bay of Pigs as such?

KENNEDY: Yes.

MARTIN: Did you raise any questions or have any doubts about it at that time?

KENNEDY: Not really, no.

MARTIN: Did you discuss it with the President after this?

KENNEDY: I discussed it with him, and then I went to a meeting the following Monday or Tuesday.

MARTIN: Can you recall your discussion with him?

KENNEDY: I can tell you generally about my feelings and what the discussions were during that period of time.

The President was making a final decision. At that time, there had been a Marine colonel who had been sent down to Nicaragua to talk to the military forces of the Cubans, with instructions from the President personally, so that they would understand that there were going to be no military forces of the United States used. It was clearly understood in all the instructions that there weren't going to be any military forces of the United States. But the President was concerned that they'd think, once they started in this, that the military forces of this country would be used. So he sent a special emissary. He also sent a fellow down to give an outside assessment of their ability to perform effectively if they were landed in Cuba. This Marine colonel came back and gave a briefing and also wrote a memorandum, which I think was the most instrumental paper in convincing the President to go ahead.

[This colonel] had been very highly decorated, had fought at Tarawa [in World War II], and was a very well-thought-of military officer. He said he had never seen such an effective military force, that they had the fighting power, the techniques, and the skills. He recommended very forcefully that they go ahead with the landing. Allen Dulles, who had participated, of course, in the Guatemala situation, said that the chances for success in this were far greater than in Guatemala.[4] Secretary McNamara was in favor of it, Secretary Rusk was in favor of it, and the Joint Chiefs of Staff were in favor of it.

I thought that it sounded like a successful operation and that we should go ahead with it. What convinced me for the most part—I suppose there were a number of factors—but what always stuck in my mind was the fact that, even if they were landed, nothing could be lost, because they could become guerrillas. They could take to the swamps and take to the mountains. The other [factor] was that Allen Dulles, who had been through these things, was enthusiastic for it. Dick Bissell, who had a good record, was enthusiastic for it. All the military people were enthusiastic for it. I learned later that William Fulbright had raised a question about it. But then I also subsequently learned that he had two meetings on it. In the first one, he raised some very serious questions about it. At the second meeting, after he received a more detailed briefing by the military and by others, he said he hadn't understood it at the first meeting. It had far more factors in favor of it than he had considered at the first meeting.

MARTIN: You said that Fulbright had a meeting on it. Did you mean to say he participated in one or two of the meetings?

KENNEDY: I wasn't there. That was before I got into it.

The one person who was strongly against it was Arthur Schlesinger. So Arthur Schlesinger came to my house sometime that week. I can remember having a conversation with him in which he said that he was opposed to it. I said that I thought everybody had made up their minds and that he was performing a disservice to bring it back to the President. I remember telling him [that] once the President had made up his mind—once it seemed to have gone this far—we should all make efforts to support him. And he [Schlesinger] should remain quiet.

The President didn't have to decide finally on this until the end of the week. I went down to speak at the Scripps Howard papers in Williamsburg. He called me from his house in the country in Virginia on Saturday and said that he was going ahead with it. Did I have any reservations? I said that I thought we should go on. I guess that was Saturday night, maybe Sunday night.

Then Monday morning I received a telephone call about ten o'clock from him, right at the end of my speech. They had landed. It wasn't going well. And he asked me to come back to Washington right away.

MARTIN: Yes. What did you do?

KENNEDY: He said, "I don't think it's going as well as it should." So I got in a plane and flew back. I spent most of the next three or four days at the White House. All of the background and the facts on Bay of Pigs is in our report.

MARTIN: Yes. We don't need to go into that here, but I think we do want to go into the President's reactions and your conversations with him. That might not be in the report.

KENNEDY: The other thing is that we conducted our interviews on tape. There were more detailed reports on all of these things. Somebody should try to put all that stuff together. I just want to make a note of that so somebody perhaps can look at that. The interviews were conducted on tape, and I think the tapes were kept.

MARTIN: You're talking about the post-mortem interviews that you conducted?

KENNEDY: Yes.

MARTIN: At the Pentagon? The CIA, primarily?

KENNEDY: At the Pentagon, I think. The report does it pretty well. It's reserved and had to have the concurrence of General [Maxwell] Taylor, Allen Dulles, [Chief of Naval Operations, Admiral] Arleigh Burke, and me. It was approved by all four. But its sharpness had to be leveled off on some occasions. I was far more critical, for instance, of the military than perhaps Maxwell Taylor wanted to be—although there is some sharp criticism of the military in the full report.

MARTIN: What we should try to center in on here is the President—his reactions—and your conversations with him that would not appear in the tapes: your relationship with him and his attitude toward the disaster while it was developing.

KENNEDY: The one thing that really struck us both was the failure of communications. It was so difficult to find out exactly what was going on. We knew that it wasn't going well, but the reports that came in were twelve or eighteen or twenty-four hours late. We'd receive the information that the situation was becoming more critical—and that might have been twelve hours before. Well, what was the situation at the present time? For instance, if we'd sent in airplanes to help, if we went in and dropped supplies, was it already too late to be of any assistance? That's what plagued us during that seventy-two-hour period. The lack of communications, the lack of intelligence information, was what was particularly disturbing.

Obviously, the President was very upset that it was going badly.

MARTIN: Whose responsibility was it?

KENNEDY: What do you mean, whose responsibility?

MARTIN: To get intelligence and keep communications.

KENNEDY: I don't think that part was planned well.

MARTIN: I see. Who should have been planning it?

KENNEDY: It's a covert operation, so it's more difficult. The fleet was off the coast of Cuba; but they didn't have any Americans on the beach, and there weren't any Americans flying over the beach the first twenty-four or thirty-six hours. Then the President authorized them to fly over the beach to see what was going on—so he would know. But by the time they communicated up here, there was a delay. So that was difficult. That's why we made a real effort afterward to improve the communications in any kind of an operation, and why, at the time of the second Cuba [the missile crisis], a whole different system was established throughout the world dealing with communications.

MARTIN: I remember that. What were the President's reactions during these four days?

KENNEDY: It was really a question of what we could do in order to save the situation. I remember Secretary Rusk was strongly against sending in any airplanes. The President had made a public announcement that no military forces of the United States would be used. Therefore, he'd be going back on his word if American forces were, in fact, used in order to save it.

MARTIN: Yes, he said that flatly and publicly before the invasion.

KENNEDY: So there was that problem. The other argument against doing anything—sending in American forces—was that we didn't know whether, in fact, airplanes going in there or bombers going in there would save the situation. Again, we didn't have enough intelligence information to know that. The third factor was that we didn't know if—and this was a very important factor—the Russians would move on Berlin.

If we used American forces, it would have to be mostly in planes at that time, because there weren't enough American military forces in the area prepared to land. And all you'd do—instead of having them destroyed in seventy-two hours, they would be destroyed in six or seven days. You would have used American military forces and still not have saved the situation. Then there was the risk that the Russians would move in Berlin while we moved in the Bay of Pigs and moved ineffectively.

MARTIN: Khrushchev said at the time, publicly, that Cuba is not alone.

KENNEDY: Yes. I don't think we often thought that he'd do anything in Cuba or that there was a great deal he could do. But we did think there was a great risk that he'd move and make it more difficult in Laos, make it more difficult in Vietnam, make it more difficult in Berlin—that he couldn't just stand by. The other thing, as I say, was we didn't even know whether it would be effective. So we sat around at these meetings—it was a most frustrating period—we sat around at the meetings without having any information and without really knowing what we could do that would be effective.

Finally, the President permitted—one night or the next morning—some planes to fly over the beach for an hour and provide air cover. At that time, there were some other Cuban planes [of the invasion force] that were supposed to come in and land at the airport that they'd captured at the Bay of Pigs. But the hour that the American planes flew over the beach was different from the time that the Cuban planes came in to land, and the result was they were gone by the time the Cuban planes came in. The Cuban planes were shot down. In fact, we found out later that, despite the President's orders that no American forces would be used, the first two people who landed in the Bay of Pigs were Americans. The CIA sent them in. I think that there's a book that's coming out now on the Bay of Pigs which was written by the leadership of the Bay of Pigs—[Eneido] Oliva, [Roberto] San Roman, Enrico Williams, and [Manuel] Artime, the four of them—that will indicate that some of the [American] officers down in Nicaragua, in Central America, had said even if the President attempted to call off the invasion of the Bay of Pigs that they would make arrangements with the Cubans [the invasion force] to turn over their arms and be captured—and that they should go ahead with the invasion in any case. Virtually treason!

The President was strongly in favor of helping in some way, but nobody could think of any way that we could help. So we went through meeting after meeting, receiving the bad news: First this part was wiped out; then the second part was wiped out. The other great problem, of course, was they were running out of ammunition. We kept getting these reports, as they were running out of ammunition, that they couldn't fight. It was a very sad, frustrating, unhappy time.

I would think that, of all the time that I saw the President during this period, the most unhappy time was the end of the week. During this period we were busy, but during the end of the week he was very upset. You know, we'd been through a lot of things together. And he was just more upset this time than he was any other.

MARTIN: As I recall it, he asked you to inquire into the reasons for the failure.

KENNEDY: The other point which kept coming back to us was why they didn't become guerrillas. Because they couldn't become guerrillas! It turned out that, when they talked about this guerrilla territory, it was guerrilla territory back in 1890. Now, it was a swamp. And Castro used to fly over in his helicopter himself and pick out these fellows who were in the swamps—and just shoot them. We sent some destroyers and some other ships in there to take some of them off. One of the destroyers almost got sunk because they weren't permitted to fire back. They'd come in, some of them with great bravery, right along the side of the beach to pick these fellows off, to try to get them off the beach and save their lives. But they couldn't fire back. Of course, by that time Castro's bigger guns had moved in, so it was a dangerous operation. Some of them escaped up along the beach. At night we'd send boats in to try to take them off. We rescued a number of them. But there were harrowing stories about Castro and the other helicopters going along—these fellows just reaching the beach, just coming out of the swamp, being shot. We were all very, very impressed, then and after making our investigation, with the great bravery with which these men fought, and their tenacity and dedication.

I was getting the reports in as quickly as possible from the beach— the cries and calls for more ammunition. The last report that I received was from Pepe San Roman, saying, "We fired our last shell. We're all taking to the swamp." It was a very sad, difficult period of time.

It was saved to a large extent—first, by all the things that we learned in this operation, and secondly, that we were able to get the men out. If all of these men, who were the cream and backbone of Cuba, had perished in jail or been shot, that would have weighed very, very heavily on everybody's conscience. But the fact that we were all able to go through that—there was some loss of life—and learn as much as was learned really revolutionized, drastically altered the President's approach to government.

I think that the Bay of Pigs might have been the best thing that happened to the administration.

MARTIN: When you say it drastically altered the President's approach to government, what do you mean?

KENNEDY: Let me see what I can say about that. The President had been used to dealing with people and having them know what they were talking about. He came into government as the successor to President Eisenhower, who was a great general, a great military figure. He came into the presidency and succeeded him. He retained the same people in all these key positions whom President Eisenhower had. Allen Dulles was there, Lemnitzer was there, the same Joint Chiefs of Staff. He didn't attempt to move any of those people out. And these were the people who were around this table when they were making the decisions. It was on their recommendations and suggestions and their intelligence information—what they found the situation to be on *their* homework—that he based his decision.

Now, he took the responsibility, which was the right thing to do. But it was based on people he had confidence in, not because he had known them himself but just because they had been there. They had had the experience; they had had the background; they were evidently trusted by his predecessor. So he thought that he could trust them. When they said this was much more apt to succeed than Guatemala, when the military looked it over and said it was a good plan, then he went ahead. The second thing was the repercussion of Eisenhower having trained these people in Central America and then bringing them back when the military said that this could be a successful plan and the intelligence people said it could be a successful plan. Allen Dulles said it would be much more effective than Guatemala. Then you'd have to bring all these Cubans back and say that we're not going to do it. Everybody said this was a great plan. It would have been sure of success.

They said afterward it was because President Kennedy was such an amateur that he went ahead. Well, if he hadn't gone ahead with it, everybody would have said it showed that he had no courage. Eisenhower trained these people; it was Eisenhower's plan; Eisenhower's people all said it would succeed—and we turned it down. Well, what ultimately came out of this was that he never substituted anybody else's judgment for his own. The second thing is that, whenever a problem or question came up, he went into the facts minutely.

MARTIN: First?

KENNEDY: Study it, yes. And everybody had to. I remember shortly afterward [the Joint Chiefs] were suggesting we send troops into Laos. I think we would have sent troops into Laos—large numbers of American troops into Laos—if it hadn't been for Cuba. Because everybody was in favor at the time, initially, of sending troops into Laos.

I remember two things that struck me at the meeting on Laos. One thing was [the Joint Chiefs of Staff] said, "We'll send troops in." The plan was: Send these men in, we'll get control of this territory, and we'll be in good shape.

[JFK] said, "Well, first, how will they get in there?"

Then they rushed around: "They're going to land at these two airports."

So he said, "How many can land at the airports?"

"If you have perfect conditions, you can land a thousand men a day."

So he said, "How many troops of the Communists are in the surrounding area?"

They said, "We guess three thousand."

"How long will it take them to bring up four?"

"They can bring up five or eight thousand, six thousand, in four more days."

So he said, "What's going to happen if on the third day you've landed three thousand—and then they bomb the airport. And then they bring up five or six thousand more! What's going to happen? Or if you land two thousand—and then they bomb the airport?"

MARTIN: Gets foggy here, right?

KENNEDY: Right, foggy. Well, then the answer was you dropped a bomb on Hanoi—and you start using atomic weapons! Which was never planned out for him in the initial plan or drawn up for him.

The second thing, [the Army representatives] started going into the diseases. He talked about the fact that you'd have thirty-five or forty percent casualties from a particular disease. I don't know whether it was jaundice—not jaundice but yellow fever. The President had them look into it and found out they'd never had a case of that kind of disease in Laos. Evidently he got the disease mixed up with another kind of disease. In other words, he just didn't know. The factual information that they presented to the President was not correct. But after Cuba he'd follow— What is it Francis Bacon said? "A wise interrogation is half the knowledge." He continuously prodded and probed to bring out all the facts. When somebody came in and made a particular recommendation—no matter what their background or what their title was—he made an effort to find out himself and required that from all of his people. It also made a great impression on everybody else, like Bob McNamara. McNamara was enthusiastically in favor of the Bay of Pigs, and he had gotten into the same position because he had accepted the military's point of view.

MARTIN: Being a layman, neither of them had gone behind the judgment of the military to the facts, as henceforward they did. Now isn't it true, Bob, with the world being as complex as it is and so many things coming to the President, as they must, that he cannot personally go behind the judgments and into the facts in every situation? Isn't this perhaps one reason why, thereafter, he brought you more centrally into major questions of this sort, to go behind the facts for him?

KENNEDY: I think so. I think that's true.

MARTIN: Did this alter your own relationship with him and with the government?

KENNEDY: I then became involved on every major and all the international questions.

MARTIN: For this reason?

KENNEDY: I think probably so.

MARTIN: Were there other reasons?

KENNEDY: I think it was probably just to have somebody to discuss some of these matters with.

MARTIN: Somebody he'd have absolute confidence in? In any case, you did come in and were very close from there on, on everything that was crucial.

KENNEDY: I was thinking of the time the Panama dispute arose.[5] I was thinking the other day that it's really the worst matter involving an international problem that I have not been in on.

There were a number of other changes made. The other impression I had from watching this develop—almost immediately the impression I had—was that there had to be one person in charge of some of these matters to pull things together. So that's when we started setting up task forces to deal with the particular problems, like Laos. As I remember, we had Ros Gilpatric and then Paul Nitze do some work on that.

What was happening was that the government, being so large and diffuse—all in various agencies, with the CIA having their responsibility, the military having their responsibility, AID [Agency for International Development] and all the rest—what you needed was a central body to pull them all together. This was too much for the President to do continuously. Somebody had to do it on his behalf, because he couldn't be expected to do it on every occasion. What had happened, what was really happening, was that everybody went their own way and there wasn't any central person or central body pulling them all together. I felt strongly about that. After we made our study in Cuba, we made some recommendations along those lines, recommendations which were not accepted by the State Department because they saw their losing a little bit of power and authority.

Those recommendations are in our report. They didn't accept them, but we were able to get them—at least to a large extent—accepted de facto. In the first place, the President started appointing individuals to head up task forces to bring everything together and then to make a report to him jointly. Not that that one person would be the only spokesman for policy, but he would have the responsibility of pulling everything together and coming up with some recommendations to the President. We did it in Southeast Asia. Right at the time when the [Taylor] group was sent to Southeast Asia, I was going to do it for him for a while—and then I thought it would be much better to have Bob McNamara or somebody appoint someone.

Let's see what else. The other thing that was changed drastically was the operation in the White House. Everybody was reporting to the President individually, and I thought that that needed to be pulled together so that you had some centralization.

MARTIN: How was this done?

KENNEDY: That was done mostly by giving more authority to Mac Bundy. We had people in turn report to him or at least receive clearance before they went up and saw the President. So that everybody knew what their responsibility was.

MARTIN: These were matters involving national security?

KENNEDY: That's right. Dick Goodwin would be in; Mike Feldman would be in; Mac Bundy would be in. The President would talk to two or three different people about the same problem, so everybody would be working on it. In the meantime, nobody would be working on this other difficulty. So what was needed was to centralize the authority in the White House and have somebody reporting directly to the President. If someone else were reporting to the President, that the one person—namely, Mac Bundy—would know about it. Mac Bundy would have his area of responsibility; Kenny O'Donnell would have his; Pierre Salinger would have his.

[O'Donnell] had the appointments—he had that quite clearly before. I think the major problem was in the foreign policy area, and there was some overlapping with Ted Sorensen and Mike Feldman.

MARTIN: What was the area of responsibility of Ted Sorensen?

KENNEDY: He did mostly domestic matters.

MARTIN: I see.

KENNEDY: But after the Bay of Pigs he was brought in on more occasions on foreign policy matters. The two of us were being brought in because [JFK] had worked with both of us before. So Ted Sorensen was brought in frequently on important foreign policy matters. Sorensen's primary responsibility was domestic matters, but it was like me: My primary responsibility was domestic matters—I mean, the Department of Justice—but when the final decision or decisions were going to be made on some foreign policy matters which had an important effect, we would be brought in just to give our views or raise questions.

MARTIN: Or ask the hard questions?

KENNEDY: Yes. It wasn't the day-to-day operation of foreign policy for either one of us. It was just on Berlin or Laos or Vietnam or Cuba. Then, as I'll explain later, there were some committees established, which I felt were important, to try to coordinate the activities of the federal government in this area and also to focus attention on problems that were going to arise in the future.

　　In the past what we were doing was concentrating on crises as they arose. There wasn't any place where you anticipated or prepared yourself for some crises. There was a crisis room established at the State Department, but that was just dealing with the problems that came to the attention of the State Department.

MARTIN: Was that Steve Smith's?

KENNEDY: Steve Smith was down there. But that wasn't an effective operation. . . . They didn't work with Defense and CIA and AID and all the rest as they should have. So that wasn't very effective. We had suggested—Maxwell Taylor and I—that a unit be set up that would anticipate what was going to go on. Well, as I say, the State Department—Dean Rusk—opposed that. But what did happen was a presidential check-sheet was given to the President every day—a checklist—and that would very effectively list the crises and the problems. That arose, again, out of the Bay of Pigs, out of the Cuban problem, and out of our own investigation. On November 22 [1963] they issued one—of course this is the highest secret; it has the highest classification in the government, but this is the first President who had used it or had put this into effect—they issued one on November 22 in which they put the poem that the President recited right after the missile crisis:

> Bullfight critics ranked in rows
> Crowd the enormous plaza full,
> But only one there is who knows,
> And he's the man who fights the bull.

MARTIN: Also, at the President's request, as I recall it, you did a lot of interviewing and checking over at the CIA and the Pentagon. This report that you've spoken of came out as a result of that. It didn't come out publicly, but I mean it was written as a result of that. Is that right?

KENNEDY: Yes.

MARTIN: Now, there were changes, personnel changes: Allen Dulles left the CIA—

KENNEDY: And Dick Bissell left the CIA.

MARTIN: —because of the Bay of Pigs?

KENNEDY: Yes, I think basically because of the Bay of Pigs. Allen Dulles handled himself awfully well, with a great deal of dignity, and never attempted to shift the blame. The President was very fond of him, as I was. Dick Bissell's greatest mistake in my judgment was the fact that he came in and repeatedly said that these people could become guerrillas when there wasn't any chance of them becoming guerrillas. And, as we found out later on, they never had been told they were to become guerrillas, and there was no territory for them to become guerrillas. That's an awfully important factor. You can say you think there's going to be an uprising in the area or you think that troops are going to be slow in getting there and all the rest of it, but when you can't tell about that—you at least could tell whether this is guerrilla territory. And to say that they've been trained, they're ready to become guerrillas, and then we find out nobody had ever told any of these people that they were to become guerrillas—

MARTIN: That's a disaster.

KENNEDY: That's pretty bad. We asked them about that—these soldiers—when we interrogated them, and we asked the Americans who'd trained them. [The Americans] said, if they'd told them they could become guerrillas, then they'd immediately think that they should fall back and become guerrillas and wouldn't continue to fight. So they never told them about that. All that should have been explained to the President. I thought that was unforgivable. Now, Dick Bissell developed the U-2 [reconnaissance plane], and he also was largely responsible for the beginning of the development of this new plane [the SR-71 high-altitude surveillance plane]. So he deserves a great deal of credit and thanks from the American people. But he did make a bad mistake.

MARTIN: He was wrong on this one. Why was [John] McCone chosen to succeed Dulles?

KENNEDY: Well, the President spoke to me about becoming head of CIA. I said I didn't want to become head of the CIA. I thought it was a bad idea to be head of CIA, because I was a Democrat and his brother. So we looked around for other people, and the first person we centered on was the man who became the head of AID.

MARTIN: Fowler Hamilton became head of AID.

KENNEDY: It centered on Fowler Hamilton. I spoke to him tentatively about becoming head of CIA. Everybody had spoken well of him and thought that he had gotten very high marks. Then we found in papers that had been uncovered—he'd worked in the Second World War in some capacity—in a code that had been broken in the Second World War, that there was a Russian spy, somebody working in the same department as he, who was delivering important information to the Communists. He was close enough to Fowler Hamilton that at least one person on the British side had thought that the information had come from Fowler Hamilton. Actually, investigating and looking into it deeply, I was convinced that it had not. He wasn't involved at all. But the British had the information. If there were somebody over there in an important position who thought so and they had to work closely together, it might even infect the relationship.

MARTIN: How did you get to McCone?

KENNEDY: Then we asked, what are we going to do with Fowler Hamilton? We had AID at that time, which wasn't going very well. So I called up Fowler Hamilton, had him in my office, and asked him if he would become head of AID. He agreed to accept that and said he'd rather have that. That got us through a rather sticky point.

I don't know who suggested John McCone originally. Maybe [Washington Senator] Scoop Jackson did. But in any case I remember I called him up and asked him to come in. Then I was called by the head of MIT [James R. Killian], who said he'd protest violently. (The committee that oversees the intelligence community [the President's Foreign Intelligence Advisory Board] is headed by Killian, and others—you know, Clark Clifford and some others—are on it. They were averse to John McCone. John McCone had made a lot of enemies.) [Killian] said he was going to put out a report against John McCone. I had to call him and had a long conversation with him. Then I think I met him down here in Washington. We finally got it straightened out, and he agreed. I think he and McCone talked, and finally it was worked out. So there wasn't any fuss about it. He's got rather a strong personality.

MARTIN: What were the qualities you were looking for? An administrator?

KENNEDY: A good administrator. I think it helped that he was a Republican, somebody whom the intelligence community generally would have confidence in; someone whose name and prestige and position would establish confidence in the CIA—which had been badly shaken. Someone, of course, who could get along with the President; someone who would be loyal to the President. There were those who were against John McCone, saying that he'd be so close to Congress that he wouldn't be loyal to the President. We had some difficulties, as a matter of fact, with him in February of 1963, right after the Bay of Pigs, when he had a very bitter, mean argument with Bob McNamara.

MARTIN: After the second Cuba [the missile crisis]?

KENNEDY: After the second Cuba.

MARTIN: Not the Bay of Pigs?

KENNEDY: The second Cuba.

MARTIN: How did Maxwell Taylor get—

KENNEDY: I don't know who suggested he come down originally, but he came down. He was up in New York and he came down. The President liked his book very much—*The Uncertain Trumpet.*

When he came down, he worked with me—or I worked with him—for three months, and we used to—

MARTIN: After the Bay of Pigs?

KENNEDY: After the Bay of Pigs. We used to have sessions from about nine o'clock in the morning to five o'clock in the afternoon. Then I would go back to the Department of Justice and work on Department of Justice affairs until about nine-thirty or ten.

MARTIN: But you were working with Taylor at the Pentagon and CIA?

KENNEDY: Yes. I was really terribly impressed with him—his intellectual ability, his judgment, his ideas. He was, with Bob McNamara, the most effective person that I had met. Looking back over the past three years, I would say that the two people who have made the greatest difference as far as the government is concerned are Bob McNamara and Maxwell Taylor. I was terrifically taken with him. So the President brought him on as his military adviser.

MARTIN: Did the military establishment, the Joint Chiefs, resist the idea of having such a person?

KENNEDY: I think to some extent there was resistance at the beginning. And he was slightly concerned about taking the job.

MARTIN: Taylor was?

KENNEDY: Yes. About the fact that he was a military man and they might feel that they were being bypassed. Bob McNamara did a lot to smooth it out. This was a very tough decision for him, because in the first place, he was making three or four times the amount of money. He had gotten an apartment up there, his wife liked New York, and he had felt that he was out of military life and out of Washington. But I think he was so taken with the President, and the President needed him so badly, and then we had developed some ideas as to how things could be handled in the government when we worked together. I thought he was enthusiastic about that.

Their philosophies about the growth of conventional forces (for instance, out of our Bay of Pigs investigation, we increased the number of Special Services men tremendously, four or five times in number) and what the President was doing about the Army, what he was doing about facing up to limited wars and not having all the emphasis on atomic firepower—this greatly appealed to [Taylor]. And, as I say, he just admired and liked the President.

MARTIN: The whole idea of redesigning the nuclear strategy to avoid reliance on massive retaliation was given a big forward push by the lessons of the Bay of Pigs?

KENNEDY: Yes, and by Maxwell Taylor's own thoughts. Of course, the theme Maxwell Taylor developed had been used by the President in the campaign. It made so much sense. The President understood it made sense. That's why Maxwell Taylor came over to the White House. It was sensitive, but every decision that the President made on foreign policy was cleared through Maxwell Taylor.

MARTIN: It was?

KENNEDY: Yes. He was in, seeing the President continuously. Then we formed some committees that dealt with some of these problems. A number of committees.

MARTIN: For example?

KENNEDY: We formed a Counterinsurgency Committee, of which he was the chairman and I was a member. We had the head of AID, the head of CIA, and Ros Gilpatric representing the Defense Department. This was the kind of committee that we wanted, bringing together all the governmental agencies.

We started out with twelve or fifteen countries. The committee is still in existence; we meet once a week and receive no publicity. It deals with insurgency problems in particular parts of the world. I think it's generally accepted that it was responsible for the preservation of the democratic system in Venezuela.[6] If it hadn't been for the work that was done by this committee and what flowed out of it, the police work, then Venezuela would have been taken over by the Communists. Also, the Ambassador from Colombia was up here, and he said that the methods that were introduced in Colombia, the police methods, worked. The other efforts that had been made had been very instrumental in bringing about relative stability to that country, so I think the Counterinsurgency Committee—

MARTIN: Is that how you refer to it—just for the record?

KENNEDY: Yes, CI. We set up a school on insurgency . . . which the top officials—ambassadors, military aides, heads of AID programs, heads of USIS [United States Information Service], teams of various countries—attended for a four-week course (originally a five-week, now a four-week course). The President made it clear he didn't want to have this course just for those who had nothing better to do. These are policy makers. I think the school's been very effective. We also established the police academy in Panama which trained police from Central and South America. We established—it's just finished its first course here—a police academy in Washington which takes heads of police departments from all over the world.

MARTIN: Yes, I remember when I was in the Dominican Republic in the spring of '62, the government lost control of the streets to the Communists. I couldn't get any help out of IAD [Inter-American Defense Board] or anywhere else to get some American policemen down there to train the Dominican police. I finally got the help only by going to the President while I was up here and asking him for this help. I said, "All I need is two good men off of [William H.] Parker's Mexican squad." He told [Special Assistant Ralph] Dungan to tell you to get them for me, and we got them right away and we got the streets back. This was *ad hoc*. What you're describing is a structured thing that would have dealt with a situation like that.

KENNEDY: I called Parker and asked him, because, I guess, AID had spoken to him and he hadn't agreed to do it. We had a friendly relationship. The same in Venezuela: they sent three fellows down to Venezuela. It's incredible what just a few people can do.

MARTIN: It is. I know. I saw it. The Bay of Pigs was obviously a major turning point in many respects, as you say. Did it have an effect on the President personally?

KENNEDY: It did at the time. I think it made him more removed and tougher about some of these things than he had been prior to that time. Then, after a system was developed over a period of a year or so, I think he was more relaxed about it. But any time he was going to make a major decision which would commit American policy or American position or American men, he was damn well going to know where it was going to lead to, what the implications were.

MARTIN: [Hugh] Sidey makes two remarks in his book.[7] He says, at the time of the Bay of Pigs, that the President really didn't trust anybody completely but you, and also that the fun seemed to have gone to some extent out of being President. Do you think those two things are true?

KENNEDY: On the first one, I think that adversity draws people closer together. We had been through a lot of problems together. It was just more natural.

On the second, I think it was temporary. I used to ask him each week about how he enjoyed being President. During that period, we had a helluva tough time—not just rising out of the Bay of Pigs but Berlin, which I don't think people really understood generally around the country. The President felt strongly, and I did, that we were very close to war at the time. He went to Vienna, and in my judgment Khrushchev thought he was dealing with a rather weak figure, that he was dealing with a young figure who had perhaps no confidence, that he was dealing with a weak person because if he wasn't weak he wouldn't have gone through the Bay of Pigs. He didn't permit [a situation like the] Bay of Pigs at the time of Hungary,[8] and he felt that if you got into a problem like Cuba, you would have just wiped them all out and ended it. That didn't happen [at the Bay of Pigs], and so I think he thought he was dealing with a weak figure.

All this pressure then was on the President for the next six months. As I say, I used to ask him each week, and during that period of time he frequently would say, "If it wasn't for the Russians, there's no question it would be the best job in the world." After '60 through the finish of '61, he always used to say that he enjoyed being President.

"A VERY TOUGH YEAR": 1961

MARTIN: Sixty-one was a—

KENNEDY: Tough year. It was tougher than people think. It wasn't just the Bay of Pigs; '61 was often a very mean year because of Berlin, what to do about Berlin, and the fact, as I say, that the Russians thought they could kick [JFK] around.

At this time I began to have a relationship with a man by the name of Georgi Bolshakov. Most of the major matters dealing with the Soviet Union and the United States were discussed and arrangements were made between Georgi Bolshakov and myself. He was Khrushchev's representative, so we used to meet maybe once every two weeks. We used to go over all this: whether the United States would stand up. We went through Berlin. We were reasonably hopeful about what would happen on the inspection for nuclear weapons, because he had indicated to me in a meeting one Sunday morning that they would permit, I think, up to twenty inspection sites in Russia. Of course, when they got to Vienna, they wouldn't agree.

MARTIN: Who was this Bolshakov and how did you happen to get in touch with him?

KENNEDY: I think Frank Holeman of the New York [Daily] News put me in touch with him first. He had played some role in the last administration. I think he'd been the one who originally suggested Nixon's trip to the Soviet Union. I'm not quite sure about that. But Frank Holeman of the New York [Daily] News had met him frequently. Finally, he said that [Bolshakov] wanted to see me.

MARTIN: Was he attached to the Russian embassy?

KENNEDY: Yes, he was attached to the Russian embassy. I think he was their public relations man.

MARTIN: What did you discuss with him, Bob? What was your relationship with him?

KENNEDY: Any time that he had some message to give to the President (or Khrushchev had) or when the President had some message to give to Khrushchev, we went through Georgi Bolshakov. I don't know why they wanted to proceed in that fashion, but they didn't want to go through their Ambassador [Mikhail Menshikov], evidently.

MARTIN: "They" meaning the Russians?

KENNEDY: Yes. The Ambassador handled the regular routine matters, and he—Bolshakov—handled other things. I suppose I saw him on the average of once every couple of weeks.

MARTIN: What kind of messages were sent? What did they say?

KENNEDY: I met with him about all kinds of things. I met with him about whether the [summit] meeting should take place, whether the President wanted to meet with Khrushchev. I met with him about what they would discuss at the meeting. When they were concerned about Berlin, he would come to me and talk about that. . . . I can remember discussing the agenda, discussing the advantages and disadvantages of the meeting, the importance of their understanding that we were committed on Berlin, and the importance of trying to reach some conclusion, some determination about the control of nuclear weapons.

MARTIN: Also on the agenda was what? Laos?

KENNEDY: Yes, we got into the problem about Laos.

MARTIN: Cuba?

KENNEDY: Yes.

MARTIN: Testing?

KENNEDY: Yes. We discussed Laos, about trying to bring their forces under control in Laos.

Remember when we had the problem about Berlin, the particular incident where they drew up their tanks?[9] Remember that? They were in their tanks. I got in touch with Bolshakov and said the President would like them to take their tanks out of there in twenty-four hours. He said he'd speak to Khrushchev, and they took their tanks out in twenty-four hours. He delivered effectively when it was a matter that was important.

He asked me, on the other hand, to see if we would withdraw the troops from Laos. Remember when we sent troops into Thailand and [Laos], when the Communists moved on Laos? I can't give you the date of it.

MARTIN: That's all right.

KENNEDY: They said how important it was, so I told them—after talking to the President—that he would have the troops out of there in sixty days. Khrushchev sent back a message that it meant a great deal. Some of these crises which were building up and which were perhaps due to misunderstandings were discussed. There was an effort made to resolve them through these kinds of discussions. They wouldn't go through the Ambassador. And when the new Ambassador [Anatoly Dobrynin] came, he was upset about it. But Georgi Bolshakov used to tell me the Ambassador [Menshikov] was not delivering the true messages reflecting the true point of view. He said that's why, ultimately, we had the confrontation of Cuba: because Khrushchev really didn't understand the United States. And that was because the Ambassador wasn't giving accurate reports.

MARTIN: What about our Ambassador? Was he similarly bypassed in Moscow?

KENNEDY: I suppose he was.

MARTIN: At that time it was Llewellyn Thompson; later it was Foy Kohler. But at both ends there was an unofficial exchange going forward?

KENNEDY: Yes. The State Department was brought up. Unfortunately, stupidly, I didn't write many of the things down. I just delivered the messages verbally to my brother, and he'd act on them. I think sometimes he'd tell the State Department—and sometimes he didn't. I can just tell you generally what we discussed.

It's an awfully important matter. I can tell you, as I'm telling you now: I remember Laos, and I remember the troops, and I remember Berlin, and I remember the tanks, and I remember nuclear inspection. I remember I emphasized to [Bolshakov] continuously that we would go to war on Berlin. He kept saying that he was sending back that message. Then he said to me afterward he didn't think the Ambassador was sending messages back.

I didn't see him after they put the Wall up for a while because I was disgusted with the fact that they had done so. Finally, I saw him, three or four months later.

MARTIN: Where did you usually see him?

KENNEDY: Mostly at my office. He came back just before the second Cuba. I didn't see him then. He, at that time, was supposed to deliver a message to me to give to the President that the Russians definitely were never going to put any missiles in Cuba. After they put the missiles in Cuba, I sent [Kennedy friend, journalist] Charlie Bartlett, who was friendly with him, to see him, and I gave Charlie Bartlett a picture of the missiles. [Bolshakov] told him at that time that the message he had been sent over to deliver was to tell the President that the missiles weren't in Cuba. He said when Khrushchev told him that, [Soviet Foreign Minister Andrei] Gromyko was present—no, Gromyko wasn't present; [Deputy Premier Anastas] Mikoyan was present. Of course, [Bolshakov] said he'd been lied to. This really was embarrassing to the Russians—embarrassing to Khrushchev—because it was clear that [Khrushchev] had sent a message over to mislead the President, mislead the American government. This was in addition to the other Russian assurances that there weren't missiles in Cuba.

I remember when we gave a farewell luncheon—Charlie Bartlett did for Bolshakov—and the first assistant to Poland went into a long spiel about the missiles and the fact that he felt very strongly that it was a misunderstanding. I said after the luncheon to Georgi, as I was driving him downtown, that he didn't speak up and support a member of the Soviet Union. He said—he was very violent and strong—"He doesn't know what I know." I always thought he was very candid with me.

The State Department didn't like having him much because this involved circumventing them, I suppose. I always found him honest with me. But after the second Cuba, that method of operation was discontinued. (Pierre and I dealt a good deal at the second Cuba with the Russian Ambassador [Dobrynin] directly and delivered him some ultimatums, particularly the one that Saturday night.[10]) The Russians felt, because Georgi Bolshakov's position had been publicized, that he'd better be recalled. Nobody's really replaced him. And I've never resumed the same position that I had before. I did for a short period of time after the second Cuba, but then they delivered a message to me, a written message, which was so insulting that I said I wouldn't give it to the President and that if they wanted to deliver that kind of a message, they should go to the State Department and not talk to me again. I wouldn't take it. Then what they did was they wrote another message, which was far different, and communicated it somehow with the State Department. That really was the end of our relationship.

MARTIN: When the President came back from his European trip, he'd met Khrushchev, De Gaulle, Macmillan—a number of people. What did he say about them and what did he say about the trip?

KENNEDY: He liked Macmillan very much, and he grew to like him more and more.

MARTIN: Why? For what reason?

KENNEDY: He liked him personally. [Macmillan] had a great sense of humor and was very bright, quick. He had a very dry way of looking at things.

I think Macmillan mistrusted the idea of Jack being President. It rather appalled him because he was so young. I learned later that he also was rather concerned because he thought that Jack would think he was so old that he wasn't worthwhile talking to. [Macmillan] had had a rather good relationship with Eisenhower. So he had entered the relationship with a good deal of concern and trepidation. But they established a very close relationship. I got a letter from Macmillan— I called him when I was in London this last time [January 1964]— and he said that Jack Kennedy was the greatest public official he'd ever met in his life. Jackie wrote him a letter telling what the President thought of him, and I told her that. If you could just make a note of that, that would be of importance about that whole relationship.

De Gaulle, I think, he greatly admired, thought he was a rather impressive figure. They got along well. All in all, he could understand De Gaulle's position, although it was frustrating. He felt that what De Gaulle was doing as far as France was concerned made some sense for them and that in the long run he'd get by with some of these problems. He also felt that the deterioration in the relationship with France and the United States was natural after the Soviet Union got so badly hurt in the second Cuba.

MARTIN: But on this first trip, his first impression of De Gaulle was a good one?

KENNEDY: He liked him, yes.

MARTIN: What was his impression of Khrushchev?

KENNEDY: He thought he was a very tough, wily, unrelenting figure— and uncompromising. For that reason and his personality, discussion was not very effective with him. Where you could talk or have an exchange with people that you disagreed with—that was something the President did better than anybody else, really—he had a difficult time doing that with Khrushchev.

MARTIN: He did?

KENNEDY: The first day, I think Khrushchev felt that he was coming in there with this young figure and that he [Khrushchev] was going to control and dominate the conversation—and did. The second day, the President decided that he was going to make sure that before he left, [Khrushchev] was going to understand the United States' point of view. So he took issue with a lot of these problems. Chip Bohlen told me afterward that, in all of the international meetings that he had had with American officials and Russians, nobody has ever handled it as effectively as the President.

MARTIN: Did he feel that the trip to Europe had been a success when he came back?

KENNEDY: Yes, he was very pleased with it. He was concerned about where we were going with the Russians, and this concern showed up in his speech. He thought, coming back from there, that we were going to have a lot of trouble with Berlin and that we should be prepared for it. There was going to be very serious trouble. They reached an agreement on Laos. That's, again, one of the bases of my conversations with Bolshakov. Whenever the agreement appeared to be broken in Laos and we wanted them to do something, I'd get in touch with Georgi Bolshakov and say, "Would you mind putting pressure on the Laotians and get them back to the conference table and get them to stop screwing around?"

MARTIN: The President and Khrushchev did reach an agreement on Laos at Vienna. And you kept it on track through Bolshakov?

KENNEDY: Yes. We had an understanding before they went that this was one of the matters that they would discuss. This was one of the areas in which Khrushchev indicated to Bolshakov that he could reach an agreement. The other thing was this test ban, which didn't turn out. Somewhere between the time they talked to me here and the time the President got to Vienna, they changed their minds. I don't know what it was, but somehow they changed their minds, because [Bolshakov] indicated to me here quite clearly that they could reach an agreement on the test ban.

MARTIN: Berlin was the thing that they could not agree on?

KENNEDY: Yes. The President thought they'd have a lot of trouble.

MARTIN: And as it turned out, they did. We'll get to that. Did they discuss Cuba, the Bay of Pigs?

KENNEDY: Yes. I remember the President telling me that he'd said something to the effect that "we admit we made mistakes over here, are capable of making mistakes. The thing that impresses me about you, Mr. Khrushchev, is that you have never erred."

And Khrushchev said, "Yes, I admitted that we made mistakes in Stalin's time."

The President said to him, "You always admit that somebody else made a mistake."

MARTIN: Do you want to talk about Chester Bowles?

KENNEDY: He was in charge of appointments in the beginning. I thought he did a pretty good job. I think some of them weren't as good as they might have been.

MARTIN: Do you mean ambassadorial appointments?

KENNEDY: Yes, ambassadorial appointments—and he tried to get people placed in the State Department. I know there was a good deal of criticism about it. It seemed to me that some of them were very good. I think he looked around for some bright, intelligent people. He had a great problem as far as the President was concerned: a great tendency of never getting to the point and talking around a subject, all long sentences and big words. The result was that he irritated the President. Then he always seemed to have some dam up the Nikon River or something—he always had some plan, a particular point that he was getting across, and he failed to focus on the immediate problem. I think it's important to have somebody like that around— and I think the President felt it—because it stimulates ideas and thought. He had a lot of ideas, but he also had a bad habit of talking to the press too much. When he disagreed with the President, he talked to the press. He was rather a weeper. I had two exchanges with him at the time of Cuba. One, after Cuba failed—

MARTIN: Which Cuba are you talking about?

KENNEDY: First Cuba. He came up in a rather whiny voice and said that he wanted to make sure that everybody understood that he was against the Bay of Pigs.

MARTIN: Had he been consulted?

KENNEDY: I didn't know that. Perhaps he was, but I hadn't known it because he wasn't present at the meeting I was present at. But I told him at that time that everybody was going to stand by the President. We had an exchange. I said that was not the time to try to pull away from this.

MARTIN: Was he suggesting that he should say something publicly?

KENNEDY: No. He was around the White House, and you know, it was depressing enough as it was. We didn't need somebody coming in and making sure that everybody understood that they weren't in favor of this in the first place. Everybody rather resented it.

Second, he came in with a plan on Cuba—which was foolish—about a week or ten days later. It was filled with generalities. It didn't make sense. I said it didn't at a National Security Council meeting.

The President was going to move him out. [Bowles] leaked to the press that he was going to be moved out, and I think that held up the transfer. So the next time when the President was going to move him, [JFK] didn't tell anyone. I think Ted Sorensen and I were the only ones who knew it. He just did it. And Chester Bowles was moved before he could complain about it. The President made up his mind, once [Bowles] acted that way, that he wasn't going to have anything more to do with him. He was going to get him out of there. I think everything quieted down, because he really irritated him, irritated me, and irritated everybody.

MARTIN: Then he later sent him as Ambassador to India.

KENNEDY: That's right.

MARTIN: Why was that?

KENNEDY: I don't know. I think he probably felt that he'd do a good job there. There are roles which Chester Bowles can really play.

MARTIN: He was very successful there as Ambassador before, I guess.

KENNEDY: Yes. You see, he resigned from Congress. He came to talk to me about resigning from Congress, about the fact that he wanted to work with Jack. Well, in fact, he was going to get beaten in Congress—at least, John Bailey thought he was going to get beaten—and he didn't want to go through that race. I think he thought that if he resigned he could be Secretary of State. He tried to make a deal with me at that time, that if he resigned, we would appoint him as Secretary of State. I said that we couldn't do that. But he was a great pusher. During the November–December period after the election, he was also attempting to get his position. So the relationship with the President wasn't a very friendly one.

MARTIN: What about George Ball? How did he come into the State Department, into the administration? He came in very early, if you recall. I believe he was sworn in at the same time the Cabinet was.

KENNEDY: I don't remember him. I mean, I remember he worked in the campaign. I don't think the President knew him particularly well. I don't know who suggested him. Of course, [Ball] had that relationship with Adlai Stevenson.

MARTIN: Did he work closely with the President?

KENNEDY: No, not particularly. I think the President was impatient with him by the end.

MARTIN: Impatient?

KENNEDY: Yes. I think he felt that several assignments he gave him were not well handled. That was just my impression of what he said. I always thought that George Ball never focused attention sufficiently on some of these matters. I know his advice to the President on certain matters was bad—and the President felt it was bad. The President didn't feel as good about him the last year as he had before.

MARTIN: Alexis Johnson [Deputy Under Secretary of State for Political Affairs]?

KENNEDY: I think the President always felt that he performed his task well.

MARTIN: There was one spot there was a terrible time filling: Assistant Secretary for Latin America.

KENNEDY: Yes. We had tried a lot of different people, and of course nobody'd ever take the job.

MARTIN: You thought [Stanford Law School Professor Carl B.] Spaeth was taking it, and then it turned out he'd changed his mind?

KENNEDY: Clark Kerr [University of California president] we tried too.

MARTIN: Did you? How did you end up with Ed Martin? Do you know?

KENNEDY: No.

MARTIN: Bob Woodward? Briefly.

KENNEDY: He was ineffective.

MARTIN: He had been Ambassador to Chile, and then he was sent to Madrid as Ambassador. There were four or five months when there was simply no Assistant Secretary.

KENNEDY: We couldn't get anybody. We tried fifteen or so people.

MARTIN: The Latin American Ambassadors were all saying nobody knew who was doing what.

KENNEDY: Tried Connally. John Connally was my candidate. He was going to take it; then he wouldn't take it. The President was going to appoint him.

MARTIN: Tom Mann had been, under Eisenhower, Assistant Secretary for Latin America, hadn't he?

KENNEDY: I guess he had. I've had some sharp exchanges with him since he's been in there. I think that's going to be a disastrous appointment. [In December 1963, Mann was appointed Assistant Secretary of State for Inter-American Affairs. In addition, he was asked to head the Alliance for Progress.]

MARTIN: There's a general impression there were an awful lot of political ambassadors or personal appointees of the President, and actually there weren't any more than there ever are.

KENNEDY: No. I think the President always felt generally that they were the most effective that he had.

MARTIN: He did? Rather than the career men?

KENNEDY: Yes. There were some good career men, but the spectacular jobs—the out-of-the-ordinary jobs—were done by people who were political appointees, particularly the ones in Africa. They always seemed to be more effective and more aware and could do better. So if he could have found more political appointees, he would have appointed more of them. Of course, the good jobs in Europe were career people. He had that struggle all the time—with somebody like Chip Bohlen and others who wanted all those good jobs to go to career people. We had a helluva time in the organization of the State Department. It was very badly organized and never has become organized. Finally, we got so disturbed about it we sent Bill Orrick over. He had been head of the Civil Division [U.S. Department of

Justice]. He was a good organizer. But the machinery and the old-timers really got the best of him. He had no support from up above. Dean Rusk doesn't take any interest in it. And George Ball gets involved to a point, and then leaves it and doesn't follow it up. So the result was that there was no organization, no direction.

I think it's a helluva job, but I think it can be done. What you have to do is be able to turn over some of these tasks to others in the State Department. Dean Rusk couldn't do that and didn't focus attention on what was really important. For instance, just lately we got into Cuba about the fishing vessels, and he doesn't come to two-thirds of the meetings on the fishing vessels and what we were going to do about cutting off the water. [In February 1964 the United States seized four Cuban fishing vessels trespassing in American waters off the Florida coast. Castro responded by cutting off the freshwater supply for the U.S. Navy base at Guantanamo.] He came to one meeting. The result was that in the final meeting, when the decision was made, one position was taken by the Secretary of Defense and the other position was taken by me. Of course, I'm just there in sufferance, the Attorney General. I was arguing a particular view which had been originally taken by the State Department. They didn't enunciate their position. The Secretary of State didn't enunciate his position at this meeting that lasted two hours. Finally, when he came out, he came out on the side of Bob McNamara and opposite what he had done originally—and he had not attended the meetings which led up to it. He didn't attend all of the meetings, for instance, on the second Cuba. He wasn't there. He didn't go to Bermuda when they were talking about [ballistic missile] Skybolt.[11] And he's not going to Vietnam. Those are things that occur to me immediately. But time after time he wouldn't be present at important meetings.

MARTIN: What was he doing?

KENNEDY: He was going to dinners, or he was going to luncheons, or he was meeting ambassadors. The result, as I said earlier, was that the Department of State wouldn't have done their homework and wouldn't have positions on major matters.

MARTIN: This never did get organized?

KENNEDY: That part didn't get organized even internally in the Department. Bill Orrick never could work it out. [William J.] Crockett succeeded him, and I think Crockett's a good fellow. But Rusk never follows up. I mean, he never lays down the law. . . . As I said, the President was very concerned about it.

For instance, when we went through all the struggle on the coup out in Vietnam, his position changed continuously. When they were thinking of having the coup out there, the President started asking questions about what if the coup comes off. How many forces do the coup people have? How many forces do the anti-coup people have? Well, they didn't know that. He never gave any direction to Henry Cabot Lodge. The result was that Lodge was running away with it.

Again, going back to the Cuban vessels, I asked the question at the first meeting: "Well, how did the Cuban vessels get into American waters? Had they been sent?" I said, "How are you going to make any decision about what you're going to do about it?" They didn't even have the answer to that. I said, "How can you sit around here making decisions?" The State Department didn't even have that [answer]. And Dean Rusk didn't.

This went on with all of these matters. The President spoke to me frequently after a meeting was over—we used to go back into his office—about how awful it was and that he should get rid of Rusk when he could. We talked about whether we could get rid of him at that moment, and I didn't feel he could. But he was talking about replacing him. McNamara was one of the people that he discussed. He might have even put in Mac Bundy, I think.

MARTIN: There was a lot of talk at various times about replacing Rusk with George Ball.

KENNEDY: No, he never was considered.

MARTIN: Somebody else was mentioned a lot in the gossip around town: Nitze.

KENNEDY: No, the President didn't like Paul Nitze at the end. He could have never had Paul Nitze. That's clear because Paul Nitze didn't even get Under Secretary of Defense.

MARTIN: What about [Averell] Harriman? Was there talk of replacing him?

KENNEDY: The President liked Harriman, spoke well of him. He was not very helpful or effective at the time of Vietnam. In fact, his advice was wrong. He started us down a road which was quite dangerous. . . .

MARTIN: On the matter of political ambassadors, some of them had trouble with the State Department, which resented them, and some of them went over the head of the Department directly to the President. I suppose Ken Galbraith is the best example of that, isn't he?

KENNEDY: Yes. Some of them did. [Galbraith] did it and, of course, had fights with a lot of people in the State Department and, I think, in the CIA too.

MARTIN: Why did Galbraith leave as Ambassador? Was he a success as Ambassador? He looked like a good appointment.

KENNEDY: I think he was. I think the President thought he did a good job there. He had a fight with Harriman and had fights with some of the others on what we should or should not do at the time of [China's] invasion [of India]. I think he just probably got fed up with it.

MARTIN: He got tired of fighting City Hall?

KENNEDY: Yes.

MARTIN: Do you think the President thought he was successful as Ambassador?

KENNEDY: Yes, I think he did. The Ambassador always could get in to see the President.

[JFK] was far more accessible, I think, than had been true in prior years, particularly with the ones that he knew.

MARTIN: In other words, he encouraged this direct line.

KENNEDY: Yes. Then a good number of them *I* knew. So if there were a particular problem, I'd have correspondence with them, whether it's Jim Wine [then Ambassador to the Ivory Coast], or Bill Attwood [Ambassador to Guinea], or [William P.] Mahoney in Ghana, and some of the others. . . .

MARTIN: We've covered the first six months of 1961. We're up to the end of June chronologically. You spent that Fourth of July weekend, that long weekend, up at the Cape with the President and some other people. Do you remember anything particular about that weekend? You had been through the first civil rights crisis; he'd been at the summit in Vienna; you'd been through the Bay of Pigs. There might have been a time, it occurs to me, when there was a reassessment between the two of you.

By early summer, I think that I recall, the sense of the newspapers was one of letdown. The hundred days that everybody—the newspapers—had talked a lot about had passed, and a lot of things hadn't happened. There had been a close election. There was some talk that the President had gone slowly on some areas because it was a close election. Less had been accomplished during the first hundred days than a lot of people thought would be. Not much had been done up to then on employment and various other problems that existed in the foreign [affairs] fields as well as the domestic field. I wonder, did the President feel this? Do you recall?

KENNEDY: Although he used to read the papers and some of these things that were written used to exasperate him, he wouldn't change his policy or change his direction or change what he was doing because papers disapproved or suggested something else. I think that he always kept in mind where he was going and that he was going to have to change the direction not only of the country but of the world, change the expectations of people, change their speed of life, and change a lot of their fundamental beliefs.

You weren't going to do that just by making a speech, and you were not going to be able to do that in the United States with the kind of Congress we had, one that was oriented in a different direction. Here were a lot of rather revolutionary ideas that were being thrust upon Congress: education, housing, and some of these other matters. You weren't going to get it done overnight.

The other thing is that, as far as foreign affairs, we never thought that through personality or persuasion we were going to affect the Russians. It was obvious at the meeting in Vienna that we were not going to be able to do it that way. So what he had thought—thought strongly—in Vienna was that what we needed was the most effective military force we could have. In the last analysis, that was what was going to appeal to the Communists.

He didn't expect that these things were going to be done right away. What he was looking for was an eight-year period in which he would change the country and change the world around a little bit. But you shouldn't expect that that was going to be done immediately under the circumstances. So people expressed impatience. He read about it, and he didn't like it. But fundamentally it didn't affect him.

It seems to me that that's the major difference between him and the present President. What the present President reads in the paper or what people are going to think is what is fundamentally important. Both of them were affected by what was written in the newspapers; you wouldn't be a political figure if you weren't. If you'd started not caring about what was written in the newspapers, then you wouldn't be in politics, wouldn't be an effective political figure.

But he'd never let what was written in the newspapers affect him.

President Kennedy never let it affect what he was going to do. For the first time since I've been here—except on some rather unimportant points or perhaps on an appointment—in the last couple of months I've heard policy decisions discussed on the basis of what it would do to the vote here in the United States. And that, in any major matter, was never a factor with President Kennedy.

MARTIN: Yes. You said earlier this morning that he came back from Vienna with a feeling that we were going to be in very serious difficulties in Berlin in the summer and that the summer was a very dangerous time. I'd like to get into that now.

I notice that you attended, on the 19th of July, something called the Steering Committee in the White House. People there were Rusk, McNamara, Dillon, Allen Dulles, Ed Murrow [then Director of the USIA], Lemnitzer, Taylor, Bundy, Sorensen, the President, and yourself. The day after that, or within a day or two, the President made a speech to the country on Berlin.[12]

KENNEDY: Oh, yes.

MARTIN: I think that may have been what that meeting was about. I wanted to ask you this: How did the Steering Committee differ from the Executive Committee and the NSC and so forth? You always refer to the Steering Committee, and it kept meeting all during this period, which was the period leading to the Berlin crisis.

KENNEDY: I think the Steering Committee rose out of our suggestions and recommendations on Cuba and finally grew into the ExComm committee. The ExComm committee was an Executive Committee of the National Security Council. The National Security Council was too large—sometimes you'd have thirty-five people there. You'd never get any business done in the National Security Council. In addition, there were people such as the head of Civil Defense [Federal Civil Defense Administration]. Then each person brought two or three assistants, so you might have thirty-five or forty people there.

The President wanted to get it down to people in whom he had confidence. I was a member of the Security Council. Ted Sorensen obviously wasn't. So we set up the Steering Committee to be a smaller group that was to do what the Security Council was supposed to have done when it was originally formed. That was that committee. From that we went to the ExComm committee, which was formed at the time of Cuba. Then there was another committee called the Standing Committee. And there was the Counterinsurgency Committee.

MARTIN: The President's speech to the country on the 25th of July was a pretty somber speech. It was really war talk. It was a talk about civilian defense, more money, a possible increase in taxes, an increase in military preparedness, and so forth. This was all related to Berlin. I think you said, in an offhand way, that you and the President both thought we were pretty close to war.

KENNEDY: Yes.

MARTIN: Do you want to go into this now in some detail—the whole Berlin crisis of that summer?

KENNEDY: We had a lot of meetings about it. Dean Acheson was brought in to make a study of it. Again, this was the same idea that grew out of the Bay of Pigs: that one person would have the responsibility of coming up with some suggestions and recommendations. We then had the struggle that took place internally in the United States on whether we needed conventional forces or whether atomic forces were sufficient.

MARTIN: Who held what view on that? That was a freaky question, wasn't it?

KENNEDY: Yes.

MARTIN: It was a redesigning of our whole defense establishment, in a sense, that was involved here?

KENNEDY: Yes. A survey was made of our conventional forces' readiness. I don't have the exact figures, but I am sure exact figures were supplied by McNamara and the President. I asked the President to get a memorandum so that we could see how we stood, so that posterity would know about it. Half the torpedoes for the submarines didn't have batteries; a third of the soldiers in Europe didn't have bullets for their guns; a fifth of the antiaircraft guns didn't work at all. It was the worst situation that you can possibly imagine. We had troops all rushing around, but they couldn't do anything.

As I say, the figures aren't correct, but they are in the area. I mean, if we were attacked, we didn't have forces that had armaments that could protect them for more than a few days. All that had to be changed. It was so obvious what we needed. Some of the old-timers protested and objected to it. But when you brought out the facts that we weren't prepared and we couldn't deal with the problem, it became far clearer—the necessity of taking certain steps to deal with the difficulties.

This obviously led to struggle. Bob McNamara was strongly in favor of it. Some of the Joint Chiefs of Staff were not enthusiastic about it. Obviously, Curt LeMay thought it was a mistake. His answer to many of these problems was to go in and drop a bomb on them: "Bomb the hell out of 'em," as he put it. But that was the fundamental question.

It was then, I think, that we sent some more troops to Europe. That was a question of whether we should send troops to Europe, how long we would say that we would send them for, and how much effort we should make to have the other countries put troops up as well. When we had the crisis in Berlin, the French gave an indication that they were strong about Berlin and that the United States might not have been as strong. But that really wasn't the question. The French were making speeches about it and refusing to talk to Khrushchev. On fundamental questions—what you would do if a plane was shot down from the ground; what steps would you take under those circumstances; would you attack that ground installation; would you attack the ground installation with what kind of bombs; if planes came out to attack you as you were attacking the ground installation, would you send fighters up; how many fighters would you send; if a plane was shot down by another plane, what would you do—on all those fundamental questions, the individuals who wanted to take strong action in case the Russians or the Communists took action against us were always opposed by the French. The French were making public pronouncements about standing up on Berlin and not giving an inch. But when it finally got to the really unpleasant part of it, they were not going to stand fast.

Charles de Gaulle always fundamentally believed that nothing would ever happen, and that if anything ever happened, then you can go in and drop a bomb. You should be ready for nuclear war. The President always felt that that should not be the first step you would take. I mean, you should see whether you could *avoid* that.

MARTIN: Early in August, Bob, you went to Africa—the Ivory Coast, I think, and other places.[13] This is before the Berlin thing began to really get serious. What was the purpose of that trip? Do you recall where you went?

KENNEDY: I just went to the Ivory Coast. The State Department felt Houphouet-Boigny, the President of the Ivory Coast, was particularly important for the leadership of all of those countries in that part of the world. He was sort of the leader of the others and had a great deal of influence on Sékou Touré [of Guinea] and possibly even

[Ghanaian President Kwame] Nkrumah. I think we wanted to indicate to him the strong feeling that President Kennedy had for him and this country had for him. So I went as the representative. I think it was really worthwhile. He's been extremely important. We dealt with him a lot.

He's very instrumental with Sékou Touré. Obviously, the Ambassador [William Attwood] did a helluva lot. And President Kennedy, whom Sékou Touré really worshiped, did a lot. But Houphouet-Boigny gave a good deal of leadership and a good deal of help. When he came to the United States, he had meetings with the President. Then he had some rather unsatisfactory meetings with the State Department. He called me up, and I went over and met with him for a couple of hours at his house, because he was about to leave the United States in a rather dismal frame of mind. Then I spoke to the President, and the President had him back in, unexpectedly, and they got some things cleared up.

MARTIN: This was your first trip outside the country for the President, wasn't it?

KENNEDY: Yes. I went for a few days.

MARTIN: Now on Berlin. Up to now the crises had been Laos, the Congo,[14] and other places on the periphery, but Berlin was really very central. The Wall went up on August 13. The immediate response from the State Department was not very much of anything. Then—suddenly—the President sent the Vice President to Berlin to reassure the Berliners that we were still with them.

KENNEDY: He had a meeting in the White House on, I think, Sunday morning. There hadn't been any meeting on the Wall or the fact that the Wall was going up prior to that time. I think the Wall went up on a Friday, as I remember, and then we had a meeting at the White House in which the various courses of action were discussed: number one, sending Lyndon Johnson to Berlin; number two, sending a regiment or group of troops across [East Germany] into Berlin. It was rather interesting because the President had thought that the troops were on the border. So he ordered it and then found out—once again he hadn't been told—that they were two days away. They didn't get to the border for another two days. That just delayed the—

MARTIN: What was the idea of sending troops to Berlin?

KENNEDY: They couldn't do anything but just to indicate a psychological—

MARTIN: A psychological lift for the Berliners?

KENNEDY: Yes, and also to indicate our own commitment to remain in Berlin.

MARTIN: It wasn't a test of Khrushchev's intentions or anything like that?

KENNEDY: No, we thought it was a dangerous time. I think it was a Saturday or a Sunday when [the troops] finally got there. The President was very relieved personally when they finally got through, because it was a nervous time. He didn't know whether [the Russians] would try to stop them.

MARTIN: There was something very odd going on around this time because Khrushchev had taken a very tough line on Berlin at Vienna. Subsequently, he had said publicly that he intended to sign a treaty with East Germany by Christmas or by the end of the year, taking a very hard line. At the same time, on July 30, Khrushchev issued a restatement of the whole Soviet-Communist thesis and said that he thought it would be possible to avoid nuclear war in this generation. This was the first basic party program since Lenin's in 1919. It also called for peaceful coexistence as an objective necessity, so to speak. Yet, at the same time, there was the public hardening on the Berlin question, you see? These are not possible for me to reconcile. Can you throw any light on them?

KENNEDY: I think it was a test of strength for President Kennedy.

MARTIN: Do you want to go on about that?

KENNEDY: I think that [Khrushchev] thought that the President was not going to be a strong figure based, in my judgment, on the fact that we didn't use American forces to crush Cuba—not that we started in Cuba, but we didn't use American forces to crush Cuba. I think when he then met him in Vienna, he thought he was a young, inexperienced figure. Read the press accounts. I think he got statements from his Ambassador here that President Kennedy didn't amount to very much, didn't have much courage. But I don't think the Ambassador at that time had much contact. He was telling Khrushchev what he'd like to hear. That's what Bolshakov told me. Bolshakov said *he* kept telling them that we would fight, we would stand up. This is on the basis of my conversation with Bolshakov. He said the Ambassador kept giving them different accounts, so they thought that they could put the pressure on Berlin, President Kennedy would collapse, and they'd take over Berlin. There wouldn't be any problem. It wouldn't be difficult.

MARTIN: What stopped that? What made Khrushchev realize—

KENNEDY: First, I think the psychological measures that were taken.

MARTIN: Such as sending—

KENNEDY: Sending the troops, but also we did a lot of things internally, in the military forces here in the United States. There were more troops that were sent to Germany.

MARTIN: You brought up some reserves?

KENNEDY: Yes, reserves were called up; some troops were moved. We took steps in a number of ways which would become known after a period of time to the Russians—we were going to be prepared for war—and yet they were not widely publicized. You might put the SAC, Strategic Air Command, on more of an alert; more submarines would be deployed in different places; troops would be moved in different directions; certain leaves would be canceled—all these kinds of things. More hardware and equipment would be landed [in Europe]. All these things indicated that we were going to stay and fight.

MARTIN: Did you and the President actually think that we were close to war?

KENNEDY: Yes.

MARTIN: You did?

KENNEDY: Much closer than anybody—
    I don't know whether we talked about the percentage. I thought it was about one chance in five or so.

MARTIN: Really?

KENNEDY: Yes . . .
    We had a lot of meetings on Berlin. I was in favor, at that time, of increasing taxes by a percentage point or a percentage-and-a-half. My brother used to say to me afterward—he turned out against it, I guess. I don't know who was in favor of it. I think we were about split on it.

MARTIN: He used to say what?

KENNEDY: When I used to remember things he'd suggested that were wrong, he used to recall that I was in favor of a tax [increase].

The President made a speech on Berlin, talking about some of these problems. We were also thinking, as well as calling up the reserves, of the percentage increase. My thought was that it was a psychological factor: that everybody would understand the seriousness of the situation, and everybody, therefore, would feel involved in it. The arguments against it: We were already in a recession; putting another percentage tax on would increase the recession, slow down the recovery—and we were just making the recovery. Therefore, maybe it would be a bad mistake.

MARTIN: You were looking for something in the way of a sacrifice to make people realize what we were in.

KENNEDY: That's right. And the [economic] viewpoint prevailed. It seems to me that we met two or three times a week during that period. We were then getting into the post–Bay of Pigs era where the relationships had changed and the degree of questioning had changed— and the sternness. It was a harder period. I don't know how to describe it exactly. It was just a tougher, harder, meaner period than that which had gone before. A lot of it rose out of the Bay of Pigs.

McNamara handled himself well, made some sense, obviously became rather dominant. This was his period of starting to become rather a dominant figure.

MARTIN: Was there anybody who held the view that we should abandon Berlin?

KENNEDY: No.

MARTIN: This was never even discussed, considered as a possibility?

KENNEDY: No. No.

MARTIN: The next main thing was the nuclear testing.

KENNEDY: You see, I was nothing but a troublemaker: I thought it was outrageous that [the Russians] resumed nuclear testing[15] and there weren't parades and demonstrations and people throwing bricks through public relations offices at the Russians—as they would have if we had started testing.

I thought if we could harness all of the energy, if we could use the elements within American society and have them get in touch with their counterparts in other countries—businessmen with businessmen, lawyers with lawyers, labor unions with labor unions, students with students, the public sector, the private sector, plus what we could do with our government (although we didn't have such a thing as an internal political party, as the Communists did, and they had some advantages)—we still could do a great deal more. So the President appointed me and Maxwell Taylor and another on a task force to make a study of it. We made a study of it and made some recommendations as to what could be done. We brought in the CIA, and Arthur Goldberg, I think, was on the committee with me.

MARTIN: I suppose we wanted to get the national, the world propaganda benefit, letting [Khrushchev] be out there all alone.

KENNEDY: Yes. There wasn't that much [benefit]. If we had done it first, the embassies would have been stoned and places would have been attacked. There would have been parades and marches and everything. I was particularly concerned about it. So the President appointed a committee to find out what we should do in order to take advantage of what they were doing. One of the things we studied particularly, which we got ready for, was—when [Khrushchev] announced that he was going to explode the hundred-megaton bomb—to see whether we could work up groups around the world to be as concerned about this as they would be if we were doing it.

I didn't feel that we were using our assets as we should have. We have businessmen who could be in contact with other businessmen, labor leaders with labor leaders, labor unions with labor unions, and students with students—to try to get some of these things across. . . . And once again we had a lot of trouble with the State Department.

Finally, the State Department, in its own inimitable way, swallowed it up by appointing Bill Jordan of *The New York Times* to handle this. Of course, Jordan, appointed to this position [on the Policy Planning Council of the State Department], was immediately sent out to Vietnam to do something else. So the whole thing collapsed. It was at this time that the President gave George McGhee the responsibility. I had two or three meetings with George McGhee. He said that everything was being done, that they were following it up. That's when I got to dislike George McGhee because he's one of those people who just—sentence after sentence, paragraph after paragraph—went on. And when you analyzed it, nothing was said. It all sounded good and it all came out in the right order, but he just said nothing. He wouldn't do anything, and he'd get nothing done, and he wouldn't follow anything up. . . .

So this battle went on for a year.

Finally, in a very badly handled way, they got rid of George McGhee by firing a rather good Ambassador, [Walter] Red Dowling, over in Germany. Dowling was so upset at the way it had been handled that he quit the Foreign Service. The President liked Dowling.

He was very helpful at some of the meetings he had attended on Berlin in 1962. I remember some meetings that I attended where he made a great deal of sense and was very effective. But he was so badly treated in the transfer that I guess he felt that he couldn't stay on. So George McGhee got that job. George McGhee was a real zero and was one of the problems with the State Department. Of course, it was greatly improved when Harriman came in. But, as I say, when you have problems at the top—

MARTIN: Now, we resumed our testing on September 15—atomic testing in Nevada. Was there great debate going on inside the government?

KENNEDY: Yes. Mostly on what kind of testing we would do: how big the bombs would be, how many we'd do, and how long they'd go on.

MARTIN: There wasn't very much doubt that we were going to resume?

KENNEDY: We thought that we had to resume.

MARTIN: For what reason? For scientific reasons?

KENNEDY: Yes, because there was a strong feeling that we had a lot to gain. There was always a strong element within the government that felt testing should be resumed, that it would be very helpful to resume testing. When the Russians resumed their testing, that position prevailed. The President was never very enthusiastic about the testing. I never heard anybody in a scientific area come in and oppose testing. But the President asked some hard questions about testing. Most of the testing was aimed at developing smaller bombs with bigger punch. He wasn't convinced that was so necessary.

MARTIN: Were there other reasons why he was rather reluctant to resume?

KENNEDY: When he finally agreed to it, he put stricter limitations because of the fallout problem, so that we'd only have about twenty-five percent of the fallout the Russians would have. I guess he felt that unless there was a real military advantage in testing, he hadn't wanted to. But they resumed. There was a strong feeling by the scientific community that we should test.

One of the strongest arguments, now that I remember, was that they might perfect an antimissile missile. That was the thing that really convinced him.

MARTIN: Did this have anything to do with testing?

KENNEDY: Yes.

MARTIN: Really?

KENNEDY: Yes. Because with an antimissile missile, part of the technique is to have an explosion in the sky which would then throw off the bombs or detonate their missiles.

MARTIN: I see. . . . On the business of the easing of tensions over Berlin, was there any particular reason, any particular thing that happened, Bob? It seemed to tail off. At the end of the year, the President said the thing was still dangerous and he thought that we were a long way from being out of the woods as far as Berlin is concerned. Nevertheless, the crisis feeling was over. What happened during the fall to change that? Do you recall?

KENNEDY: I think that there were a number of things. First, the response of the President and the country during the fall—the sending of the troops, the obvious intentions of the President to fight, if necessary, on Berlin. We spent a good deal of our time going through the various alternatives.

MARTIN: Such as what?

KENNEDY: What we would do if a missile from the ground shot a plane; what we would do if a plane of the Communists shot a plane of ours down; what we would do if—

MARTIN: What would you do?

KENNEDY: We had various alternatives. But the problem was to get all of the Allies in agreement. That's what really brought home to us a lesson during that period of time: what an advantage the Communists or a dictatorship had—you just decide what your policy is going to be and you don't have to publicize it.

During that period of time, it was hailed in the papers: Why weren't we as tough as the French? Because the French were standing up to Khrushchev, they were going to stand up for Berlin, and the United States was rather weak and rather vacillating. In fact, when we got down to the particular individual issues or questions, the French were the ones who gave the most difficulties. The British were not much better. But the French! If you'd start to determine or decide what you were going to do if a particular incident occurred, the French would never, or very rarely, give their concurrence if you'd fight back. They always wanted to meet about it. They didn't want to reach any conclusion as to taking any definitive steps. That made it so difficult.

The second great problem in planning during this period of time was the fact that, once you discuss this, once you reach a determination, you have to discuss it with other countries. We always had the feeling that it would either get in the newspapers or it would get back to the Communists so that they would know our every move. There's the advantage Khrushchev had: He'd just decide what he'd do. He could push it right to the wall, and then when it got to the wall—I don't mean the Berlin Wall—he could push it that far and then he could decide himself whether he wanted to pull back or not. When we were taking any steps or making any maneuvers, we couldn't move and take that step or move to that wall without consulting with all the Allies and getting their concurrence; then we couldn't pull back without consulting all the Allies and getting a concurrence. It was such a great disadvantage. [Khrushchev] could seem to play almost a yo-yo with us. We had a very difficult time responding. And the ones who really caused us the most difficulty during that period of time were the French.

MARTIN: When you say "the French," you mean De Gaulle?

KENNEDY: I suppose he's the one who was making the decisions. But it wasn't consultation individually with him, but with the French Ambassador and their representative.

MARTIN: Who were the people whom you were consulting with? How did this work?

KENNEDY: For some of the decisions it was all the NATO countries. Others, it was just the French. Particularly on Berlin, it was the French and the British. But, as I say, the French caused us the greatest difficulty. When I went to Berlin in early 1962, the [U.S.] commandant there said they had the same problem in taking individual steps in Berlin in order to deal with problems: that it was always the French who weren't willing to go along—although the public pronouncements and all the columns at the time were writing that the ones who really would stand up to the Russians and the ones who were really tough were the French.

This gets back to our basic strategy, which was starting to be developed during this period of time. What the President was attempting to do was [ensure] that we wouldn't have to respond to a smaller step by them with an atomic war. De Gaulle had reached the conclusion—the French had, and to some extent the British—largely because of what we had been selling them over the period of the last ten years, that the reaction to any step that the Russians might take would be the use of atomic weapons. What concerned him was, maybe you'd eventually come to atomic weapons and maybe you'd come down to twenty-four or forty-eight hours, but shouldn't there be some room for maneuver during that period of time when you used just conventional forces? If they send a platoon in, do you respond with an atomic bomb on Moscow or do you respond with two platoons? If they send a brigade in, how do you respond?

The result was that the French weren't willing to work out any responsive action to a particular incident—what happened to a plane or what happened if our troops were stopped going in—because they never thought about it, really. They thought it would just eventually evolve into atomic warfare. The President always thought this was not only a dangerous but also a weak position. It didn't give us any flexibility. The Germans, of course—Adenauer particularly—were concerned about our strategy and talked to me in a good deal of detail when I was over there in '62.

MARTIN: Was he opposed to our view?

KENNEDY: Yes. Basically because he thought or envisioned that while [the Russians] moved in troops through West Germany—captured Cologne—to the Rhine River, we would be discussing and negotiating. In the meantime, they would have taken over most of Germany. That would have been the status quo by the time the war ended, where you could negotiate the ending of the war. They had stronger conventional forces than we did, would always have stronger conventional forces; therefore, they would capture Germany. We would eventually talk them into stopping, but by that time Germany would be under their control. What [Adenauer] wanted was—if they moved at all—to drop an atomic bomb. So that everybody understood that they couldn't afford to move, because otherwise, you'd have worldwide atomic war.

MARTIN: What was the British position?

KENNEDY: They were a little bit more flexible. I think, over the period of time, now everybody is more flexible about it. But one of the great problems was that we had always been selling them this idea. Our whole philosophy was this idea of the use of atomic weapons.

MARTIN: You're talking now about the Eisenhower administration, the massive retaliation policy?

KENNEDY: Yes. That's right.

MARTIN: This is a basic foreign policy shift that you're now discussing.

KENNEDY: That's right. And it was really brought about by, basically, the President. The most influential figure in it was Maxwell Taylor.

MARTIN: He was?

KENNEDY: It was his feeling, as you remember, that we should build up these other forces. After our investigation of the Bay of Pigs, we made a major effort to build up the Special Forces. We did that. Also, the conventional forces, so that we would have troops over in Germany to respond. There were some rather strong, vigorous debates in which Dean Acheson participated. He was given the assignment by the President during the [spring] of 1961 of making a study and coming in with a report and some recommendations as to what should be done. He wanted to send more troops—many, many more troops—over in 1961.

MARTIN: Conventional forces?

KENNEDY: Yes. There was some compromise on that. This goes back to the original question of why there was an easing of tension. We called up some troops, enlarged the Army. Also, tremendous steps were taken to make our armed forces more efficient and better equipped. There was a real effort, an expensive effort, to build up so that our forces would be equipped properly. We had a lot of forces on paper, but they didn't really mean anything. I think this was one point.

The second point was that, by putting up the Wall, the Russians had eased their own problems, because what concerned them was the fact that people were just flowing out of East Germany and flowing out of Berlin—all the best people. Well, this was where they went to: How they got out was through West Berlin. And by putting up the Wall, they stopped that. Therefore, there wasn't such a cancer on their side. I think that those two factors had eased tensions.

I couldn't stress sufficiently the concern the President had, and the concern all of us who were involved in those discussions had, about the possibility of war. I think this was the first effort by Khrushchev to test the President, figuring that after the Bay of Pigs he was going to back down on everything. So he was going to put the President to the test. And he found out. I kept telling Georgi Bolshakov that we'd fight. He said he kept reporting it.

MARTIN: Who was negotiating for us with the British and the French Ambassadors?

KENNEDY: Somebody from the State Department. We'd have these meetings at the White House—it wasn't really a National Security Council meeting but a smaller unit—and go over what steps we'd take under each set of circumstances. Then that decision would be transmitted for negotiation. Paul Nitze, I think, did most of that.

He had to get everybody ready so that they could get the tests over in the shortest possible period of time and with the least fallout possible. There was tremendous fallout from Khrushchev's testing.

The second point was that we were very concerned—the President appointed a committee, which didn't do much and should have done more—about the fact that he, Khrushchev, was able to announce the testing and get on with the testing, and there wasn't really any world outcry.

MARTIN: . . . There must be an awful lot of things that a President wants done—good ideas—but they never get done. Before he can follow it up himself, he's got ten other crises he has to deal with. Was this a problem that he talked to you about?

KENNEDY: Yes.

MARTIN: What did he try to do about it?

KENNEDY: Well, he wrote an awful lot of memos. Going up on the plane to the Cape, for instance, he'd always sit with his machine and just dictate. We'd be reading documents, and he'd be dictating memos to people in various departments. It would be up to the staff in the White House. It got far more efficient at the end.

MARTIN: Did it succeed, this follow-through? That seemed to me the hardest thing in executing policy: to get follow-through.

KENNEDY: I think it succeeded in some cases. But it was very, very tough to move the State Department: first, the bad organization in the State Department; secondly, Dean Rusk, whom he was going to replace in '65. It really began to irritate the President by the last six months because it was so obvious then that, almost inevitably, the ideas that [Rusk] came in with—particularly, for instance, on Vietnam at the end—almost always turned out wrong. . . .

It was terrifically frustrating for the President. [Rusk] would never follow anything up. He'd never initiate ideas. There would never be any initiative that would come from the State Department. I would think sixty percent of new concepts or new ideas or plans about matters came from the President; maybe eighty percent came from the President and the White House, of which probably sixty of the eighty percent came from the President himself. The other twenty percent came from the State Department and other places. It was a most frustrating experience.

He got a lot of things done, but he always felt that in the next four years, the second term, he'd be able to do something with the State Department to pull it together. The major area which was frustrating to him was the operation of the State Department and the fact that they didn't produce. He always felt that, with ten or twelve people over at the White House, he was producing more than the whole State Department. When we had letters with Khrushchev, he would either have to rewrite them himself or have somebody in the White House rewrite them. They not only didn't have any ideas, but they were badly written.

MARTIN: During this same fall, Bob, Vietnam started heating up. He sent Maxwell Taylor over there. The press reported that the President was strongly against sending any combat troops to Vietnam. Do you recall any discussions with him during that time on this?

KENNEDY: Yes . . . One of the alternatives that had been suggested was to send troops into Vietnam, as the French had, and fight the war in Vietnam. General [Douglas] MacArthur, when he came down to see the President, was strongly against sending any troops into Southeast Asia. He said that you'd just get lost there, that it would be a very bad mistake. So the Taylor mission, when it went out there, that was one of the alternatives that was discussed and considered. The President had been there in 1951 and had been impressed with the toughness of the French soldiers. A lot of them were Foreign Legion. There were paratroopers, and they were very impressive. They had several hundreds of thousands. And they were beaten. [Taylor] came back and made a speech about that: that you have to have the approval, the support, of the people. One of the suggestions by some of the military was that we send troops in there—you know, several divisions—and help fight the war. So when [JFK] said that there wouldn't be troops used, that was what he had in mind. The people that we did send eventually—there've been some sixteen thousand, seventeen thousand—have been in the form of advisers.

MARTIN: Did the President feel that we would have to go into Vietnam in a big way?

KENNEDY: We certainly considered what would be the result if you abandon Vietnam, even Southeast Asia, and whether it was worthwhile trying to keep and hold on to.

MARTIN: What did he say? What did he think?

KENNEDY: He reached the conclusion that probably it was worthwhile for psychological, political reasons more than anything else.

MARTIN: World political reasons?

KENNEDY: Yes.

MARTIN: Because there aren't many votes in that at home.

KENNEDY: No. We had a lot of bad intelligence at that time, again, about what the situation was there. I mentioned the fact that they got the diseases mixed up and all the rest of the business. About sending troops into Laos—I think I mentioned the airport, trying to get there. By this time Maxwell Taylor was beginning to play a more and more important part. The reorganizations that came out of Cuba were beginning to take place. So we were getting a little bit better at dealing with some of these matters.

We sent some other task forces out there, too—Laos and Vietnam—during that period of time.

MARTIN: To collect information?

KENNEDY: Yes.

MARTIN: Where did you get them?

KENNEDY: I think Paul Nitze went. I think Ros Gilpatric was one. It was, once again, this idea of centralizing authority and bringing in all the various government agencies under one individual who would then make a report to the President. That was the idea that grew out of Cuba.

I would say that if it hadn't been for Cuba, we probably would have sent large numbers of troops into Laos and Vietnam. That would have been very damaging. I think it was the fact that the President kept going back and back and back—asking questions, attempting to get answers, not just taking a person's opinion or conclusion, no matter how high their position—that eventually evolved the policy that we followed.

MARTIN: During the fall the President sent the Congress the new trade and tariff bill.[17] This was all to tie us tighter to the European Common Market. Apparently, this was the purpose of it. This was also part of our effort to concert ourselves with the Allies in Western Europe. Is that so? Or was this something that the President felt was important as an economic matter solely?

KENNEDY: I don't know whether he separated it in his own mind. I think he thought it was important economically but, obviously, also politically. I don't know where he'd put the emphasis, really.

MARTIN: Okay. He went to Venezuela and Colombia that fall. Why to those two countries? Why to Latin America at all?

KENNEDY: He wanted to put more emphasis on Latin America. This was a keystone of foreign policy. I think he felt particularly close to Venezuela and Colombia because of some of the assets that existed as far as friendliness toward the United States.

MARTIN: That trip was a great success, wasn't it?

KENNEDY: Yes, it really was.

General [Godfrey] McHugh [USAF] was the one of his aides who was the least efficient—sometimes more humorous—and who had rather a fight with Lyndon Johnson on the day of the President's—on November 22nd [1963]. In any case, he had one of his triumphant moments when the President, in order to get his suits, asked him to find out what the temperature was. So [McHugh] came back and—this was before he took the trip—gave him the mean temperature in Caracas. It would be sixty-five during the day and, I don't know, sixty at night or something. So the President brought rather, you know, medium-heavy suits. Then, as they were going on their way, he asked him for another report. He gave him another report: it was sixty-eight at the airport. Anyway, they got out of the plane: it was eighty-nine or something! The President couldn't believe what had happened. It finally evolved that what Colonel McHugh had gotten was the average temperature in Caracas for the year—including the night and in the shade. From then on, there was always a thermometer placed in the sun at the airport where he would arrive. Very funny. But the President never forgave him.

MARTIN: In 1961 there was some antiracketeering legislation proposed. Do you want to get into the whole question of the antiracketeering legislation and on the Justice Department's activities about organized crime?

KENNEDY: Generally, there wasn't anything [that had been] done. There had been a good deal of conversation, but there was no coordination between the various governmental departments. That's what I did first when I became Attorney General—even before I became Attorney General: I met Douglas Dillon, J. Edgar Hoover, and Mort Caplin, and got them all to agree.

MARTIN: But nothing, really, ever did come of this, did it?

KENNEDY: Absolutely. There is complete coordination now between all the governmental agencies—which never existed before. Also, on the major racketeers in the United States, there's an overall list which is supplied by all governmental agencies and departments in which they gather any information. That's all sent to the Organized Crime

Section of the Department of Justice. There it's catalogued and disseminated. We have an intelligence division, plus we have about sixty lawyers in the Organized Crime Section alone who do work on these major criminal cases.

MARTIN: Have there been a lot of major prosecutions?

KENNEDY: Oh, yes. In the first place, convictions in organized crime are up about seven hundred percent. Indictments are up seven hundred or eight hundred percent. And the major figures who have been convicted around the country are very impressive. A good deal of work has been done. The coordinated effort has made a major difference. Also, we obtained the passage of several antiracketeering bills which were very, very helpful and made a major difference. So I think it's the passage of the legislation, plus coordination, plus the emphasis. We've tried to bring in some of the best lawyers on these problems rather than the worst lawyers. I think it's had a helluva difference around the country.

MARTIN: Did you spend much time on this yourself?

KENNEDY: Yes. I spent a lot of time on it.

MARTIN: What was the Sheridan group?

KENNEDY: The Sheridan group, which is made up of about sixteen or eighteen attorneys, went into, particularly, the Teamsters Union.

MARTIN: That's Walt Sheridan, who used to be the investigator for the Rackets Committee?

KENNEDY: Yes. It's concentrated chiefly on the Teamsters, where nothing had been for years. Their work has resulted in convictions of about a hundred Teamster officials and financial associates of Hoffa, and about sixty or seventy more are presently under indictment. So it's made a helluva impact around the country.

MARTIN: What do you think of J. Edgar Hoover?

KENNEDY: I think that probably, because of the fact that the President and I were brothers, it is the first time he's really had somebody that he had to pay attention to as Attorney General. He was the more important figure in the Department of Justice prior to that. I think two things really affected him in his relationship with me: number one, our concentration on organized crime, because he'd always denied that it existed. He said that there was no organized crime. That's the importance of Valachi. Because for the first time the FBI changed their whole concept of crime in the United States. They had to admit that—everybody, down the line. Of course, he won't admit it publicly, but he'd always argued with the Bureau of Narcotics and everybody else that there wasn't such a thing. So Valachi, plus the other investigations that have been made around the country by the FBI, indicated now that there was such a thing as organized crime and how it was directed and controlled. That was damned important.

Secondly, he's put [in more people]. Here in New York, for instance, prior to the time I became Attorney General, there were about ten FBI agents working on organized crime. Now there are one hundred and fifteen. In Chicago, it's also increased one thousand percent, and in the major cities around the country. They've been taken from some of these old Communist cases. Now it's known as the elite squad in all of these major cities. They've got the best people. They're really doing a lot of work and have made a helluva difference. A helluva difference. The FBI, reluctantly at first, got into it mostly because they didn't have any choice.

The second area where they hadn't done a helluva lot was civil rights, and they had to get into that too. Of course they'd jealously guarded their relationship with the police officers in the South and with the southern Congressmen and Senators, and suddenly they were thrust into this struggle. This was difficult—although [Hoover] couldn't complain about it: There wasn't any place to go. He had to follow what I wanted done. And he got it done. When they worked, they did it well. It's the best organized operation within the federal government. . . .

Bill Lambert, with whom I worked on the Rackets Committee, who was a reporter and got the Pulitzer Prize out in Portland, Oregon, in 1957, works for *Life* magazine now. He came across a fellow down in Florida—I think he's down in Florida now—who used to be a clerk at a hotel out near the race track where Hoover goes to stay every month. When he left in 1958—he'd been there from '53 to '58—he took the records with him. They showed that up to that time— and, of course, Hoover has stayed there every year since then—he stayed in a hundred-dollar-a-day suite and that the bill at the end of each month was picked up and paid for by the Murchisons.[18]

MARTIN: Really?

KENNEDY: The total for that five-year period was, I think, something like eighty-five hundred dollars—which I thought was interesting.

MARTIN: I'll say it is.

KENNEDY: But they made such an effort over him. They had grape arbors around the house. Grapes were out of season. So every morning early they would come and tie grapes to the trees so that when he came out he'd be able to pluck the grapes. . . .

He acts in such a strange, peculiar way.

MARTIN: Toward the end of that year, there was a wiretapping bill introduced in Congress. [The 1962 wiretapping bill introduced by the Kennedy administration attempted to outlaw warrantless wiretapping with the exception of cases involving national security.]

It was said in the papers that your own views had changed about wiretapping. Do you remember this? What was that all about?

KENNEDY: The bill was generally the bill that had been introduced before.

(I don't think it was as good a bill as the one we introduced later.) I asked all of the Assistant Attorneys General to get together and see if we could come up with a bill. Burke Marshall, Lou Oberdorfer, and Nick came up with that bill. I always have felt that what we should have is the concurrence of the court.

The FBI indicated that, if we introduced a wiretapping bill—I mean, virtually said it—a wiretapping bill where you had to get the court approval on espionage and sabotage cases, they would not support it. The result was that they would go around and tell everybody not to vote for the bill.

Of course it wouldn't have any chance or possibility to pass. So we introduced the bill that generally had been introduced in the past. Then, in 1962, we got a better bill, which had far more protection— and which [the FBI] would go along with. That's the bill that's been up there for the last three years.

Discussion or talk about wiretapping, of course, sends some people through the roof. I have much more authority and power at the present time. I mean I can decide whose phone is going to be tapped.

MARTIN: But you can't use anything in evidence?

KENNEDY: No. I don't think that's the important thing, though.

MARTIN: You don't?

KENNEDY: It's not the fact it's going to be used in evidence, but just the fact that I can tap somebody's telephone and listen in. It could be used for blackmail purposes. I could stick a tap on your telephone.

MARTIN: You wouldn't hear anything.

KENNEDY: But I think the important thing is the fact that there are now people around listening to people's telephone conversations. With the bill that I introduced in '62 and '63 and '64, we couldn't do that. In addition, we'd have to continuously make reports to the court as to what we were doing. Now there's no check on what I do whatsoever. Except for the most serious kinds of cases—sabotage and espionage—we'd have to get court approval. It continues the same practice, but we still have to make a report to Congress. So I think the bill's better. It was supported by [Francis] Biddle, the head of the ADA [Americans for Democratic Action] or whatever he is, and it was supported by *The New York Times.* Joe Rauh and some of the others bitterly fought it. It's been very controversial. It's been an indication to liberal groups that I'm not in favor of civil liberties.

MARTIN: The ACLU did support the bill finally, didn't they?

KENNEDY: Biddle did.

MARTIN: Not as a body though?

KENNEDY: No. Most of those liberal organizations were against it.

MARTIN: Yes. Well, they would naturally be, on principle.
    During the fall of '61, [Prime Minister] Cheddi Jagan from British Guiana came to Washington. The President seems to have gone to a good deal of trouble to be nice to him. Was he very much concerned about that?

KENNEDY: Yes. He was concerned about it.

MARTIN: Why was it so important?

KENNEDY: I think the idea was that you had Cuba, and if you had another stronghold for Communists in the Western Hemisphere, it would just create that many more difficulties. He was convinced that Jagan was probably a Communist.

MARTIN: But he wanted to give it a try?

KENNEDY: Yes, and see whether we could work something out with him which would keep him—

MARTIN: That was impossible?

KENNEDY: That was impossible.

MARTIN: What did the President have in mind? What did he think he might be able to do?

KENNEDY: There were various plans we went through—which I became involved in—of trying to get the British to come up with something.

MARTIN: For example, what?

KENNEDY: I think there was an election coming on there, and [we discussed] whether we should support his opponent; whether the labor unions should support his opponent; whether Great Britain should give up any of its control there or should continue its control. There were various papers that were prepared by the CIA and by other organizations there about how to deal with him. It mostly revolved around the British. Most of our efforts were to try to get the British to recognize the concern that we had and ask them to take action to control the situation. They were reluctant.

MARTIN: Why were they?

KENNEDY: They were not as concerned about him and about the situation.

MARTIN: They couldn't see why we were worried?

KENNEDY: Yes.

MARTIN: From the standpoint of domestic politics, that's where the importance of it lay?

KENNEDY: And the future of South America.

MARTIN: But it's a very small country.

KENNEDY: Well, I suppose Cuba is too. It's caused us a lot of trouble.

MARTIN: It's caused us trouble most people don't understand. Castro has unnaturally strengthened the military right. That's what happened there. Dictators were on their way out when he came along.

KENNEDY: Yes.

MARTIN: There's a speech the President made in October of that year at the University of North Carolina in which he [said], "Anybody who thinks you can get total victory or total defeat is just wrong—and this is a dangerous delusion." This is a theme that ran through both the campaign and the presidency, isn't it?

KENNEDY: I think so. I think probably more during the presidency because of the assessments that they were making at the time of Berlin: the fact that so many people were going to get killed; the fact that you could have a war and we'd drop a bomb on the Soviet Union and destroy them. Each year there's a group that studies what happens in the United States and what happens in the Soviet Union if a war comes. They make a report each year to the President. That's very bloodcurdling.

MARTIN: Yes, it must be.

KENNEDY: It goes through the cities: what happens in the Soviet Union when they have a strike, what happens when we have a strike, what happens if you concentrate on the more populated areas, what happens if you concentrate on the military. That's why there was so much discussion in 1963 about seeing whether we could concentrate on the military targets rather than the people.

MARTIN: At about this time, or it may have been a little earlier, George Kennan had proposed a whole new idea—which he called disengagement—in Europe. Rusk made a speech rejecting the idea. Did the President ever consider it seriously?

KENNEDY: I think what he felt was that it was impractical at that time, that perhaps our policy was too much dominated by the Germans and what they wanted or didn't want. That was a practical reality of the times. Adenauer was rather suspicious of President Kennedy. His number-one statesman of the world was John Foster Dulles. [Adenauer] always caused a good deal of trouble for us, because he'd complain to someone about the President. When he came over here, he liked the President. All the personal visits were fine. But he complained to me and he complained to others. Finally, in 1963, I think, the President wrote him a very sharp letter about all the complaining he was doing, about the fact that it was the United States who had the troops over there, it was the United States who was carrying the burden, the United States who was putting the money in.

But I think that, on that plan and other suggestions that were made, the President felt, at least for the first term, he would have to deal with the political realities of the day.

MARTIN: General Walker resigned late in the fall. [A right-wing critic of the Kennedy administration, Major General Edwin A. Walker claimed that there were Communist influences in government and military circles. Walker resigned from the Army in November 1961.] This was part of this whole rightist upsurge. Was the President very concerned about the rightist upsurge?

KENNEDY: Not really, no.

MARTIN: Birchites [members of the John Birch Society] and the rest?

KENNEDY: No.

MARTIN: He didn't regard it as a serious political force?

KENNEDY: No. He thought it was silly, that Walker was crazy, and a lot of the others were pains in the butt. But it was more humorous than anything else.

MARTIN: That's when—November of '61—he appointed [Teodoro] Moscoso Coordinator of the Alliance for Progress. He had been Ambassador to Venezuela, do you recall? What did he think of Moscoso?

KENNEDY: He liked him personally. By the end he didn't think he was much of an administrator.

MARTIN: He had a lot of company in that view.

KENNEDY: It was difficult for him to get anybody to take it over. I think I might have gotten more involved in Latin America myself.

MARTIN: Wish you had?

KENNEDY: In the second term, anyway. But it was a question of trying to get somebody—we certainly didn't have that feeling in the beginning; it was gradual—to replace Moscoso. And that created all kinds of problems.

Did I mention how we got the head of AID? Fowler Hamilton. I think I mentioned about the fact that he was going to be head of CIA. Hamilton turned out badly. I mentioned the fact that everybody was disappointed with him. He went around and made a lot of speeches.

MARTIN: Moscoso did too.

KENNEDY: Yes. So the whole thing fell down. When the President wanted to get rid of [Fowler Hamilton] and he was ready to resign, the President asked Sargent Shriver to head it up. [Shriver] made a study of it and thought he couldn't run AID. He thought it was difficult because you couldn't fire people and some other things. He wouldn't do that. So then the President asked Dave Bell [then Director, Bureau of the Budget].

MARTIN: I sent a letter of sympathy to Dave Bell when he was appointed. It was a swamp, AID.

KENNEDY: He's done a good job.

MARTIN: I'm sure he has. If anybody can run AID, Dave can.

KENNEDY: When we used to have our meetings on counterinsurgency, Fowler Hamilton used to come. Then he used to send [AID Deputy Administrator] Frank Coffin. Neither one of them ever knew the answers to any of the questions. All the problems we had were basically on AID.

MARTIN: What happened to the Alliance for Progress? It started out so well. What do you think went wrong?

KENNEDY: I don't think [Moscoso] was the best administrator. It was tough to get good people. Then it's tough to move some of those countries. The opposition came not only from the Communists but from the right-wingers. So it was tough. We had to get the best kind of people ourselves, we had to have the best possible administration, and then we had to have some cooperation. All those elements weren't there. They were there to a lesser or greater extent in any particular country. Some places it worked well. We didn't know what kind of programs we were going to get into. I think it's trial and error. And, as I say, I don't think we've had the best possible people.

MARTIN: Was there any program?

KENNEDY: The President thought we were moving in the right direction, thought it was the right concept, and was disappointed that it didn't work better. He thought that he could get it to work well.

MARTIN: He did? That's what I really wanted to ask you. He was not ready to just let it die a natural death?

KENNEDY: No, no.

MARTIN: He was ready to go ahead and push forward to make it work?

KENNEDY: Yes.

MARTIN: During this fall, the United Nations had one of its perennial debates on the admission of Red China to the U.N.

KENNEDY: Yes.

MARTIN: Did you ever talk to the President about this? I'm not talking now about the tactics in the U.N. or anything. But did you ever have a general conversation about the future?

KENNEDY: You mean about the future of China?

MARTIN: Sooner or later they'd have to get in.

KENNEDY: Yes.

MARTIN: What was the future of Red China and our relations with them?

KENNEDY: I took it for granted that they were going to get in, that it wasn't helpful in our foreign policy that they get in at the present time—and it certainly wasn't helpful domestically. It was in our interest, at least at the present time, to oppose that. I gathered [JFK] had the same viewpoint. We'd had so many other problems without sitting down wondering what was going to happen to Red China. I don't know that he had any great long-range concepts of what we'd do as far as Red China is concerned. With the immediate problems that we had that were taking so much attention and energy, I think he felt that things like that could be put more into the second term, that you could really concentrate more on them once you got the world going in a generally satisfactory direction—which it really wasn't in early 1961.

No matter what might be the feeling about what is happening now, it was far different at the end of 1963 than it was in the beginning of 1961. With all of these things, it seemed that every day there was a new problem.

MARTIN: I got the impression from what you just said, Bob, and other things you've said, that during 1961 it was almost a matter of putting out fires and trying to survive day to day as the crises kept piling up. Is that about right?

KENNEDY: Yes. We had the Bay of Pigs, we had Berlin, and then we had Laos and Vietnam. That was a helluva burden to carry in '61, as well as reorganizing the government, picking the right people for all these jobs, fighting with Chester Bowles, and getting judges. You know, just all together, each day. I mentioned I used to ask my brother each week whether he liked the job, and during that period of time he'd say what a fantastic job it would be if you didn't have the Russians.

MARTIN: How did he feel by the end of 1961? Do you recall?

KENNEDY: I think he thought we were making some progress, but it was awfully tough sledding. Then, in addition to the things I mentioned, there were the fights with Congress, the newspapers saying that nothing was being done. All of these things. He was really, you know, sort of an optimist.

MARTIN: I always had a contrary feeling, that he was deeply pessimistic.

KENNEDY: No, not really. I think he—a little bit like my father—always saw the bright side of things. He recognized the problems, but he really assessed what was happening—what he was doing—over a period of years, even though he'd get upset with what the newspapers were writing, because he was a perfectionist. He always wanted to be well-thought-of at the time and didn't want anybody to make a mistake. If he read in the paper a criticism, he'd always call up to get an explanation of it. He was calling people continuously, all the time. He wanted to make sure it was done well.

But after you say that, that's not sufficient, because I think he saw that what he was doing—over a period of eight years, a decade maybe—would have an effect for many, many years to come. Little things that he was doing—his relationship with a President of a country or his relationship with an Ambassador—were chipping away at what had happened before and starting us on an entirely different course. That road that we were going on: You couldn't get on it immediately; or you could get on it but you couldn't go far on it immediately. But each step you were taking made a difference. What he saw was that, over an extended period of time, it would really make a difference. Although concerned by the day-to-day events, he never lost sight of the major picture.

I see the difference between [then and] now: Although there's no major matter where we're falling, we're not doing the little things that used to get us up. Instead, we're going flatter, going down. Secondly, I can't think of any matter of any significance that was decided based on how it would help us politically in the United States. When we went through this last Cuba crisis about cutting off the water, that and other matters seemed to be determined a good deal by what the effect politically was going to look like that day. That never was important to the President, even though he was a past master in politics. I don't know whether that's all clear.

What he thought was that—at least, for the first few years—because things had been going so badly against us, he had to concentrate all his energies (and there wasn't any alternative, because each day was a new crisis) on foreign affairs. He thought that a good deal more needed to be done domestically. The major issue was the question of civil rights, which, except in crisis matters, he left pretty much to me, once he gave general guidelines to everybody.

Secondly, he thought that we really had to begin to make a major effort to deal with unemployment and the poor in the United States. He thought that was going to cost several billions of dollars each year, and that if he wanted to get the tax bill by, he couldn't then come in with a program which was going to cost even a billion dollars. So he was going to wait until he got the tax bill by before he tried to take some action to deal with that. But I don't think it would be right to say that he thought everything would take care of itself domestically. I don't think he did.

The crises were in the foreign policy field. I think all the other problems—the flow of gold or something—were of tremendous concern to him. We started to take action. We lost three hundred and fifty million dollars in January alone of 1961, just in the month that he took over, up to January 20. So he put in almost two dozen different measures over a period of two and a half years.

I think more was done for business in the United States during the last three years than has ever been done. Yet it's not recognized. I think, when the story is eventually written, it will be rather impressive.

I would say there's another matter in which I had a different position than my brother—I mentioned it before—which was that I was in favor of a tax.

MARTIN: You're talking about income tax?

KENNEDY: Yes. Because I thought it would bring home to the American people the crisis, the importance, and the fact that everybody was making a sacrifice. Economists generally were against it—I can't tell you quite how it split down—but they felt that we were making some progress, a recovery, and if we put in an increase in taxes, it would have a very adverse effect. That argument finally prevailed.

MARTIN: The straight economic argument that it would be an inflationary measure?

KENNEDY: Yes. When I was talking to [JFK] about the fact that I had been opposed to appointing Henry Cabot Lodge—I said that Henry Cabot Lodge in Vietnam would cause him a lot of difficulty in six months—he said that was terrific because I could always remember when I was right. He said, "Do you remember when you were in favor of a tax increase and that would have had a very adverse effect? That's when you weren't right."

MARTIN: Your idea was, I suppose, to bring home the thing that he'd said in the inaugural address?

KENNEDY: Yes, that's right.

MARTIN: "What you can do for your country?"

KENNEDY: That's right.

MARTIN: I think at the time the general impression was that you were alone in this position.

KENNEDY: Yes. The other fight or argument I had—for the interests of history—was in '61, on the building of the dam in Ghana [the Volta Dam project]. I don't know whether it was '61 or '62—it might have been '62—but I was involved in the discussion about building a dam in Ghana.[19] First, I was concerned about the fact that we'd have that investment there and lose the investment. They worked up the details in such a way that it would appear that we could invest each year and have control over it through 1965. We needn't be concerned about that aspect of it. I think, based on some of the problems we've had in the last few weeks on Ghana, that hasn't proved completely accurate. And I think it's very difficult to get out of it now.

In any case, we had some meetings on it. I had thought that if we had that much money to invest, it would be better to invest it with friends of ours in that part of the world. It was awfully difficult to explain to the Ivory Coast—or even Guinea or Togo, some of those other countries—why they had difficulty getting one, two, or three million dollars when we were putting ninety-six million dollars in Ghana.

MARTIN: Is that what the thing cost, ninety-six?

KENNEDY: Ninety-six over a five- or six-year period.

I thought that was the biggest problem. Secondly, I thought about the question of losing the investment. Third, all the reports were that [Nkrumah] was going Communist, that the country would be turning Communist. We'd put the dam up there, and then the Communists would take it over. I didn't see that that was any great asset.

The argument on the other side was helping the people, raising their standard of living. If we pulled out of it then, it would have a very adverse effect there and also around the world. I said that we'd take the money—we'd say that we weren't going to take it out of there but that we were going to continue to invest the money or give that money to other countries. In any case, the President finally decided to put the dam in Ghana, and we had some spirited arguments about it. He made some remark about my cross little face looking over his shoulder while he was doing this. But he did it. I think, looking at it in retrospect, that it was the correct decision.

MARTIN: Yes. I don't know. We could have used that money in the Dominican Republic.

KENNEDY: Yes.

MARTIN: It could have built a couple of dams.

KENNEDY: Yes, but I suppose it would have had an adverse effect.

MARTIN: Were there [other issues] that you recall that you were in disagreement on?

KENNEDY: We were in disagreement on some timing on matters, or I was undecided about something and he decided immediately.

MARTIN: Can you think of an example?

KENNEDY: That's the great thing about doing an oral history or writing a book: You can always think of things when you were reasonably right. There were a number of examples where I'd have a problem and he'd make up his mind right away about what we should do, and appeared to be completely correct to me—which over a period of time used to impress me. The second thing is where we'd have alternatives or I'd sort of be leaning in a certain direction. There were some on the civil rights matters. There were other times when we'd make a decision about what we would do, the two of us (particularly in civil rights), and then I'd think about it some more and know that it wasn't the right decision and do something differently. I'd figure in my own mind I knew what was right, so we didn't do it. I'm thinking of some of the dealings with Alabama and the racial problems.

MARTIN: Anything specific?

KENNEDY: I think one was on the question of what time we would call out the [National] Guard. I think we left the White House with the understanding we'd call out the Guard the next day, twenty-four hours before.

MARTIN: You changed your mind?

KENNEDY: I changed my mind.

MARTIN: In that instance, did you just change your mind and so order it?

KENNEDY: Just changed it.

MARTIN: You didn't go back to him?

KENNEDY: I just never did. It became clear that—if I had a problem or if he had a strong feeling toward a particular position, if we'd discussed it and both reached a conclusion, and then if I thought about it some more and reached a contrary conclusion—I might just decide on my own to do it. If he felt strongly about something and then I reached a different conclusion when I came back to my office, I'd call him. But I remember in the morning, on the Alabama thing again, we were going to wait until the Governor moved before calling up the troops. Then I thought maybe we should call up the troops that morning. So I called him about doing that. He said, "Let's just stay with what we decided originally"—which was the right decision. The most indecisive time we ever had was in the selection of the Vice President.

MARTIN: Was it?

KENNEDY: Yes. Now that was just terrible. We changed our minds eight times during the course of it.

MARTIN: Among whom?

KENNEDY: Just my brother Jack and myself.

MARTIN: No, no, I know, but whom were you talking about?

KENNEDY: Whether we wanted Lyndon Johnson on the ticket or not.

MARTIN: What were the alternatives?

KENNEDY: We thought either [Scoop] Jackson or [Stuart] Symington. I don't know whether we'd concentrated [on anyone], but I think Symington probably at that time. . . . We changed and rechanged our minds probably seven times. The only people who were involved in the discussions were Jack and myself. Nobody else was involved in it.

MARTIN: Whatever happened to the missile gap? I ran across a story in *The New York Times* in December '61 saying the Atomic Energy Commission said that we're ahead and everything is fine. But the missile gap in the campaign was very large and very real. What the hell happened here? It always was a good issue.

KENNEDY: I think it was based on CIA reports as to what existed and what they assessed the Russians had. The CIA reports during that period of time assessed the fact that they were way, way ahead of us as far as missiles were concerned. Then we were able to send over some satellites, which took pictures in '61 and, more importantly, in 1962 and '63, and found out they didn't have missiles. Where they were constructing them, the satellites could do just a helluva job—almost as good as the U-2—and take pictures.

This report in 1963—it was the worst leak that we had during President Kennedy's administration—was by Hanson Baldwin, who wrote a story in *The New York Times* about the missiles: our satellites taking pictures, knowing which of the Russian missiles were embedded in concrete, which were not, and giving us an assessment. The result was that the Soviet Union since then has changed its whole concept. They started putting them in concrete and hiding them, and this caused tremendous difficulty for our intelligence. We started looking into who gave Hanson Baldwin the information. Hanson Baldwin raised a big fuss. *The New York Times* raised a big fuss. Yet the President's Advisory Council on Intelligence,[20] which is independent of the President but advises him, made an assessment and said this was the worst leak that they had seen. . . .

Hanson Baldwin was very bitter against me and against the President. It showed up in his writings during 1963 because he was always very critical and called it a police state. But it was terribly, terribly serious. Finally, the President talked to [publisher Orville E.] Dryfoos, or whoever was there, and gave him the report of the intelligence bureau. What happened afterward was most unfortunate because [the Russians] just realigned their whole strategic efforts because of the story. He was very unpleasant, Hanson Baldwin.

MARTIN: Do you think in your own mind there ever was a missile gap?

KENNEDY: No.

MARTIN: The President didn't think so either? He thought so at the time he was campaigning and concluded, after he got in the White House, there hadn't been. Is that right?

KENNEDY: That's right. We were and we are way ahead, considerably ahead, of the Russians now in missiles. I think it's what led them to back down [during the missile crisis], one of the points that led them to back down, because we really would have destroyed them. Our lead will get smaller and smaller each year.

MARTIN: It will?

KENNEDY: Yes, until 1968 and '69, when we won't have any.

MARTIN: Really? Then what happens?

KENNEDY: We'll have different kinds of missiles, and they're going to have more atomic power. (Ours are going to be spread better.) It just means that they can kill us better than we can kill them.

MARTIN: In December there was fighting in the Congo between Katanga troops and the U.N. troops. The President took the initiative to try to stop it. This struck me, on the face of it, as somewhat unusual in that it was already in the U.N. and the President stepped into it himself directly. Do you remember any reason why? He was really sticking his neck out, it appears, where he didn't need to.

KENNEDY: His policy on the Congo generally was based on the fact that if you had two independent states in the Congo—Katanga and the rest of the Congo—the Katanga would be rich and powerful, and the rest of the Congo would go Communist. The only way you could have a viable country was to have one independent country. Belgium and the rest of them were making a bad mistake. In order to prevent the Communists from becoming embedded in the central part of Africa, we had to prevent the Congo from splitting up. We had to do everything to prevent that.

MARTIN: I think that's the answer.

KENNEDY: He became completely committed to doing that. Then the President sent out Ed Gullion—or he was made Ambassador. He was the fellow we met in Vietnam in 1951, when we were there, who so impressed the President. He became Ambassador.

MARTIN: I know him very slightly. He seems like a terrific fellow.

KENNEDY: The President became very impressed with him and said that, if he [JFK] was a Foreign Service officer, how much more he'd rather be sent to a place like the Congo or a country in South America than Paris or London or any of the other countries where you just become almost a messenger.

MARTIN: Absolutely.

KENNEDY: In the last analysis, in these countries, a good deal depends on what the Ambassador does. He thought very highly of Ed Gullion. . . .

MARTIN: There was opposition rising in Congress to the whole U.N. operation costing so much in the Congo. There was a bond issue. The President went down the lines for the bond issue, didn't he?

KENNEDY: Yes, he did. He also had seen some polls that had been taken around the United States, and individual polls, which showed that the United Nations was terribly popular in the United States. So not only did he think it was right, but he felt that he had the support of the people.

MARTIN: That he was on solid ground, not out on a limb?

KENNEDY: That's right. He made himself unpopular on the Congo matter, particularly with columnists like Arthur Krock and David

Lawrence. But he thought that the alternative was going to be complete chaos in Africa.

MARTIN: He placed a lot of reliance on the United Nations?

KENNEDY: He thought it was our one major hope. Primary reliance was on our own power, position, prestige.

MARTIN: This was basic in his policy thinking?

KENNEDY: Yes. But hand in hand with that—

MARTIN: I don't mean to downgrade the U.N., but in his thinking—

KENNEDY: That was what we had.

MARTIN: That was what we had.

What was this curious business of the editor of *Izvestia* who came over here and talked to the President? The interview was printed in Moscow, and Salinger was involved in it. Do you remember that?

KENNEDY: [Alekei] Adzhubei.

MARTIN: Was there anything that hasn't been published and is of interest in connection with that episode?

KENNEDY: They got along well. [Adzhubei] went up to the Cape and talked to the President. I think he was very impressed with the President. He came out to see me at the house and had lunch. He's a tough Communist, and I didn't like him much. The President liked him pretty well. His wife came over with him. It was just arranged for an exchange of views. I don't think there's any more.

MARTIN: Nothing much in it, nothing that isn't generally known? That's all I was looking for.

KENNEDY: No.

MARTIN: It was announced at the end of the year that [Abraham] Ribicoff would resign [from HEW]. Ribicoff hadn't been very effective anyway, had he?

KENNEDY: No, he hadn't.

MARTIN: He hadn't been interested, had he, in HEW?

KENNEDY: No, and he didn't have much contact with the President. I think he tried hard, and I think he was loyal. I spoke about the fact that the President offered him Attorney General. It was rather a frustrating experience. He was involved in the disputes on church and state, Medicare—it's just such a difficult department to run. He had a difficult time coping with it. . . .

MARTIN: How did [Ribicoff's successor, Cleveland Mayor Anthony J.] Celebrezze happen to be appointed?

KENNEDY: We were looking around for a number of people.

There were about four or five people who were suggested. He had a pretty good reputation. Kenny O'Donnell was strongly in favor of Celebrezze. He had a good reputation out in Cleveland, and the fact that he was Italian was a major factor to be considered. It was an election year.

MARTIN: Yes. The story I heard was that you were having trouble with the Italian vote in Massachusetts in Teddy [Kennedy's senatorial] campaign. This was why he was appointed?

KENNEDY: No.

MARTIN: It's not true?

KENNEDY: No. A major factor in his appointment was the fact that he was Italian, but it wasn't with the eye on Massachusetts at all. We did have a saying after that: "Celebrezze makes it easy." He was very helpful in the congressional elections around the country, because he got the Italians. . . .

MARTIN: At the end of the year, the President met with Macmillan in Bermuda. Anything particular happen that you know about?

KENNEDY: Well, the Skybolt was a big—

MARTIN: Was that the Skybolt or was that later?

KENNEDY: It was '61, Bermuda. All of that has been written up in great detail by [Kennedy adviser Professor Richard] Dick Neustadt, whom the President asked to make an investigation. The President took it on his trip to Dallas, Texas, and told Jackie it was (he asked me to read it) like a detective novel. It really is. It goes into all of the ramifications of Skybolt.

The President had a lot of humorous stories about Macmillan. He liked Macmillan very much. He had a great dry sense of humor. [JFK] had a number of stories that he told of what Macmillan said. I think he wrote them all down or told Mrs. [Evelyn] Lincoln [the President's secretary]. They were awfully funny, but unfortunately, I didn't write them down. And I can't remember.

MARTIN: You keep coming up to these climaxes—and then say that you can't remember! That's all right.

It was then that your father had the stroke?

KENNEDY: That was at Christmas.

MARTIN: It was right about this time?

KENNEDY: Yes. He saw the President off at the airport to come back to Washington, I think on the 22nd or 21st of December. The President got back here, and he had his stroke that morning, that noon. We all went down to Florida that night. . . .

MARTIN: Did this make a lot of difference to the President? Of course it made a difference. But did he change?

KENNEDY: No, he didn't change. It made a difference, particularly during the steel dispute. He often said how much he wished my father was well. On the tax bill and other matters that he would ordinarily talk to my father about, he could not do that any longer. It was distressing to him, as it was to everybody, to see my father in that condition when he'd been so active and able.

[JFK] was almost the best with my father because he really made him laugh and said outrageous things to him. My father used to sit out there Friday afternoon waiting for the helicopter to arrive. He used to get excited. And Jack used to come over and spend some time with him. It really made a big difference in his life. Then on Sunday afternoon he'd take off. My father'd come out and see him leave in the helicopter.

1962

MARTIN: There are a whole lot of things which start in '62. One of the first that came along was the trade and tariff bill. How much importance did the President assign to it? It was hailed as a major turning point in American policy. Did the President think of it that way?

KENNEDY: He thought it was very important. I don't know whether he thought so at the end, after the French and the British—

MARTIN: The whole thing fell apart when England was refused admittance to the Common Market.

KENNEDY: I think he had far greater hopes for it at the beginning.

MARTIN: It turned out not to be of much importance, didn't it?

KENNEDY: Well, now, I can't say that.

MARTIN: Earlier than that, Khrushchev was making a speech about Russia as an affluent society. This was really a turnaround.

KENNEDY: Let me just say that, talking about Khrushchev's speeches, the speech that impressed the President most by Khrushchev was his speech on January 6, 1961, about wars of liberation. When we were talking earlier about reassessing the military forces and strategic forces, the speech of January 6, 1961, was a major factor. The President made everybody on the National Security Council read the speech. He also made all the military people read the speech.

This speech was important. Wars were not going to come in an exchange of atomic bombs. Khrushchev talked about the wars of liberation that were going to be done through subversion, through overthrow of governments, through civil war, civil disobedience. The President felt that our actions should be tailored to meet those kinds of problems, that too much in the past we had been ready to [use] the big bomb with the big buck—or whatever.

MARTIN: Yes, the bigger bang for a buck.

KENNEDY: What we needed were people who could shoot guns and make an effort along those lines. Our [Counterinsurgency] Committee, when taking it up six months after Cuba, tried to assess what needed to be done. One of the things that we thought should be done was to have a school established to teach about insurgency and teach about Communism. The President felt very strongly it shouldn't be a school just for those who didn't have anything better to do, but for people who had really important positions or were going to have positions of responsibility. So that school was formed, with about fifty or sixty students. At first, it was a five-week course; now, it's a four-week course. I go and speak to it in each course. It's under our Counterinsurgency Committee.

Then we increased the size of the Special Forces by four hundred percent. The President gave them their green berets.

MARTIN: Was that his idea?

KENNEDY: I think the green beret was his idea. I arranged for them to come to the funeral to march because he felt very strongly about the Special Forces. . . .

MARTIN: The January 6, 1961, speech of Khrushchev's was a very important factor in this. A year later, he was beginning to make noises like a capitalist. He was talking about the affluent society. The whole tone of the Russian dialogue had changed. I think by that time he was having trouble with the Chicoms [Chinese Communists] and with Albania. But also, everything we'd been doing in '61 must have begun to have some effect on him. I wonder if you recall whether you talked to [JFK] about a real—apparently—change in Khrushchev's general attitude. Do you recall?

KENNEDY: I think we reached the conclusion, whether it was then or later on, that all of this was used for some purpose. [Khrushchev] would be friendly and then unfriendly, friendly and unfriendly, so that he'd keep everybody on the hook. He was friendly in '62, but by the end of '62 he was sending missiles into Cuba. At the end of '61, we had the Berlin crisis, and then we were having problems with Laos. I think it was just a question of how we were going to react under pressure.

MARTIN: You thought this was all tactics?

KENNEDY: Yes.

MARTIN: Not a basic shift?

KENNEDY: Yes.
   I think that Cuba also proved that he didn't want to have a war with the United States. He's got that much sense. If anything changed his opinion, it came at the end of 1962, because I think he would have put the screws on or reapplied the screws.

MARTIN: End of '62? You mean second Cuba?

KENNEDY: Yes.

MARTIN: In 1962 the State of the Union speech emphasized domestic affairs, promised a balanced budget, and talked a lot about welfare programs and other domestic matters. Is there any particular reason why the emphasis went on the domestic side in 1962? It was an election year.

KENNEDY: No. The unfinished business that he could do something about was domestic matters. The President, of course, was interested in a lot of domestic programs, some of which got through and some of which were stalled.

MARTIN: Why didn't he do better with Congress than he did?

KENNEDY: I think he did very well.

MARTIN: Do you think he did better than most people think?

KENNEDY: Very well, I think. We got a helluva lot of bills by. A lot of important legislation was passed.

MARTIN: You think the record is better than the general impression of it?

KENNEDY: Yes, much. Consider what you're working with: considering that, when you had the fight in the Rules Committee, we only won it by four or five votes and that was *with* the prestige of Sam Rayburn, with everybody lined up, with some southerners—and we still only won that by a very narrow margin—then I think it was remarkably successful.

MARTIN: You're speaking generally, every year now?

KENNEDY: Yes, I mean overall. I think probably the best person to discuss that is Ted Sorensen. He's got it down because the President had him assess that, so I would think that he knows the situation. But I think, actually, the record is damn good.

MARTIN: Do you want to talk about your trip? Why did you go? What happened? What impressed you? What was the importance of it? What did you think of the people you met? Your relationship with [Indonesian President] Sukarno may have begun then.

KENNEDY: Reischauer, the Ambassador [to Japan], came in '61 to my office and said that he'd like to have me come. He went and made a big pitch for it with the State Department.

We had met, when we were out in the Far East in '51, a man by the name of Hosono [Gunji, a Japanese businessman], who then proceeded to correspond with my brother and myself and my sister Pat continuously over the period of the next ten years. He took an interest in us when we arrived [in 1951]. The Congressman was descending on Tokyo with his brother and sister; nobody was very interested. Mr. Hosono, who was Japanese, an old man who was interested in Japanese-American friendship, became very interested and talked to us and brought us out and everything.

He corresponded with us. Then the President ran for the Senate in '52. [Hosono] is the one who got the captain of the *Amuri*—that's the ship that sunk [the World War II PT boat commanded by] the President—to write a letter. We got a lot of publicity out of that. We took some pictures, and all the rest of it. He was a good friend.

We wrote him back, and he wrote. When the President was inaugurated, he invited Mr. Hosono to come and sit in the stand with him. So he came with his daughter. It was a rather nice relationship, all based on the fact that he had been nice to this Congressman in '51.

[Hosono] was very anxious for me to come out. So he spoke to the Ambassador, and they raised a big fuss about it. The President became interested, and they decided that I'd go. It was decided that, as long as I was going there, I'd also go to Indonesia. At that time they were starting, or continuing, their efforts over West New Guinea.[21] That was the big problem.

MARTIN: You had to go to Holland as well.

KENNEDY: Yes. My mission really was to see if I could get them [the Dutch and the Indonesians] to sit down at a conference table and discuss their grievances. Also, I had a second mission: There was a pilot by the name of [Allen L.] Pope, who had been captured in the '58 [Indonesian] rebellion and had initially been sentenced to death. He had been a CIA man, and they were trying to get him out. He was the one American who was held. He'd never talked. He'd been very brave. His wife came to see me, and I was tremendously impressed with her. She talked about the children, the fact that the children were fighting with one another, that one child had never seen her father. So I was really very taken up with it.

I went first to Japan and spent six days there. I sent John Seigenthaler out first with another young fellow from the State Department, Brandon Grove, to be advance men, because I didn't want to just go around to a lot of cocktail parties. It was established that I would come and spend one day, or a day and a half, visiting officials of the Japanese government. The rest of the time would be an unofficial visit.

We toured Japan in a bus, went to a lot of odd places, did strange things, ate peculiar food, and all the rest of it. I went to universities and schools and spent a lot of time with the students, a lot of time with the factory workers, and a lot of time with intellectuals and professors.

MARTIN: How did you find the students? Friendly?

KENNEDY: Yes, very.

MARTIN: Or some of them hostile?

KENNEDY: No, no. For the most part, friendly. Some, I suppose the most part, were neutral; some, very friendly; and some, very hostile.

We had a near riot at Waseda University. But it was caused mostly by just about two hundred students.

MARTIN: I was interested in how you handle students who are hostile. I had this problem in the Dominican Republic as the Ambassador, because we had a Communist-infiltrated student movement there. When I'd go out whistle-stopping, as you did in Japan, I ran into a lot of hostility. I was never really sure that I was handling it right. I wondered if you had any thoughts in general on how you did it.

KENNEDY: If they are there just to break up the meeting, I think it's very difficult to handle it.

MARTIN: It's impossible, really.

KENNEDY: Because they're just going to yell. Then somebody yells at them; then they yell back—and so you never can be heard. I don't know that there's any future in that. That's what happened at my meeting. They were there just to make sure I didn't speak. This was all on live television all across Japan. When they started yelling, I invited their spokesman up on the stage and said, "Why don't you speak for five minutes. Then I'll speak for five minutes."

MARTIN: Did that work?

KENNEDY: It worked out very successfully, because then they started yelling when I spoke. I mean, it was difficult there. People all across Japan saw what the Communists did. They saw that I was willing to give them a chance to speak their piece. All I wanted was a chance to speak mine. And they wouldn't let me. It was the best thing that happened in my trip. It was very, very successful because everybody was so humiliated and embarrassed that I'd been invited and then couldn't speak.

But if they just want to break it up, I don't know that you can do a helluva lot. I went back to Waseda University this last time [January 1964], and they had filled the hall. They had twenty to thirty thousand students outside the hall—just this sea of humanity. They were really excited about the fact that I came back. There wasn't any incident.

MARTIN: Did you ever have private conversations with hostile students?

KENNEDY: Yes.

MARTIN: Did you find that useful? Or were their minds so closed you couldn't get through to them?

KENNEDY: No, you couldn't get through.

MARTIN: That was the trouble I always had.

KENNEDY: If they're Communists, you can't get through to them.

I met with different groups all at one time, for instance, and I would go around the table and talk to each of them. It is helpful, to some extent, to have one group that's hostile. Even though they won't listen, they ask hostile questions. If you're able to answer them and discuss it intelligently, then I think that it makes a difference.

Then I went to Indonesia and met with Sukarno. I got along with him.

MARTIN: Was that the first time you'd met him?

KENNEDY: Yes. I didn't like him from what I had heard of him, I didn't like him when I was there, and I haven't liked him since.

MARTIN: Really?

KENNEDY: I don't have respect for him. I think that he's bright. I think he's completely immoral, that he's untrustworthy.

MARTIN: Is he a liar?

KENNEDY: I think he's a liar. I think he's got very few redeeming features. He speaks like hell. He's a demagogue; he's not a Communist. I think he's antiwhite. But I think he liked the President; he likes, he admires the United States; and I think he liked me and Ethel.

MARTIN: What were you supposed to do with him?

KENNEDY: Two things. First, nobody had visited Indonesia. I went to offset what was happening there: the fact that all the Chinese officials and Russian officials and Khrushchev had spent some time there. I went around to the universities and spoke and got into arguments and fights every place.

MARTIN: Did you get anywhere on the substance of West Irian?

KENNEDY: Yes. At the universities I did. I think it made a helluva difference with the universities—as I do with Indonesia. I think that was well worthwhile. The second thing I did was get [Sukarno] to agree to sit down with the Dutch to discuss it.

MARTIN: And did he?

KENNEDY: Yes, he did it, and they resolved it. They avoided a war. They would have had a war.

MARTIN: Do you think so?

KENNEDY: Yes. It would have been the white men against the Africans, the Asians, and the Communists. It would have been a very bad, very dangerous situation. So, if for no other reason, that trip was worthwhile—just to get him to agree to that. The war was called off, postponed; and eventually the issue was settled. The Dutch wanted to get out of there. The person who was causing the trouble was [Dutch Foreign Affairs Minister Joseph] Luns, but such pressure built up that they agreed to sit down and talk over their difficulties and troubles. Pressure built up on Luns.

It was quite different from the Malaysian dispute now, where Indonesia doesn't have the support of any of the other countries. Sukarno's almost isolated. But that wasn't the situation in West New Guinea. Number two: The difference in West New Guinea is that at the time of independence the Dutch had promised them that they would take some steps to deal with this problem—and nothing had ever been done in fifteen years. Number three: The Dutch wanted to get rid of West New Guinea. Again, that is another difference between Malaysia and North Borneo. You can't equate the two. It was very important that that matter be settled, because it would have been a very unpleasant war to get involved in. The Russians want them to settle Malaysia. They think this is silly, to enter this dispute. And I did also.

I did have a rather bitter fight—in which I walked out of a room—with [Sukarno] on the question of Pope, the pilot, because I asked him the first day I was there about releasing Pope. He had told the President earlier that he would release Pope. When I got there, he said, "I'll tell you at the end of the week." At the end of the week, it was quite obvious that what he was going to do was use Pope as a bargaining [chip] for our position on West New Guinea. I explained to him that that was not going to be possible. He could take Pope out and shoot him and it wouldn't affect what we did on West New Guinea, because we were going to do what was in the interests of the United States and in the interests of justice. So he couldn't do that. Secondly, I told him that I thought he was trying to string us along. And I got up and walked out. The American Ambassador [Howard Jones] said, "You can't do that. It's going to destroy or break relations." So I went back and said I was sorry that I got so upset about it, though I did not apologize for what I said, because I thought that that was correct.

Then the Foreign Minister got in touch with me and said they would let Pope out in six weeks. Six weeks went by, and they still hadn't let him out. So I got back in touch with him and said that he was lying: He told us he'd let Pope out and he wasn't letting him out. About three weeks later they let Pope out with the understanding that there would be no publicity. He got back in the United States. There wasn't any publicity. He was out. We put him away in a hideaway for a month. Finally it was publicized that he was released. He eventually came to see me to thank me. He's a good-looking fellow, the soldier-of-fortune type. He was going back out to the Far East. I said how wonderful his wife had been. I said, "Is she going with you?" He said, "No, she's not going. We don't live together. We've been separated for some time."

MARTIN: No kidding?

KENNEDY: So I said, "Well, I have all the more respect for her, because even though you're not living together, she made a major effort."

MARTIN: Where else did you go on this trip?

KENNEDY: We went to Hong Kong for a day, and then we went to Thailand.

MARTIN: What for?

KENNEDY: I stayed there for a day and visited with some students again. Then I went to Rome.

MARTIN: Iran?

KENNEDY: No, I didn't go to Iran. They asked me to go to Iran. The trip was arranged for Iran. But I said if I went to Iran, I wanted to visit the university and visit students. They said I couldn't visit students. So I said I wouldn't go to Iran. That caused a major fuss in the State Department. They said, "You've got to go to Iran." I said, "I'm not going to go unless I can go where I want to go." So they canceled that. That's why, I guess, they put Thailand in instead. They said I had to go to Thailand. I don't know what excuse they made.

Then I went to Rome and arrived there on the day when [astronaut] John Glenn made his trip. We went to Berlin because of the problems that existed [there]. It was felt that it would be helpful to have somebody else go there. General [Lucius D.] Clay [then presidential envoy to Berlin] had come to see me and asked me to go to Berlin.

MARTIN: Did he have a basic disagreement with the President on policy?

KENNEDY: No.

MARTIN: There was a lot of newspaper stuff about it.

KENNEDY: No, [Clay] didn't. He had a disagreement fundamentally—it wasn't with the President—with the State Department, as I recollect. He wanted more authority for himself in Berlin. He kept having to go through the State Department before they'd permit him to take any action. The result was there were a lot of delays in what he thought he should be able to decide for himself as the officer on the scene.

When I got to Berlin, I talked to him about it. I talked to him a number of other times about it. The President tried to smooth it over as much as he could. I think [Clay] liked the President, liked what we were doing in Berlin, and the President made a real effort. But I think there wasn't a helluva lot for him to do afterward. He got there, and he was a symbol—and he was damned good in that—but then it started to fade off as to what he actually could accomplish. It was one of those unpleasant things. I was quite friendly with him personally and used to visit with him frequently. When he had problems of this kind, he'd frequently come to see me. We'd just discuss them.

So I went to Berlin and got a helluva reception in Berlin—different from the reception any other place. People were really emotional, large crowds all the way in from the airport and in the square where we spoke. Of course, it wasn't comparable to what the President received, but it was the same emotion, the same feeling. I told my brother about it when I got back, and he found the same thing when he went there.

MARTIN: Did you talk with Adenauer?

KENNEDY: I talked to Adenauer.

MARTIN: Did you make any progress?

KENNEDY: I think I did. It helped

MARTIN: You said earlier he was always suspicious.

KENNEDY: Yes, I just think [he was suspicious] with young people— the fact that there wasn't a John Foster Dulles—and then generally with our position on these matters. The idea of conventional forces—he didn't like that. Of course, we'd tried to get the other countries to build up the conventional forces because of Berlin's problems. And none of them really contributed. We carried the whole burden there.

A lot of it, as I say, goes back to the fundamental concepts that they had about what should be done in Germany, what should be done to meet the Communist threat—[concepts] which became quite different from ours. So we had to reeducate them. Now, I think that that education had been partially successful.

[General Lauris] Norstad [Supreme Commander of Allied Forces in Europe] was not very helpful in all of this because he had the old ideas. He didn't really agree with what the President was doing, and he didn't really agree with Maxwell Taylor. He was good during the Cuban crisis of '62—his ideas were good. The President didn't like him much before that because they fundamentally disagreed and he caused so much fuss all the time. He was rather a prima donna. I met him for some period of time. I think that was helpful.

And then I went to Paris and saw De Gaulle.

MARTIN: What did you think of him?

KENNEDY: He wasn't nearly as warm as Adenauer. He was cold and tough and unfriendly. He spoke about not meeting the Russians, how opposed he was to meeting with the Russians. He said, "At the appropriate time, I'll be prepared to meet with the Russians, but it's going to be on my terms and when we're ready to solve the problems of the world, not individual problems."

MARTIN: You came back and you reported to the President. What did you tell him when you reported to him?

KENNEDY: I reported to him just so that they'd know I was back in the country. Rusk was there. We talked a little bit about Indonesia and a little bit about Japan.

Then a number of things happened afterward. There were a number of things that had to be done. First, get the machinery started on trying to do something about the Indonesian-Dutch dispute. I had also gone to Holland. I met Luns again in Paris to try to get them conferring. Ultimately, [career diplomat] Ellsworth Bunker was brought in; he was the arbitrator. Through the pressures that we placed on the Dutch and on the Indonesians, they sat down in a house in Virginia and settled their dispute. It was quite clear that we wanted them to settle it, and we put a lot of pressure on the Dutch to get it settled.

MARTIN: How? What kind?

KENNEDY: Mostly political pressure, telling them that they should sit down, that we didn't want to support this kind of a war, that we didn't want to get involved in it. They didn't want West New Guinea. They wanted to get out of West New Guinea, as I said. It was just a question of saving face. The face-saver would be an election that would be held in ten years. All that was involved, really, was how long the United Nations would stay there and when the election would be held. It was a helluva thing to be fighting a war about. And in the last analysis we'd have to bear the burden. So we made it quite clear that we thought, when it came down that close, they should settle it. I was quite frank about that with the Dutch when I was in Holland.

The other thing is, I thought much more should have been done about the youth that was ignored. We formed this youth committee which has been operating for the last two and a half years around the world. It was to promote the exchange of books, personnel, and cultural exchanges.

MARTIN: Has it accomplished anything?

KENNEDY: Yes, I think it has. In a lot of countries where they would not have done anything, they are now doing something. They've got programs.

MARTIN: I could never get anything started on that. I thought it was one of the most important things we should be doing and one of the areas of our greatest failure. Couldn't get it done through the normal—

KENNEDY: Why?

MARTIN: —State Department and USIS channels. Ten years from now, maybe in Fiscal Year 1974, they'll do something.

KENNEDY: In some countries they did good jobs, and in some countries they didn't.

MARTIN: It really was effective, though, in some places?

KENNEDY: In some places it was. I have sent my administrative assistant out on trips with two or three other people twice now. They reported back that in some places it's very bad; some places, it's quite good.

But at least they know we're interested. It's being pushed.

MARTIN: Well, that about winds up your trip?

KENNEDY: Yes. Now, we never covered the Dominican crisis, did we?
It is interesting to think back on all these things going on. I was involved in more things than I thought.

The President was out of the country when [Dominican dictator Rafael] Trujillo—

MARTIN: [JFK] was in Paris, on his way to Vienna. Salinger broke the story from Paris that Trujillo had been assassinated.

KENNEDY: Yes. I talked to him by phone as to what we should do. The other question was, we had had some contingency plans if the Communists attempted to take over the Dominican Republic. We had the fleet off the coast. The big question was, when Trujillo was assassinated, who was going to take over the country. That was my concern. Nobody was around at that time. I don't know if Rusk was here.

MARTIN: Yes, he was.

KENNEDY: In any case, nobody seemed to be doing anything. I talked to the President. I guess I had the major responsibility of trying to work out some plans or at least getting people to sit down and start to think of what they were going to do. We moved the fleet in closer. One of the great problems was the fact that there was no communication. You couldn't tell what was going on in the country. The CIA had some people there, but they couldn't get any information out.

Then I finally found out that a newspaperman had gone in and landed and was reporting out. So I suggested, why didn't they telephone? They put a dime in the telephone, called down there, and got right through.

We had all kinds of things like that. But the most frustrating thing was that you knew a little bit about what was going on in the capital but nothing about what was going on elsewhere in the island. Based on that experience, I asked them to reorganize the communications so that we would know more and have people, particularly in South America. Well, that wasn't done very effectively. We went through the same thing again when the Cuba crisis came along.

MARTIN: That's right, I know we did.

KENNEDY: So then, again, I spoke to my brother, and he appointed a committee of our ExComm committee to come up with a real good communications plan, no matter what the cost, the energy. I think that they really did.

MARTIN: It didn't work usually. That was the red phone that I got after the second Cuba.

KENNEDY: I suppose.

MARTIN: The first time I tried to use it, when the egg hit the fan, I couldn't get anybody. As you say, I put a dime in the machine and got right straight through.

KENNEDY: In any case, it's one of the things that came out of Cuba. In some places it's been effective. Communications have improved.

Anyway, we had meetings that went on continuously, with the most frustrating thing being the lack of communication—the failure to know, the inability to know what was going on. I talked to the President a couple of times about it, and we followed it up to see what we should do. We brought, as I say, the fleet in closer. Then it gradually evolved itself: [Dominican President Joaquin] Balaguer took over, and we worked with him.

MARTIN: The Trujillos came back—Ramfis, his son.[22] There was a meeting at the White House on August 28 to set Dominican policy. You met with a couple of Dominicans earlier in the same day.

KENNEDY: What day?

MARTIN: On the 28th of August. One of them was named Luis Manuel Baquero; the other, I think, was one Johnny Vicini. Steve Smith brought them over to you. Then you went to the White House meeting. This is how I got in the act. The day after that meeting, Steve Smith called me and asked me to go down. I came to Washington. The President sent me down on a fact-finding mission in the Dominican Republic. I was there all through September and came back. Bob Murphy had been sent down earlier in the spring, before Trujillo's assassination. He was at the White House meeting.

KENNEDY: Well, what came out of that meeting was an effort to get along with Balaguer. The understanding was that Ramfis was going to keep his uncles out. He was going to get rid of the bad guys. He was going to withdraw himself, and then they were going to have an election. That was the assurance. We played along with that for a period of time, just because there didn't seem to be any kind of alternative.

MARTIN: That's what I recommended, roughly. I recommended throwing him out if we couldn't negotiate him out, but keep him and use him as long as we needed him. That is what our policy became, I think.

KENNEDY: Yes. That's it. During that period of time, we were talking to [Porfirio] Rubirosa, who was close to Ramfis and was anxious that we have a policy where you could keep Ramfis. But he always assured us that Ramfis, who was his pal, was going to get out of there. Again, I don't think there was much alternative at the moment. We didn't know where it was going to turn. Reports from you, or whoever it was, on Balaguer weren't that bad.

MARTIN: No, my reports on Balaguer were bad. John Hill's were good. He was the consul down there at the time. His reports on Balaguer were good.

KENNEDY: In any case, that was generally what we were doing. Then the President came back. There wasn't any major crisis. It all worked out.

MARTIN: You sent the fleet on November 19 and threw the Trujillos out—which is what I recommended in the first place.

KENNEDY: Yes. Who were the two who came to see me?

MARTIN: Luis Manuel Baquero. He's a psychiatrist and one of the leaders of the UNC [National Civic Union], which was the major political party or group at that time. The other fellow's name was Johnny Vicini. He's the head of the biggest Dominican sugar interest in the Republic. Steve Smith brought them in to see you. As I recall it—I wasn't present—but I've heard that you thought, "We can't do business with these fellows. They're crazy." You went over to the White House meeting and said this. As a result of that, the President decided he didn't have enough facts to go on and asked me to go down on a fact-finding job.

The thing that I think might be interesting to history, though, is why did the President think this was so important? It's a little country, the Dominican Republic.

KENNEDY: Talk about a little country—you see a little country like Cuba, the problems and trouble it caused. If [Castro] had the Dominican Republic, it meant the whole part of the Caribbean would be hard to hold. That was the major concern. You know, we were happy the Trujillos were thrown out, happy to get rid of him, just like you'd be happy to get rid of the fellow from Haiti [François "Papa Doc" Duvalier].

But then to try to guide the government that comes in, to democratic ways, to not just to have a dictatorship and then another revolution, [is difficult]. Ultimately, people become so discouraged and disgusted that they turn to Communism. That's what you have to avoid. Of course, there was some conflict within our own administration that it doesn't matter what kind of a government, what kind of system, you have in another country as long as it's anti-Communist—which was against the philosophy of the President and against mine and against, I think, the majority of us. But that's what you're contending with. Some people feel it doesn't matter, just as long as they're anti-Communist. [JFK's] whole effort was to try to have something more than that: to get rid of the dictatorships, to get rid of the cruel, inhuman governments, but to avoid replacing them with Communists. The specter that was always raised to us in the Dominican Republic was that if you'd go in any other direction, you're going to have a Communist regime.

MARTIN: That's right, sure. That's what they finally overthrew [1963 Dominican President Juan] Bosch with—raising the McCarthy specter of Communism. They kept blackmailing us all the time. I was there as the Ambassador with this: Help us or we'll all go Communist. There's just enough people in the United States government who feel that way. That makes it so effective. I'm afraid it's prevailing now. That's the trouble.

KENNEDY: Some of them are, like Bosch was, so ineffective.

MARTIN: It was terrible, I know. The President did, however, think this was an important country and continued to think so, didn't he?

KENNEDY: Very. When you talk about a little country, that reminds me of a later situation. I've had a major effort in the last four months to try to get somebody to do something about Zanzibar.[23] I kept thinking something should be done about Zanzibar. Averell Harriman wrote a memorandum that something should be done about Zanzibar. George Ball wrote back and said it was foolish to waste our time, it was such a small country, and added that, if God could take care of the little swallows in the skies, He certainly could take care of a little country like that.

MARTIN: A little bit idiotic.

KENNEDY: Imagine that?

MARTIN: No, I really can't.

KENNEDY: Well, he wrote that in a memo.

MARTIN: I've never really heard George say anything quite that flat. He usually had an anchor to windward.

I don't know how the President thought we were doing during 1962 and 1963. I don't know what he thought of Bosch.

KENNEDY: I don't think he had a very high opinion of him, but I never really got into much discussion about it after that.

MARTIN: Now, there's one thing that you did do: that was get me two cops from [William H.] Parker's Mexican squad to straighten out the street riots. That was in April of '62. That's the last time you got directly into it, I think.

KENNEDY: That's right. I didn't have much to do with it.

MARTIN: I asked the President for two cops, and he asked Dungan to get you to get them. You apparently called Parker, and we got them. The government had lost control of the streets to the left [wing]. That's how we got it back.

KENNEDY: We did the same thing in Caracas. We sent three down there. They saved that situation.

MARTIN: It saved us in the [Dominican Republic]. We wouldn't have gotten through that spring. Two cops held that country for us.

KENNEDY: Fantastic, isn't it?

MARTIN: It's also fantastic that you had to go to the President of the United States to get that. I'd been asking AID for a public safety mission ever since I got there. Nothing had happened. So I finally went to the President.

KENNEDY: That's a critical course our Counterinsurgency Committee is supposed to work with.

MARTIN: No, you got them for me. I know you saved that one. We got that quieted down in 1962 in the Dominican Republic. We did succeed in holding the first election since 1924. And we did prop up the provisional government until the elections. We made them hold elections. And we got the elected President [Bosch] to the palace alive, on schedule. Those were our three policy objectives, and we succeeded.

Were you in on the contingency planning about Trujillo before the assassination?

KENNEDY: Yes.

MARTIN: Do you want to put that in the history record?

KENNEDY: It was just a question about whether we'd move troops in, under what circumstances we'd move troops in, where they'd land, how far off the water they'd be.

MARTIN: Do you want to get into the assassination of Trujillo?

KENNEDY: Our policy was that we couldn't live with a Communist country. We'd have to stop that one way or another. We were going to stop it.

MARTIN: Do you want to get into the actual assassination of Trujillo?

KENNEDY: Well, I know that there were plans about the assassination that came up all the time, that various people were meeting. But I never knew.

MARTIN: It's been published in the United States and is generally believed in the Dominican Republic that we engineered the assassination.

KENNEDY: That's not true.

MARTIN: I don't know whether it's true or not because I didn't want to know while I was down there.

KENNEDY: It's not true. To my knowledge, this isn't true. I got into that planning, and I expect I probably would have known. I knew everything that [JFK] knew about that.

MARTIN: I don't think they'd plan to assassinate a chief of state without telling the President.

KENNEDY: No. That's what I think. They wouldn't have done it without telling me.

MARTIN: As far as you know, we did not engineer the assassination or assist the assassin.

KENNEDY: No. I might say that, on the assassination, I had never heard up until you told me that the United States was supposed to have had some responsibility. When Diem was overthrown, President Kennedy was against it because he didn't think the people knew where they were going. As a matter of fact, he was against the revolution taking place at that time.

MARTIN: Was he?

KENNEDY: Yes. Subsequently, Lyndon Johnson said to Pierre Salinger that he wasn't sure but that the assassination of President Kennedy didn't take place in retribution for his participation in the assassinations of Trujillo and President Diem.

MARTIN: Did he mean divine retribution? Or was he suggesting conspiracy?

KENNEDY: No, divine retribution. He said that. Then he went on and said that, when he was growing up, somebody he knew—who had misbehaved—was on a sled or something, ran into a tree, hit his head, and became cross-eyed. He said that was God's retribution for people who were bad. So you should be careful of cross-eyed people because God put his mark on them. And that this might very well be God's retribution to President Kennedy for his participation in the assassination of these two people.

MARTIN: I never heard that.

KENNEDY: No, I know. But, otherwise, it's a friendly relationship!

MARTIN: What about the disarmament conference? The Seventeen Nation Disarmament Conference began in March in 1962 at Geneva. Did you talk to the President about this?

KENNEDY: I was present at the meeting that preceded it.

MARTIN: Do you know what the President's views of this were? How hopeful was he? Did you talk to him about it in that sense?

KENNEDY: During '62 he was very concerned about the fallout. He was very concerned about continued testing. He had a study made to see what other countries had the bomb. The report came in, I think about that period of time, that approximately sixteen countries could have the bomb within the next ten years. He thought it meant one thing when a country that, although antagonistic, appeared to be reasonably responsible—such as the Soviet Union—had it. But if Israel had it, and Egypt had it—

MARTIN: Sukarno.

KENNEDY: Indonesia could make it. There's a list of the sixteen countries. He thought that all of our energies and all of our efforts should be toward getting control over the distribution of the knowledge of making atomic weapons, the construction and the testing of atomic weapons. His greatest disappointment through '62 and '63 was the fact that we hadn't done that, hadn't been able to get any [agreement].

He was willing to go back and go back and go back—and walk, as he described it, the last mile.

David Ormsby-Gore was an influential figure because he always felt that we had not done nearly what we could have done in the past. He had been the U.K. representative in Geneva, and he didn't think we knew what we were talking about frequently. We really hadn't made a very good case and hadn't handled it very well. He was, of course, a close friend of the President. He had been appointed at the end of '61—both the President and I suggested to Macmillan what a great difference he'd make—and he was very influential. The President felt that he wanted to do everything possible to keep the discussions going—not that you'd get general disarmament, but you could get control of atomic weapons.

MARTIN: Now, when you say control, I think we ought to make sure it's clear. Was this a reversion to the past, when the whole emphasis was on secrecy and keeping secret the methods of making atomic and nuclear weapons? Or was the emphasis on getting a treaty not to test them?

KENNEDY: The emphasis was on [three] things: on not distributing weapons; not distributing the information or knowledge for the construction so you could make weapons; and, three, to not permit testing of weapons—which would therefore make the construction of a weapon useless because you couldn't test it. It didn't make much sense.

MARTIN: Early in that same spring, '62, it was announced that Teddy was going to run for the Senate in Massachusetts. Do you want to tell me something about the history of that decision?

KENNEDY: None of us were opposed. The person who was primarily interested in having him run was my father, who felt—just as I would never have been Attorney General if it hadn't been for him, I don't think my younger brother would have been Senator nor my older brother President—but he just felt that Teddy had worked all this time during the campaign and sacrificed himself for his older brother, that we had our positions, and so he should have the right to run. He felt that it was a mistake to run for any position lower than [U.S. Senator]. Certainly, he was as qualified as Eddie McCormack[24] to run for the Senate or anybody else who was being mentioned in Massachusetts, [people] who were perhaps older but weren't particularly outstanding figures. Therefore, he should have an opportunity to run.

I think if it were left up to [Teddy], he probably would have run for Attorney General [an elective office in Massachusetts] and was tempted to run during the course of the campaign for Attorney General rather than the Senate. But he finally decided to run for the Senate, and then, particularly after my father became ill, he was committed to that. But there wasn't any opposition by any of us. Some of the people at the White House sort of mumbled about the fact that he shouldn't run or it would hurt the President. But as far as the President and I were concerned, I was pleased that he was running, and I think the President was pleased that he was running.

MARTIN: Neither of you thought that this would hurt the President? Politically in the U.S.?

KENNEDY: No, no.

MARTIN: And neither of you thought that it would damage the President's relations with [John] McCormack or seriously affect the Congressman?

KENNEDY: No, because initially at least, we thought that Eddie McCormack would get out of the contest. But he didn't get out of the contest.

MARTIN: Why did you think he would?

KENNEDY: Just because we felt that Teddy'd beat him and he probably wouldn't want to stay in there. I was anxious, actually, to have him stay.

MARTIN: Why?

KENNEDY: Because I thought it would help having a primary fight and beating somebody—it didn't leave everything to the latter part— and then to get him known. He could go around and campaign. In the meantime, I thought [Republican senatorial candidate] George Lodge was going to be tough to beat. I thought that it would be good to have a primary fight. I thought primary fights had helped *us*. It would have meant all the focus of attention was on the battle and would help [Teddy] get his name known—what kind of a person he was prior to the time he had the final election.

As it turned out, I think he won the election with the first debate against Eddie McCormack.

MARTIN: I saw that. I remember that because there was so much attention on that.

KENNEDY: And Eddie McCormack did so badly. All the sympathy was so much for Teddy that the second debate made less of a difference. But Eddie McCormack was ruined, and George Lodge could never catch up. So the result was that Teddy won the election on the first debate. . . .

MARTIN: Did the dynasty issue make any difference up there?

KENNEDY: No. No, I think it helps in Massachusetts.

MARTIN: And in the country at large, you don't think it would hurt any?

KENNEDY: I think it had some effect, generally, in the country—the dynasty business—but I don't think it cost us any votes. I was never very concerned about it. What did cost us and what was costing us was the great dislike for me in the South particularly, but in certain other [areas]. That was far more costly. In fact, I spoke to my brother about resigning or saying I was going to get out.

MARTIN: Did you? When, Bob?

KENNEDY: Oh, September or October of '63. I thought first, as a possibility, of getting out just to manage the campaign. Of course that wouldn't have helped a helluva lot, because then they would have thought I was still in there, still important. But if I got out under some other pretext that said I was going around to make speeches—

But [JFK] said no. You know, the fact that I wasn't going to be around as Attorney General would have, I thought, helped.

MARTIN: What did he say about this?

KENNEDY: He said that he thought that it would have appeared to everybody that the Kennedys were running out on something that we had committed to.

So I said that I thought we should watch it politically, and then we could decide as we went along—whether it was helpful. You know the terrible, strong feeling that they had in the South: it had changed from just *me* in '62 and '63 to both of *us*—"the Kennedy brothers" —which he brought up on frequent occasions, the fact that it was switching from Bobby Kennedy to "the Kennedy boys" in Alabama and Mississippi, you see. That was the major reason I didn't want to become Attorney General. Because I anticipated the fact that with the same last name—I saw Bill Rogers having to hide in the plane in South Carolina—how much worse it would be with the same name and how difficult that made it for [JFK]. It was an unnecessary burden, in my judgment. Eisenhower avoided it. Not that they did anything, but he still avoided the dislike that they had for Rogers. But with the same name—with this relationship—we couldn't avoid it.

MARTIN: Talking about civil rights and your being a liability and so on: In the early part of the administration, you took the heat and were out in front, the front runner on this issue, weren't you?

KENNEDY: Yes.

MARTIN: Doing dirty work, in other words, for the President?

KENNEDY: Yes. I think that we had the chief responsibility.

The Department of Justice was very inactive in the field of civil rights before 1961—criminally so. So we brought a lot of cases, did a lot of things. I never brought a case without trying to get it resolved beforehand by local authorities, bringing it to their attention. I knew a lot of the local authorities because I'd worked with them in the campaign. I was a major asset in the South in 1961. When I testified [at RFK's confirmation hearing], the people who were for me were John McClellan and Sam Ervin and all the southerners—Jim Eastland— and all the others who spoke for me and recommended my approval. I spoke a lot in the South, my area of chief responsibility even as campaign manager. I had a special responsibility in the South, a lot of friends in the South. And there was also the fact that I had worked against corruption in labor unions. A lot of them thought, "Well, he must be against labor unions generally."

MARTIN: You very soon became a liability, and this rather quickly— after a year, at least by 1963—had rubbed off on the President?

KENNEDY: That's right.

MARTIN: What really nailed it down was the great speech that he made in the summer of '63[25], isn't that right?

KENNEDY: That's right.

MARTIN: That's when he really just put it all right on the line.

KENNEDY: Plus the use of the troops.

MARTIN: I wanted to ask you about that. You sent federal troops to the University of Mississippi at the Meredith time. Why did you have to do it there but did not have to do it at Montgomery? You didn't send them to Montgomery, as I recall it, Bob.

KENNEDY: As far as Oxford, Mississippi, we sent them there because there was a violation of a court order. We wouldn't have had the authority, really, unless law and order broke down in Montgomery, Alabama, to send troops to Montgomery. We sent troops subsequently to the outskirts of Birmingham because we said we might have to use them if law and order broke down. I don't know if you remember that in '62. There was a big fuss I raised about whether we had authority to do that. But we did it on the basis that the situation was getting out of hand in Birmingham at the time, and we felt we had authority to—not because they were picketing a lunch counter or a department store, but just on the question of a whole breakdown of law and order.

MARTIN: . . . How about the steel crisis?[26] U.S. Steel and the price rise? [U.S. Steel's chairman,] Roger Blough? What happened?

KENNEDY: The President was making an effort to try—feeling, like all the economists, that what happened in steel affected the rest of the economy—to make it unnecessary for steel to raise their prices. So therefore, he put a good deal of pressure on [union president] Dave McDonald and the Steelworkers [Union] to keep their demands within limits. He had Arthur Goldberg meet with them, and then he would report back to the steel companies as to what had been done, what progress had been made. This went on for some period of time. Finally an agreement was reached between the steel companies and the union which was a noninflationary contract—at least, it was described as such in the newspapers and by economists—and so it was felt, therefore, that it wasn't necessary for the steel companies to raise their prices. All of the efforts had been made by the President during this period of time, and by Arthur Goldberg and by others, toward the objective of permitting steel companies to sign a contract which would not require them to raise their prices. And the steel companies—Roger Blough and all the others—understood his efforts were along those lines.

MARTIN: So he had an understanding with Blough?

KENNEDY: Without it being specified. I mean, nobody said to anybody: "If I can keep the steel unions from making excessive demands, will you agree not to raise your prices?" But he would say to them: "I think we're going to be able to keep the steel unions from making excessive demands." Now, the only reason, the only purpose of that, obviously, was that the steel companies wouldn't have to raise their prices. So he went through all of that, and it was sold to the steel union on that basis: It was a contribution they could make to the government and to the country and all the rest of it.

Well, then Roger Blough walks into his office and said, "I'm going to make this statement in a few hours." And it was a statement saying he was going to raise the price of steel!

The President called me up right away, right after they left. He was mad. I don't remember exactly his words, but I think something like: "You won't believe what they've done." Then, I think, he asked me to come over, and we had meetings from then on as to what should be done—how we could deal with the problem. It was a difficult, touchy battle. And it was a real battle.

We were trying to get in touch with the steel companies to bring pressure that way. The Defense Department was trying to see what they could do, indicating where they were going to buy their steel—if you kept your prices low. And we started the grand jury, which caused the major furor. Our whole point was to try to prevent them from raising their prices.

We were trying to play hardball with this effort.

MARTIN: Looking back, do you think it was (a) justified and (b) politically wise?

KENNEDY: Yes. I think both. [Given] the kind of a person and the kind of a President that President Kennedy was going to be, it would have been out of character to do otherwise. And it would have been bad for the country—it would have been bad internally—and it would have been bad all around the world, because it would have indicated that the country was run by a few manufacturers. I don't think we would ever have reestablished ourselves.

And the President felt that he had been double-crossed.

MARTIN: How did you finally get Inland [Steel] to break? That's what started the turnaround. That was the icebreaker, wasn't it?

KENNEDY: They didn't want to raise their prices. They were very good. . . .

MARTIN: Were you or the President close to [Inland Steel's president, Joseph] Block himself?

KENNEDY: No. I think the President knew him. But the President kept saying, pointing out (this really became clear to us) that the Kennedys and many of the Kennedy associates don't know anybody in business—although my father was in business and would know them all. I mean, when you finally get down to it, we looked over the names of the people in the steel companies and everything, and we didn't know people.

But, you know, I had the grand jury. We looked over all of them as individuals. We were going to go for broke: their expense accounts and where they'd been and what they were doing. I picked up all their records and I told the FBI to interview them all—march into their offices the next day. We weren't going to go slowly. I said to have them done all over the country. All of them were hit with meetings the next morning by agents. All of them were subpoenaed for their personal records. All of them were subpoenaed for their company records.

I agree it was a tough way to operate. But under the circumstances, we couldn't afford to lose.

MARTIN: It's kind of an awesome power.

KENNEDY: Yes, it is, and rather scary. There's no question about that. *There's no question about that.* And it can be abused and misused.

MARTIN: I'm not suggesting this was an abuse of it, but the potential is there.

KENNEDY: No, but I mean somebody would. There's no question. That potential, as far as the Attorney General of the United States, rests in a thousand ways. I mean the power. That's what the idea of the wiretap bill is suddenly getting into: the abuses that could take place by the Attorney General of the United States. Even the fact that he can order an investigation of somebody: If I started an investigation of you in your community, you're ruined. The FBI coming around and asking all the neighbors: "What do you know about John Bartlow Martin?" Going to pick up your bank accounts. Going into the stores where you do business. You'd never recover. Or arrest you? Or a grand jury? So when you talk about the abuse of power, there's no question.

MARTIN: It's a big country and a powerful country, and it's all centered in a few offices. There's no way around it.

KENNEDY: We all worked hard. Bob McNamara. John McCone called people. Clark Clifford played an intimate role in it. Arthur Goldberg met with some of the steel companies. Charlie Bartlett was involved indirectly with some of these people. Each person will describe what we did, but in my judgment the fact that the President channeled all of these things together and directed it himself was number one. Number two, getting Inland Steel was a terribly important factor. It really broke their backs. Number three was all the power and authority of the federal government being brought to bear. Number four was all the meetings and efforts by Clark Clifford and others to try to bring sense to these people who had made such a mistake.

MARTIN: The President was his own field general on [the steel crisis]?

KENNEDY: Yes, yes, yes.

MARTIN: He was running it?

KENNEDY: Oh, yes. The reports all went to him. I read someplace that Ted Sorensen was the field general in this. That was in *Life* magazine.

MARTIN: That's not true?

KENNEDY: No, the President ran it himself.

MARTIN: This was quite a victory. Did he enjoy it?

KENNEDY: Yes. He was very pleased that it came out that way. You know, he liked fights. And he liked to *win*. And *he* won it.

I remember his talking at the White House correspondents' dinner that spring and doing a takeoff on himself. One of the points he made was: "And when the reporters are awakened in the middle of the night to be given the news, things have come to a pretty pass!" It was very funny.

MARTIN: What did he say when he knew he'd won? Do you recall? Was he elated?

KENNEDY: Yes, very pleased. It was one of the five or six major matters in which we were involved in which he was very concerned personally and very anxious that it would come out properly.

MARTIN: What were the others? You said five or six.

KENNEDY: Well, let's see: the Berlin crisis in '61, the Berlin crisis in '62, the Bay of Pigs, the Cuban crisis of '62, steel, Oxford, Mississippi.

MARTIN: Of the civil rights crises, Oxford was the one in which he felt the most deeply engaged and involved?

KENNEDY: Well, no, I didn't mean that so much. Some of the others he was involved in, as far as time is concerned, you know, but this was one where it was so critical because people were being killed. And also there was a possibility of our marshals being wiped out or having to start to shoot students.

MARTIN: He didn't feel the same way about the signing of the nuclear test ban treaty, which was another major accomplishment?

KENNEDY: No. I think it was a major—and he thought it was—a major accomplishment. But I think that there wasn't the element of crisis about it.

I think he felt stronger about that question [civil rights] almost than anything else and felt that up through 1962 his major failure had been not making more progress in this field. That was the area where no breakthrough was forthcoming.

Disarmament? As I say, there wasn't the same feeling of crisis or emergency that existed, especially as we'd been through the disarmament conference and discussions so frequently.

MARTIN: It was a slow culmination of a long chain of events and a lot of hard work. And a lot of homework. I noticed that [delegation chairman] Arthur Dean went to Geneva with what was described by the press, at least, as the most complete preparation and planning for a disarmament conference that any American had ever taken there.

KENNEDY: I think, also, the influence of David Ormsby-Gore in this was considerable. We had always been unprepared and had a very negative attitude at the Geneva [disarmament] conferences. And David Ormsby-Gore, having watched what we were doing and what we were not doing—what our responses were, what actions we took—felt that we were not very helpful, not very constructive. So the President made a major effort in 1961 to make sure people knew their homework, that they just weren't going through the motions, and to see if we could do something that would be more productive. He felt very strongly about it and went into these matters in considerable detail himself. . . .

MARTIN: Back now in the spring of 1962. At that time, [JFK] said that Lyndon Johnson would be renominated if he chose to run in '64. Was there a particular reason for his saying that?

KENNEDY: There were stories—it seemed to me '63 rather than '62—that [Johnson] was going to be dropped.

MARTIN: This came up again in '63.

KENNEDY: I think that that's the reason the statement was made. There was never any intention of dropping him. There was never even any discussion about dropping him. There was, you know, discussion about his personality.

MARTIN: But there was no serious thought given to dropping him?

KENNEDY: Dropping him? No.

MARTIN: At that same time, England was renewing negotiations to get into the European Common Market. Was this something the President was deeply concerned with? Did he feel that his whole tariff and trade policy, which he'd worked hard to get through Congress, was endangered by the European Common Market's refusal to admit England? Did he do anything about it?

KENNEDY: I think he was concerned about it, but this is not the kind of thing that really aroused the President emotionally. These things gradually work themselves out.

MARTIN: On the 13th of May or the 12th of May in '62, we moved the fleet toward Laos and actually said that we might land troops and put them into Laos—which, of course, would have been a very difficult damned thing to do since there wasn't any seaport.

KENNEDY: Didn't we move them into Thailand?

MARTIN: Yes, we did move some into Thailand. [Llewellyn] Thompson at that time was talking to Khrushchev, and by the 17th—four or five days later—things looked a little better. Now, this indicates that Khrushchev was using his influence to try to keep the neutralist coalition[27] stuck together. Is that right?

KENNEDY: Yes, that's true.

MARTIN: Was this being done through normal diplomatic channels?

KENNEDY: I had some conversations with Georgi Bolshakov also during that period of time.

MARTIN: And you think they had some effect on this?

KENNEDY: Yes. Eventually the troops were taken out of Thailand because of the conversations I had with him. During that period of time, there were two or three different occasions when the agreement that had been made at Vienna appeared to be breaking down and that the Soviet Union really should use whatever authority or position they had in order to straighten out the situation.

MARTIN: About the same time, something in the United States happened: the stock market took a real nosedive, a real crack, in May of '62.[28] There was some talk of the President intervening and doing something about it. He finally decided not to. Do you remember anything about that that hasn't been published?

KENNEDY: Yes, the "Kennedy stock market." As the President said: "When the market went down, it's the Kennedy stock market; and when it goes up, it's the free enterprise system."

But there wasn't anything that anybody really thought that could be done. I think those who were around the White House advising felt that stocks had been overpriced at the time, that this was bound to come, and that perhaps the steel dispute stimulated its coming and brought it to a focal point. We used to discuss the value of the stock versus the amount of earnings, and it appeared that a good number of these stocks were way overvalued and were bound eventually to come down.

MARTIN: There was widespread feeling that a Great Depression like the 1930s couldn't occur again in the United States because built-in safeguards had been erected. Did the President generally feel that way?

KENNEDY: Yes.

MARTIN: In July he sent Foy Kohler to Moscow [as Ambassador]. Any background on that? I take it that [Thompson] wanted to leave. There wasn't any uproar or commotion over his departure?

KENNEDY: That's right.

MARTIN: There was a lot of talk about a great search for the best man.

KENNEDY: There was a conflict between the Foreign Service, who wanted Foy Kohler, and the people such as myself who were not impressed with Foy Kohler and would like to have had someone else. Now, I can't remember who my candidate was. But I had some exchange with Chip Bohlen. Finally, my brother said that I had to come up with a candidate, and if I could come up with a decent candidate, he'd send him. I couldn't come up, really, with anybody who knew Russian and could get along. The reason there was such a delay was that we were trying to avoid sending Foy Kohler. We couldn't come up with an alternative, so Foy Kohler was sent. But, as I say, the Foreign Service felt very strongly about Foy Kohler going. I had been involved in a lot of conferences with Foy Kohler, and I was not impressed with him at all. . . . He gave me the creeps. I didn't think he'd be the kind of person who could really get anything done with the Russians.

MARTIN: Does the Ambassador to Russia make any difference?

KENNEDY: I don't know whether he does. I think that they had some confidence in Thompson. I don't know whether he becomes just a messenger. Perhaps for the first two or three months he has some effect, when they think he's in touch with the President. The President spoke to me once about sending me—learning Russian and going.

MARTIN: Why didn't you do it?

KENNEDY: In the first place I couldn't possibly learn Russian, because I spent ten years learning second-year French. And secondly, for the first couple of months I might have done something; but after that I don't think it's my forte. I don't think the amount of good that it would have done would have remained or stayed. But this was when we were trying to get somebody other than Foy Kohler.

MARTIN: At that time, Congress had said they weren't going to give any more aid to Yugoslavia and Poland. [Ambassador to Yugoslavia George] Kennan came home, [Ambassador to Poland] John Moors Cabot raised hell, and the White House began a strenuous effort to get this reversed in the Congress—and succeeded to a limited extent. Were you involved in this at all?

KENNEDY: I came in the plane when Kennan came. That was the end of my trip.

MARTIN: What do you think of him, Bob?

KENNEDY: I liked him very much. I think he made a lot of sense.

MARTIN: He resigned over this ultimately, didn't he? He felt that Congress had undermined his position.

KENNEDY: I think to some extent. I didn't really get into much of the reason for his resignation. He liked the President very much. You know, he was very devoted.

He had some ideas about what was happening in Yugoslavia.[29] Sometimes the ambassadors come back and get shunted aside in the State Department, and they never get close to the President or the President doesn't know they're there. So I made sure they got together. [Kennan] had written some papers which were of some significance as to what was happening in Yugoslavia, which were not very optimistic about the trend in Yugoslavia. They impressed me. I read them coming back in the plane. And I wanted him to see the President. He changed them some, because I think he thought they were overly pessimistic. But he did see the fact that we really weren't making much of an impression on [Yugoslav President] Tito.

MARTIN: At that time the coup occurred in Peru. . . . [The Peruvian military seized power after the 1962 presidential election, in which

Haya de la Torre won a plurality of the votes but not the one-third vote required for election.] Was the President upset about this? Was this something he considered very important or not?

KENNEDY: Yes, I think he did. He felt it was important. He took a lot of steps, took whatever steps we could, to try to bring pressure, and I think that he felt, in the final analysis, that they were successful. I mean, eventually we recognized the regime, but the steps that were taken forced Peru and the government to agree to certain conditions. He felt strongly about it.

MARTIN: And he did feel that he had achieved something?

KENNEDY: He did. It was always described in the newspapers as if he had capitulated after holding out, but in fact, all those who were involved with him, and he himself, felt that they had achieved something.

MARTIN: . . . About this time, the Senate and House authorized a four-billion-dollar foreign aid [package]. Later they cut it, and there was a summer-long fight over foreign aid that year—that was '62—and an even worse one in 1963. Did the President take a really active role in pushing for foreign aid? In either year?

KENNEDY: Yes. He called and worried and was concerned and had businessmen in and did all those matters. I was not involved in what the strategy was or what he was doing particularly, other than just the conversation I might have about it occasionally as to what SOBs they were in the House for cutting foreign aid and what he was trying to do, whom he was trying to get help from.

MARTIN: That August, the Russians got two spaceships in orbit. During this time, we were getting people in orbit. This got an awful lot of play, of course, in the press all the way through the Kennedy administration. How much importance did he attach to the space race?

KENNEDY: He thought it was very important. As he used to say, it compared to the explorers in our own country, Lewis and Clark—what needed to be done in space. I think that made a profound impression on him. Secondly, he thought that we needed to do it for our own position throughout the world, that our efforts should be for excellence and that we should do whatever was necessary. He frequently said that had he realized how much money would be involved and how important it was going to be, he never would have made Jim Webb the head of it.

MARTIN: Really?

KENNEDY: Jim Webb was suggested by Lyndon Johnson and was awful—talked all the time and was rather a blabbermouth. . . . Anyway, the President was very dissatisfied with him. He was the kind of person who talked too much, and the President always disliked people who said in fifty words what they could say in seven words. It made him impatient.

MARTIN: . . . On this feeling he had, that the space race was important as a matter of prestige and discovery, we had two nuclear submarines rendezvous at the North Pole at that time. He made a big thing about it, and it got a big play in the press. Did the same feeling apply here? Was he genuinely very pleased himself?

KENNEDY: He was always very pleased when the United States did something extraordinary. Where it required not only brains and ability but courage.

The characteristic that he admired the most was courage. When he saw it in a human being one way or another, he was always impressed with it and always, especially, in an American. It always moved him.

MARTIN: Goldberg was appointed to the Supreme Court on the 30th of August, '62. Why? Why Goldberg? Why not someone else? Why not, for example, [Judge David L.] Bazelon, who was also Jewish and who had been on the bench a long time? Or was there much discussion at all?

KENNEDY: No, there wasn't. It was much quicker than the other [Supreme Court appointment]. He just decided on Goldberg. There wasn't any reason not to. First, I think it basically was going to come to a Jew. There was some talk that maybe somebody would resign later on and you could put a non-Jew on this time and then a Jew later on. But I think that the Jewish matter certainly had an effect. If you were going to appoint a Jewish lawyer, certainly Arthur Goldberg is awfully smart. There wasn't any reason to go outside and try to find someone else whom you didn't know. He'd been loyal, was a good lawyer, and there wasn't any reason to try in some other direction. I think, even if the Jewish aspect of it hadn't been involved, Arthur Goldberg would have been high on the list of lawyers who would have been considered. But that was a factor. There wasn't really a very great deal of discussion about other possibilities.

MARTIN: . . . On the 22nd of September the President opened the 1962 campaign, as far as he was concerned, with a speech at Harrisburg. Then he did some campaigning in the fall. I wanted to ask you in general how he felt about campaigning? Did he enjoy it? This was the first one since he'd been elected.

KENNEDY: He liked it very much. He loved getting out of Washington. It really exhilarated him.

MARTIN: Of course, he was interrupted by Cuba, but was he pleased with the results?

KENNEDY: You mean, that campaign?

MARTIN: The '62 congressional campaign.

KENNEDY: Yes. And we were awfully pleased that Birch Bayh won out in Indiana against [incumbent Senator Homer] Capehart, who was an awful man.

MARTIN: Now, in that election, Dirksen won in Illinois.

KENNEDY: George McGovern won South Dakota.

MARTIN: There was a lot of talk at the time about the President's helping Dirksen or not really opposing Dirksen in throwing all his support behind Yates. Was there any truth in that? Dirksen had been very helpful in the Senate.

KENNEDY: The President didn't want to become so personally involved that it would antagonize Dirksen. He thought that, as far as working with the Republicans, it was as easy to work with Dirksen as it was with anybody else. He had a sort of rapport and relationship with Dirksen; and if Dirksen got beat, you would have somebody else in there. So I don't think, when Dirksen won, that it was "Isn't it too bad I don't have Yates in the Senate?" But there wasn't anything going on behind the scenes. There weren't any discussions with Dirksen or anything. [JFK] felt a responsibility to Yates because Yates was a Democrat, and so he went through with it—but he didn't have any personal excitement about trying to beat Dirksen or elect Yates.

MARTIN: In that election, Nixon was beaten. Did the President think that this finished Nixon politically?

KENNEDY: No, as I remember, I think he thought it finished him at least for a period of time. Not permanently.

MARTIN: For '64? He thought it finished him for that one?

KENNEDY: I gathered he did.

MARTIN: [New York Governor Nelson] Rockefeller was reelected. [Pennsylvania Governor William] Scranton and Romney were elected. Did he have any thoughts about them as [Republican] candidates in '64? He must have been thinking about whom the Republicans would nominate.

KENNEDY: The one he feared the most and the one who concerned him the most and the one he thought would be the most difficult to beat was Romney.

MARTIN: Really?

KENNEDY: He was very concerned that Romney was going to win. He never discussed it with anyone, I think, other than perhaps myself. He was very concerned that Romney would get the nomination because he thought he had this appeal to, I don't know what it is, God and country and all of these matters. The people were very exercised and worked up by some of the things the President stood for and was working for, particularly in the field of civil rights. And here is an answer to everything, a solution to all these problems, a panacea. He spoke well, looked well. He perhaps could cause some trouble in the South, where we were in trouble anyway. He could pick up some of the states in the Rocky Mountains. And he could pick up, maybe, Michigan. That was a pretty good combination. Put together, that could cause you a good deal of trouble.

So that concerned him. That's why Romney was never mentioned, why we never talked about Romney.

MARTIN: I see. He didn't think Rockefeller would be very hard to beat?

KENNEDY: No.

MARTIN: Because of the divorce?

KENNEDY: I guess because of the divorce, the fact he'd been very badly discredited in New York for that, and for all of his activities in New York.

I always thought Rockefeller had shown he had no guts. He showed it in 1960; he showed it on his position on foreign aid, he showed it by backing away on New Hampshire in 1960, and he showed it on the platform. When it really came down to what was difficult and hard, he wasn't there. That really was his demise. It was spelled out a number of years ago. When it really became difficult, he didn't have it anyway. I don't think people understand what a difficult game this is until they get involved in it. It's not the same at the federal level as it is at the state level. You can be finished off very quickly.

MARTIN: Scranton was then completely unknown.

KENNEDY: The President always thought that was a laugh.

MARTIN: He did?

KENNEDY: I mean, mostly from his own personal experience—that they talked about *him* being inexperienced. He'd been in Congress all those years and he had been in the Senate all those years and had all this other experience and background. And here was . . . Scranton. One-term Congressman, two-year Governor. Not even halfway through his term as Governor. And he was going to be the presidential candidate!

[JFK] thought he'd win the election. When he was in Washington, it depressed him a little bit. Not depressed him—that's too strong a word. But you read all those columns, and none of them were very enthusiastic for him. [*New York Times* columnist James B.] Scotty Reston was always knocking him, and all the rest of the people who might have been his friends. Everybody was, you know, sort of finding fault with him. It was only when he got out in the country—

When you asked me about campaigning, that's why he loved it so much. Every time he came back, he said, "It's a different country." It's just that you can't tell when you're in Washington. That's why the people in Washington really missed the depth of his popularity and didn't understand when he died why— I mean, they couldn't predict this. That's what makes me so bitter about people like Scotty Reston now. I just don't think that they understand it anymore in their buildup of Lyndon Johnson, comparing him to the President. I just think that they miss the whole point—what went on for three years—and miss the whole feeling of the country.

They don't understand the country at all, really. And you know, they said the President wasn't going to get the nomination. The reason they would "know" is they were talking to Senators and Congressmen who were also in Washington, who were also out of touch.

MARTIN: Now, that congressional election was generally considered a great victory for the Democratic party and a personal victory for the

President. But the fact was that [the Democrats] lost some big states that were awfully important in the North, the governorships particularly. Was he concerned about that?

KENNEDY: No.

MARTIN: He wasn't? There are a lot of jobs, Bob. You know, organization and patronage in the states.

KENNEDY: What they were doing about organization and patronage never really involved him. Look at what happened just in 1960 in the country. People talk that way, and they write about that and say, "Well, if you can control the governorship— " But, for instance, if you take California: Pat Brown won [the governorship of] California by, I don't know, four or five hundred thousand votes, and then, later on, by a million votes (or maybe he won it by eight hundred thousand before) and we lost it by forty thousand.

MARTIN: [Illinois Governor Otto] Kerner won by four hundred thousand, and we won by six thousand in Illinois.

KENNEDY: Six thousand. If you take the six big states, there were two or three which were under Democrats that we lost, and there were a couple under Republicans that we won. I think a Democratic Governor can alienate people. I mean, they raise taxes, like [Governor Matthew E.] Welsh in Indiana. And the people are going to be mad at the Democrats. It's a very unpleasant, unattractive job. So I think that it's not quite that simple—that it's so valuable having a Governor in. Frequently it can cause you more difficulty. I was just trying to think of some of the others. If you looked at it from across the country, [there were] maybe ten or twelve of the major states, like Wisconsin, [where] we had a Democratic Governor and we lost the state. There were some other states where there were Republican Governors and we won the state. Like Mike DiSalle in Ohio: There's a Democratic Governor and we lost the state.

So I don't think that there's necessarily a direct relation, and it wasn't really of great concern to us. Because I don't think it's bad running against a Governor as well as for the national office on some occasions. It's very difficult to be a popular Governor of a state. I don't know any. And I think that's why there were so many turnovers in 1962. The Republican states, I mean New Hampshire and Vermont, go Democrat; then the major industrial states become Republican, like Pennsylvania. It's just because a Governor—you don't have enough money to run your state anymore.

MARTIN: Actually, the state doesn't and can't do what everybody thinks it ought to do, as power moves to Washington.

During that campaign, Eisenhower himself made one speech attacking the "callow youth" in the administration and another speech accusing the President of making what he called a "power grab." Do you remember any reaction from the President on this?

KENNEDY: Oh, I don't think he ever had a great deal of respect for Eisenhower. It used to irritate him. And we used to know that these things were coming up, because John McCone would write a report back that Eisenhower would be getting madder and madder and be filled with all of this sort of poison about the President.

The liaison with Eisenhower was John McCone. John McCone was very helpful in this. And John McCone became very close to both Ethel and to me and became close personal friends. When his wife died, Ethel went over and spent some time over there and was the person who became the closest to him. So I would think he likes her almost more than anybody in the world. Then he became very close to me. He then performed this function for the President of being the liaison with Eisenhower. And he, because of his relationship, I think, primarily with Ethel and to some extent with me—but also, obviously, he became a great admirer of the President—was very, very helpful. He was also very loyal. He had an interest that was greater than the interests of President Kennedy—which was his own. Sometimes there was a conflict. There was that conflict [on the missiles in Cuba], for instance, in early 1963. . . .

MARTIN: You said on some occasions McCone was helpful with Eisenhower. Can you instance that?

KENNEDY: He briefed [Eisenhower]. You see, he liked Jack so much, he admired President Kennedy—so he conveyed this. He pacified Eisenhower. He was the one influence with Eisenhower which was giving him another side and moderating what Eisenhower was hearing all the time. He used to say to me that Eisenhower would sit out there—he was not informed—and he'd just be filled with poison by all of these people who would tell him things and make things up. And it shocked John McCone that Eisenhower knew, really, so little about some of the problems. But, as John McCone said, [Eisenhower's] reactions are good, or what he wants or desires is right, and so he could work with him or at least reason with him a little bit. That was the only thing that saved the situation at all. He became more and more interested in politics. He missed—Eisenhower did—he missed political life. He missed the adulation. So he kept wanting to get back in, and this was sort of a way of getting back in. He said that—in 1962—he was much more interested in politics and the campaign than he had been even when he was President.

MARTIN: At the same time the Cuban [missile] crisis was heating up in October, the Chinese Communists attacked India heavily, and pretty quickly Nehru got rid of [Defense Minister] Krishna Menon. Were you involved in that at all?

KENNEDY: I was involved in National Security Council meetings in connection with the supply of India, in sending over the airlift. I guess it was the Harriman mission.[30] There was a conflict, of course, between him—Harriman—and [Ambassador] Galbraith as to how it should be handled. It was really a political matter, once the decision was made that we'd try to help in whatever way possible.

MARTIN: . . . Now, I want to go back in '62 and pick up a few loose ends. Congress killed the bill for the Urban Affairs Agency.[31] Do you remember any reaction of the President's to that?

KENNEDY: Just impatience with Congress and a feeling that perhaps it hadn't been as well handled as it might have been by us.

MARTIN: The press mentioned a technique the President used in trying to persuade people to come to work for the United States government by bringing them into Washington in groups for an all-day briefing lunch at the White House. Did this amount to anything?

KENNEDY: We were trying, particularly, to get people in the AID program to try to take on good people. I don't know how this evolved. I know I was involved to some extent in the planning, in getting a group of people to do it. The idea was to get various groups down there and explain the need for personnel and see if they would make some people available for a couple of years. And that's what we did. We recruited people. Some of them turned out well, some of them did not. It wasn't any more of a program other than several meetings; and from then on, it was picked up by people of the lower echelon. But we explained the problem and asked the executives to see if they could suggest people to take on these jobs—not people whom they just wanted to get rid of from their companies, but people who could actually accomplish something.

MARTIN: What level would they go into at AID?

KENNEDY: They would be people who'd be placed first or second, as head of some of these programs in the various countries. That's where we didn't have people, where the problem existed.

MARTIN: Any reaction of the President on the release of [Francis Gary] Powers, who had flown the U-2 over Russia? This happened February 10, '62.

KENNEDY: I signed the papers on that before I went on my trip. And it was accomplished, of course, while I was gone. We worked on it for—I don't know for how many months. The person who would know the most about it in the Department of Justice is Andy Oehmann [Executive Assistant to the Attorney General]. He had the discussions with [James B.] Donovan.[32]

MARTIN: Any reaction of the President to the expropriation in Brazil of the IT&T [International Telephone and Telegraph] properties?

KENNEDY: Not that I've ever discussed with him. He sent me down to Brazil, and I brought that up with [Brazilian President João] Goulart. Goulart had told him earlier that he would straighten that matter out. And it hadn't been straightened out. I brought it up with Goulart, and Goulart assured me he would—and he did—do it. And IT&T was recompensed for seizure of the property.

MARTIN: What was your impression of Goulart, by the way?

KENNEDY: I didn't like him. He looks and acts— Well, he looks, of course, a great deal like a Brazilian Jimmy Hoffa.
    I didn't dislike him as much as I disliked Sukarno. But I didn't like him. I didn't think he could be trusted, and I thought there were a lot of problems in connection with him. I went through, when I was down there, all the difficulties about putting these leftists and Communists in positions of power. And he wanted names and the areas. We gave him some. The other problem was the fact that they weren't doing anything about economics.
    Do you want to go into that trip now?

MARTIN: Let's save it till you come to it, all right?
    In March of '62, Nixon said that the President had endangered national security by calling for a Cuban invasion in the 1960 campaign when he knew that they had something going. Did the President have a reaction to this?

KENNEDY: He hadn't. He got Allen Dulles to put out a statement saying that it was untrue, that the President never knew about it.

MARTIN: The Senate approved the poll tax amendment. [The Twenty-fourth Amendment to the U.S. Constitution prohibits poll taxes in federal elections.] Did the President attach a lot of importance to this or not?

KENNEDY: Yes. He pushed it. He had a lot of discussions about it. Pushed it. Senator Holland, you know, was the one who was behind it.

Then [JFK] was very anxious to get states to ratify it. When there were any problems about it as they came up in the states, he used to make telephone calls. And we sent telegrams to all the states urging their taking action on it.

MARTIN: About that same time there was a lot of agitation for a pardon for Junius Scales. [Junius Scales was the only Communist sent to prison under the membership clause of the Smith Act. His sentence was commuted by Robert Kennedy in 1962.] Do you want to tell me about that?

KENNEDY: Well, I think there was some fuss about it. [Socialist party leader] Norman Thomas and a lot of other people came to see me at various times or wrote me letters. I said that I would take a look at it. But I wasn't going to take a look at it if they picketed or made it appear that it was going to be advisable because of political reasons, because of all the efforts that were put in. So I just asked them that nobody would get in touch with me for a period of time and that I would take a look at it; and if I thought it should be done, I'd do it. And nobody did do anything. I never heard for a period of time. And I looked at it, I think, at Christmas. Based on the penalties for others, the amount of time of his sentence, and problems that he had at home [his wife was ill], I had his sentence commuted. I never discussed it with the President.

MARTIN: That April the President gave a dinner for the Nobel Prize winners in the hemisphere. Were you there?

KENNEDY: Yes.

MARTIN: Was it a good thing?

KENNEDY: Terrific, very impressive.

MARTIN: I was thinking: Did [JFK] enjoy that sort of thing?

KENNEDY: Oh, yes, very much. That was Dick Goodwin's idea. It was wonderful.

MARTIN: One of the highlights apparently was the reading of a Hemingway chapter.

KENNEDY: Yes, Fredric March did it. And Fredric March was telling me there were a lot of very obscene words in it that Mrs. [Mary Welsh] Hemingway didn't want him to change—and he changed anyway. He described his conversation with Mrs. Hemingway at dinner about these terribly crude words: her saying, "Well, what can you do?" and his saying, "Why don't we substitute this for that."

She said, "That's fine because, even so, everybody'll know what you mean."

I thought that the President's toast was the highlight. . . .

MARTIN: I worked on that speech a little that afternoon with Arthur Schlesinger. In our draft, we had the line that "this is the greatest assembly"—just a routine, dull, hack line—that "this is the greatest assembly of talent and brains ever assembled in the White House." Was it the President who added "except perhaps when Thomas Jefferson dined here alone"?

KENNEDY: Yes, it was. You can see his notes. He had the speech there, and there were some notes on the speech or on the menu card that I've seen.

MARTIN: That was a marvelous thing. He enjoyed this kind of an evening?

KENNEDY: Very much. Oh, yes. Then I suggested he try to get the Medal of Honor winners down and do a similar thing, and they had a reception for the Medal of Honor winners.

MARTIN: Was that good too?

KENNEDY: Oh, it was wonderful. The President said afterward about the Nobel [Prize dinner], "You know, they can criticize Dick Goodwin, but he came up with two ideas: one, the Alliance for Progress, and the other one was this."

MARTIN: What'd he think of Dick, anyway?

KENNEDY: I think he liked him, thought he was very bright and able.

MARTIN: Well, why'd they let him get kicked around so? I mean, Dick took a terrible beating for a while. They moved him clear out of the White House first, and put him under [Robert] Woodward.

KENNEDY: That wasn't being kicked downstairs.

MARTIN: He thought he was going to get Bob Woodward's job as Assistant Secretary for Latin America, and what happened was that George Ball moved Bob Woodward up and put Ed Martin in, apparently for the express purpose of sitting on Dick Goodwin. And Ed Martin sat on him.

KENNEDY: Well, I wouldn't have made Dick Goodwin Assistant Secretary of State, I'll tell you that. I mean, I like Dick Goodwin, but I wouldn't have made him Assistant Secretary of State. I'm sure he might have thought he was going to do that, but certainly the President never indicated to him he was going to make him Assistant Secretary of State. He was working on Latin America, so he went over to the State Department to continue his work on Latin America. But I don't think anybody had ever indicated he could make it. I mean, that would have made absolutely no sense whatsoever.

Then he had a difficult time. He used to come over and talk to me, and I talked to the President a number of times about it. You know, he was over there, and once you get in that terribly difficult maze— the State Department—they swallow you up. It was difficult. I mean, the President can make it clear—just as he made it clear: "I think he should get rid of George McGhee, and I don't think George Ball is handling this"—but, I mean, to stay on it day after day, and say, "This is what should be done with Dick Goodwin"—

He'd still consult with Dick Goodwin, and he'd talk with him himself. His role over there became more and more difficult. It was awfully tough for the President to try to follow up, with all the other problems he had, to make sure that Dick Goodwin was being treated properly.

MARTIN: . . . In May the President—this is after the steel crisis—the President made a speech before the United States Chamber of Commerce, and the press said he had a cool reception. Do you remember this?

KENNEDY: Yes.

MARTIN: Did it bother him?

KENNEDY: Well, he never liked them. He just always felt that you couldn't do anything with them; there's no way to influence them. We were brought up thinking that they were— My father thought businessmen didn't have any public responsibility. And we just found that they were antagonistic and you couldn't do anything with them.

Lyndon Johnson's been able to do something with them. But we couldn't. But I think that Lyndon Johnson has been able to do something with them based on what [JFK] did for them. Which makes it even more ironic.

MARTIN: In the spring of '62 the United States committed five Polaris missiles to NATO. Were you in on this? Or did you ever talk to the President about the importance of Polaris and the importance of NATO itself?

KENNEDY: No, no. I mean, I know what he thought of Polaris submarines.

MARTIN: What'd he think of them?

KENNEDY: Well, very highly. I was in the conversation about the multilateral force: whether we'd have mixed crews on the Polaris submarines. And it was after our conversations with Admiral— What's his name, from the Polaris submarine? . . . [Hyman] Rickover, who was opposed to it. But the President decided that they'd try to stick them on a cruiser. Isn't that what we finally did?

MARTIN: I think so.

KENNEDY: And keep them off the Polaris submarines because Rickover said it wasn't practical. The President was impressed with Rickover, number one; but number two, he also thought that if Rickover was opposed to it and we tried to do it, not only would we create problems anyway, but secondly, we'd just have a helluva political problem in the United States. So therefore, he never pressed that. Then they tried to work out some alternatives to that, none of which, I think, turned out very satisfactorily, although I didn't get involved in much of the conversation after that. The reason behind that was because of Skybolt and all the problems that grew out of that, to try to come up with an alternative idea.

I got into the conversation with Georgi Bolshakov because all this concerned the Russians, who felt that we were bringing the West Germans in closer to the control of nuclear weapons. And this genuinely concerned them. There was that basic conflict: the President trying to bring a more peaceful relationship with Russians and with the Communists and at the same time having the conflict of the Skybolt, trying to bring the Allies in Europe into a closer relationship. Then, of course, the French stepped in, and by 1963 it was more confused than ever. I don't think it was just the Skybolt. I think it was also due to what the French were doing.

The French were saying that these other countries weren't playing a big enough role, and they could, under a different kind of arrangement. So the idea was to try to get them into a closer relationship and yet not antagonize the Communists to such an extent that it would break down any possibility of success, and reaching a rapprochement with them.

MARTIN: Did you ever talk to him about the future of NATO as such? What I mean is, Bob, it seemed to me during that period in '62 that the old postwar alliances on both sides were breaking up, that ours was and so was the Soviet's and the whole Communist alliance. You could see this pretty early in '62, and of course it's become pretty awfully obvious by now. I just wondered if you ever had any conversations with the President about this.

KENNEDY: We talked about the realities of it.

MARTIN: What'd he say?

KENNEDY: Just what it would necessitate our doing—at least, at that point—to try to get through the next year or so. And I think he was basically just very understanding that our alliances would change and be altered. A lot of it, he felt, was due to the Cuban missile crisis: that it was natural that everybody felt safer and therefore would go off in their independent way. We had to adapt to it.

As to what it was going to lead to in the long run, it was just a question of our continuing our strength and being able to adapt to changes. I don't think that he felt that he was in a position, really, to move on those things so quickly after the Cuban missile crisis or now, the end of '63 and '64, at a time [near] the election. He visualized that maybe he could start to try to come up with some different answers in the second term—to this and a lot of our domestic problems.

I go back and I keep thinking about it now, about all the problems that faced us in '61. I compare it with the problems that face Lyndon Johnson in 1964. It's just fantastic, the difference in the world, the differences: domestically, the balance of payments or economic growth; or the relationship with the Communists or the relationship in Berlin— the situation in all parts of the world then, as compared to now. That just didn't happen overnight.

MARTIN: The President came into office after eight years of Eisenhower— when everything had been postponed for eight years—and he had it all fall in his lap. Johnson came into office when nothing had been postponed. Everything had been acted on. Is this the difference?

KENNEDY: As MacArthur said to the President: "What has happened after eight years of Eisenhower is that the chickens have come home to roost. And you live in the chicken house."

MARTIN: And what concerns me is whether the United States can stand another eight years of an Eisenhower, even though he has the Democratic party with him.

KENNEDY: I don't know. Of course, there hasn't been a crisis yet. The only major matter was Panama [the January 1964 riots in the Canal Zone]. That was not very impressively handled. And then Cuba. I disagreed with what they did on that. On the cutting off the—

MARTIN: The Guantanamo cutting of pipe?

KENNEDY: Yes.

MARTIN: All this nonsense.
   Were you involved in the Billie Sol Estes case? [Billie Sol Estes, a Texas businessman involved in Democratic party affairs, was convicted on state and federal charges of fraud, theft, and conspiracy in 1962–1963.]

KENNEDY: Yes.

MARTIN: Is it worth talking about?

KENNEDY: It's worth talking about just from the fact that there was this major effort to build it up into a scandal within the administration, and it wasn't a major scandal in the administration. The [New York] Herald Tribune wrote patently false articles about it. . . . It was built up in the country as another Teapot Dome. And there wasn't anything to it. There were a couple of people who took a thousand bucks or something in gifts. I don't know if that much. It rattled Orville Freeman. I think the efforts of the Department of Justice really saved him because we put him through a very stiff cross-examination, so that when he finally went up there [before the Permanent Investigations Subcommittee of the Government Operations Committee] he knew his business. [Under Secretary of Agriculture] Charles Murphy hadn't handled it as well; he's a little more calculating. But we did the same thing with him. And he came out of it.
   Everybody, you know, was comparing it to Teapot Dome: Orville Freeman's going to have to resign. Of course, Orville Freeman handled it well—and he's an honest man—but it's a tough department to operate. There wasn't any major scandal attached to it or

associated with it. We prosecuted it, and [Estes] was convicted, and we also made available—which is the only time we've ever done it—all the FBI reports as we uncovered things. We made them available to the congressional committee. I think they were disappointed they didn't come up with more. But there wasn't anything more.

MARTIN: You mentioned the *New York Herald Tribune*. Did the President cut that off, stop his subscription?

KENNEDY: Yes.

MARTIN: Was he the one who did it?

KENNEDY: Oh, yes, he did.

MARTIN: Was he sore, really sore?

KENNEDY: Oh, he was just fed up. I don't remember what it was at that particular time, but they wrote so many really false articles. . . . But it was just day after day reading this material on Billie Sol Estes and other matters which were just completely inaccurate . . . But it just got frustrating for [JFK]. He figured, why bother going on reading it?

And he never did read it.

MARTIN: Did he do this in a moment of anger? Or did he do it deliberately in a calculating way?

KENNEDY: He did it deliberately and was glad. He was happy that he did it afterward. And he didn't cut it off and sneak off, sneak away somewhere and read it. He just wouldn't read it—nobody in the White House would. But I think he was sorry that he gave the *Herald Tribune* so much publicity.

MARTIN: Anything on Medicare that you can add?

KENNEDY: I know he wanted Medicare passed. He felt strongly about Medicare. He felt that all the polls showed it was a major issue still. And so for his own personal reasons and for political reasons, he wanted something done about Medicare.

MARTIN: He supported [New York Congressman Charles A.] Buckley here in New York, in spite of [New York City Mayor Robert] Wagner, didn't he?

KENNEDY: Yes.

MARTIN: How much did he get involved in New York politics?

KENNEDY: Well, not very much. I got involved in it probably more.

MARTIN: Did you?

KENNEDY: Because I knew all the people up here. First, getting rid of Carmine De Sapio and [New York State Democratic Committee chairman] Mike Prendergast, who I didn't think much of—not because of dishonesty, but I just thought they were incompetent. Mike Prendergast, particularly, was just incompetent, handled the campaign badly, and threw his weight around in an unpleasant way. And then, of course, there was the conflict with Mrs. [Eleanor] Roosevelt and [former New York Governor and Senator] Herbert Lehman: The reformers were worse than Prendergast and the regulars. I'd rather deal with the regulars than the reformers; they were more power crazy and less responsible. But Prendergast became arrogant and difficult. So we had this conflict with him.

MARTIN: And then what about Wagner?

KENNEDY: Well, we had a friendly relationship with Wagner. We knew the people upstate, I think better than he did, because we worked upstate. I had two people upstate during the whole campaign—Ben Smith and Paul Corbin. And after the campaign was over, we reorganized a lot of those counties and put a lot of young people in. It made a helluva difference and got rid of some of the crooks. So we did a lot, and we had a lot of those contacts.

Now, I suppose, if you name the three or four people who were more responsible—political leaders—for getting the President the nomination, Charlie Buckley would be at the top, just about the top of the list. Lyndon Johnson had Carmine De Sapio and Mike Prendergast, and I guess he said to somebody afterward: "I thought Mike Prendergast and Carmine De Sapio ran New York—and I find it's Charlie Buckley!" Then, of course, we got Peter Crotty in Buffalo, and Dan O'Connell in Albany, and Bill Posner in Rochester, and John English in Long Island.

When the election came along, *The New York Times* and everybody was opposed to Charlie Buckley. But we weren't going to forget our friends. He was good to us when we needed help, and so we were good to him; we made an effort for him, and we're going to make an effort this time too. We really made an effort because he was our friend. He helped us.

I think that's one thing that's understood in political life. Because you're apt to meet people—on that ladder you're going up and down—you meet people while you're on your way down you pushed when they were on their way up. I think the most important ingredient in politics, in political life, is loyalty and that relationship. And frequently it doesn't exist. One of the basic reasons that we were able to build up some kind of a machine or following was because the President was loyal, and I think all of us were loyal, to people who were helpful or at least made an effort—and not always successfully, but at least made an effort.

Charlie Buckley and some of these other people understood that. The second thing was that everybody's so pompous about him and *The New York Times* used to write such strong editorials about him that it was a great deal of pleasure to be for him, because it used to make them so mad. . . .

MARTIN: You were probably involved in the Dr. Soblen case: the spy who jumped bail.[33] It was [Chief U.S. Marshal] Jim McShane who lost him in London and so on. Is that worth going into?

KENNEDY: He fled the country.

MARTIN: Yes, he jumped bail and went to Israel, and Israel put him on a plane and shipped him to London.

KENNEDY: We didn't have control over him then. I sent McShane over. But [Soblen] couldn't be in our custody. So there wasn't anything to be done. He sat there, but [McShane] couldn't lay hands on him or do anything to him. When [Soblen] wanted to go to the men's room or go someplace, under ordinary circumstances [McShane would] go with him. But he couldn't go with him. So [Soblen] went in and did what he did: slit his wrists or did whatever he did—took pills.

MARTIN: Took an overdose of barbiturates.

KENNEDY: That wasn't a very bright day in all of our lives.

MARTIN: How about the sugar bill in '62? I was sure as hell deep in that—I can tell you that—down in the Dominican Republic.

KENNEDY: I was involved in it too.

MARTIN: Sixty-two was when the administration tried to go to the world quota system and abandon the country quota system.

KENNEDY: In '61 we started an investigation. We had a lot of information that people in Congress were getting money from the sugar interests in the Dominican Republic and elsewhere. We made a major investigation of it. We came up with some names but were never able to prove it.

MARTIN: Your only indictment was Cassini. Is that right? [Igor Cassini allegedly accepted illegal payments from the Trujillo regime in the Dominican Republic. Investigated by the FBI by order of Robert Kennedy, Cassini ultimately pled nolo contendere to four counts of failure to register as an agent of the Dominican Republic and paid a $10,000 fine.]

KENNEDY: Yes, but that didn't come out of this investigation.

MARTIN: Oh, it came later as an unregistered foreign agent. At that time, [New York Times correspondent] Tad Szulc published a story saying that [Igor] Cassini and Bob Murphy had gone down to the Dominican Republic after your father had told Cassini that the Communists might take over after Trujillo fell. They'd done this before Trujillo was killed. They'd gone down just before the assassination of Trujillo, about four months before, I think—no, about six weeks before. The White House confirmed this. Do you remember?

KENNEDY: I was involved in all of that.

MARTIN: You were?

KENNEDY: Yes.

MARTIN: Do you want to tell about it?

KENNEDY: Basically, the way you described it is correct. The additional part is that Cassini said that he had a close relationship with Trujillo and that Trujillo was—I don't know whether willing to get out, but at least willing to make adjustments in the Dominican Republic. [Cassini] said he could talk to him and try to work and develop this. So Murphy went down, talked to him, and came back and reported it to the State Department and the President.

MARTIN: What was the relationship originally between Cassini and your father?

KENNEDY: Cassini said that he knew Trujillo—

MARTIN: But how did he happen to know your father?

KENNEDY: Oh, I don't know. I don't know how. I suppose he just saw him around. He didn't know my father well. He had never been in my house or anything.

MARTIN: In other words, Cassini made it appear he was much closer to your father and to your family than he really was?

KENNEDY: Yes. As I say, I don't think he was ever in the house. He certainly wasn't at any meal. Now, I don't know whether he came to the house. I think he talked to my father. . . .

MARTIN: Now, he was married, wasn't he, to [oil baron Charles] Wrightsman's daughter [Charlene]? And she later committed suicide. This was a terrible story, this whole thing.

KENNEDY: It is terrible. It was too bad. She had a difficult time because he was so odd. Her father cut her off and wouldn't help her. Then, when [Igor Cassini] got into difficulty with me and with the Department of Justice, [Wrightsman] wouldn't help them with the legal bills, so that his brother ended up paying the legal bills. The President liked his brother.

MARTIN: That's Oleg, the dress designer.

KENNEDY: Oleg Cassini, yes. And he did visit. You wouldn't say he was a friend, but at least he was around. He came to White House parties on occasion and everything. He ended up paying the bills. It became a very unpleasant business because I was prosecuting his brother and then we were investigating him because he was involved— and then Charlie Wrightsman's daughter commits suicide.

MARTIN: Mr. Wrightsman was a friend of your family, too, wasn't he?

KENNEDY: Yes. All in all it was an unpleasant case. And then there was the fact that it involved Bob Murphy. And he was not sympathetic to our investigation. That was an unpleasant case. Of the unpleasant cases that I've had—
Should I name the unpleasant ones?

MARTIN: Yes.

KENNEDY: That was unpleasant. [New York Congressman] Gene Keogh was another. If I had to name, again, about five people who were most helpful to the President in the election, Congressman Keogh's one of them. Then I prosecuted his brother [James Vincent Keogh], who was a judge of the Supreme Court in the state of New York and was convicted with three or four others for taking bribes.[34]

And then: Another person who was responsible for obtaining the Indiana delegation for us was the Mayor of the city of Gary, Indiana, Mayor [George] Chacharis, who was being mentioned as the Greek Ambassador and was at the White House for the dinner for the Greek Prime Minister or whatever it was. [Chacharis pled guilty to a federal indictment charging him with receiving payoffs which he failed to report on his income tax return.]

MARTIN: A friend of [Indiana Congressman] John Brademas.

KENNEDY: Yes. We prosecuted him for taking money too. He's in jail, as is Keogh. Oh, we've had a lot of politicians, mostly Democrats. But I would say that those are probably the three most difficult.

There was an awful lot of pressure, obviously, not to prosecute him.

MARTIN: Cassini?

KENNEDY: Yes. . . . As a matter of fact, the only investigation I've called off since I've been Attorney General I called off on Cassini because his brother came down and swore to me—and then swore to Bob Murphy—that [Igor] wasn't involved in this, that he wasn't getting any money. You see, I'd heard a rumor of that. And [Igor] said, "I've performed this function, you know, with Murphy. And then I come back, and somebody starts a rumor, and you start an investigation"—we had carried on the investigation for six weeks or so and didn't come up with anything—"and you carry on this investigation, and it's hurting me with my papers. It's hurting me with everybody that's associated with me!" Which is all understandable.

He said, "It's just finishing me, and I swear"—and they're not coming up with anything—"and I swear to God." So I notified the FBI not to continue with it. . . . Finally, I went back into it. I got some more information, and I went back into it.

MARTIN: Was this later when the Fulbright [Senate Foreign Relations] Committee began investigating?

KENNEDY: We had something before that.

MARTIN: When [committee investigator Walter] Pincus went down?

KENNEDY: When Pincus went down. He had some information.

MARTIN: You sent a couple of people down to my embassy, and then Pincus came down from the Fulbright committee. I had more damn investigators down there than I had attachés.

KENNEDY: I don't remember how it was that we came up with some material, but we came up with the material about this thing.

MARTIN: I think I got your fellows into the palace files down there, Bob. I think that's what it was. And I sent you something myself.

KENNEDY: Some material. That's right.

MARTIN: I got a CIA fellow to pull that file for you.

KENNEDY: I felt really fooled. [Igor Cassini] had been not only playing with his own future, but with the integrity of the government—the integrity of the President, and mine, and everything else. So I was going to prosecute him and I told him that. I mean, I never—I could never forgive him. I didn't care whether they registered or not. But it was a bad situation. It was an unpleasant one too.

That's one of the reasons I didn't want to be Attorney General—just that people might be involved and that people might ask me to do favors. Somebody like Mayor Chacharis. We had so many people who came in and detailed all they had done for the President. And I worked with [Chacharis]; I worked with him closely. You know, he's sending in money for the campaign. Suddenly, he sends in ten thousand dollars in cash in the campaign, and you take the cash in the campaign—and then you're prosecuting him for money! And he says, "Well, I gave it to you in the campaign." You have to go through it, but it's very, very unpleasant.

As I say, it was one of the reasons I was rather reluctant to become Attorney General—because I knew I'd get into these kinds of cases, as well as somebody who wanted to be a judge and all the other business. That's why I think it's dangerous for a person involved in politics to be Attorney General. It is a position that should be removed completely from politics, or as completely as it can be.

MARTIN: I don't think it can be, really.

KENNEDY: I think it's awfully difficult at times.

MARTIN: During your time, Alcatraz was closed. Were you for that?

KENNEDY: Yes.

MARTIN: Why?

KENNEDY: Because it was a waste of money and cost us ten times as much, or eight times as much, to keep prisoners out there as any place in our other prisons. We could build a tight security prison elsewhere at much less expense. To renovate this would have cost us five million dollars more. It was a sacred cow to a lot of Congressmen and that presented, again, some problems.

MARTIN: [U.S. Bureau of Prisons Director] Jim Bennett's retiring, isn't he?

KENNEDY: Yes, yes.

MARTIN: He's good, isn't he?

KENNEDY: He was good. I think he's gotten a little old the last few years, but I had a very good relationship with him. I think we did quite a bit: these halfway houses and some of these other matters.

MARTIN: Does that interest you?

KENNEDY: Yes. I hate the idea of going to a prison, and I've gone to a good number of them.

MARTIN: I have, too, and I just hate the places.

KENNEDY: But [Bennett] has done a terrific job in there.

On pardons and commutations, we've made a major effort and a major breakthrough. President Eisenhower didn't believe in them because he thought it was interfering with judicial prerogatives. It might be worthwhile for somebody to interview the head of our board, just on what had been done on pardons and commutations. I was talking to him the other day, and it's an impressive record.

Then there are the halfway houses. The changes that have been made in the prison system since this administration came, particularly in the operation of our halfway houses, have been very helpful to young people.

MARTIN: [James] Gavin resigned as Ambassador to France. Why? The reason given was he needed money.

KENNEDY: I think that was the reason. He wasn't very happy over there anyway, because he had a lot of conflicts with the State Department. It just didn't work out very well. He made recommendations. I think he felt that there was more in what General de Gaulle said than the State Department thought, and I think, also, he took De Gaulle and his program more seriously than the State Department did originally. So he didn't enjoy it very much. And it was costing him money.

The President liked him—gave him a party at the White House when he came back—and admired him.

MARTIN: What about the President's relations with other ambassadors of other countries? We've talked of David Ormsby-Gore.

KENNEDY: David Ormsby-Gore—that's the closest. He made a big difference. He was part of the family, really.

MARTIN: Were there others?

KENNEDY: No. [French Ambassador Hervé] Alphand he didn't like.

MARTIN: Did not like?

KENNEDY: No. I mean, not actively dislike, but he just didn't think much of him. He didn't think he really spoke for France very much. The only one he really had a close relationship with at all was Ormsby-Gore. A lot of the others he sort of liked and enjoyed talking to. I think he liked the fellow from Yugoslavia.[35]

MARTIN: Any Latin Americans?

KENNEDY: I don't remember him saying, particularly. I don't know how much contact he had with them.

MARTIN: Toward the end of 1962, Senator Goldwater said that Schlesinger and Stevenson, Bowles and Goodwin had to go because they were soft on Communism. Do you remember any reaction of the President's to this?

KENNEDY: No. I mean, he wouldn't have any reaction.

MARTIN: A piece in the paper about the same time said that you and he donated your salaries to charity. Is this true?

KENNEDY: Yes.

MARTIN: Had it always been true?

KENNEDY: Yes.

MARTIN: Ever since either of you had been in public office?

KENNEDY: Well, I don't know. When he became President.

MARTIN: When he became President? And when you became Attorney General?

KENNEDY: Yes.

MARTIN: Previously, you had not done it? I want to get the record clear on this. There are different versions published.

KENNEDY: Yes. And, actually, it didn't really make much difference because we gave more than that money to charity, in any case.

MARTIN: I know that. I'm just trying to clear the historic record.

KENNEDY: Oh, I know. I understand.

MARTIN: Because various things had been published.

KENNEDY: Yes. That's correct.

MARTIN: In the fall, also, *The Washington Post* published and at the same time denied a story that the President had once been secretly married. Do you remember this?

KENNEDY: Oh, yes.

MARTIN: Anything on that that you want to get into the record?

KENNEDY: No, there were rumors and stories around it for a year prior to that time. I don't remember the name. Was it DuPont? Or what was the name? Shevlin.

MARTIN: I don't know the story, Bob.

KENNEDY: The Shevlin girl [Durie Malcolm Desloge Shevlin].

MARTIN: Once and for all, though, it was not true?

KENNEDY: No, it wasn't true.

MARTIN: I have a few things in 1962 left over. You went down to see [President João] Goulart in Brazil that December, Bob. What was the purpose of that trip?

KENNEDY: It was a question of whether we were going to continue our financial assistance and our relationship with Goulart.

MARTIN: What were the President's views on this?

KENNEDY: There were two problems. One was the problem of the inflation, which was eating away any monetary or financial aid that we would give them. Second was the number of Communists in important positions—in the labor unions, in the military, and in government generally. We had reached a critical stage as to whether we would continue aid or whether we would pull away from Brazil with all that implied. Ambassador [to Brazil Lincoln] Gordon thought the only person who could talk to him—Goulart—and have him understand the seriousness was me.

MARTIN: Did you tell him this? Did you tell Goulart?

KENNEDY: [Gordon] asked if I'd come down. I guess he asked Ralph Dungan and the State Department. They asked the President, and the President said, "Fine." So I was briefed. I went down for twenty-four hours, and I told [Goulart] all this.

MARTIN: What did he say?

KENNEDY: He wanted to know the names of people who were Communists. We gave him some examples of those. He said that he'd put in certain steps to deal with inflation, that he didn't want to have Communists in positions of control, and that he'd take the steps that we wanted him to take. It appeared that we had made some progress with him. I also talked to him about AT&T, the property that he had seized.

MARTIN: Was it AT&T or IT&T?

KENNEDY: IT&T. It's all the same, isn't it? He had indicated earlier that he'd pay for that, which he never had done. I said that for confidence in the business community in the United States and general confidence, you have to keep your word. And shortly after that they made retributions. They paid IT&T in a manner that was satisfactory. So that was worked out. Then they put in certain steps. Certain things they didn't do, but certain steps they did do. We had to wait until, as I remember it, after the election, and then he put in his Finance Minister.[36] He was very good, and people had confidence in him. (There were some others who weren't quite as good.) [Goulart] came to Washington, and I saw him. I think that was about four months later. He was going to fight inflation; he was going to deal with the problems. We made a financial arrangement with him because we had confidence in him: He said that he'd deal with these problems. That went on for several months. Then it collapsed. Ultimately, that man was fired.

They changed the Cabinet around, and there were some good people and some bad people again. The situation gradually was deteriorating. We'd sent down a committee to study Brazil—our Counterinsurgency Committee—and they'd come back with a rather disquieting report about it. That was another thing that stimulated interest.

MARTIN: Did [Goulart] give you any commitment on removing the Communists from his government?

KENNEDY: He said that he'd deal with that and that he didn't want Communists in his government.

MARTIN: Did he deal with it? Did he make good on his commitment to you?

KENNEDY: I think temporarily he did by bringing in some good people. Gordon (I saw him afterward) said that he thought that we made a good deal of progress. But, gradually, over the period of last year, the situation deteriorated until it was even worse than when I went down there.

MARTIN: Do you think it could have been saved?

KENNEDY: With Goulart?

MARTIN: Yes.

KENNEDY: No. I didn't like Goulart, nor did I trust him.

MARTIN: Do you think sooner or later, in any case, he would have gone? I mean, we couldn't have continued our support of him.

KENNEDY: No. I think Brazil would have gone Communist.

MARTIN: About that same time, Tanganyika became a republic. Did the President have any general views on the new African nations that he ever expressed to you?

KENNEDY: No. We talked about Ghana, of course, and we talked about the Ivory Coast. But it was more about particular problems and particular countries rather than in more general terms. We talked about the problem of Angola and Mozambique, and I was involved in what our position would be before the United Nations in connection with that. [In the early 1960s both countries witnessed the struggle of nationalist movements for independence from the Portuguese.]

MARTIN: Was there any general feeling that we should limit our commitments, not try to do everything, maybe stay out of Africa—

KENNEDY: No.

MARTIN: —and concentrate on Latin America and Southeast Asia?

KENNEDY: No, not really. I suppose my own feelings obviously had a bearing on this. It had been the policy, before, that England would take care of her former colonies, France would take care of hers, and we'd stay out of it. I felt very strongly that we should become more involved.

MARTIN: And the President also?

KENNEDY: I don't know, really. I think he wanted to get involved. I never had a discussion about that particular problem with him. It came up before our Counterinsurgency Committee as to what we would do in some of these areas. I was always in favor of becoming more involved and getting our police people involved in training their police.

I had, you know, a number of conversations with Houphouet-Boigny of the Ivory Coast. He felt it would be helpful if they could have some place to go other than the French, to not be completely dependent on the French. It had been the policy of the State Department and the government to stay out of those areas. I think the European desk in the State Department was anxious for us to stay out. So there was this conflict. I think that it came to the fore, to the climax, when Zanzibar went Communist and we didn't have any assets there. We didn't have any information, so we were completely dependent on what the British wanted to do. The British wouldn't do anything.

That was, of course, after November 22, but it involved me in rather a strong fight with the State Department, and then the CIA, to try to get them to do something. They ultimately came up with some plans dealing with the joining of Tanganyika and Zanzibar. But George Ball wrote that memorandum to Averell Harriman when Averell Harriman raised a question about this. He said, "If God can take care of those sparrows and the lilies in the field, He certainly can take care of countries such as this. So why should you worry about it?" That was their philosophy. And Dean Rusk had no interest in it particularly.

It was a question of combating that. I thought that we could do something where there weren't expensive programs. You do have programs, particularly in the police field and perhaps to some extent in the military field, which could be very valuable if anything became serious there. Then we wouldn't be completely dependent upon the French, particularly as the French were antagonistic to us in the last year and a half. And the British under [Secretary of State for the Colonies, Lord] Duncan Sandys were so frequently completely unreliable.

MARTIN: In the last few weeks or months, it's appeared that the French and the English are going back to Africa. The British put down the mutiny in Kenya and Tanganyika after Zanzibar. The French went back to Gabon and put down a mutiny. This looks like a return to the old policy of letting Europe handle Africa and we'll stand aside. This has happened since November 22. Do you think it might not have otherwise?

KENNEDY: No, I think it would have happened before.

MARTIN: In any case?

KENNEDY: I think that they were unique situations. You had a request from Kenya and you had a request from Tanganyika to go in there. There wasn't an interest by Sandys and by the British, and you had really a very difficult situation in Zanzibar until we kept pressing it. As far as Gabon, I just think the French don't want to lose any of those countries and their financial outlets and economic markets at the moment.

MARTIN: Yes, I think that's right.

KENNEDY: There wasn't any urging on our part. The fact is that the French kept it together.

MARTIN: One domestic item left in '62. On November 20 the President signed an executive order forbidding segregation in public housing that involved federal funds. This was the "stroke of the pen" thing which he had spoken about during the 1960 campaign. Why did it take him two years to get around to doing it, if I can put it in a hostile way?

KENNEDY: You can put it in a hostile way.

MARTIN: This is what was said, if you recall.

KENNEDY: Oh, yes. I think the basic reason was that it was felt that to have done it any earlier would have caused such antagonism and controversy that it would have been unacceptable. The advantages or the gains made would not have been worthwhile. Secondly, it took a considerable amount of time to see what areas of housing you could actually have control over. There were a lot of disputes: what areas could be covered and what areas could not.

We went through '62. An awful lot of people were anxious that we not do it before the election of 1962. We went through '61 and didn't do it. We were doing so much else in '61, and we were involved in so many things in civil rights: the Freedom Riders and this complete desegregation of transportation. Then in '62 we were involved in Oxford, Mississippi. We were up to our necks in civil rights, in any case, and the amount of good that was going to be accomplished by this was marginal.

Even when the President signed it, it didn't cover all housing. It covered future housing, and as I say, politically, some of the Congressmen in some of the northern communities, so-called "liberal" Congressmen, were very anxious that we not do it.

MARTIN: They were?

KENNEDY: Some of the ones from Michigan, for instance. . . .

We talked about the appointment of Thurgood Marshall, didn't we? And the delay.

MARTIN: Yes.

KENNEDY: And my assurance from Jim Eastland that he'd put it through.

MARTIN: No. Not about that.

KENNEDY: Well, we appointed Thurgood Marshall, and there was a long delay on his finally being confirmed.

[New York Senators] Keating and [Jacob] Javits raised a fuss continuously. We didn't raise too much because I'd had a conversation with Jim Eastland that before it was over he'd put it through. There wasn't any reason to get all excited about it. I told Thurgood Marshall that he'd be appointed. So he was relaxed. And eventually it went through.

MARTIN: Eastland did say okay?

KENNEDY: Yes. He never kept back any Negro judge. He might have delayed them, but he never caused us any trouble. . . .

1963

MARTIN: Moving into 1963, in the beginning of the year, the first day or two: Larry O'Brien said the fight on the Rules Committee would decide the legislative program; Senator [Robert] Kerr died; and everybody said the big bill was going to be the tax bill. These were the three main Congressional items on the agenda at the beginning of '63.

First, you won the fight on the Rules Committee. Were you involved in that? Do you know how it was won?

KENNEDY: I didn't have a very significant role.

As far as Kerr is concerned, the President got along with Kerr well. I didn't. He was a very unfortunate loss as far as the [Finance] Committee is concerned, because at least they could work with him. Dillon liked him.

MARTIN: And the President liked him?

KENNEDY: A terrific ego. Impossible. His great interest was money.

MARTIN: Why didn't you like him, Bob?

KENNEDY: Because I didn't think he had any integrity. I thought that his only interest was money and advancing his own and his friends' economic well-being. I just didn't like him.

MARTIN: The tax cut was something you had opposed earlier, right?

KENNEDY: No, it wasn't a tax cut earlier. It was an increase in taxes I had been in favor of.

MARTIN: You didn't oppose the tax cut in '63?

KENNEDY: No, I didn't. We had a meeting about it in the beginning of '63. It was a Cabinet meeting. That's the only time I really got into it at all. Everybody thought that we'd been so committed to a tax cut that we had to go for it. I just raised the point that I didn't think we had been so committed that it made it essential. It should be decided on its merits. But I never got into it beyond that.

MARTIN: The TFX scandal just began to see the light of day, also, in January.

KENNEDY: I don't think I'd accept the appellation of "TFX scandal." I don't think it was a scandal. It was a selection of an airplane and the kind of an airplane. I think, again [the congressional investigators] started out thinking they were going to get something very sinister. It really was a decision by McNamara as to what kind of a plane he wanted. Now, I can't get into all the pros and cons and why one plane's better than the other plane.

MARTIN: No, no. Not the technicalities.

KENNEDY: I talked to him after the committee had its hearings and after he looked into it again. Because I think he made the decision without going into it as deeply as he might have if he had known that there was going to be so much fuss about it. But he said that, looking it over, there's no question that they selected the right contractor and the right plane. If he had to do it over again, he would have done the exact same thing. So there wasn't any scandal. People were looking— John McClellan was looking—for a scandal, but even he got off that. It came down to just bad judgment. Well, I don't know how John McClellan and Jerry Adlerman [chief counsel, Senate Permanent Subcommittee on Investigations] can decide that they had better judgment. The President tried to do something with McClellan, said that we would examine it, make a report to him, and that we should get on with it. It was having an adverse effect on the military. We were fighting the war in Vietnam, we had all these other problems, and this was taking up a good deal of McNamara's time and a good deal of Gilpatric's time. And of course, McClellan still never called McNamara. Our relationship with McClellan deteriorated very badly during this period of time, and I had a bitter exchange with Jerry Adlerman.

MARTIN: Did you? I remember him through the Rackets Committee. You gave him his start, really.

KENNEDY: Gave him his start. [White House special assistant] Carmine Bellino talked to [the Senate Committee]. But they became just impossible about it and said they were going to run McNamara out of town.

MARTIN: Really? Why in the hell would they do that, Bob?

KENNEDY: I think they thought [McNamara] was arrogant, tried to push his weight around. And I think McClellan just got carried away by years and years of publicity and attention.

MARTIN: Was McNamara arrogant? Did he handle himself badly in front of the committee?

KENNEDY: I think the Defense Department handled itself badly. I think the Defense Department made some mistakes.

MARTIN: Who? Gilpatric?

KENNEDY: Gilpatric, I think. I don't think he was as frank as he might have been with them. Then there was a story that was put out by— Who's the public relations man?

MARTIN: You mean for Defense? Arthur Sylvester.

KENNEDY: Arthur Sylvester. A story questioning the integrity of the committee, and they resented that.

MARTIN: [Secretary of the Navy Fred] Korth finally resigned, didn't he?

KENNEDY: Yes, but that didn't have anything to do with the TFX, really. Basically [Korth] had an exchange in correspondence with a bank about taking customers of his out on the *Sequoia* (which is a Navy boat) in order to help the bank get customers. He was taking an interest in matters in which the bank had an interest. Now, there wasn't a direct conflict of interest, but I thought that the letters were so bad that he should resign. Lyndon Johnson didn't think he should resign, although he never said it to me. [Johnson] said it to the President. Kenny O'Donnell was against his resigning, and Clark Clifford was against his resigning. I felt strongly he should resign.

MARTIN: Did you tell him so?

KENNEDY: Yes. I also told his lawyer, who was Abe Fortas, and he, I think, has resented it.

MARTIN: You didn't think it was a real conflict of interest. Why did you think he should resign?

KENNEDY: Because I thought it was such bad judgment, and I thought it violated the ethics that were established by the President in 1961 and the whole spirit of the administration. So I didn't think he should stay there. Now, when [Korth] got out, he said that he hadn't been fired, that he was going back because of private business. He'd never talk about being fired.

MARTIN: But he actually was?

KENNEDY: He was fired. He was told to resign. McNamara was against his leaving initially and then, I think, came around to my position.

MARTIN: . . . And you were the one who pushed it—the resignation?

KENNEDY: Yes, yes.

MARTIN: The President agreed with you?

KENNEDY: Yes. Yes, he did. . . .

MARTIN: Do you want to talk generally about the President's relations with the press?

KENNEDY: I think his relationship with the working press was very good. He liked them, and I think they liked him generally. He grew to dislike Arthur Krock, grew to not have as much respect for Scotty Reston because he thought that he never suggested anything. He disagreed with Walter Lippmann, but he thought at least he had alternatives to suggest. He liked Joe Alsop. . . .

MARTIN: What about Rowly Evans?

KENNEDY: He said he wrote one of the most readable and one of the most inaccurate columns in Washington.

MARTIN: Whom did he admire or respect among the press? Or maybe none.

KENNEDY: He liked them all reasonably well. I just don't think he was very impressed with any of them terribly. He thought Walt Lippmann wrote so well. Walt Lippmann wrote an article on Barry Goldwater, I think in the spring of '63. [JFK] asked somebody to call Walter Lippmann up and tell him not to do that because he had destroyed Barry Goldwater. He thought it was too early to accomplish that.

MARTIN: Did he telephone them himself a good deal?

KENNEDY: No.

MARTIN: This impression was around at the time.

KENNEDY: No, no. I don't think so.

MARTIN: What about the *Time* people?

KENNEDY: Well, he liked Hugh Sidey. [Washington bureau chief] John Steele he didn't see very much. Anne Chamberlin he liked. [*Time* founder] Henry Luce knocked [JFK's] brains out every week and then invited him to their dinner. He refused to go to that.

MARTIN: Really?

KENNEDY: Wanted him to be their guest speaker—you know, that anniversary dinner they had.

MARTIN: Yes.

KENNEDY: I didn't go either. [From *The Washington Post*:] Phil Graham he liked. . . . [Diplomatic correspondent] Chalmers Roberts he didn't like. [White House correspondent] Carroll Kilpatrick he liked. [Managing editor] Al Friendly he didn't like.

MARTIN: Did not?

KENNEDY: Not much. [White House correspondent] Eddie Folliard he liked very much. Maggie Higgins he didn't like much.

MARTIN: Who was the woman's society writer?

KENNEDY: Betty Beale [of the *Washington Evening Star*]?

MARTIN: Is that the one who was always—

KENNEDY: Didn't like her.

MARTIN: —getting a lot of people into a lot of trouble?

KENNEDY: She wasn't much.

MARTIN: He liked Joe Alsop, you said?

KENNEDY: Yes. Arthur Krock he thought really was unfair.

MARTIN: I thought [JFK] used the press about as effectively as anybody I've ever seen use the press. He was just a master at it. He devoted a good deal of time and thought to this, did he not? And how to use it? He was conscious of the possibilities inherent here?

KENNEDY: I think that's true.

MARTIN: You weren't in the foreign aid fight in '63, I suppose? How did the Clay report happen?[37]

KENNEDY: I don't know how it happened. The President thought it was a mistake at the end, mostly because of the language. The report itself wasn't so bad.

MARTIN: I know that. I read it. You're right.

KENNEDY: But he thought that the way it came out had been a mistake. It hurt. He tried to get Clay to recoup. Clay did work at it

MARTIN: Clay finally came out and said, maybe they could cut five hundred million—but no more.

KENNEDY: But then it was too late. What I said earlier about its effects are, really, what the President felt about it. I talked to him about it, and what I said is what he thought. He said his feeling later on was that it'd really be adverse and really hurt.

MARTIN: The liberals in the Senate lost the fight to change Rule 22, the filibuster rule.[38] How did the President feel about the filibuster rule, anyway?

KENNEDY: He didn't feel strongly about it. I think he thought it was a matter for the Senate. He wasn't going to get involved in it.

We never went through the Bay of Pigs, did we—I mean, into getting the prisoners out?

MARTIN: No, I don't think we did. Do you want to go ahead?

KENNEDY: Yes. I might say, I think that Haynes Johnson has written a book called *The Bay of Pigs,* which is a pretty accurate account.[39] (I know that some of my people in the Department of Justice—Oberdorfer and some of the others—are working on it and having some interviews. I think they're going to interview me in connection with it.) I might just say that we felt a responsibility. The one thing that really hung over from the Bay of Pigs was the fact that those eleven hundred and fifty or so prisoners remained in jail. They were going to die. Not only did we have the responsibility for carrying out the Bay of Pigs in an ineffective way but also for the lives of all of these men. So we wanted to do whatever was necessary, whatever we could, to get them out. I felt strongly about it. And the President felt strongly about it. We really worked on it for a year and a half, and finally it was successful. And we tried to pull it off before Christmas—which we did.

MARTIN: The President made a speech to them, didn't he?

KENNEDY: Yes.

MARTIN: Quite an emotional thing. He said, "This flag will go back to Cuba some day"—something like that.

KENNEDY: Yes, that's right.

MARTIN: Do you know what he thought would be the ultimate solution as far as Cuba is concerned, Bob?

KENNEDY: No, I don't think he knew what would be the solution. After the missiles, Dean Rusk said that Castro would collapse or be replaced within two months.

MARTIN: Did you ever have a talk with [JFK] about how maybe we're going to have to make some deal with Castro or learn how to live with him?

KENNEDY: We always discussed that as a possibility. It was a question of trying to work it out. There were some tentative feelers that were put out by [Castro] which were accepted by us—which were done through Bill Attwood. Bill Attwood got in touch with me, and then I had him get in touch with Mac Bundy at the White House. Ultimately, I think, the President gave the go-ahead. He was to go to Havana—I don't know, in December of last year or January of this year—and see Castro and see what could be done. We had certain things that were required: the end of the military presence of the Russians and the Communists, the cutoff of ties with the Communists by Cuba, and the end of the exportation of revolution. In return for those basic points and perhaps more, there would be normalization of the relationship. We discussed that as a possibility. In addition, we were also making more of an effort through espionage and sabotage in August, September, October. It was better organized than it had been before and was having quite an effect. I mean, there were ten or twenty tons of sugar cane that were being burned every week through internal uprisings.

MARTIN: Which we were assisting?

KENNEDY: We were assisting just psychologically by some of these landings, some of these other acts of sabotage that were taking place, and the contact with some of these people.

MARTIN: You told the Cuban exiles they had to get together and get united. Miro Cardona stepped down out of the leadership of the revolutionary junta. About that time—that was in the spring—we were stopping Cuban raiders. But, as you say, along toward the end of the summer and the early fall, they were moving. Did you have any Cubans whom you used particularly? I remember meeting one at your birthday party who kept in touch with me for a while.

KENNEDY: Enrico Williams.

MARTIN: Yes. What was he supposed to be? He wanted to go to the Dominican Republic and do something from there. We talked about it.

KENNEDY: He participated in the Bay of Pigs. Very bright fellow. He was the head engineer and general manager of the biggest mining company in Cuba. He was very brave and had very good judgment. There were a lot of them involved. Cardona was losing his support because he couldn't really produce anything. There wasn't anything to produce. There were all these conflicts between the various Cuban groups.

MARTIN: On the question of the economic pressure, did the President or did you think this was going to be effective in the long run, that it was being effective?

KENNEDY: Yes, it was being effective, making it more difficult for [Castro]. And it was.

MARTIN: I had a theory that Khrushchev would give you Castro sometime during 1964 to make absolutely sure the President would be reelected. Was there anything like that in the wind?

KENNEDY: No.

MARTIN: Do you think there might have been?

KENNEDY: No.

MARTIN: You think it would be impossible for Khrushchev to do it? Why wouldn't he do it?

KENNEDY: Because I think it's an important ploy for him, having this base here. It gives him a lot of possibilities in South America, Latin America. Why give those all up?

MARTIN: Of course, Castro would then just turn to the [Chinese Communists] rather than us.

KENNEDY: Yes. It's more difficult, because transportation from China is almost impossible.

MARTIN: There'd be advantages for Khrushchev if we would support him against Peking. There were difficulties there. It just seemed to me something that might be in the wind for 1964.

KENNEDY: Well, no. There wasn't anything.

MARTIN: Okay. Jack Crimmins was in charge of the Cuban Task Force in the State Department?

KENNEDY: Yes.

MARTIN: What was he doing?

KENNEDY: He was trying to coordinate the various activities. It didn't work out very well. I don't think it had that support, sufficient support, like a lot of those things. People don't pay attention to it. They have a tough or a difficult time ever getting anything done. So they weren't a very effective group or organization. It was supposed to come up with ideas. It didn't work out very well.

MARTIN: Were you trying to do anything?

KENNEDY: Yes, I was involved in it all the time—Cuba. I was trying to do things, mostly trying to get them to come up with some ideas about things to be done. The people the CIA had originally were not very good. Then they put this fellow Fitzgerald on, Des Fitzgerald, who I thought was much better. We had a terrible experience with the ones who were handling it at the time of the missile crisis. They were going to send sixty people into Cuba right during the missile crisis. Nobody knew what they were doing. They never told or explained. I just heard about it because one of the fellows who was going to go wrote me, or got in touch with me, and said, "We don't mind going, but we want to make sure we're going because *you* think it's worthwhile." I checked into it. And nobody knew about it.

The CIA didn't. The top officials didn't. We pinned it down to the fellow who was supposed to be in charge [William K. Harvey]. He said we planned it because the military wanted it done. I asked the military, and they never heard of it.

MARTIN: Oh, my God.

KENNEDY: This is the same fellow who put the tunnel under Berlin. Remember that tunnel in 1948? They constructed a tunnel and built it up into intelligence offices—which was a helluva project. But he did that better than he did this. We'd been working with him for a year—and no accomplishments. Then we had [Air Force] General [Edward] Lansdale, whom I got to take this on. He was supposed to go to Vietnam. I thought he'd done so well in the Philippines and was impressed with him, so I got the President to assign him. He started developing some programs, but then he came to cross-purposes with the CIA. They didn't like his interference. Then the military got upset. So that thing collapsed.

This other man they put on it was the fellow who'd been the

Berlin expert, who had had this great achievement. He ended in disaster by working out this program. Of course, I was furious. I said you were dealing with people's lives—the best of the Cubans. They're the ones who volunteer. And then you're going to go off with a half-assed operation like this. We had a meeting at the Pentagon on it. I've never seen him since. . . .

Des Fitzgerald came up with some ideas. At least, we got some projects going. But then every time he got a project ready, nobody wants to have a go. Got scared of it. So, since November, we haven't really done anything.

MARTIN: What kind of projects, Bob?

KENNEDY: Well, just going in, blowing up a mine or blowing up a bridge. You know, some of them ended in disaster. People were captured, tried—and confessed. It wasn't very helpful.

MARTIN: Any direct assassination attempts on Castro?

KENNEDY: No.

MARTIN: No one tried?

KENNEDY: No.

MARTIN: Contemplated?

KENNEDY: No.

MARTIN: Just sabotage. This is something I kept running into in the Dominican Republic: travelers from Cuba who would come through and wonder why we didn't do that. Because [Castro] was not guarded. It would have been so easy, according to these people. I don't have any way of knowing whether that's true.

Most of the publicity at the time came from the Republican side, because of course they were yelling: "Let's get the Russians out of Cuba!" The President was more concerned about other things than that?

KENNEDY: I don't know why there was a political matter to be concerned about—the Russians in Cuba—because they weren't posing any threat, really. I didn't see what the problem was—the Russians in Cuba. I mean, I'd rather have the Russians running the SAM sites than the Cubans running them.

MARTIN: I was going to say! As a matter of fact, right now we're worried because the Russians are leaving—and leaving the missiles in the hands of Fidel.

KENNEDY: Yes. Khrushchev said—his correspondence and also his communications during the missile crisis—that he was going to get the Russians out of Cuba. Out of Cuba. He never put a date on it. That's what caused some of the problems. I had some conversations with the [Soviet] Ambassador [Dobrynin] about it. He always indicated they'd get them out. It was just a question of working out the time. It was the pressure from Keating which slowed them up in getting them out because they thought, then, it looked like they were getting them out under pressure.

MARTIN: So every now and then Khrushchev would make a tough speech about how, if we attack Cuba, it'd mean war. He had to do it because of the counterpressure here?

KENNEDY: Yes.

MARTIN: Because, actually, things were going pretty well with Khrushchev.

KENNEDY: Yes, they were fine, except that Ken Keating raised all this fuss with a lot of inaccurate information.

MARTIN: The hot line was put in about that time, wasn't it?

KENNEDY: Yes.

MARTIN: Was it used?

KENNEDY: No, not that I know of.

MARTIN: Was it secure? Was there a scrambler on it?

KENNEDY: I don't know.

MARTIN: [Venezuelan President Romulo] Betancourt came here early in '63. What did the President think of him?

KENNEDY: He liked him. He admired him very much.

MARTIN: He did?

KENNEDY: Yes. I think it was the only diplomatic reception I went to.

MARTIN: What'd you think of him?

KENNEDY: I admired him. I talked to him this last time he was here. He was very discouraged about the Alliance for Progress and what our policy was in South America—felt that President Kennedy had started something and it was deteriorating. Also, the Ambassador[40] said he couldn't even get in to see Lyndon Johnson. So I called Mac Bundy. He said he'd arrange it, and finally he did.

Did we discuss the security arrangements we made when [JFK] went to Caracas? I got involved in it, to try to make sure that there was proper security. We had a real check on whether all the Communists and fellow travelers were picked up and the guards were adequate. We really spent a good deal of time in the State Department and elsewhere to make sure it was well handled. I often thought that's the kind of arrangement when you were going into a crazy city like Dallas, Texas. It should have been done.

MARTIN: That's right. Absolutely. And Stevenson having been there the week before.

The President said in a speech in May that the number one domestic problem in the United States was unemployment. He repeated this at the Americana Hotel to the AFL-CIO in November and, at that time, said flatly it was more important than civil rights. Why?

KENNEDY: I think, in the long run, civil rights is just a narrow part of unemployment.

MARTIN: Really? I'd put it the other way 'round.

KENNEDY: It probably can be put the other way, too, as I think of it. But I mean, if you have full employment, and everybody has jobs, and everybody's trained well enough to have a job, the problems that exist as far as civil rights are concerned gradually disappear, especially many of the major problems. The problems in the South you can solve with some of this legislation that would permit people to go to a drugstore or stay in a hotel. But the more difficult, complex problems which are going to cause difficulty in many parts of the United States over an extended period of time can only be defeated by adequate jobs. Civil rights legislation is not going to make the ghettos disappear and give employment to Negroes in New York or Chicago or Los Angeles. I don't know what [JFK] had in mind particularly, but I think that that's generally what he was concerned with. The heads of one out of every four families in Chicago—Negro families—are unemployed. There's no legislation you can pass in Congress that is going to deal with that. You've got enough laws on the books.

MARTIN: Most of them are unemployable in a technical, industrial society.

KENNEDY: Therefore, employment really is the answer. I never discussed it with [JFK]. That's what I would think.

MARTIN: You went before the Supreme Court for the first time. What was that on?

KENNEDY: Georgia reapportionment case—congressional districting.[41]

MARTIN: Why'd you do it?

KENNEDY: Just because I hadn't done it and wanted to do it before I left. So I spent three weeks or a month getting ready for it.

MARTIN: Were you thinking of leaving? This was in January.

KENNEDY: No. No, but I just wanted to do it once.

MARTIN: I see.

KENNEDY: I didn't want to do it on a civil rights case, so I selected an apportionment case.

MARTIN: Why not on civil rights, Bob?

KENNEDY: I had done so much on civil rights. I was just up to my ears in civil rights. So I did another case. I was glad when it was over. They never ask an Attorney General questions by tradition. So I made arrangements that they'd ask questions.

MARTIN: Did you enjoy it?

KENNEDY: I did. As I say, I was happy when it was over.

MARTIN: Why were you happy when it was over?

KENNEDY: Oh, just because it's a strain.

MARTIN: The President went into Alabama and Tennessee in May, just a week after there'd been disorders down there, and was well received. That was interesting.

KENNEDY: Yes.

MARTIN: Did you and he discuss that?

KENNEDY: We discussed his going.

MARTIN: Did you advise him to go or not to go?

KENNEDY: I advised him to go. I had been down there myself, you see, in April, and I was very well received in Montgomery and Birmingham and in South Carolina. I went to the law school of South Carolina and to Georgia. I always thought the more contacts [the better]. I wanted him to take a trip throughout the South, go to Virginia, and go to some of these other states.

MARTIN: He did, didn't he?

KENNEDY: He didn't do it in that form. We talked so much about civil rights, we wanted to let it cool off a little bit. So he never did that kind of a trip, although he was prepared to. He was going to do this after he got back from his trip in Europe, but then we thought it was probably inadvisable.

MARTIN: In the end of May, Rusk said that the Russians had shown no interest in the nuclear test ban treaty or discussions. But a few weeks later, the treaty was signed—or initialed, I should say. What the hell was the reason for that?

KENNEDY: I don't know why Rusk said that. I think that the speech that the President made at American University had a profound effect on the Russians.

MARTIN: What do you base that on, Bob?

KENNEDY: From reports that we received that [Khrushchev] followed it carefully, that it changed his opinion as to what the United States wanted. It had a profound effect. Second, what we were trying to obtain before was a test ban treaty for nuclear tests of any kind. Finally, we had to abandon that.

MARTIN: You went for a limited test ban?

KENNEDY: A limited test ban. All the effort prior to that was to how many [verification] posts you would have on Russian soil. They wanted three; we wanted twenty. All of the work and effort had gone into that.

It was only, finally, the speech at American University and then the realization that we couldn't get that; and wasn't it better to get something, a fallback position, and then go ahead? Everybody tested underground if they wanted.

MARTIN: I suppose that Moscow's trouble with Peking had something to do with this, too, didn't it?

KENNEDY: Well, that I don't know.

MARTIN: Did Harriman come out the hero in this matter?

KENNEDY: Yes.

MARTIN: Did he deserve all the credit that he got?

KENNEDY: Yes. Yes, he did. The fellow from Britain wasn't any good.

MARTIN: But it wasn't all done before [Harriman] got there?

KENNEDY: No, not a bit. In fact, I think that there wasn't any assurance that he'd be successful.

MARTIN: Really? I assumed it was already set.

KENNEDY: I remember, before he went, that there wasn't any great feeling that he could accomplish it.

MARTIN: That's wonderful.
   The President made a trip to Europe. He went to Berlin, England, Italy, the Vatican, and so forth, in June that year. This was a great success, was it not?

KENNEDY: Yes, it was.

MARTIN: One of the best trips of all.

KENNEDY: Yes.

MARTIN: You were not along?

KENNEDY: No, I wasn't.

MARTIN: Were you in on the planning of it?

KENNEDY: No. No, I was not.

MARTIN: Didn't you have anything to do with this?

KENNEDY: I talked to [JFK] informally about going to Berlin and about whether he should make a speech in German when they got off the plane. We talked about going to Ireland. He'd always wanted to go to Ireland. We talked about going to visit my sister's grave in England[42]—you know, just family matters. But I wasn't involved in any of it formally. But that was, I suppose, the happiest time of his administration, particularly his trip to Ireland. He had the movies of his trip to Ireland, and he showed them, I guess, every night when he got home.

MARTIN: Is that right?

KENNEDY: Everybody had to go in and watch the movie.

MARTIN: When he said we would risk our cities to defend Berlin, would we?

KENNEDY: Yes.

MARTIN: De Gaulle never believed it, I guess.

Did you ever talk to [JFK] about the Peking-Moscow split, the future course it might take?

KENNEDY: No.

MARTIN: And the opportunities it might open to us?

KENNEDY: No.

MARTIN: He said once, if this continued and the Chicoms got the bomb and went ahead in the direction they were heading, in the seventies this world would be even more dangerous than it was now.

KENNEDY: That's why he was so anxious to get the control of nuclear weapons, of the testing—because of the fact that the indications were that sixteen nations could make the bomb and could have the bomb within a few years. If they couldn't test, they would not. I think that was the whole purpose.

MARTIN: He went to see the Pope [Paul VI], didn't he? When he was in Rome?

KENNEDY: Yes.

MARTIN: Did he ever meet Pope John [XXIII]?

KENNEDY: No.

MARTIN: Did you ever hear him discuss the two Popes?

KENNEDY: He liked this Pope [Paul VI]. I don't think he was over-whelmed by him, but he thought he was a nice fellow. Jackie met John [XXIII]. I met John. I liked him very much. I thought he was wonderful. He made a great impression.

MARTIN: Early in the summer of 1963, the President was said to be contemplating changes in the Alliance for Progress. There were newspaper stories about how he was going to get a new committee appointed and get more Latin American participation. Were you involved in this? Do you know what the President had in mind?

KENNEDY: Just indirectly. I knew he was dissatisfied with the adminis-trative ability of [Teodoro] Moscoso. He'd hate to get rid of

Moscoso—he liked him, and of course he knew that the Latin Americans liked him—but he didn't feel it was going very well. He was quite [eager] to get some better personnel to run it.

MARTIN: They were going to appoint a committee—which I think subsequently had been appointed—of Latin Americans to supervise it.

KENNEDY: Yes.

MARTIN: During the late spring and early summer of '63, there was a dispute between the Dominican Republic and Haiti. [In April 1963, Haiti refused to grant safe-conduct visas to opponents of Duvalier who had taken refuge in the embassy of the Dominican Republic. When Haitian soldiers surrounded the embassy, the Dominican Republic protested this action as a violation of diplomatic immunity.] At one point we pulled all our people; we evacuated the women and children from our missions in Port-au-Prince. Subsequently, there was a rebellion of some Haitians there, and Duvalier accused the Dominican Republic and us of being involved. Were you in on this? Do you know much about it?

KENNEDY: No. No, I wasn't. Again, I was involved on the periphery. I don't think I ever discussed it with the President, [only] the fact that we'd all like to get rid of Duvalier and how to do that.

MARTIN: You weren't in on any of the CIA operations, though?

KENNEDY: No, I wasn't.

MARTIN: It was said several times that the administration did not want an East-West nonaggression pact. This is in July, August '63. Why not?

KENNEDY: The question was a nonaggression pact between NATO and—

MARTIN: The Warsaw Pact.

KENNEDY: Yes. I think it would have, as I remember, entailed the recognition of East Germany. The [Soviet] Ambassador, Dobrynin, and Georgi Bolshakov used to suggest this all the time. Of course, I reported it. It just didn't seem to ever go anywhere. I never got into a conversation particularly about why we didn't. But I thought it was because of East Germany.

MARTIN: Now, in September, Khrushchev asked for a seventeen-nation summit conference the next year for discussion of general and complete disarmament. The President replied in a speech to the United Nations, talking about a joint venture to the moon. Do you know what the President thought the prospects were for general and complete disarmament? This is after the limited test ban treaty was signed, Bob.

KENNEDY: I don't think he thought there were any immediate prospects. He always felt that there had been a possibility of at least working out an inspection system of some kind within the Soviet Union for underground testing and that progress was made for a period of time. Then I think he felt that the Russians went back and took a more adamant position. But he certainly didn't think there was anything going to go on for another year.

I might say that the announcement by Lyndon Johnson last month about the twenty-five percent nuclear material—that was all worked out in August 1963.

MARTIN: It was?

KENNEDY: Yes.

MARTIN: You asked me whether I thought people in general knew that Johnson was getting credit for a lot of things that President Kennedy had done. I don't think so.

In the Dominican Republic, the Bosch government fell on the night of the 25th of September. Were you involved in any of that? Do you know what the President's reactions were?

KENNEDY: No, I don't think I was.

MARTIN: He fell on a Wednesday morning, and I came out on Saturday, the 28th of September.

The last night, when my nerve was going, I asked for a carrier—[Bosch] asked me for one. I transmitted the request and got an answer saying that they wouldn't send one except to prevent a Communist takeover. They wouldn't send it to prop up Bosch. You don't know anything about that? Did you get in on the negotiations that went on all fall on recognition of the military junta that had overthrown Bosch?

KENNEDY: No.

MARTIN: I never saw you at any of the meetings but I didn't know whether you were—

KENNEDY: No, I did not.

MARTIN: On September 30, the President said that Goldwater might very well be nominated. Any particular reason for him to say that? You told me a while back that the one that you were really concerned about was Romney.

KENNEDY: Romney. No, I think he probably thought [Goldwater would] be the easiest to beat, and he wanted to build him up a little bit.

MARTIN: Who'd he think really would be nominated? Do you know?

KENNEDY: Romney.

MARTIN: He did think so?

KENNEDY: Yes.

MARTIN: I've thought all along it'd be Nixon.

How about the wheat sale to the Soviet Union, Bob? Were you in on that [the October 1963 sale of American wheat to the Soviet Union]?

KENNEDY: Yes. There was a split. I think the political people, Kenny O'Donnell and Larry O'Brien, were against it. I was in favor of it—Averell Harriman was in favor of it—basically because I felt that it was difficult to turn down a request for the purchase of food for the Soviet Union.

MARTIN: Because it was for the people of the Soviet Union?

KENNEDY: The people. Also, the Cold War had diminished somewhat. The problems hadn't diminished, but the Cold War had. Trade had some advantage to it. Secondly, as I say, it is difficult to turn down food. Third, it was quite clear that the wheat that we would sell to Germany was repackaged, or was going to be repackaged, and sold by the West Germans to the Russians in one form or another. We had examples of that. So we weren't gaining anything particularly. And it would help the economy.

We had one meeting at the White House in which discussions went back and forth. In any case, I think the President came out with the feeling that he should go ahead and sell it. There were some other meetings after that, and I became less and less involved.

It was a question of how it was going to be worked out: working it out with the unions, working it out with the companies, whether there'd be government sales or company sales, whether they'd be competing with one another, whether they'd be subsidized, and all that. I didn't get into it, other than just hearing generally that those were the problems. After that, they were handled by Luther Hodges, Bill Wirtz, and Orville Freeman.

I had the feeling as we went along that the ball dropped somewhere in connection with some of the discussions and negotiations. I don't know exactly where or how or why. The expectation of the sale was greater than what actually materialized. Why that was, exactly, and if it was somebody's fault, again I just don't know. I do think it wasn't clear with the unions what was going to be done as far as carrying how much in American ships and what ships were available. That was questionable.

I think that the President was uncertain at the beginning. I think he was ultimately convinced by those three factors I mentioned. Number one, that somebody would make a profit and it'd probably be with American wheat. Number two, to turn down the sale of food didn't make any sense. And three, it would help the farm economy by four or five hundred [million], six hundred [million], perhaps a billion dollars.

MARTIN: The Bobby Baker case broke in November. Do you want to go into the Bobby Baker case?

KENNEDY: I can go into it. I really didn't follow it particularly or get into it very much. The newspapers had a number of articles, *The Washington Post* particularly. I had always heard stories about Bobby Baker, about all his money and free use of money. My relationship with him always had been reasonably friendly, although I didn't have much to do with him. Even though he was opposed to President Kennedy—he was working for Lyndon Johnson—he was always quite reasonable about it. He certainly didn't create any bitterness on our part. So I was reasonably friendly toward him.

Our first involvement in it came, I suppose, in a conversation I had with Ben Bradlee [then the Washington Bureau Chief of *Newsweek*], who had some information. I can't remember exactly what it was, but they printed it in *Newsweek*. He asked me if we would look into it, and I said we would look into it.

Subsequently, there were a lot of stories that my brother and I were interested in dumping Lyndon Johnson and that I'd started the Bobby Baker case in order to give us a handle to dump Lyndon Johnson. Well, number one, there was no plan to dump Lyndon Johnson. That didn't make any sense. Number two, I hadn't gotten really involved in the Bobby Baker case until after a good number of newspaper stories had appeared about it. There really wasn't any choice but to look into some of the allegations, which were allegations of violations of law. Some weeks after that, I called [Baker]—I suppose sometime in November—and said that I just wanted to assure him that he'd get a fair shake. If there were any problem, he could send his lawyer to the Department of Justice and he would be fairly treated. Abe Fortas was his lawyer. There were a lot of stories then, after November 22, that the Bobby Baker case was really stimulated by me and that this was part of my plan to get something on Johnson. That wasn't correct.

MARTIN: *The New York Times,* on the 13th of November, said that there'd been a three-hour meeting at the White House on the '64 campaign strategy: what its themes would be, where to concentrate, and so on. I assume you were present, weren't you?

KENNEDY: Yes, I was.

MARTIN: Can you tell me about that? I think it'd be very interesting. Civil rights as an issue would be something, I suppose, you were talking about, [as well as] what kind of a campaign it was going to be, whether it would be a landslide, what the prospects were, and so on. And the problems.

KENNEDY: Well, there were a number of conflicts over at the Democratic National Committee. I had made arrangements for Steve Smith to go over there. Some of the people who had been involved in Washington for a little period of time began to have their own empires and began to develop their own loyalties. I thought it would be helpful to have somebody over there who was just interested in President Kennedy. Dick Maguire was Kenny O'Donnell's man and had sort of been running the National Committee because John Bailey was rather weak. . . .

So Stephen Smith went over there. I was anxious to have it clear throughout the campaign that Steve Smith was going to be running things and people should be reporting to him. That was one of the major purposes for the President to say that people should report to Steve Smith. And that's what they did. He then said that Steve Smith would in turn report to John Bailey. John Bailey by this time had become almost a figurehead.

MARTIN: Would Steve have been the campaign manager?

KENNEDY: I suppose he would have, yes. We never discussed it, but I expect he probably would have.

Second, the President said that the campaign themes were going to be peace and prosperity. The prospects of having the longest period of time in the nation's history of prosperity were very good. What's her name, the one who writes the financial column? Porter?

MARTIN: Yes, Sylvia Porter.

KENNEDY: She was one of the President's favorites. He quoted from her frequently. She pointed out that already it had gone thirty-six months and that thirty-eight was the record or something. It looked like we could get the tax bill by. We were going to have prosperity. He said, "We'll have peace and prosperity. And if we don't have peace, we damn well better win the war." That was going to be the theme.

He had a feeling at that time that he had not gotten himself across as a person with much compassion, that people didn't feel personally involved with him enough. He thought that he should give some thought to what should be done so that he came across a little bit more.

We were talking about who was going to be in charge of registration, who was going to be in charge of the convention. Most of the meeting was taken up with change in the delegate strength from each state. There were various ideas about increasing the delegate strength of each state and making more allowance for some of the industrial states.

There was an extreme position which would give much more strength to the industrial states. It was felt that you couldn't go that far because it would look like we were trying to turn the National Committee over to me. There was an in-between position. And there was a third position not to change it at all. We took a rather in-between position. Every state got a few more delegates; but the ones in the northern industrial states, which had a greater voting population, received a greater increase, percentage-wise, of strength. That's basically what we discussed.

[New Jersey Secretary of State] Bob Burkhardt was going to be brought in from New Jersey. Dave Hackett [Special Assistant to the Attorney General] was going to go to work organizing the delegates as he had done in '60 and be the right-hand man of the fellow from Georgia [Bob Troutman], who'd always done it. Bob Troutman was going to be brought back in—a lot of the same people that we'd used before. All this was discussed.

MARTIN: What was the President's estimate of the civil rights issue?

KENNEDY: He always thought that it cost votes, but that by the time it shook down in the election, it wasn't going to be that serious.

MARTIN: Even in the suburbs or in the big cities in the North?

KENNEDY: Yes, it would cost votes.

MARTIN: That's where it would hurt most.

KENNEDY: But he thought that, if he was running against Goldwater, it wasn't going to be a problem. If he was going to run against Rockefeller, it was going to be less of a problem, too, because Rockefeller would have to take the same position. It wasn't going to hurt that much. If he was going to run against Goldwater, he'd pick up so many other votes to offset the losses in this area. And then we all felt—we had worked with Goldwater—we just knew he was not a very smart man. He's just going to destroy himself. [The President] was concerned that he would destroy himself too early and not get the nomination.

MARTIN: What were his feelings about how big he would win?

KENNEDY: We didn't discuss it.

MARTIN: You didn't? Do you know what they were, though, even though you didn't discuss it at that meeting?

KENNEDY: No, I don't. We didn't really discuss it. We discussed civil rights and also my own position. I had thought during that period of time—and I talked to him, I think, in November—about resigning at an appropriate time.

MARTIN: Did you decide anything?

KENNEDY: He thought it was a bad idea, because it would make it appear that we were running out on civil rights. The Negroes would be upset. But I thought that I'd become such a liability and the campaign was getting so bitter and mean. People were saying so many things, and it was getting to more and more of the family. We felt it was going to be a very mean, very bitter campaign.

MARTIN: You did? What did you think would be the main attack lines?

KENNEDY: Well, I suppose, the power. We saw all this literature that was coming out and the letters that poured in. You know, there was just real hatred. . . .

Readers may have considerable difficulty equating Robert Kennedy's passionate opposition to the war in Vietnam—which was a main theme of his campaign for the presidency—with the hardline views on American involvement that he expresses here, in the doleful spring of 1964. Although Robert Kennedy went on record in the previous autumn as questioning whether a Communist takeover could be resisted successfully by the Diem-Nhu regime—or any other government of South Vietnam—when John Bartlow Martin asked him in 1964 why President Kennedy had felt there was an overwhelming reason for the United States to pursue victory in Vietnam, he said:

"The loss of all of Southeast Asia if you lost Vietnam. I think everybody [in the administration] was quite clear that the rest of Southeast Asia would fall. . . . It would just have profound effects on our position throughout the world."

Four years later, in announcing his candidacy for the presidency, he pledged to end the conflict.

"The reality of recent events in Vietnam," he said, "has been glossed over with illusions. . . . In private talks and in public, I have tried in vain to alter our course in Vietnam before it further saps our spirit and our manpower, further raises the risk of wider war, and further destroys the country and the people it was meant to save. I cannot stand aside from the contest that will decide our nation's future and our children's future."

The 180-degree difference between those two statements measures the distance that Robert Kennedy traveled from supporter to opponent of American involvement in the war, but not the political turmoil or the vexing second thoughts that were borne down on him by his turnabout. When the following interview was conducted in 1964 he still thought it was possible, despite the overthrow of the Diem brothers, that South Vietnamese forces could overcome Viet Cong guerrilla warfare and end the Communist threat by relying less on conventional military tactics and by pushing the strategic village program to secure the countryside step by step. But as the political situation deteriorated in South Vietnam and the effectiveness of its forces weakened, doubts began to gnaw at him. When President Johnson opted for a military solution and it became clear that increasing numbers of American soldiers, sailors, airmen, and marines—not the South Vietnamese—were carrying the major burden of the fighting, RFK's opposition mounted and he came to believe that our course in Vietnam was insanely wrong, morally as well as tactically.

To put the following conversations in context, suffice it to say that the Robert Kennedy who responded to John Bartlow Martin's questions in 1964 was not the same Robert Kennedy who ran for the presidency in 1968.

VIETNAM

MARTIN: Vietnam now began appearing rather prominently in the papers—and of course still is—and was, all through '63. In January the Vietnamese killed three Americans and shot down five helicopters.

KENNEDY: Viet Cong, you mean.

MARTIN: That's right. That's what I mean, Viet Cong.
   A little later [Senator Mike] Mansfield said that this thing was turning into an American war and wasn't justified by our national interest: We hadn't any business going in so deep, but we kept going in deeper. We seemed to have our lines crossed. I mean, the Majority Leader in the Senate, Mansfield, was saying this was not an American war, and he didn't think it should be an American war. He didn't think our heavy commitment there was justified. How did you feel about it? How did the President feel about it? And at what point did we get our lines straightened out?

KENNEDY: I don't think the fact that Senator Mansfield or somebody in the Senate takes a position necessarily means—

MARTIN: Well, he *was* Majority Leader.

KENNEDY: But he's frequently taken that line or that position on some of these matters. I don't think the fact that he has an independent view from the executive branch of the government, particularly on Southeast Asia, indicates that the lines aren't straight. The President felt that he had a strong, overwhelming reason for being in Vietnam and that we should win the war in Vietnam.

MARTIN: What was the overwhelming reason?

KENNEDY: The loss of all of Southeast Asia if you lost Vietnam. I think everybody was quite clear that the rest of Southeast Asia would fall.

MARTIN: What if it did?

KENNEDY: It would just have profound effects on our position through-out the world and our position in a rather vital part of the world. It would affect what happened in India, of course, which in turn has an effect on the Middle East. It would have, everybody felt, a very adverse effect. It would have an effect on Indonesia, with a hundred million population. All of these countries would be affected by the fall of Vietnam to the Communists, particularly as we had made such a fuss in the United States both under President Eisenhower and President Kennedy about the preservation of the integrity of Vietnam.

MARTIN: There was never any consideration given to pulling out?

KENNEDY: No.

MARTIN: But, at the same time, no disposition to go in—

KENNEDY: No.

MARTIN: —in an all-out way, as we went into Korea. We were trying to avoid a Korea—is that correct?

KENNEDY: Yes, because everybody, including General MacArthur, felt that land conflict between our troops—white troops and Asian—would only end in disaster. So we went in as advisers to try to get the Vietnamese to fight, themselves, because we couldn't win the war for them. They had to win the war for themselves.

MARTIN: That's generally true all over the world, whether it's in a shooting war or a different kind of a war. But the President was convinced that we had to stay in there?

KENNEDY: Yes.

MARTIN: And we couldn't lose it?

KENNEDY: Yes.

MARTIN: And if the Vietnamese were about to lose it, would he pro-pose to go in on land if he had to?

KENNEDY: We'd face that when we came to it.

MARTIN: Or go with air strikes direct from carriers—something like that?

KENNEDY: It didn't have to be faced at that time. In the first place, we were winning the war in 1962 and 1963. Up until May or so of 1963, the situation was getting progressively better.

MARTIN: But then it started going downhill, didn't it?

KENNEDY: Yes. Then we had all the problems with the Buddhists. [In response to government suppression of Buddhist activities, at least eight monks publicly burned themselves to death in protest. The protests received worldwide media attention.]

MARTIN: Why did [things] go downhill? Why did they get bad, Bob?

KENNEDY: Well, I just think he—Diem—wouldn't make even the slightest concessions. He was difficult to reason with.

And then it was built up tremendously in an adverse fashion here in the United States, and that was played back in Vietnam. I think the people themselves became concerned about it. The situation began to deteriorate in the spring of 1963. I think David Halberstam's— from *The New York Times*—articles had a strong effect on molding public opinion: the fact that the situation was unsatisfactory.

Our problem was that the important thing was to try to get somebody who could replace [Diem], somebody who could continue the war and keep the country united. And that was far more difficult. That was what was of great concern to all of us during this period of time. Nobody liked Diem, particularly. But how to get rid of him and get somebody who would continue the war, not split the country in two and, therefore, lose not only the war but the country: That was the great problem.

MARTIN: I see. Wasn't [Frederick B.] Nolting our Ambassador there?

KENNEDY: Yes, he was.

MARTIN: Was he effective?

KENNEDY: There was mixed opinion about it. He was close to Diem when he came back and Lodge was sent out there. His advice was quite good, and he put it effectively. And he had some courage. He opposed the State Department.

Most of the people in the State Department—at least, initially— were in favor of a coup. And [JFK] was against it, until we found out where it was going to go and what was going to be done. But one weekend about six or eight weeks before the actual coup took place, the President was away. Mike Forrestal, Averell Harriman (they had a Far Eastern desk) got together—and I think they might have talked to somebody from the military—but they, working it out with Henry Cabot Lodge, approved of going ahead with the coup. The President was up at the Cape and they gave him a telegram. He thought that it had been approved by McNamara and Maxwell Taylor and everybody else. It had not. It went out on a Monday. I became much more intimately involved in it then, because I saw the telegram and raised a question about what direction they were going to go: Who was going to take over, and who was going to run the coup, and how many soldiers they had on either side.

We had a meeting on that Wednesday, I think, and all these questions were put on the table, mostly by McNamara. Nobody had the answers to them. The fact that Maxwell Taylor and McNamara and John McCone hadn't been brought in on this created a great fuss. The government split in two. It was the only time, really, in three years that the government was broken in two in a very disturbing way. John McCone hated Henry Cabot Lodge, and so he became an ally of McNamara—rather, healed that breach.

MARTIN: Who wanted the coup?

KENNEDY: Harriman, Mike Forrestal, what's his name from the Far East desk who was fired?

MARTIN: Hilsman?

KENNEDY: Roger Hilsman. And the anti-coup [people] were Maxwell Taylor, McNamara, John McCone.

MARTIN: Who was supposed to pull off this coup, Bob? The military?

KENNEDY: Oh, they had been talking to some fellow who, in turn, talked to the generals. It was rather nebulous.

MARTIN: Jesus!

KENNEDY: And then the coup never came off, of course.

MARTIN: Well, it ultimately came off.

KENNEDY: But then the story got out that we were interested in a coup. So that was publicized all over. That was embarrassing for the country. This situation gradually deteriorated because Lodge thought the best way of proceeding was to make it difficult for Diem and never talk to him. He would never communicate with Diem nor talk with him in any way. So we didn't have any communication with Diem for eight weeks to speak of. They might have spoken twice.

MARTIN: The coup was before [Lodge] went out, before Nolting was replaced by Lodge. Is that correct?

KENNEDY: No, no. Shortly after.

MARTIN: No, I mean, the cable authorizing the coup.

KENNEDY: Shortly after.

MARTIN: Shortly after Lodge went?

KENNEDY: Yes.

MARTIN: I see.

KENNEDY: And it was at the request of Lodge or with his concurrence.

MARTIN: He was in favor of the coup?

KENNEDY: Yes.

MARTIN: Lodge was?

KENNEDY: And he wouldn't talk to [General Paul] Harkins.

MARTIN: Our military commander. Well, who the hell was he? He wasn't talking to anybody.

KENNEDY: Lodge wasn't. Lodge sent telegrams back about the military situation which he'd never clear or talk about with Harkins. So the bitterness between the military and State grew. And I don't know what Rusk was doing. . . . He didn't bring the situation under control at all, so it just started to drift badly during that period of time.

MARTIN: This was right after Lodge went?

KENNEDY: Yes.

MARTIN: It was drifting. And [Lodge] apparently was fighting with a CIA man, the station chief [John Richardson].

KENNEDY: [Lodge] exposed him and gave his name publicly to the newspapers. That resulted in McCone becoming even more bitter. . . .

MARTIN: Actually, we did not authorize that coup?

KENNEDY: No.

MARTIN: Though we had encouraged it earlier?

KENNEDY: Well, there was all this conflict back and forth about the coup. Every week there was a story about the coup.

Then there was a question—you see, we told the people out there that we welcomed a coup.

MARTIN: You mean in the original cable?

KENNEDY: Yes. So then the problem was to get—some of them were risking their lives—to tell them not to have a coup.

In fact, this fellow [Diem] was bad and it would be nice to have a better government, but we didn't want to have a coup when nobody knew what kind of government you were going to have and whether you'd just have a bloody riot out there. So we tried to throw some cold water on them by finding out who they had who was going to take over, what their forces were—asking all those questions.

My impression was that Henry Cabot Lodge didn't pay much attention to it because he wanted a coup. But the President sent out requests for all that and got not very satisfactory answers, usually.

And then, just suddenly, the coup took place.

MARTIN: That was while Madame Nhu was in New York, or in the States. [Madame Ngo Dinh Nhu was married to Diem's brother, Ngo Dinh Nhu, and served as the official family hostess.]

KENNEDY: Yes, in the States.

MARTIN: Now, earlier, on August 20, the Diems had said that a coup was inevitable and that Lodge was going to throw it off—that's what he was there for. Then Mrs. Nhu saw Ted—Teddy Kennedy—in Belgrade. Now, what was that all about?

KENNEDY: Well, nothing. They just ran into each other. I don't think there was anything that took place, particularly.

MARTIN: There wasn't?

KENNEDY: No. I mean, nothing very meaningful. He thought she was very attractive.

MARTIN: Why did she come to the States?

KENNEDY: I don't know. I don't know why she came.

MARTIN: Whose idea was that?

KENNEDY: Well, we were not in favor of it, but I don't think anybody said that she couldn't come, because they knew that she'd raise a fuss. It was her own idea. We tried to discourage it, but could not. They were also close to Johnson. That's, I think, one of the major reasons Hilsman got fired: because he was in favor of the coup and Lyndon Johnson was against, strongly against, having a coup. And he was bitter about it.

MARTIN: What was the President's position? Pro- or anti-coup?

KENNEDY: He would have liked to have gotten rid of Diem if he could get rid of him and get somebody proper to replace him. He was against getting rid of him until you knew what was going to come along, whether the government that was going to replace it had any stability, whether it would, in fact, be a successful coup.

But he didn't know—I mean, other than the fact that there were rumors about coups all the time. He had no idea that this particular coup was going to take place, other than what I've described. This looked more serious, but he had sent out and asked for certain information before any coup should take place. Henry Cabot Lodge was going to come home during this period of time; and it was felt that he should delay his departure but still act as if he were going home, because otherwise, it would disturb everybody.

We had the difficult problem that, in fact, people had been encouraged to have a coup and now to pull the rug out from under them meant their death. That complicated the problem. And then what really brought the coup on—I guess, from what I've read since then—is the fact that Diem planned a coup himself, a fake coup: He was going to pick up all these people and arrest them and say they were participating in a coup and then execute them.

MARTIN: It's the old Trujillo trick. An *agent provocateur*.

KENNEDY: The fellow who was supposed to do all that squealed, and that's what brought on this.

MARTIN: I see. Why did the President appoint Lodge as the Ambassador out there?

KENNEDY: Well, Lodge was interested in going someplace where there was a difficult problem. They needed somebody who could work with the military, spoke French, had some diplomatic experience. So he fit into it.

Ted Sorensen heard about it. They said [Lodge] was being appointed to Vietnam. [Sorensen] said, "You mean, North Vietnam?"

I thought that, as I said to the President, he'd get into difficulty some way. He wouldn't talk to the military out there, and he had a bad effect on the CIA. He talked to the newspapers all the time— Lodge—and he didn't do his homework. He was very difficult to deal with and heartily disliked by McNamara, by McCone, by Maxwell Taylor. [Taylor] liked him initially but didn't like him afterward. Maxwell Taylor's close to General Harkins, and Harkins and Lodge didn't get along at all.

MARTIN: When the appointment was announced—Lodge, I mean—I had a feeling that we were going to lose Vietnam and we were trying to distribute the responsibility politically.

KENNEDY: No. No. Because—at least, I thought—we were winning the war in Vietnam.

MARTIN: Even at that time? I mean, he wasn't appointed until pretty late in the game.

KENNEDY: No. That was not a factor.

MARTIN: That was not true? Distributing the responsibility, political responsibility?

KENNEDY: Not a bit.

MARTIN: Did the President have a high regard for [Lodge]?

KENNEDY: I think a fair regard.

MARTIN: It was a helluva hot spot, Bob. That's all I'm trying to suggest.

KENNEDY: I think he thought he might do the job satisfactorily.

MARTIN: It's turned out to build him up as a presidential possibility. Do you think Lodge had that in mind at the time?

KENNEDY: No. He could never run against the President. I'm not sure it's built him up as a presidential possibility.

MARTIN: You're not?

KENNEDY: No. He could have gotten publicity some other way. I think, mostly, he's being built up now because the other candidates are so bad, not because of what he's doing in Vietnam. I don't think that's a very popular war among Americans generally or among the Republicans particularly. I don't think that helps him with delegates. In fact, he's carrying out the Democrats' policy, the Democratic policy in Vietnam.

MARTIN: If he's not the candidate, I presume this will become a campaign issue.

I notice that McNamara, the other day, called this, accepted this as McNamara's war—which I didn't think, incidentally, was very good politics.

KENNEDY: No.

MARTIN: Congress declares war.

The President sent Taylor and McNamara out to Vietnam in September [1963], pretty late in September. Was this because of the things you've been describing, that the President wasn't satisfied with Lodge's reports?

KENNEDY: They came back and gave an account that the war was going well, that the efforts by the Buddhists and the internal struggles were not having an adverse effect on the carrying out of the war, that they could win the war under the present circumstances.

MARTIN: This doesn't seem to have been true.

KENNEDY: No.

MARTIN: They must have been misled by people in the field.

KENNEDY: I don't know whether they were just misled or misread the signs. I think they went out with a preconceived notion that all was fine.

MARTIN: Would Taylor do that? And McNamara?

KENNEDY: I suppose it's partially due to the bitterness that had been created. It just got to be a difficult period. Nobody was looking at it very objectively during this period.

MARTIN: That's one of the real problems in government, isn't it? Once you get a policy set, it's awfully hard to unset it.

KENNEDY: Yes. Everybody was committed.

MARTIN: Everybody gets himself personally committed.

KENNEDY: Particularly Harkins. You see, that played such a role: that the military were being mistreated by Lodge. So they'd take one position and Lodge another. And each one became more extreme. They weren't working together. And the result was difficult.

MARTIN: Is there anything else on Vietnam? Any conversations between you and the President that you can recall?

KENNEDY: I had a lot of conversations about Henry Cabot Lodge.

MARTIN: What'd he say about him?

KENNEDY: We were going to try to get rid of Henry Cabot Lodge. He was supposed to come home—if that coup hadn't taken place, he was going to come home—and we were trying to work out how he could be fired, how we could get rid of him. [Lodge] had a fellow out there who was, I think, handling his press, and he was leaking everything to the papers, everything that appeared in the newspapers.

He didn't have answers to questions. It was just a difficult business.

MARTIN: But he never did come home?

KENNEDY: He didn't.

The President wasn't very impressed by the end with Roger Hilsman.

MARTIN: Wasn't he?

KENNEDY: Averell Harriman had come back from the great success of the test ban treaty. Then he had mishandled this business on Vietnam. And the result was that he was rather cut off.

He had done so well. He felt very strongly about a coup, but again, he hadn't thought it through very carefully. It became an emotional matter. He got involved in this early coup without really going through the President and without discussing it sufficiently with others. He gradually was listened to less, and I think his advice was sought less. He felt, unfortunately, during those last few months that he was a little bit out. I think the President brought him back in the last week or ten days of November—before November 22—but prior to that time it was unfortunate, because he had done so well and then had gone downhill on this.

But you can see . . . Bob McNamara and Maxwell Taylor so involved with the military and General Harkins that they didn't see things correctly; the State Department committed to one point of view, Dean Rusk not really helping at all. (I don't know, to tell you the truth, where [Rusk] stood. He was for a coup and then he was against it. He was all over the lot.) There wasn't anybody. And Mac Bundy wasn't particularly helpful.

MARTIN: This was really his area in the White House, wasn't it?

KENNEDY: Yes.

MARTIN: Why wasn't he helpful or effective on this?

KENNEDY: Because it was so difficult to deal with all of these things. Perhaps it should have been watched more carefully or closer. I don't know that our meetings were as frequent as they might have been.

MARTIN: You think this is one that the administration bobbled? How would you assess the whole thing?

KENNEDY: I suppose it is. I suppose you'd think that [JFK] bobbled. If you look back on it, if it had been handled properly, I don't know what we would have done. Assume first that you have Henry Cabot Lodge out there. You have an Ambassador out there, particularly as the situation was deteriorating, who wouldn't talk to Diem. Well, what do you do? You'd have to fire him.

MARTIN: Yes, but we had a different Ambassador—Nolting.

KENNEDY: Yes.

MARTIN: Let's assume you just left him and then took his advice. I don't know Nolting, Bob.

KENNEDY: I think it was just the feeling that he'd been out there so long and that we should have a more critical look. He was very close to Diem, Diem's brother [Ngo Dinh Nhu]. The change came at the wrong time. My only point is, assuming that it had been smoothly handled and well handled, looking back on it, I don't know exactly what we would have done that would have improved the situation.

Diem was corrupt and a bad leader. It would have been much better that we didn't have him. But we inherited him. He came with the job. So what do you do? I mean, it's better if you don't have him, but you have to have somebody who can win the war—and who is that?—and to try to select him. Well, it's pretty tough to have the United States select. It's a bad policy to get into, for us to run a coup out there and replace somebody we don't like with somebody we do, because it would just make every other country nervous as can be that we were running coups in and out. As you say, I'm sure it wasn't well handled, but assuming it *was* well handled, I'm not sure that—

MARTIN: You know, I think there are two basic things involved here: first, Diem's own failings in his refusal to deal with the Buddhist problem. Correct me if I'm wrong: I wonder if the Buddhist immolations didn't have a good deal to do with the deep emotional involvement that people felt here—when the monks were actually burning themselves.

KENNEDY: It was played up here. I don't know if you realize that there've been, I don't know, eight or ten of those burnings since this coup took place.

MARTIN: Yes, I do.

KENNEDY: Of course, nobody writes about them anymore. They were all, at that time, used to show that Diem was so bad. But they have gone on. I don't know what they prove now. I think that to some extent it was a major campaign to show how terrible he was.

MARTIN: In addition to the built-in problems out there, you have another basic problem in it. That's the limits on American power. I mean, we just can't do everything that we'd like to.

KENNEDY: That's right. The advantage of the Communist system over our system is the fact that they don't have to pay attention to your allies. They don't have newspapers that leak, to whom things are leaked—and only things that they want appear in papers.

Consider the Cuban [missile] crisis: If that ever happened in the United States, you'd have the President of the United States impeached. He could never have done that secretly and then withdrawn [the missiles] under those circumstances. Think about the Berlin crisis. You have to talk to each one of your allies as to what they want. Would they agree to fire a missile back if a missile is fired at you? And under what circumstances? One disagrees; what do you do about them? You can't fight a war in Europe if you don't have the support of France. You can't fight if you don't have the support of Germany. Well, what if they disagreed with one another? The fact that you have to get all those countries to go along is very difficult. So, vis-à-vis the Soviet Union or Communism, you have certain weaknesses in the system.

Secondly, just inherently, you can use the mass of power only under certain circumstances. I think that was really why the President emphasized other aspects of possible power over the period of the last three years—because he knew that our reliance almost solely on the use of atomic weapons to secure what we thought was necessary, and what could be helpful, just was a very fallible policy. The buildup of our conventional forces, the buildup of our Special Services, and the efforts that we made in a lot of different areas were based on that. Still, there are limitations diplomatically as to what you can do.

ON HIS OWN

MARTIN: We're down to the 22nd, Bob. Do you want to do it?

KENNEDY: No, I don't think I need to go into that.

Do you want to discuss after that? There were four or five matters that arose during the period of November 22 to November 27 or so which made me bitter—unhappy at least—with Lyndon Johnson. Events involving the treatment of Jackie on the plane trip back and all that kind of business. And then he came to the White House on Saturday and started moving all my brother's things out Saturday morning at nine o'clock. I went over and asked him to wait, at least until Sunday or Monday. Then he wanted to give the State of the Union message on Tuesday—the day after the funeral. But in any case, there were about four or five things.

So then he wanted to see me afterward. Sargent Shriver went to him and told him that I was unhappy—no, told Bill Moyers, who then told him. And then he asked to see me. And I went over to see him before Jackie left the White House, and he said, "Your people are talking about me," or something. He went through some of these things and gave explanations for them. He left a message that he'd like to see me anytime. I didn't feel like seeing him in December, so I never went to see him. I went away for about four days, and then I came back and I went to work. But I didn't feel like seeing him. I went away at Christmastime, and he sent me a telegram at Christmas, saying that he hoped I'd see him when I came back. I sent back a telegram wishing him a happy Christmas.

We went through January, and I never had any extensive conversation about any matter.

Then, I think in January or February, after a Cabinet meeting, he said he wanted to see me. We went into his office, and he got into a conversation about Paul Corbin, who was over at the Democratic National Committee. It was a bitter, mean conversation. It was the meanest tone that I've heard. He said that Paul Corbin had been up in New Hampshire and that he wanted Paul Corbin out of there, out of the Democratic National Committee. Paul Corbin had come to work for us in Wisconsin and was extremely loyal to me, . . . somewhat loyal to President Kennedy, and didn't like Lyndon Johnson.

He said, "I know he's been up in New Hampshire. I've received reports that he's been around New Hampshire. He's got to get out of there."

I said, "Well, why don't you find out? I didn't know he'd been in New Hampshire."

And he said, "I don't want to have anybody up there. I don't want anybody working over there that's interested—well, do you understand?"

I said, "You're not talking— I don't want to talk to you like that. And you could find out—you could ask Paul Corbin." I suggested that he find out himself whether that story was true. So I said, "I'm not going to. I don't want to have this kind of conversation with you."

That was, as I say, in January or February. Actually, Paul Corbin had never been up to New Hampshire. But he was a great booster of mine and, I think, very indiscreet about the fact that I should be Vice President. Since then—really, since January—I haven't had any dealings with Johnson.

It was probably a conscious effort to separate himself, to establish his own identity—and not to be involved with President Kennedy and therefore, to some extent, with me. He used to tell Kenny and Larry and all the others that he thought I hated him, and what could he do to get me to like him, and why did I dislike him?—everybody else in the Kennedys liked him, but I didn't seem to like him—and whether he should have me over for a drink or have some conversation with me. I didn't have any interest, really, in becoming involved with him.

I thought that an awful lot of things were going on that President Kennedy did that [Johnson] was getting the credit for—and wasn't saying enough about the fact that President Kennedy was responsible. Then some of the people who were closely involved with President Kennedy—like Bob McNamara and Mac Bundy—I didn't think stood up enough on some of these matters.

We got into one rather violent argument, a substantive argument on what to do about Cuba at the time the two or three fishing vessels arrived in Florida, in [U.S.] territorial waters. I was invited to a National Security Council meeting on that matter. The whole basis of our policy was built on the fact that these vessels had been sent in by Castro. I raised the question: what proof we had of that. I thought that we should find that out first. We had a meeting at three o'clock in the afternoon in which John McCone and others reported that they really couldn't prove that; maybe the fishing vessels just arrived there. I said that I thought this whole business about the fishing vessels was foolish. It's like a speeding ticket. Why don't they just tell them to get out of there and go on home? If you wanted to fine them a couple of hundred bucks, fine them. But the idea of locking them up and creating a national issue about it and creating a major crisis about it was foolish.

My major argument at that time was with Tom Mann and with Bob McNamara. I said that I thought [the Cuban vessels] should be sent back. Ultimately, that point of view prevailed. Then it was a question of what we were going to do with Cuba. All of us were in favor of cutting off the water and supplying our own water [at

Guantanamo], so they couldn't keep cutting it off or putting it on. The major question was what to do about the employees. There were several thousand [Cuban] employees down there. And Tom Mann was in favor of firing the employees. He said they brought in ten million dollars a year to the Cuban government, or five million dollars. It didn't make any sense to give to the Cuban government. They were security risks. And he said that this would cost the Cuban government money. He said that what we should do was make them spend all their money in PX's on the base, so that they couldn't take any of the money back—or fire them.

I said, if they had to spend the money on the base, how could they pay for rent? And how could they buy clothing and other things? And [Mann] said, "Well, they don't need any of that, because they'll still be living much better than most people in South America, even if they haven't got any money for housing." I said I didn't think that made any sense.

Subsequently, he said that the reason we should fire them was that the only thing the South Americans understood was money. And when you took this money away from the Castro government, it would be a sign to the rest of the countries of Latin America that this was a new administration, which was going to stand up to them, that money was going to be involved, and that if they misbehaved, they would lose economically. He said that this is the one major question in all of their minds: that they were far different from people in the United States and this is the one matter that would most impress them.

I said I thought he sounded like Barry Goldwater making a speech at the Economics Club, that this policy of the United States had gone out fifty years before.

Bob McNamara thought they should be fired. I asked him—this was subsequently in the Cabinet meeting with Lyndon Johnson—why Johnson wanted them fired. It was my feeling that they'd all arranged it beforehand and that they were going to be fired, and we were just whistling in the dark or blowing in the breeze, or whatever it might be.

But he said, well, they might be security risks; Lyndon Johnson said they might be security risks.

I said, "Well, if they're security risks, why didn't we fire them back in October of 1962? If they're security risks, can you tell me why we kept security risks on our base for all this period of time?"

I didn't think that made any sense. I wasn't firmly convinced of my position before they started arguing why they should be fired. It was after I heard Bob McNamara and Thomas Mann. But it got rather bitter and mean by the end of it. Mac Bundy then became more involved. He hadn't taken a position, really, at the beginning, and then he became more involved and had a rather strong exchange.

MARTIN: Where'd he come out? Where did Bundy come out?

KENNEDY: He came out on my side, finally. I was, interestingly enough, the spokesman for keeping the employees. The State Department—George Ball and Alex Johnson—at the first meeting, before the meeting with Lyndon Johnson, were on my side. By the time they finished the meeting, they and Dean Rusk were on the other side. Dean Rusk didn't come to the earlier meeting. And then John McCone was on my side, interestingly enough. And he was the other spokesman.

MARTIN: I'll be damned.

KENNEDY: Although I've been to National Security Council meetings and the ExComm—I mean, it was the last time I really got involved.

MARTIN: Is Johnson still using the ExComm?

KENNEDY: Yes, we have meetings. But, for instance, the last meeting we had was on what we should do if they shot down a U-2.[43] He came for five minutes of that meeting. I thought the meeting really missed the point. I won't go into the details of it, but it shocked me: first, the fact he wasn't there, and secondly, that I didn't think they really focused on the whole question. Because the major question was, if you used a certain kind of equipment, you had a fifty-fifty chance of avoiding being shot down by a missile. If you didn't use the equipment, chances were ninety-five percent that you'd be shot down. Well, if you put the equipment on, what if they shot at the plane and didn't shoot it down, then what would you do? I mean, that was a very important point which never was considered. Anyway, [Johnson] came there for five minutes.

Then we had a Cabinet meeting that followed it, on economy in government, and he came for an hour and a half to that. We went around the table, and Luther Hodges, Douglas Dillon, Gene Foley [of the Small Business Administration]—each person spent twenty minutes saying how they were having meetings and what they were doing to cut down on expenses in their departments.

MARTIN: You say this was the last substantive meeting that you—

KENNEDY: This was just a week ago. But the contrast between President Kennedy and President Johnson to me was striking.

MARTIN: In what way?

KENNEDY: Because this was a very important matter on what we were going to do when U-2 flights were shot down, what we would do if a U-2 plane was shot at and wasn't shot down. To go into that in some great detail and know what we were going to do, what our policies were, I thought was rather significant and rather important. And to go around and have such questions as "Everybody raise his hand who has put a freeze on employees on outlying bases"—

MARTIN: Turning out the lights.

KENNEDY: And Cabinet members were putting up their hands. I heard Bob McNamara say to one of the other Cabinet members: "That was a fine meeting."

And then, you see, the A-11 plane was started under Eisenhower, but it was really pushed and was the favorite of the President [JFK], and they didn't mention President Kennedy's name. I raised the question with Bob McNamara. He said he'd get it out, and he never really got it out very clearly. That made me upset. Mac Bundy came up and said, well, he didn't know whether President Kennedy was very interested in it, or some words to that effect. And I had heard the President discuss it so much. I'd known he was very responsible for it.

Then the things about the fissionable material: The destruction of that had been developed by the President [JFK] back in August. Then all of what had been done in the economy, really, had been developed over the period of the last three years. I didn't think there was ever any mention of that.

Nor did I think that those who were closely identified with President Kennedy who came to work for Lyndon Johnson—I thought that they felt: "The king was dead, and long live the king." . . .

I think probably it's important to what my relationship has been with him—

MARTIN: With Johnson you mean.

KENNEDY: —historically. I'm affected considerably by, I suppose, what we thought of him, what the President thought of him, particularly by the time of October or November of '62. He very rarely helped when he could help when we were trying to get votes in the Senate. He was against sending any civil rights legislation up.

MARTIN: He was?

KENNEDY: Yes. He was against our policy on Cuba in October of '62—although I never knew quite what he was *for*; he was just against it. He was just brought in on the last day, but he was against it. He was shaking his head, mad. (He had been in an earlier meeting. I guess he went out to Hawaii or something. Then he came back in for the last meeting.)

When the President was going down to Texas, trying to get the political situation settled in Texas, Lyndon Johnson would be no help. That made it difficult for the President. The President was looking forward to his trip to Texas just because of the fact that there was so much trouble in Texas. He thought it would make it more exciting, more interesting—which he said to me. . . .

And he said to Jackie, talking about him, that Lyndon Johnson was incapable of telling the truth. And then I had these terrible experiences with him coming back—when he lied again and where he treated Jackie, the whole business, very badly. . . .

Ralph Dungan was trying to work out appointments. He was in charge of that under the President. And [Johnson] said he wanted to make sure that everybody who was at all interested called him personally and ask him for the person to be appointed so that they would know that they'd be personally indebted to him as President. . . .

MARTIN: What about the White House staff? The new ones who came in and the old ones who stayed on?

KENNEDY: Well, Bill Moyers [then Special Assistant] is good. All of them are good, from what I understand. I haven't had many personal dealings with them. [Special Assistant] Walter Jenkins seems like a good fellow.

MARTIN: Does he?

KENNEDY: I think he got involved terribly in that Bobby Baker business, but I think he was taking the rap. Ted Sorensen asked me initially when it first came up—he was supposed to be handling it—and I said that I thought that Walter Jenkins should request an opportunity to testify. I think he obviously was in difficulty, and that's why he didn't. But he's a good fellow, everybody says.

Bill Moyers is a smart fellow and an honorable man, from what I understand. And [Press Secretary] George Reedy's fine. You know, they're all scared, of course, of Lyndon. I guess [aide Jack] Valenti's a nice fellow.

MARTIN: Is he?

KENNEDY: Yes. They've all treated me very well. I think, generally, the people [Johnson] has immediately around him look good.

MARTIN: How's Mann? How's Mann doing?

KENNEDY: He's a disaster, in my judgment—based on that meeting with him. Anybody who says that about the money must have been—indicates a very bad figure.

Lyndon talks about everybody, you see, with everybody. And of course that's dangerous. You know, he doesn't think anything of a lot of people. And he yells at his staff. He treats them just terribly. Very mean. He's a very mean, mean figure.

MARTIN: What were the feelings of the people who left and the people who stayed?

KENNEDY: I think Ted Sorensen got along with [Johnson] reasonably well. He thought that Lyndon Johnson was good, that his reactions were good on matters. He thought that if he stayed, he'd probably have an argument with him because Ted Sorensen's very outspoken and wouldn't have any respect for Lyndon Johnson—I mean, he had nothing like he had with the President. . . .

MARTIN: How about Schlesinger?

KENNEDY: Art Schlesinger. They just don't get along, and Arthur Schlesinger, I think, became too vocal in his criticisms. He used to go around and say how much he disliked Lyndon Johnson, disliked Mann. But that probably didn't accomplish a great deal of good. I don't think he left on the best of terms. Lyndon didn't like him very much at the end.

MARTIN: What about Pierre [Salinger]?

KENNEDY: . . . He started to talk about the fact that he couldn't stand it over there. He wanted to get out. It was a question of when he could get out. Then this idea of running for the Senate came to him.

He thought he had some time to make up his mind and then found out that he had to file immediately. He went out and did it without any discussion with Johnson beforehand.

MARTIN: Did he talk to you about it?

KENNEDY: He talked to me on a Monday before—to me and to Jackie—but then he thought at that time he had about three weeks to decide. I said he should find out what the newspapers were going to do and what kind of support he could get out there [in California] and also what kind of money. I didn't think he should make up his mind before he found out. The next thing he did was call me Thursday and said that he was going to have to resign the next day because he found he had to file on Friday.

MARTIN: What about the ones who stayed on, Dungan and Kenny O'Donnell?

KENNEDY: Dungan's unhappy. Kenny, I think, was on a reasonably good relationship up until about two weeks ago. Now, he sounds like he's getting mad. But I don't know what he was trying to prove. You know, he was talking about how he was going to do it for the Democratic party, but I didn't quite understand it. He would never see Johnson socially. He'd never go swimming with him—[Johnson] wanted him to always go swimming—or he'd never go to lunch with him; he'd never go over with him at night. [Johnson] always wants somebody to come with him and have a drink at night and swim, do something. . . . [O'Donnell] never would do that. He was independent. I think it's gradually caught up with him.

MARTIN: Well, in the beginning Kenny was the one we were all so worried about.

KENNEDY: Oh, you mean because he was so affected?

MARTIN: Yes, yes. And is he functioning in the White House?

KENNEDY: Yes, but he's doing a lot of work at the Democratic National Committee. I think that this gradually just deteriorated. He—Lyndon—knows [O'Donnell's] my friend and he has got these contacts all over the country. It worries [Johnson]. Because the one thing Lyndon Johnson doesn't want is me as Vice President, and he's concerned about whether he's going to be forced into that. He started out, one, to try to avoid it by having Sargent Shriver. And that's fallen—

MARTIN: Has it?

KENNEDY: It doesn't make a helluva lot of sense. So then he started on Bob McNamara, and that's not having a very happy time, either. Because it's going to be tough for the Democrats to accept Bob McNamara.

I think he's hysterical about how he's going to try to avoid having me or having to ask me. That's what he spends most of his time on, from what I understand: figuring out how he's going to avoid me.

MARTIN: Well, what is going to happen to the Kennedy wing of the Democratic party?

KENNEDY: That's tough to tell. I suppose if I got out of government now or went into some independent base, then that would be far different than if I stayed as Vice President.

MARTIN: I do too.

KENNEDY: I'm just trying to make up my mind what I'm going to do. I think it's a great problem, of course, if I stayed as Vice President and was forced on him. It would be an unpleasant relationship, number one. Number two, I would lose all ability to ever take any independent positions on matters. Lyndon Johnson has explained quite clearly that it's not the Democratic party anymore; it's an all-American party. The businessmen like it. All the people who were opposed to the President like it. I don't like it much.

MARTIN: That isn't true, anyway. I mean, if that's what he says, it's not true. I mean, the businessmen don't like the Democratic party, for God's sake.

KENNEDY: But they like Lyndon.

MARTIN: Oh, I don't know. I'm not sure they'll vote for him.

KENNEDY: No, I mean, that's what the point is at the present time.

MARTIN: He's trying to get them, but that's another question.

KENNEDY: Yes. That's right.

MARTIN: And he's kidding himself if he believes it.

KENNEDY: Well, I think he believes it.

MARTIN: He just can't go that conservative and still hold the Democratic base that he's got to have. He can't do it.

KENNEDY: I don't think so. I think he doesn't think they have any place to go and they don't have anything to tie on to at the moment.

MARTIN: Well, that's now. But they will in October. They'll have a candidate. If he believes that, I think he's deluding himself. And I also think it's damned important that the Kennedy wing—or whatever you want to call it—of the party continue to be a very important force in the party.

KENNEDY: Yes, I know. So do I.

MARTIN: And I'm not sure, either, that, if you were elected Vice President, that would end your ability to do things and exert an influence. I don't think that is necessarily true.

KENNEDY: Is that right?

MARTIN: Yes. I don't see why it's true. Your position is not just that of a man who happened to become Vice President by some curious trade in the convention or something like that. You have a unique position—and not just in the party but in the minds of the American people. And I think for that reason that you as Vice President would be a different Vice President from almost anyone else.

KENNEDY: I've seen, though, what he could do and what he has done in the last three months. If I didn't have the Department of Justice, I'd be—
The fact is that he's able to eat people up, even people who are considered rather strong figures. I mean, as I say, Mac Bundy or Bob McNamara: There's nothing left of them.

MARTIN: Yes, but you're not "they." It doesn't seem to me that a junior Senator from New York would have as much influence on executive policy as the Vice President would.

KENNEDY: I don't think you can have any influence. Lyndon Johnson didn't have any influence. I wouldn't have any. I don't have any real influence. I mean, I have some influence because I have contact with Averell Harriman, or I'm on the Counterinsurgency Committee or something. But I don't really have anything. The influence is just infinitesimal compared to the influence I had before. And as Vice President, I'm not going to have any influence. He's not going to have to pay any attention to me whatsoever anymore.

MARTIN: I think he is. I don't think he could afford to break with you now. I don't think he could afford to break with you while he's President either.

KENNEDY: Well, I suppose if he's not doing anything for the Alliance for Progress, or if he's not paying proper attention to Panama or Brazil—I mean, like the Panama thing.[44] If I was in the United States Senate, I would have raised a fuss about Panama.

MARTIN: Well, yes, but you're just one. There are ninety-nine other Senators.

KENNEDY: I'd not be just a Senator. I'd be the Senator from New York. And I'm head of the Kennedy wing of the Democratic party.

MARTIN: I'd think you'd have a better chance of staying head of the Kennedy wing of the party as Governor of New York than you would as Senator.

KENNEDY: Yes, but I can't be Governor.

MARTIN: Why? In two years you can run.

KENNEDY: No, I have to live here five years.

MARTIN: You do? Is there any chance of Secretary of State?

KENNEDY: No. He won't make me Secretary of State.

MARTIN: He wouldn't? You're sure? If you could give him a vice-presidential candidate he'd want?

KENNEDY: I don't think he would.

MARTIN: I don't know. Who do you think he'll—

KENNEDY: Mac Bundy, I think.

MARTIN: You do?

KENNEDY: Or Bob McNamara, if he doesn't make him Vice President.

MARTIN: He's going to have a helluva time, I think, making him Vice President, don't you? McNamara?

KENNEDY: Yes. And I don't think anybody's going to be very enthusiastic about Hubert Humphrey.

MARTIN: They don't seem to be. I should think that'd be a default kind of thing, a fallback.

KENNEDY: So that's why it's tougher for him.

MARTIN: You described in an earlier interview how Johnson almost forced himself upon you and the President in the convention last time. And I think you could do the same thing here now. Don't you think so?

KENNEDY: Yes, but our President was a gentleman and a human being. As I described here, this man is not. . . . He's mean, bitter, vicious—an animal in many ways. You know, as I say, I think his reaction on a lot of things is correct, but I think he's got this other side of him in his relationship with human beings which makes it very difficult, unless you want to kiss his behind all the time. That's what Bob McNamara suggested to me a couple of weeks ago, if I wanted to get along.

MARTIN: Oh, well, I think that's silly, and you're not going to do it anyway. So there's no use talking about that.

KENNEDY: No, I can't do that, and so, therefore, I think it's probably difficult to get along.

MARTIN: I don't think there's anything that's very easy. I'm sure it's difficult, Bob.

KENNEDY: I'm not sure that it's possible, really.

MARTIN: To have an influence or to get it?

KENNEDY: I think it's possible to be Vice President.

MARTIN: You do?

KENNEDY: Yes.

MARTIN: Well, then I think you should.

KENNEDY: But who am I going to have influence with? He's not going to pay any attention to me.

MARTIN: You're going to have influence with the people of the United States.

KENNEDY: Yes, but I can't go out and speak against the policies of the President.

MARTIN: No, but you can let it be known that, if he doesn't change them, you might. He knows that you're tied to some extent, but he also knows you're not tied entirely, because he knows you, what kind of person you are.

KENNEDY: Yes, but I don't know that it's possible, really. I mean, I couldn't.

MARTIN: I know, I know how difficult and unpleasant it would be for you, Bob.

KENNEDY: I don't know that I could speak out—you know, and start criticizing what he's doing in South America, what he's doing in Southeast Asia—as Vice President of the United States.

MARTIN: You can do a lot of things quietly, short of making a speech. You know better than I do.

KENNEDY: Boy, that's a pretty disloyal operation.

MARTIN: Well? Disloyal to whom? I mean, it's a disloyal operation, you may say, to him, but not to the country. Or the people? Or everybody else in the party who's interested in the things that you are. I just think you have an opportunity here. . . .

KENNEDY: Well, anyway, that's the future.

MARTIN: Okay. Let's see. I've got a bunch of loose ends. Do you want to just start plowing through them?

KENNEDY: All right.

MARTIN: Well, one of the things that isn't really a loose end at all is what the President [Kennedy] thought of the people around him as he saw them operating in particular situations. Do you want to talk about that? His Cabinet and his staff?

KENNEDY: Well, I think he thought very highly of Bob McNamara, very highly of him. He thought that Mac Bundy was competent. . . . I think he thought a lot of Bill Wirtz. . . . Dave Bell he liked very, very much. Sargent Shriver he thought was very competent. . . .

MARTIN: Steve Smith?

KENNEDY: I think he thought he was good. I think he thought he was fine. He liked Steve Smith.

MARTIN: You said a minute ago that the Shriver [vice-presidential candidacy] idea had fallen apart. Why did you say that?

KENNEDY: Oh, I just think that it never caught on sufficiently. I don't think it was acceptable sufficiently among Democrats. I think they [thought] they could get a Kennedy without having a bad Kennedy.

MARTIN: What about the White House staff?

KENNEDY: [JFK] liked Kenny O'Donnell. He liked being with Kenny. His judgment was good—although frequently he didn't accept it. . . . Kenny O'Donnell was so loyal to him. Ralph Dungan he liked very much. He thought he was good. Not in the same category, not as brilliant as Mac Bundy. Mike Feldman he liked. All those people over there.

As far as the military aides: General [Chester V.] Clifton was the most competent, and the general from the Air Force was the most incompetent.

MARTIN: Sorensen?

KENNEDY: Ted Sorensen, he liked very much. . . .

MARTIN: Stevenson?

KENNEDY: Adlai Stevenson? Oh, he didn't like Adlai Stevenson. [Stevenson] used to drive him out of his mind.

MARTIN: How about Arthur Schlesinger?

KENNEDY: He liked Arthur Schlesinger, but he thought he was a little bit of a nut sometimes. He thought he was sort of a gadfly and that he was having a helluva good time in Washington. He didn't do a helluva lot, but he was good to have around. He was a valuable contact, and he's also contributed some very stimulating, valuable ideas at various times. That made it well worthwhile. He wasn't brought in on any major policy matters, but he'd work on drafts of speeches. Also, he used to stimulate people all around the government by writing them memos, what they should be doing and what they should be thinking of, and frequently made a lot of sense. I think he was a valuable addition, Arthur Schlesinger, and I think the President thought so too.

MARTIN: Mike Feldman?

KENNEDY: Very good.

MARTIN: The President thought very well of him—very highly of him?

KENNEDY: Yes. His major interest was Israel rather than the United States. But he did an awful lot of valuable, helpful, worthwhile work.

MARTIN: How about Heller? Walter Heller [Chairman of the Council of Economic Advisers]?

KENNEDY: He thought he was very good. He always talked to the press too much. It used to irritate the President.

MARTIN: How about Dillon?

KENNEDY: He thought he was a brilliant man. [Dillon's] forecasts about what was going on in the economy were not very accurate. Douglas Dillon he liked very much. He thought he was a very substantive, valuable figure. And he liked having him at meetings. He was always very valuable. He was in our ExComm committee.

MARTIN: . . . How about Harriman?

KENNEDY: Averell Harriman he did like, until he made the goof in Vietnam that I spoke to you about. But he liked him, and he thought he was good, and he did very well in Southeast Asia.

And he liked Tommy Thompson. This is obviously influenced by my personal opinion, you know, and I expect it's based on the conversations that we had. Tommy Thompson he thought was outstanding. I also thought he was outstanding. He made a major difference. The most valuable people during the Cuban crisis were Bob McNamara and Tommy Thompson, I thought.

MARTIN: How about Ed Martin?

KENNEDY: He liked him very much. And he liked Ed Murrow very, very much.

MARTIN: Don Wilson?

KENNEDY: I think he thought he was good. Don Wilson handled the USIA at the time of the Cuban crisis and did a very good job. He liked Ed Murrow. Ed Murrow never spoke, you know, at meetings unless he had something to say. When he said something, it always made sense. He was damn good. Mike Forrestal he liked, although, again, Mike Forrestal was involved in the Vietnam fiasco and that rather colored his opinion. Nick Katzenbach he thought was outstanding. Burke Marshall he thought was outstanding.

MARTIN: Freeman? Orville Freeman?

KENNEDY: I think he valued him highly.

MARTIN: What about in the Senate?

KENNEDY: Well, he liked Dirksen. He liked Kerr—I went into that. He liked Kerr and I didn't.

MARTIN: Hubert Humphrey?

KENNEDY: I think he thought Hubert Humphrey had his place. But, as [JFK] said, "When I think of Hubert Humphrey and the way he acts, I realize I shouldn't be too mad, because if he acted better, he'd be President and I wouldn't be. If he didn't act like he did, then he would be President of the United States." But I see (in meetings I've had in the last two weeks) he just, number one, talks too much. Number two, he hasn't got— I don't know whether it's a fundamental strength that gets you through or the ability to see what the problems are going to be in the future in the state and stand fast on something that's important—just because it makes sense or it's important in the future. I think probably he'd stand fast if he knew it was going to be helpful politically in the future. But you know, he just wobbles away. And so that's scary. I think he must be much better now than he used to be.

Dirksen he liked, I told you.

MARTIN: Yes. Mansfield?

KENNEDY: He loved—yes, he liked Mansfield very much.

MARTIN: Did he?

KENNEDY: I don't think he thought [Mansfield] was the best under certain circumstances, but at other times he was loyal. [JFK] often said how lucky he was to have Lyndon Johnson as Vice President, because otherwise, Lyndon Johnson would be Majority Leader and that would be just impossible. Lyndon Johnson would screw him all the time. Mike Mansfield was loyal to him, and Lyndon Johnson never would have been loyal to him. So he was very pleased. He was more pleased about having Lyndon Johnson Vice President because he was out of the Senate than he was having him as Vice President.

MARTIN: Who do you think influenced him most on policy? Who did he turn to or count on when it was really serious?

KENNEDY: I think that Ted Sorensen was a very important figure. Bob McNamara, as I said, was an important figure. I think, on general matters, that they were the significant figures. Kenny used to bounce some of these ideas—not foreign policy matters so much—if it came to a crunch.

MARTIN: That's what I mean.

KENNEDY: Kenny'd be involved. He'd be discussing it with him. In the area of foreign policy or defense, obviously, it was Bob McNamara, not Dean Rusk. And Ted Sorensen he used to bring in on a wide variety of subjects. Mac Bundy, too.

MARTIN: If you had to list four, would it be Sorensen, McNamara, Kenny, and yourself?

KENNEDY: Well, it's different fields. It's difficult. If it's foreign policy and what to do about, I mean, the coup in Vietnam, he wouldn't bring Kenny O'Donnell in. If he were talking about what ship was going into Cuba, he might have Kenny. I mean, Kenny wasn't involved in any of the ExComm committee meetings. In the last few days [of the missile crisis] he was brought in, just when we were about to go to war. He was rather a strong figure; and no matter what the President decided, he would be with him. That was different than Bob McNamara, who'd be brought in more on substantive questions and substantive issues. And Ted Sorensen, whenever it became a difficult matter, whether it was domestic or a foreign policy question—if it was difficult, Ted Sorensen was brought in.

MARTIN: It would be you and Ted, really, wouldn't it? More than any other two, then?

KENNEDY: . . . There was just a mixture. Bob McNamara was brought in later. The fact was that we had grown up together and had gone through all these things. I would be involved. Each person had sort of a different role.

MARTIN: Where would you usually see him? At the White House?

KENNEDY: Yes. I'd see him when he'd have a meeting. I'd stop by; we'd have a chat. After a Cabinet meeting or a National Security Council meeting or a meeting on other matters, we'd usually have a talk. That might be maybe once or twice a day or several times a week—whatever it might be. I knew what was going on.

MARTIN: What times stand out? What occasions stand out in your mind when he came to you, when it came right down to the crunch? When you were deeply and closely involved?

KENNEDY: Well, I think that the major, most difficult times were Cuba—Bay of Pigs and Cuba '62. Then I had the responsibility for Oxford, Mississippi, of course, which was my personal responsibility. That was unpleasant.

MARTIN: Those three stand out in your mind as the major times.

KENNEDY: Well, the first one was where he was unhappy. The second one was where he was really concerned. And with Oxford, Mississippi, he was concerned and disturbed. The Army hadn't arrived, two people had been killed, and it was really a question of whether it was going to come down to the fact that it had been mishandled and therefore going to be our responsibility—some responsibility of his. There were different kinds of things, but I suppose those were the three most difficult periods.

MARTIN: Would you add Berlin, or not?

KENNEDY: I suppose Berlin '61, but there's no one particular day—over an extended period of time.

MARTIN: What'd he like most about the job?

KENNEDY: I think being able to accomplish something.

Every week or day he was involved in major matters that affected a lot of different people. He could have influence. It's the Greek definition of happiness: "exercise of vital powers along the lines of excellence, and a life affording them scope." And that's what it was. It was happiness.

As far as the comforts of the presidency, he said the only thing that he'd like to take with him was the White House operator. Everything else you could have anyway. But you couldn't have the White House operators.

NOTES

INTERVIEWS WITH JOHN BARTLOW MARTIN ON
MARCH 1, APRIL 13 AND 30, AND
MAY 14, 1964

1) **Theodore H. White,** *The Making of the President, 1960* (New York, Atheneum, 1961). A chronicle of the 1960 campaign.

2) **Thirteen Days**: *A Memoir of the Cuban Missile Crisis* by Robert F. Kennedy, (New York, Norton, 1969).

3) **Isle of Pines.** The landing site for the invasion forces.

4) **Guatemala situation.** In 1955 a CIA-sponsored exile army helped topple the government of Guatemalan President Jacobo Arbenz.

5) **the Panama dispute arose.** In January 1964, rioting broke out in Panama in opposition to American control of the Panama Canal. Panama suspended diplomatic relations with the United States and demanded a revision of the 1903 Canal Zone treaty.

6) **Venezuela.** United States technical assistance helped Venezuelan leader Romulo Betancourt resist a Cuban-sponsored insurgency in 1963.

7) **Sidey . . . his book.** White House correspondent, *Time*, 1961–1969; chief, Washington bureau, *Time*, 1969–1978; author of *John F. Kennedy*, (New York, Atheneum, 1963)

8) **time of Hungary.** In the fall of 1956 the Soviet Union dispatched troops and tanks to Hungary in order to suppress anti-Communist elements attempting to institute a multiparty parliament and weaken Hungary's ties with the Soviet bloc.

9) **they drew up their tanks.** American and Russian tanks faced down one another in a tense confrontation on the Berlin border on October 27, 1961.

10) **that Saturday night.** Robert Kennedy met with Anatoly Dobrynin on the evening of October 27, 1962. According to Kennedy's version of the meeting: "We had to have a commitment by at least tomorrow. This was not an ultimatum, I said, but just a statement of fact."

11) **Skybolt.** Skybolt was a two-stage ballistic missile launched from a bomber. In 1962, John Kennedy canceled a 1960 agreement between Eisenhower and Macmillan for the supply of Skybolt missiles to Britain.

12) **speech to the country on Berlin.** President Kennedy spoke to the nation on July 25, 1961, in response to the Berlin crisis: "We cannot and will not permit the Communists to drive us out of Berlin. . . . [But] we do not abandon our duty to mankind to seek a peaceful solution."

13) **you went to Africa.** Robert Kennedy headed the U.S. delegation to the independence celebration of the Ivory Coast in August 1961.

14) **Congo.** The July 1960 independence of the Congo brought immediate chaos to the country. The pro-Belgian province of Katanga, under the leadership of President Moise Tshombe, declared itself a republic and seceded from the central government. Kennedy supported U.N. efforts in the region.

15) **[the Russians] resumed nuclear testing.** The Soviets announced their resumption of nuclear testing on August 30, 1961.

16) **Khrushchev was having trouble with Peking.** The early 1960s witnessed an increasingly severe ideological rift between Peking and Moscow.

17) **the new trade and tariff bill.** The Trade Expansion Act was signed by the President in October 1962.

18) **Murchisons.** On his yearly summer visits to Florida and California, J. Edgar Hoover was the guest of Texas oil man Clint Murchison.

19) **dam in Ghana.** Throughout 1961, Robert Kennedy objected to American investment in the Volta Dam project.

20) **the President's Advisory Council on Intelligence.** The Foreign Intelligence Advisory Board.

21) **their efforts over West New Guinea.** The United States was interested in preventing serious hostilities between Indonesia and the Netherlands over West New Guinea (or West Irian, as the Indonesians preferred), a territory held by the Dutch but claimed by Indonesia.

22) **Ramfis.** The younger Trujillo, head of the armed forces since May, precipitated a political crisis when he left the Dominican Republic in November 1961. It was widely believed that Ramfis's two uncles, brothers of the assassinated leader, planned to overthrow the government of Joaquin Balaguer.

23) **Zanzibar.** Zanzibar became independent on December 10, 1963. A leftist revolt overthrew the coalition government on January 12, 1964. On April 27, 1964, Zanzibar and Tanganyika merged to form Tanzania.

24) **Eddie McCormack.** Edward J. McCormack, Jr., was the nephew of John McCormack, Democratic Representative from Massachusetts and Speaker of the House. The younger McCormack opposed Edward M. (Teddy) Kennedy in the 1962 Democratic primary for Senator from Massachusetts.

25) **speech that he made in the summer of '63.** The reference is to John F. Kennedy's June 11, 1963, nationally televised address on civil rights.

26) **the steel crisis.** On April 10, 1962, the U.S. Steel Corporation announced a $6-per-ton price increase. Other companies followed, sparking vigorous protest from the Kennedy administration.

27) **neutralist coalition.** On July 23, 1962, fourteen nations had signed accords at Geneva guaranteeing the future neutrality of Laos. A provisional coalition government was established under the premiership of Souvanna Phouma.

28) **a real nosedive ... in May of '62.** On May 28, 1962, the stock market experienced what was then the largest one-day drop in prices since the crash of 1929.

29) **what was happening in Yugoslavia.** After an open split between Yugoslavia and the Soviet bloc in 1948, the Yugoslav Communist party went on to develop an approach to Communism which emphasized decentralization of political and economic authority. By the early 1960s, Yugoslavia had reestablished independent contacts with the West and had emerged as a leader of the "nonaligned" movement.

30) **Harriman mission.** In response to Communist China's invasion of India's northern frontier in October 1962, Averell Harriman was dispatched to evaluate Indian needs for American support.

31) **Urban Affairs Agency.** The House Rules Committee killed John F. Kennedy's 1962 legislative effort to elevate the Housing and Home Finance Agency to Cabinet status as a Department of Urban Affairs.

32) **Donovan.** A former general counsel of the OSS (Office of Strategic Services) during World War II, James B. Donovan was largely responsible for the negotiations which resulted in the exchange of Soviet spy Colonel Rudolf Abel for Francis Gary Powers.

33) **Dr. Soblen case.** A convicted Soviet spy, Soblen committed suicide while awaiting extradition.

34) **for taking bribes.** New York Supreme Court Justice James Vincent Keogh was convicted on charges of conspiring to fix a federal court sentence in June 1962.

35) **the fellow from Yugoslavia.** The reference is probably to Veljko Micunovic, Ambassador to the United States from Yugoslavia.

36) **his Finance Minister.** The reference is probably to Francisco Clementino de San Thiago Dantas, who served as Finance Minister for Brazil, January 1963–April 1964.

37) **the Clay report.** On March 21, 1963, a commission headed by General Lucius Clay issued its report recommending improvements in foreign aid programs and a reduction in aid expenditures.

38) **Rule 22, the filibuster rule.** The attempt to amend the filibuster rule failed in January 1963.

39) **Haynes Johnson.** *The Bay of Pigs* (New York: Norton, 1964).

40) **the Ambassador.** The reference is probably to Ignacio Borges Iribarren, Ambassador to the United States from Venezuela.

41) **congressional districting.** On March 18, 1963, the Supreme Court struck down the country unit system, a system that heavily favored low-population rural counties, in *Gray v. Sanders*.

42) **my sister's grave in England.** Kathleen Kennedy Hartington is buried at her husband's family estate, Chatsworth.

43) **U-2.** In 1956 the CIA began using the new U-2 espionage plane for high-altitude reconnaissance flights over the Soviet Union and the Middle East. On May 1, 1960, the U-2 piloted by Francis Gary Powers was shot down deep inside the Soviet Union. Powers, who pled guilty to espionage, was released by the Soviet Union on February 10, 1962.

44) **the Panama thing.** The reference is to the January 1964 riots in the Panama Canal Zone. Diplomatic relations between the United States and Panama were resumed on April 4, 1987.

APPENDIX

APPENDIX

The following interview with Robert Kennedy was conducted by John Stewart on July 20, 1967, and August 1, 1967. Because it is largely concerned with the years 1952–1956, it is presented here separately and without annotation.

STEWART: Why don't we start by my asking you what you recall of President Kennedy's decision to enter politics right after the war.

KENNEDY: I was in the Navy at the time. He got out of the Navy, I think, in 1944 or '45, and he was in the hospital for a while. He was thinking of what he was going to do and whether he was going into political life. I always had felt that he'd be very effective in politics. I think really that in many ways he could do some of these things as well or better than my oldest brother, Joe, who was the one sort of designated for—or the one who had showed the greatest interest in being active in—political life. But when the vacancy occurred in the Eleventh Congressional District [in Massachusetts], or when there was an indication that the vacancy would occur in the Eleventh Congressional District, I think that [JFK] felt it was natural that he run for Congress.

STEWART: What about a career in journalism? Did this have any appeal to him?

KENNEDY: I think some, but I think he'd always rather have gone into politics. And so it was quite natural and easy for him to make the transition.

STEWART: Did he have any reservations about the race in the Eleventh District, do you remember?

KENNEDY: No, it was just a question of his residency. He had a room at the Bellevue Hotel, but there was always the question raised of whether he really lived in the Eleventh Congressional District.

STEWART: Do you know if there was any real consideration of the opposition that he would have in the race in the district?

KENNEDY: No. He felt that he had a chance because there were so many opponents and none of them had strength outside his own area, whether it was Mike Neville in Cambridge or Mrs.— I can't remember all of the names.

STEWART: Falvey.

KENNEDY: Yes.

STEWART: She was a major in the WACs.

KENNEDY: And it was difficult trying to campaign against her.

STEWART: Why do you say that?

KENNEDY: She used to make some personal statements about him. I remember campaigning with him on one occasion in which she made a personal attack on him and then sat down and leaned over to him and said, "I hope you understand this is just politics." And he got up and responded strongly and very effectively to what she'd said.

STEWART: There was a report that people, especially Maurice Tobin, were urging him to run for Lieutenant Governor.

KENNEDY: Yes. I think that is true.

STEWART: Did he seriously consider this?

KENNEDY: Yes. He just decided that he was interested in foreign affairs and that Congress had some great possibilities. So he moved in that direction.

STEWART: What precisely was your role in the campaign?

KENNEDY: I handled East Cambridge—Wards One, Two, and Three in East Cambridge. I got out of the Navy about that period of time. So I handled the area that was unpleasant and difficult and where we hoped that we'd cut down the margin of what we expected to lose by: from five-to-one, we'd cut it down maybe to two-and-a-half- or three-to-one—which is about what we did.

STEWART: That was primarily Italian, wasn't it?

KENNEDY: It was primarily Italian, and it was the hometown, the strongest area, I believe, of Neville. That's my recollection. So we gave it a lot of personal attention, and I had a headquarters in East Cambridge. I spent most of my time there.

STEWART: Was it your impression that this campaign, as has frequently been stated, was viewed as a fight between young and old, between the pros and the amateurs—this type of thing? Did you feel that at the time?

KENNEDY: No, not particularly. I was, of course, quite young myself. I suppose there was some of that. He was taking on some of the old political figures within the city.

STEWART: Mark Dalton was the—

KENNEDY: Campaign manager. And he was a very effective figure, well liked and highly respected by all of us.

STEWART: How about Joseph Kane?

KENNEDY: Yes, I worked a lot with him. I had had some personal relationships with him prior to that time.

STEWART: He was, of course, quite old, wasn't he?

KENNEDY: He was quite old, but he was a very wise, wily figure. He had some good ideas and was helpful in many ways.

STEWART: Do you recall what kind of a role your grandfather, Mr. [John Francis] Fitzgerald, played in the campaign?

KENNEDY: My feeling was, really, it was mostly John Kennedy. My grandfather, of course, felt very strongly about it, and he felt very close to my brother. But I think that his effectiveness in some of these areas was not overwhelming. He had some important introductions and contacts which were significant. But the appeal that John Kennedy had was to an entirely different group. It was to young people, and it was to people who had not been involved in politics and to a lot of servicemen. My grandfather Fitzgerald was a help in offsetting some of the problems that would have otherwise existed, but I think that the campaign ultimately came down to what John Kennedy did himself.

STEWART: What, do you recall, did he consider his major strengths and his major weaknesses as a campaigner? There again, there's been a lot written as to how he was somewhat reserved and somewhat shy and that his appearance wasn't what people normally expected in an active campaigner. Was this a fact?

KENNEDY: I think so. Yes. It didn't occur to us. I always thought he was very effective and everybody liked him. I think that was appealing. I never thought there was any great problem from a personal point of view. I think he was a very attractive figure.

STEWART: Was there ever a fear of overstressing his war record?

KENNEDY: No. I don't remember any.

STEWART: It would appeal to veterans, of course.

KENNEDY: Yes, but I don't remember any concern over that.

STEWART: As far as issues were concerned, were there any problems regarding his stands?

KENNEDY: I don't remember any, but I was involved mostly just in organizational work. It was mostly a personal appeal. He got around a lot, worked very hard, had a lot of people working for him who were enthusiastic, and was able to be successful, I suppose, because of his strong personality, his name, and that effort, I think, rather than any issue.

STEWART: Were there any individuals, that you recall, who stood out?

KENNEDY: I worked with DeGuglielmo myself, who used to be Mayor of Cambridge. That was helpful. He was an Italian. He was very helpful. We had a couple of fellows, Peter Cloherty and Jimmy Kelley. Peter Cloherty was very close to my brother, his closest associate. And then he turned out to be his most violent enemy in Massachusetts. He was one of the spokesmen for John McCormack in the fight in 1955 and 1956. And then also he caused a lot of other problems at various times, or tried to cause them. He is still around and is active and is associated with, I think, the McCormack family somehow.

STEWART: He's from Brighton, isn't he?

KENNEDY: I think so. But he was close. And then Jimmy Kelley was close.

STEWART: From East Boston.

KENNEDY: And that relationship deteriorated shortly after the campaign. It was very good for a period of time, but then a feeling of distrust was created there. Patsy Mulkern, of course.

STEWART: Patsy passed away very recently.

KENNEDY: Yes, that's right. And Frank Morrissey. Mark Dalton, I remember. I remember Lem Billings handled Cambridge.

STEWART: Dave Powers, of course.

KENNEDY: Dave Powers.

STEWART: Tom Broderick.

KENNEDY: Tom Broderick. He had all those people.

STEWART: Ted Reardon, of course, was there.

KENNEDY: Yes, out in Somerville. He had the first three wards in Somerville.

STEWART: How did [JFK] do in the wards?

KENNEDY: I think he lost by about two-and-a-half- or three-to-one.

STEWART: Then this was better than expected?

KENNEDY: Better than he had anticipated doing. [JFK] did better in Cambridge as a whole than he had anticipated doing.

STEWART: What, do you recall, did the President feel were the chief reasons that he won?

KENNEDY: I don't think he analyzed it much. I'd say my judgment, my recollection, my feeling was that it was just his own personality, plus the fact that he had the Kennedy name—and that was highly respected—and the fact that a lot of young people worked for him. It was the wave of the future right after the war.

STEWART: Do you recall having a relatively easy time getting workers?

KENNEDY: No. I was in a tough area, so there was a good deal of antagonism toward him and toward, I suppose, me and the operation. But we worked very hard. We always felt that every vote there counted two. That's the philosophy that I worked under. I had a little headquarters and worked out of there with some Italian families.

STEWART: As far as the whole campaign was concerned, were the people in each area relatively independent or was it a fairly tight organization overall?

KENNEDY: There was a relatively tight organization. I worked with Billings in Cambridge and then, I think, with Mark Dalton. We did the organizational work. My wife, Ethel Skakel Kennedy, came and got involved a little bit—she wasn't my wife at that time—and my sisters. I stayed at the Bellevue Hotel during that period.

STEWART: . . . What happened to Billy Sutton? He didn't last, did he?

KENNEDY: No, he didn't. It just wasn't a very satisfactory relationship. He was a rather amusing but not a very substantial figure. So I think it just gradually deteriorated. He amused my brother, but he didn't contribute very much.

STEWART: Do you ever recall him [JFK] commenting about the possibilities of a longer career in the House? Did he fairly early decide that this wasn't for him for very long?

KENNEDY: Yes. He liked it, and it was rather an easy job without a great deal of pressure. He rather enjoyed the whole life, but I don't think he felt that he wanted to stay there. He was going to get out when he could.

STEWART: . . . Was it somewhat frustrating that he couldn't get more involved in foreign affairs in the House?

KENNEDY: No. I used to think he rather enjoyed it and took everything rather lightly. He was living with my sister Eunice at that time. I don't remember any great problems.

STEWART: . . . In 1951, you accompanied him on a trip around the world.

KENNEDY: Yes.

STEWART: Was the prime purpose of this for the 1952 race?

KENNEDY: Yes, and so that he could talk about foreign policy.

STEWART: Do you recall any particular reactions that he had on this trip or anything that made any lasting impact on him?

KENNEDY: Yes, I suppose quite a few things.

We went to the Middle East for just a very short period of time and met Franklin Roosevelt [Jr.] there, who received all the attention. It was almost as if we weren't there. Congressman Kennedy— they didn't care at all about him. They cared just about Congressman Roosevelt, who was the major figure and sort of led us around. We weren't there very long.

We went to Pakistan, and we met the Prime Minister, who a couple of days later was murdered—Liaquat Ali Khan—and then went to see Nehru. He didn't pay the slightest attention to my brother but was just destroyed by my sister Pat. He wouldn't talk to President Kennedy at all. He just talked to my sister Pat and directed everything to her. My brother always remembered that. It was very funny, you know, and we really laughed about it. It was so interesting about him. President Kennedy never liked Nehru. He didn't like him much then—not just because of that, but just because he was so superior, and his personality was rather offensive. He really disliked Nehru when he came—when was it, '62?—whenever it was he came to the United States. Everybody thought—the stories were that they got along so well. But [JFK] thought he was—he really disliked him as a personality.

I suppose the major impression that came out of it was the fact that these countries were struggling for independence, or had just gained their independence, and were trying to right themselves and create a future for themselves.

The major matter after that was in Vietnam. We went to Saigon, where he was tremendously affected by Ed Gullion.

STEWART: Had he known Ed Gullion before?

KENNEDY: I don't know whether he knew him before. It seems to me that he did, but I'm not sure of that. But he was very impressed with Ed Gullion. He didn't— None of us thought very much of Ambassador Heath. [JFK] thought American policy was disastrous—that the war was going to ultimately be won by the people against the French, and the French had operated a very selfish regime. We were wined and dined by the Emperor in the palace, the three of us—my sister Pat was there—and the three of us slept in one room, which was the only room with air conditioning. My brother slept on the floor because of his back. The two of us slept in beds.

Also, he greatly admired General de Lattre. We went up to Hanoi and flew over the area in which the Foreign Legion was fighting. General de Lattre spent a good deal of time, took us up to Hanoi. They had a big parade welcoming us into the city with all of the children of Hanoi coming out and waving flags. Ironic.

STEWART: Do you recall what about General de Lattre particularly impressed [JFK]?

KENNEDY: Well, he was just a very noble figure, a very brave man obviously, and very determined and very patriotic. He was a very, very impressive figure. Although disagreeing with the French policy in Indochina, we admired him as an individual.

And as President Kennedy said, though, when he came back (without going into all the details), he thought that the policy was a disaster and our representation was disastrous, that we didn't have the right policy and that we were going to get into a great deal of difficulty. Generally, in all of these countries, he was very critical of Foreign Service representation. He felt it was very second-rate. People associated themselves just with the leaders to some degree and not with the people or the aspirations of the people.

STEWART: Do you recall any heated discussions with any of these diplomats?

KENNEDY: Not particularly, no. It was mostly their response to questions: their lack of knowledge, of information about what was going on in their country; their lack of feeling for the people; and their general attitude or philosophy, which was quite different from his.

Then we went to Malaysia. The war was going on there too. And MacDonald was the High Commissioner, I think. We went to Singapore, and we went to Kuala Lumpur, which was under siege at the time. We went out to Kuala Lumpur in a tank.

STEWART: [JFK] became ill somewhere.

KENNEDY: He was going to go to Korea, and I went to Japan. He was a little sick at the time, but then he got [very] sick. I made arrangements for him to be flown to Okinawa. He went to the hospital in Okinawa. He had a temperature of about a hundred and six or a hundred and seven. They didn't think he could possibly live. So that was very worrisome. He survived that one night where his temperature went up so high that they thought he'd die. And everybody there just expected that he'd die. He survived that and then stayed a few days there. Then we flew back.

STEWART: Was he generally satisfied with all that he found or the depth to which he was able to probe into things in these countries?

KENNEDY: No, I don't think [he was] satisfied at all. No, he felt the trip was a success. He'd learned a great deal, and it made a major impression upon him, about these countries from the Mediterranean to the South China Sea all having gained their independence—really, from the West Coast of Africa all the way through—all of these countries having gained their independence, searching for a future: what their relationship was going to be to the United States; what we were going to do in our relationship with them; the importance of the right kind of representation; the importance of associating ourselves with the people rather than just the governments, which might be transitional, transitory; the mistake of the war in Indochina; the mistake of the French policy; the failure of the United States to back the people rather than what we were doing. It made a great impression upon him—a very, very major impression upon him.

STEWART: Moving on to 1952, there was some consideration of his running for Governor in Massachusetts. Do you recall this period of indecision—if it was indecision?

KENNEDY: Yes, I think there was a good deal of interest in having him run for Governor.

STEWART: Did it have any particular appeal to him?

KENNEDY: Some. He struggled with it for some period of time. During that time, '51, after we came back, I was working in Brooklyn with the grand jury, and he was in Congress. I would go up during the week to Brooklyn and come back on weekends to campaign in Massachusetts. So we shared a house, which he used during the week and I used during the weekend. He was getting ready to run. There was an interest in running for Governor. Who was Governor at the time?

STEWART: Paul Dever.

KENNEDY: The problem was that [JFK] had to not only beat a Democrat in the primary, which would be unpleasant and have a major effect on the party and his relationship with the party in the future, but secondly, it took him out of what he enjoyed the most—which was Washington. But he very, very seriously considered it.

STEWART: The big question was whether Dever was going to run for reelection or for the Senate. Did he talk about opposing Dever in a primary for the Senate if Dever chose to do that?

KENNEDY: As I remember—and I'm not certain about it—[JFK] finally decided that he'd run for the Senate. He said that he was going to run for the Senate. He was going to take anybody on at that moment.

STEWART: Even if Dever had planned to?

KENNEDY: Yes. I think so. That's my recollection.

STEWART: I guess Dever just saw the writing on the wall.

KENNEDY: President Kennedy decided he'd run—no matter what—for the Senate finally. I think that helped Dever make up his mind. The polls showed that he would do very well if he ran against Dever, that he could beat him if he ran against him. I just don't think— My recollection is that [Dever] didn't want to take him on.

STEWART: How, generally, would you describe the relations between the President and Paul Dever at this time?

KENNEDY: Well, with Dever it obviously was better later on. It was not warm. You know, Dever always had a better relationship with my father. A lot of those people had better relations with my father than they did with my brother.

STEWART: Were many people, do you recall, counseling against taking on [Henry Cabot] Lodge?

KENNEDY: Yes. A lot of people thought it would be very, very tough. My father was in favor of him running against Lodge because he thought that, first, you haven't got much even if you become Governor—and [JFK] wouldn't like it as much—but secondly, that Lodge was the major figure in the state and perhaps in the country. When you beat him, you beat the number one person; and it made John Kennedy a major figure overnight. So he was very strong for that. Maurice Tobin and my father were friends. As I remember, Maurice Tobin was considering running at the time, but I don't think that he had any great support.

STEWART: I think he died shortly after that. What, in the beginning, was the feeling as far as Lodge's biggest assets or main problems? Was it a fact that there would be no real distinction in a campaign between Lodge and the President as far as general voting records and general personality, would you say? Was this the big problem in running against Lodge—that there would be no real contrast?

KENNEDY: Part of it, yes. The biggest problem was that, on top of the fact that Lodge was a popular figure in the state, he had been primarily responsible for Eisenhower getting the nomination. So the Republicans would use a lot of power to get him reelected.

STEWART: How, to your recollection, did the feud with Foster Furcolo begin? Was it strictly because of Larry O'Brien leaving?

KENNEDY: No, I don't think it was. Larry O'Brien never liked Foster Furcolo, but I don't think that had much of an effect on President Kennedy. To some extent it did. Larry O'Brien wasn't that close to John Kennedy at the time—'52. I don't think Foster Furcolo was very anxious to support him, and his reluctance created a problem. When it really came to [a] head was in—

STEWART: Fifty-four.

KENNEDY: When Furcolo was running?

STEWART: Fifty-four, when he ran against Saltonstall.

KENNEDY: President Kennedy (Senator Kennedy, then) didn't feel well—he was having a lot of trouble with his back—but agreed to get involved in this campaign, went to the television station. Foster Furcolo said, "This is what you're going to say. This is what I'm telling you you're going to say." But he was so officious and so offensive that that created the break that was never healed.

STEWART: What about the whole matter of running an independent campaign aside from Dever's campaign? Was this decided very early in the game? Was there ever any consideration of running a more combined operation?

KENNEDY: Well, there was the interest on their part to run a combined operation—Dever and John E. Powers. I got into a lot of struggles about that. . . . I was working in Brooklyn at the time, so I came up. I got a friend of mine, Kenny O'Donnell, to get involved in it. The campaign wasn't going anyplace, and the [campaign] stuff was sitting on the floor. It was just ineffective, and no decisions were being made. So I came up and got involved in the campaign then, maybe April or May.

John E. Powers was doing the overall campaign in the city of Boston. I had a very stormy meeting with Paul Dever about running our own campaign. He wanted to run a joint campaign. And then he got furious at me and almost broke off any kind of relationship with us, except it was patched up, really, by my father, whom he liked. It was rather a big debacle. He dismissed me and dismissed us as being a lot of young "whatever we were," describing us as such. But in any case we ran our own campaign—which is all that I wanted.

STEWART: Did you have any reservations at all about taking it over?

KENNEDY: No.

STEWART: Did you anticipate all of the criticism that you would get because of your age?

KENNEDY: It wasn't really voiced at the time. I mean, voiced perhaps—people didn't like me—but it wasn't written about particularly at that time because it wasn't that major a matter. It's been written about a good deal since. But it never bothered me, and I never cared. That wasn't at all important to me. I knew what we were doing was right. I knew that we would have to do a much more effective operation than had been done in the past, and I knew the people whom they were relying on were not going to do any work. Nobody had ever done any work in a political campaign during the summer, and we had to do work in the summer if we wanted to win the campaign. We couldn't rely on the older people who said that you don't ever get started until after Labor Day. We wouldn't win under those circumstances. And the Democratic party never organized outside the city of Boston. We couldn't win relying on the Democratic political machine, so we had to build up our own machine. That's what we spent all summer doing. So what people were saying about me was rather unimportant. And the people we were asking to work—I mean [for example] the labor unions—were critical. So I gave them stickers to put on their members' automobiles. And I'd go around to the plants, and they didn't have their stickers on. So when they came and criticized the next time, then I blew up.

STEWART: What about that story, true or not, about the Boston politicians who came to the headquarters and you didn't recognize them—and tried to put them to work?

KENNEDY: I think it's very conceivable, possible. I don't remember.

STEWART: What about your relations with John Powers? He was the manager.

KENNEDY: I liked him. I thought he was the most effective of the people who operated for Dever. I didn't have a good personal relationship with him, but I mean, unlike a lot of the others, I thought he knew what he was doing. I had some fights with him. But I thought that he worked hard and he was an effective operator.

STEWART: He was also working for your people, though, wasn't he?

KENNEDY: Yes. He did Boston for both of us. But you know, he was primarily Dever's friend. We had our own sort of operation in Boston, simultaneously with him. So it was a little ticklish. But I thought he was effective.

STEWART: Do you recall many problems that you got involved in as far as the secretaries throughout the state and their relationship with local party people?

KENNEDY: Yes, some. But mostly the Democratic party never had an organization outside [Boston], except in Springfield, Worcester, Fitchburg. But they didn't have much of an organization outside the city of Boston, and they weren't prepared to do any work outside the city of Boston. That's where we stole the march on them. In fact that's what won, because we came out of Boston with the same margin that Dever did, perhaps a little bit behind him, but we did five percent better than he did in every one of those communities—again, as I remember the figures. He did five percent worse than we did. That was the margin of winning—by sixty-nine thousand votes or seventy thousand votes.

You know, they didn't have computers on television or radio at that time. We had a slide rule that I'd learned to run, so we were able to tell as the evening wore on—two or three or four o'clock in the morning—that we were five percent ahead in each one of these communities that came in. So Dever lost by twenty-five thousand—is that it?

STEWART: Approximately.

KENNEDY: And we won by seventy thousand. Maybe he lost by fifty thousand.

STEWART: What about the relationship with John Hynes? Was he at all a factor at that time? He was Mayor.

KENNEDY: Yes, but he didn't work particularly hard. I had some respect for him. We had to take some care with him. He was not particularly friendly, but we had to take some care with him because he was known as the honest Mayor and had a good reputation. It was fine, you know. Really, we went about doing our own business, which was trying to get a lot of people interested and a lot of activity around the state, organizing all kinds of groups—lawyers and Italians and chefs and physicians and doctors or whatever it might be—just trying to get as many organizations going as possible and in as many areas as possible. There was duplication and overlapping. But it never, as I say, had never been done before or tried before. But it was what paid off.

STEWART: Were there a significant number of disgruntled Taft people helping you?

KENNEDY: Well, I think the important one, really, was Basil Brewer. He made a big difference. But they were not a very effective group.

STEWART: I've heard it said that there were many, many battles about positions on issues in that campaign. Were you at all involved in these?

KENNEDY: Not really, not much.

STEWART: The decision as to whether to go to the left or to the right of Lodge on particular things or to just stay with the New England problems?

KENNEDY: I was mostly in organization. I didn't get much involved with issues.

STEWART: Were you at all involved or aware of the problems with John Fox and the *Boston Post*?

KENNEDY: Yes, to some extent.

STEWART: What do you recall about that?

KENNEDY: Well, the *Boston Post* had almost been a Kennedy house organ, because they were always friendly and always favorable, and we needed their support. He was a very difficult and unpleasant man, John Fox. My father went down to see him, and I don't know whether he arranged for him to get a loan or got him a loan or what. I don't remember the details, but the *Boston Post* supported John Kennedy—and there was a connection between the two events. I don't know what was involved or specifically what was involved, but I know he was an unsavory figure.

STEWART: Was the question of Senator McCarthy—Joseph R. McCarthy— a big one as far as enlisting support from union people, and people around Harvard and other universities?

KENNEDY: I never found it as such. I mean, he was a highly regarded figure in Massachusetts in 1952—Joe McCarthy was.

STEWART: There was always a question as to whether he was going to come and campaign for Lodge—which he never did.

KENNEDY: He never did. Lodge asked him to come in. Or at least, Joe McCarthy told me he asked him.

STEWART: Really? Why didn't he?

KENNEDY: Because he didn't like Henry Cabot Lodge.

STEWART: I never heard that.

KENNEDY: I forget. Maybe he didn't tell me the truth. He said that he wouldn't come in because he just didn't like Henry Cabot Lodge.

STEWART: To what extent, if at all, were you involved in fund-raising? And in what major problems?

KENNEDY: I wasn't involved in it.

STEWART: What about relationships with the Stevenson people at the national campaign? Was Stevenson generally viewed as a drag?

KENNEDY: Yes.

STEWART: Did you have any problem with the Stevenson people?

KENNEDY: Yes, some. We made an effort for Adlai Stevenson in the state. We were the only ones who did. John Powers didn't want to do anything for him in Boston. He was a drag around the rest of the state, but we made an effort. My brother liked him a lot or admired him a good deal. We tried on his behalf in 1952. The people who were for Adlai Stevenson were not the people with the widest range of support in the state. They alienated people rather than bringing people to his side—not that it was a factor.

STEWART: Did [President Harry] Truman campaign at all in the state?

KENNEDY: I think he came in. Yes.

STEWART: He probably would have been a great drag, wouldn't he, in 1951?

KENNEDY: Yes.

STEWART: What was the President's attitude personally about Henry Cabot Lodge as a campaigner, as a political figure?

KENNEDY: I think in any political campaign you end up not liking the person you're running against. It just gets unpleasant. Campaigns always do.

STEWART: Was there much regard for Eisenhower's strength as a campaigner? Did he campaign there much?

KENNEDY: I don't remember how much he did. I think Lodge thought he was going to win. [Lodge] went away and took a vacation right after the Republican convention. While we were working all summer, he wasn't doing anything.

When he came back, he was behind, his position was in great jeopardy, and he didn't catch up. That was a great problem for him.

I don't know how much Eisenhower came in. But [Lodge] never was able to organize his campaign, never was able to organize himself. He got caught really. He devoted all his energies to Eisenhower; and then, when he got Eisenhower the nomination, he went away and took a vacation when he should have come back to the state. It was a mistake. He was a lazy man, always a very, very lazy man as a campaigner.

Our headquarters were right across the street from his. And he came out on Election Day, election morning. We didn't really know [the result]. We were still there, my brother and I. A lot of the people left at two o'clock in the morning because they thought we were going to lose. The place emptied. Patsy Mulkern stood outside the window and yelled, "You're dead! You're finished! Give up! Give up!" As I say, I had my little slide rule and thought that, although we'd go down, we'd come back again. Then [Lodge] conceded, came out of his headquarters about seven-thirty, walked across the street right in front of our window. I suppose that was, in that election, one of the most dramatic moments.

STEWART: Was he genuinely surprised?

KENNEDY: I think he was.

STEWART: Among other things, someone cited the fact that—I think the week before Election Day—the Cardinal had christened your first son.

KENNEDY: That's right.

STEWART: And this was a good deal of publicity.

KENNEDY: Yes, that's right. We were aware of that.

STEWART: What about the tea parties? Where did this idea originate, do you recall?

KENNEDY: The people who ran it and made it effective were Helen Keyes, Polly Fitzgerald, and their groups. They're the ones who pulled them together—and Eunice Ford. They worked very hard and spent a lot of time together. I can't remember how it originated.

STEWART: There's no doubt in your mind that these were tremendously effective?

KENNEDY: Yes. My mother was a very important factor.

STEWART: John Powers was telling me about the campaigning he did with her in Boston, taking her around to eight or a dozen places at night.

KENNEDY: She was very good. And the girls were very good. They worked very hard. Everybody in the family worked very hard.

STEWART: Did you travel considerably?

KENNEDY: I did, yes, setting up these organizations. I spoke to these organizations. I spent a lot of time in Boston. Physically, I think it's almost the toughest campaign I've ever been in. We spent a lot of hours, you see. We started early in the morning and we worked until late at night—seven days a week. I lost ten or twelve pounds. We never took any time off.

STEWART: Looking back on it, what do you feel, if anything, were the major mistakes you made as far as the organization?

KENNEDY: I don't think there were any. That's a funny thing to say, but I don't think, really, we made mistakes, major mistakes.

STEWART: Were you and others around you conscious of your inexperience?

KENNEDY: No. I don't think politics requires much except effort. I mean, there's strategy and in the last analysis the judgment of the candidate—perhaps with the advice of those around him, but his analysis and his judgment. But beyond that, politics is no great— I mean, you've got to do some work. And we did a lot of work. It's a more effective campaign if you can get a lot of people working. What we did was to get large numbers of people to work, doing lots of different kinds of jobs. And that was the philosophy of the campaign. We were able to put this together. We didn't have any paid people, really—Kenny O'Donnell, who had never been involved in a political campaign, really; myself; and then Larry O'Brien came down a couple of days a week.

STEWART: . . . To what extent was the President [JFK] interested in analyzing the reasons for his victory? Was there any detailed analysis?

KENNEDY: No, no. He asked me to write up an organization of the campaign—but I never did it—what we did from the organizational point of view and the kinds of things we got involved in. I really never got around to doing it—which I should have done.

STEWART: To your knowledge, were many of the secretaries or many of the organization people in various localities replaced after the campaign because of their ineffectiveness?

KENNEDY: No, no, not really. No, some of them just received more attention and some of them just fell by the wayside. But they weren't replaced, because they weren't being paid or anything. They were there just as volunteers.

STEWART: There was never any question of the need to maintain some kind of an organization across the state?

KENNEDY: No, we always thought it was effective and had made the difference in his campaign and that, therefore, we should keep in contact with them because they were a very useful outlet into the local community.

Women did most of the work. We got a lot of volunteer workers from the teas and the sisters. It was made up mostly of volunteers. There were very few paid workers, none really on the organizational level that I can think of. Kenny O'Donnell was very valuable, although he hadn't participated in campaigns before. Larry O'Brien came down two or three times a week, and his advice and ideas were helpful. But for the most part, it was just the fact that there were a lot of people who felt strongly and used their energy to promote the campaign and to be involved in the campaign rather than having any great knowledge or background in political life.

STEWART: Did you find many people who really surprised themselves with what they could do?

KENNEDY: Yes, an awful lot of people in these local communities had never participated before and were very excited about it. The fact that this was their first campaign and the first time they'd been involved was a very rewarding experience for them. And then there were some wonderful people both in the city of Boston and outside the city who became actively involved in the campaign and who were very competent.

We organized each precinct. The philosophy was to see if we could get as many groups as possible going and active. Perhaps there would be overlapping. A woman might be an Italian and she might be twenty-one, so she'd be in a young person's club for John Kennedy, she'd be in the Italians' Club for John Kennedy, and she'd be in the Women's Club for John Kennedy. People would leave things at hairdressers and on buses, so that there'd be material and information about John Kennedy. There was a great spirit in the campaign that I don't think had existed prior to that time in the state of Massachusetts.

The speeches, what would be done on television, what he'd say publicly, and what would appear in ads, my brother worked on himself, instead of me. He had advisers, and he made the decisions. The organizational part—the teas or the coffee hours or the men's clubs or the secretaries or what we'd do in the city of Boston—was left pretty much in my hands. We communicated, but it wasn't even necessary to do that frequently. That aspect of it was left for us to do, and he expected that it would be done, so that he really didn't become involved in it or didn't worry about it or concern himself.

STEWART: Was there a problem of too many people, or people of the type you really didn't feel were essential, trying to get heavily involved in the campaign?

KENNEDY: Not really, no. I think they wouldn't want to become particularly heavily involved with what I was doing. They were much more apt to want to be involved with taking a trip with John Kennedy, appearing with him on a platform, or whatever it might be. The rest of it was—well, what we were doing was very, very unglamorous, and nobody got their pictures in the paper, and nobody wrote any articles about any of the people. So someone who was like that—rather a four-flusher, a faker—then they would want to be with the candidate all the time rather than with me or with what we were doing.

STEWART: . . . Do you recall when you first began discussing the possibilities of [JFK's] trying for the [vice-presidential] nomination in '56? I think that the first notice that I've come across was some mention in the late fall of '55. It had appeared in the papers, and I think there was an item in *Newsweek* probably around December or January of '56 that he was really being considered and was a real possibility. Do you think there was any discussion of it much before that?

KENNEDY: Not much. No, I didn't hear it particularly. It's hard for me to focus on when it was first discussed. I know during the course of '56 it was discussed, but just as sort of a rather remote possibility.

STEWART: Ted Sorensen, in his book, says that the President's interest in the nomination grew more out of a sense of competition than of conviction.

KENNEDY: I think that was true. There were a lot of drawbacks. I think he just wanted to see what it looked like, to put his foot in the water and see how cold it was. But he hadn't made up his mind that he wanted to swim, by any means.

STEWART: Did he always feel that religion would be the highest obstacle?

KENNEDY: A major barrier and, I suppose, probably the biggest one, but there were a number of others as well.

STEWART: Was there ever any question of the President's supporting Adlai Stevenson in '56?

KENNEDY: No. He liked Adlai Stevenson—then.

STEWART: Do you recall why the President was chosen to narrate the film produced by Dore Schary? I think Senator [Ed] Muskie had been the original choice, but for some reason he backed down. You don't know why?

KENNEDY: I don't know. I don't know why he backed down. I know the President—Senator Kennedy—was interested in participating, taking some part in the convention, and he was able to obtain that spot. He thought it was advisable and helpful because it would focus a good deal of attention on him. But how that was arranged I just don't know, and I'd never heard that there was somebody else who had been enlisted for it originally.

STEWART: Was he generally satisfied with his performance on this film?

KENNEDY: Yes. Wasn't it well done? As I remember, it was.

STEWART: Was it always assumed the President would have no chance for the nomination if [Senator Estes] Kefauver or Harriman were nominated [for President] by the convention? To your knowledge, was there ever any discussion with Kefauver or Harriman people about the nomination?

KENNEDY: No. Not to my knowledge. No. Senator Kennedy was pledged to Adlai Stevenson, so I don't think he got involved with any of the others at all. It was quite clear that Adlai Stevenson was going to get the nomination.

STEWART: Do you recall when you first became aware of the possibility of an open race for the vice-presidential nomination? John Sharon, I guess, was the first person to really push this whole idea.

KENNEDY: It was out there, and we decided one night—five or six of us and President Kennedy—that we'd make it. We had a meeting with John Bailey and—

STEWART: You mean at the convention?

KENNEDY: At the convention, [and decided] that we'd get involved in it and try to obtain the nomination. I remember going around the room, trying to get everybody there who might support him to find out what they thought they could deliver, whether they thought it was a good idea that he run. John Bailey was a very strong, stalwart figure, interestingly enough. The feeling now is, of course, that he's not a very strong leader of the [Democratic] National Committee, but during those meetings he was much stronger, for instance, than Abe Ribicoff.

STEWART: Then there was considerable activity even before the convention. For example, Ted Sorensen wrote what became known as the "Bailey Memorandum" on the whole religious problem. You weren't heavily involved in it?

KENNEDY: I knew about the memorandum, but I didn't have anything to do with drawing up the memorandum. I was involved then as the counsel for the Senate investigating committee, so that took my full time almost. I'd talked with my brother, but I didn't have anything to do with the drawing up of the memorandum.

STEWART: Were you at all involved in the fight in Massachusetts for the state party chairman?

KENNEDY: No. No. I got Kenny O'Donnell and some others sort of into it and talked with them but in a rather distant way. I mean, I talked with them about what was being done and what they were doing and the role they were playing and whether they thought they could pull it off, but the decision to go into it and the direction of strategy was almost solely with President Kennedy.

STEWART: You know why he felt he should do it at that time? There have been a number of reasons: that he felt, in order to make an impression for the convention, he had to show his strength in Massachusetts; then, of course, all the stories about a conflict between him and Speaker McCormack—I think those were probably the two primary ones.

KENNEDY: The people who were associated with McCormack were not friendly to [JFK]. He thought that if he was going to move ahead at all in the national scene, he had to control his own state. There were forces within the state, which perhaps to some extent received their birth during the '52 campaign—there was some bitterness that came out of that—there were forces within the regular Democratic party antagonistic to him, and they were all identified with this other group. Larry O'Brien and Kenny O'Donnell and some others who felt strongly about John Kennedy were sitting up in Massachusetts with idle hands, and they felt strongly about getting into this kind of fight. I think he just sort of got involved in it from that point of view—that it would help him, that he would always have trouble in the state if it were left like it was, and that they felt that they could win and they were contacting all these people. So I think it was a combination of a lot of things, not the least of which was the fact that Larry and Kenny, who had been involved in our '52 campaign, wanted to get into another struggle in Massachusetts and have the Kennedy voices mean something in the Democratic political structure of that state.

STEWART: Was the President at all fearful of damaging his relations with McCormack—of totally damaging his relations with McCormack?

KENNEDY: There was some concern about that, but I don't think that he thought that that was a very warm relationship in any case.

STEWART: It hadn't been, even up until that time?

KENNEDY: No. It was with my father and my mother, but not particularly with us.

STEWART: The President was frequently criticized for not getting more involved in local Massachusetts Democratic activities. To your knowledge, did he ever seriously consider getting more personally involved?

KENNEDY: Not really, because I think he always felt—all of us did—that it was unwise, that there wasn't anything to be gained from it, considering perhaps the possibilities for him in the future. It was a lesson that we learned; it was, at least, taught to us when we were very, very young. It was one of the reasons that he ran for the Senate rather than Governor. It's an endless morass from which it is very difficult to extricate oneself. And you can be much more effective and accomplish a great deal more by having general support in the state and working on state issues and national issues, which can make a difference for people, and not to try and go back to determine who's going to be the sheriff of Middlesex County, who's going to be the ward committeemen, and trying to settle all the fights and struggles that are going on within a state—where you always make enemies.

You're either going to get into the problems of Algeria or you're going to get into the problems of Worcester. To get into that and make all the enemies that you're bound to make didn't seem ever, to any of us, to make a great deal of sense. When I say "any of us," I say "us" because we talked about this long before he went into politics—that it didn't make a great deal of sense to get into all of those kinds of fights in a state, because after a period of time, it sucked away all of your strength. Governors are weakened national political figures because they get involved in the morass of their local party fights, difficulties, troubles.

GLOSSARY OF NAMES

Abernathy, Reverend Ralph D.: b. 1926; secretary-treasurer, Southern Christian Leadership Conference, 1957–1965; vice-president, Southern Christian Leadership Conference, 1965–1968

Abrams, Creighton W., Jr.: 1914–1974; commander, U.S. Military Assistance Command, South Vietnam, 1968–1972. Abrams played a significant role in the use of federal troops in the American South to avert racial violence in the early 1960s.

Acheson, Dean G.: 1893–1971; Secretary of State, 1949–1953; foreign policy adviser during the Kennedy administration

Adenauer, Konrad: 1876–1967; Chancellor of the Federal Republic of Germany, 1949–1963

Adlerman, Jerome S. (Jerry): 1902?–1975; chief counsel, Senate Permanent Subcommittee on Investigations, 1960–1972

Adzhubei, Aleksei I.: b. 1924; Soviet journalist; editor in chief, *Izvestia*, 1959–1964; editorial staff member, *Soviet Union*, 1964–1971

Aiken, George D.: 1892–1984; Republican Senator from Vermont, 1941–1975

Ainsworth, Robert A., Jr.: 1910–1981; judge, U.S. District Court, Louisiana, 1961–1966; judge, U.S. Court of Appeals, 5th Circuit, 1966–1981

Alexander, Henry C.: 1902–1969; chairman of the executive committee, Morgan Guaranty Trust, 1959–1967

Allgood, Clarence W.: b. 1902; senior judge, U.S. District Court, Northern District of Alabama, 1961–present

Alphand, Hervé: b. 1907; French economist and diplomat; French Ambassador to U.S., 1956–1965; Secretary General, French Foreign Office, 1965–1972

Alsop, Joseph W., Jr. (Joe): b. 1910; journalist and close associate of John F. Kennedy

Anderson, George W., Jr.: b. 1906; Chief of Naval Operations, August 1961–July 1963

Anslinger, Harry J.: 1892–1975; U.S. Commissioner of Narcotics, 1930–1962

Arends, Leslie C.: 1895–1985; Republican Representative from Illinois, 1935–1975, House Republican Whip, 1943–1975

Attwood, William (Bill): b. 1919; journalist; Kennedy campaign aide, 1960; Ambassador to Guinea, 1961–1963

Baker, Robert G. (Bobby): b. 1928; secretary to the Senate Majority Leader, January 1955–October 1963

Balaguer, Joaquin: b. 1906; President of the Dominican Republic, 1960–1962

Baldwin, Hanson W.: b. 1903; Military Editor, *The New York Times*

Baldwin, James: 1924–1987; black author and civil rights advocate

Barnett, Ross R.: b. 1898; Democratic Governor of Mississippi, 1960–1964

Bartlett, Charles: b. 1921; correspondent, *Chattanooga Times* 1948–1962; columnist, Field Syndicate 1962–1981

Battle, William C. (Bill): b. 1920; member, U.S. Civil Rights Commission, 1957–1959; Ambassador to Australia, 1962–1964

Bayh, Birch: b. 1928; Democratic Senator from Indiana, 1963–1981

Bazelon, David L.: b. 1909; judge, U.S. Court of Appeals, District of Columbia Circuit, 1949–present

Beale, Betty: b. 1912?; columnist, *The Washington Post*, 1937–1940; reporter and columnist, *Washington Evening Star*, 1945–1981; weekly columnist, News American Syndicate (formerly Publishers Hall Syndicate), 1953–present

Belafonte, Harry: b. 1927; singer and actor; member, board of directors, Southern Christian Leadership Conference

Bell, David E. (Dave): b. 1910; Director, Bureau of the Budget, January 1961–November 1962; Administrator, Agency for International Development, January 1963–July 1966

Bell, Griffin B.: b. 1918; chief of staff for Governor Vandiver of Georgia, 1959–1961; judge, U.S. Court of Appeals, 5th Circuit, 1961–1976; U.S. Attorney General, 1977–1979

Bellino, Carmine S.: b. 1905; Special Agent, FBI, 1934–1945; accounting consultant, Senate Labor Rackets Committee, 1956–1960; special assistant to the Kennedy White House

Bennett, James Jefferson (Jeff): b. 1920; administrative vice-president, University of Alabama, 1960–1968

Bennett, James V. (Jim): 1894–1978; Director, U.S. Bureau of Prisons, 1937–1964

Berle, Adolph A., Jr.: 1895–1971; Chairman, Interdepartmental Task Force on Latin America, January–July 1961

Betancourt, Romulo: 1908–1981; President of Venezuela, 1945–1948, 1959–1964

Biddle, Francis: 1886–1968; judge, U.S. Court of Appeals, 3rd Circuit, 1939–1940; U.S. Solicitor General, 1940–1941; U.S. Attorney General, 1941–1945; member, International Military Tribunal, 1950–1951; national chairman, Americans for Democratic Action, 1950–1953; adviser to the American Civil Liberties Union

Bissell, Richard M. (Dick): 1909–1977; Deputy Director of Plans, CIA, 1959–1962

Blair, William M., Jr. (Bill): b. 1916; Ambassador to Denmark, 1961–1964; Ambassador to the Philippines, 1964–1967

Block, Joseph L.: b. 1902; President Inland Steel, 1953–1959; CEO, 1959–1967

Blough, Roger M.: b. 1904; chairman, United States Steel Corporation, 1955–1969

Bohanon, Luther L.: b. 1902; U.S. district judge for the northern, eastern, and western districts of Oklahoma, 1961–1974; senior judge, 1974–present

Bohlen, Charles E. (Chip): 1904–1974; Special Assistant for Soviet Affairs, State Department, June 1960–August 1962; Ambassador to France, August 1962–December 1967

Bolling, Richard W. (Dick): b. 1916; Democratic Representative from Missouri, 1949–1983

Bolshakov, Georgi: b. 1902; Soviet Deputy Chairman, State Committee for Cultural Relations with Foreign Countries

Booker, Simeon: b. 1918; chief, Washington bureau, Johnson Publications (*Ebony* and *Jet* magazines)

Bootle, William A.: b. 1902; senior judge, U.S. District Court, Middle District of Georgia, 1954–1981

Bosch, Juan: b. 1909; President of the Dominican Republic, February–September 1963

Boutin, Bernard L. (Bernie): b. 1923; Administrator, General Services Administration, 1961–1964; Deputy Director, Office of Economic Opportunity, 1965–1966

Bowles, Chester: b. 1901; Under Secretary of State, January 1961–December 1961; President's Special Representative and adviser on Asian, African, and Latin American Affairs, December 1961–April 1963; Ambassador to India, May 1963–April 1969

Brademas, John: b. 1927; Democratic Representative from Indiana, 1957–1981

Bradlee, Benjamin C. (Ben): b. 1921; author; senior editor, *Newsweek*, 1961–1965; managing editor, *The Washington Post*, 1965–1968; executive editor, *The Washington Post*, 1968–present

Branch, Harllee, Jr.: b. 1906; public utilities executive; president, The Southern Company, 1957–1969

Brown, Edmund G., Sr. (Pat): b. 1905; Democratic Governor of California, 1959–1967

Bruce, David E.: 1898–1977; Ambassador to Great Britain, February 1961–March 1969

Buckley, Charles A.: 1890–1967; Democratic Representative from New York, 1935–1965

Bunche, Ralph J.: 1904–1971; United Nations Under Secretary for Special Political Affairs, 1958–1971

Bundy, McGeorge (Mac): b. 1919; Special Assistant to the President for National Security Affairs, January 1961–February 1966

Bunker, Ellsworth: b. 1894; Ambassador to India, 1956–1961

Burke, Admiral Arleigh A.: b. 1901; Chief of Naval Operations, June 1955–August 1961

Burkhardt, Robert J.: b. 1916; campaign director, New Jersey State Democratic Committee, 1961–1962; Secretary of State of New Jersey, 1962–1964

Byrd, Harry F.: 1887–1966; Democratic Senator from Virginia, 1933–1965

Cabot, John Moors: 1901–1981; Ambassador to Brazil, May 1959–August 1961; Ambassador to Poland, January 1962–August 1965

Capehart, Homer E.: 1897–1979; Republican Senator from Indiana, 1945–1963

Caplin, Mortimer M. (Mort): b. 1916; Commissioner of Internal Revenue, February 1961–July 1964

Cardona, José Miró: 1903–1974; first Cuban prime minister under Fidel Castro; fled to the U.S.; one-time president of the U.S.-based National Revolutionary Council

Case, Clifford P.: 1904–1982; Republican Senator from New Jersey, 1955–1979

Cassini, Igor: b. 1915; news columnist for International News and King Feature Syndicate

Cassini, Oleg: b. 1913; fashion designer

Castro, Fidel: b. 1926; Premier of Cuba, 1959–present

Celebrezze, Anthony J.: b. 1910; Mayor of Cleveland, Ohio, 1954–1962; Secretary of Health, Education, and Welfare, July 1962–August 1965

Celler, Emanuel: 1888–1981; Democratic Representative from New York, 1923–1973

Chacharis, George: 1908–1983; Mayor of Gary, Indiana, July 1958–December 1962

Chamberlin, Anne Nevin: b. 1917; Washington correspondent, *Time* magazine

Chaney, James: one of three young civil rights workers reported missing on June 21, 1964, in Philadelphia, Mississippi. His body was found on August 4, 1964.

Clark, Joseph S. (Joe): b. 1901; Democratic Senator from Pennsylvania, 1957–1969

Clark, Kenneth B.: b. 1914; author, educator, and psychologist; leader in the civil rights movement; distinguished professor, City College of New York, 1945–1975

Clark, Ramsey: b. 1927; Assistant U.S. Attorney General, 1961–1965

Clay, Lucius D.: 1897–1978; presidential envoy to Berlin, August 1961–May 1962. During the 1950s, Clay advised the Eisenhower administration on German affairs. In December 1962, John Kennedy appointed Clay to head a special committee to study foreign aid proposals.

Clifford, Clark M.: b. 1906; lawyer and presidential adviser; liaison to Eisenhower administration; member and chairman, Foreign Intelligence Advisory Board under Kennedy and Johnson; Secretary of Defense, 1968–1969

Clifton, General Chester V.: b. 1913; military aide to John F. Kennedy, 1961–1963

Coffin, Frank M.: b. 1919; Democratic Representative from Maine, 1957–1961; Deputy Administrator, Agency for International Development, 1961–1964

Coffin, Reverend William Sloane, Jr. (Bill): b. 1924; clergyman and social activist, participant in numerous civil rights and peace demonstrations, including the Freedom Rides

Cohn, Roy M.: 1927–1986; Chief Counsel to Joseph McCarthy; Associate at law firm of Saxe, Bacon, Bolan in New York

Coleman, James P.: b. 1914; Democratic Governor of Mississippi, 1956–1960; judge, U.S. Court of Appeals, 5th Circuit, appointed in 1965

Connally, John B., Jr.: b. 1917; Secretary of the Navy, January 1961–December 1961; Democratic Governor of Texas, 1963–1969

Connor, (Theophilus) Eugene ("Bull"): 1897–1973; Commissioner of Public Safety, Birmingham, Alabama, 1937–1953, 1957–1963

Corbin, Paul: Kennedy campaign worker, 1960; political aide to Robert F. Kennedy, 1961–1968; staff, Democratic National Committee, 1961–1964

Costello, Frank: 1891–1973; an organized crime figure investigated for racketeering

Cox, Archibald (Archie): b. 1912; U.S. Solicitor General, January 1961–July 1965

Cox, William H.: 1901–1988; senior judge, U.S. District Court, Southern District of Mississippi, appointed 1961

Crimmins, John H. (Jack): Foreign Service officer; Director, Office of Caribbean and Mexican Affairs

Crockett, William J.: b. 1914; Deputy Assistant Secretary of State for Budget and Finance, 1960–1961; Assistant Secretary of State for Administration, 1961–1963; Deputy Under Secretary of State for Administration, 1963–1968

Crotty, Peter J.: b. 1910; chairman, Erie County (New York) Democratic Committee, 1954–1965

Currier, Stephen: executive director of the Taconic Foundation

Daley, Richard J. (Dick): 1902–1976; Mayor of Chicago, Illinois, 1955–1976

Darden, Colgate: 1897–1981; Democratic Representative from Virginia, 1933–1937, 1939–1941; Governor of Virginia, 1942–1946; president, University of Virginia, 1947–1959

Dawson, William Levi: 1886–1970; Democratic Representative from Illinois, 1943–1970

Day, J. Edward (Ed): b. 1914; head of western operations, Prudential Insurance Company, 1957–1960; Postmaster General, January 1961–August 1963

Dean, Arthur Hobson: b. 1898; chairman, U.S. Delegation to the Conference on Discontinuance of Nuclear Weapons Tests, February 1961–January 1962; chairman, U.S. Delegation to the 17 Nation U.N. Disarmament Conference, April 1962–February 1963

De Gaulle, Charles A.: 1890–1970; President of France, 1958–1969

DeLoach, Cartha D.: b. 1920; Assistant Director, Crime Records Division, FBI, 1959–1965; Assistant to the Director, FBI, 1965–1970

De Sapio, Carmine G.: b. 1908; chairman, New York County Democratic Committee, 1949–1961; New York committeeman, National Democratic Committee, 1954–1964

Diefenbaker, John G.: 1896–1979; Canadian political leader; leader of the Progressive Conservative party, 1956–1967; Prime Minister, 1957–1963

Diem, Ngo Dinh: 1901–1963; Prime Minister of South Vietnam, 1954–1963

Dillon, C(larence) Douglas: b. 1909; Secretary of the Treasury, January 1961–March 1965

Dirksen, Everett M.: 1895–1969; Republican Senator from Illinois, 1951–1969; Senate Minority Leader, 1959–1969

DiSalle, Michael V. (Mike): 1908–1981; Democratic Governor of Ohio, 1959–1963

Doar, John M.: b. 1921; Deputy Assistant Attorney General, Civil Rights Division, Justice Department, 1960–1964; head, Civil Rights Division, Justice Department, 1965–1967

Dobrynin, Anatoly F.: b. 1919; head of the American Department, Soviet Ministry of Foreign Affairs, 1958–1961; Soviet Ambassador to the United States, 1962–1986

Dolan, Joseph F. (Joe): b. 1921; Assistant Deputy U.S. Attorney General, 1961–1965; administrative assistant to Robert F. Kennedy, 1965–1968

Douglas, C. H.: Mayor of McComb, Mississippi, 1957–1963

Douglas, John W.: b. 1921; Assistant Attorney General, Civil Division, Justice Department, 1963–1966

Douglas, William O. (Bill): 1898–1980; Associate Justice, U.S. Supreme Court, 1939–1975

Dowling, Walter (Red): 1906–1977; Ambassador to the Federal Republic of Germany, 1959–1963

Dryfoos, Orville E.: 1912–1963; publisher, *The New York Times*, 1961–1963

Dulles, Allen W.: 1893–1969; Director of Central Intelligence, CIA, 1953–1961

Dulles, John Foster: 1888–1959; Secretary of State, 1953–1959

Duncan-Sandys, Duncan (Lord): 1908–1987; British Secretary of State for Commonwealth Relations, 1960–1964; Secretary of State for the Colonies, 1962–1964

Dungan, Ralph A.: b. 1923; Special Assistant to the President, January 1961–October 1964

Dutton, Frederick G.: b. 1923; Special Assistant to the President, January 1961–November 1961; Assistant Secretary of State for Congressional Relations, November 1961–December 1964

Duvalier, François ("Papa Doc"): 1907–1971; President of Haiti, 1957–1971

Eastland, James O. (Jim): 1904–1986; Democratic Senator from Mississippi, 1941, 1943–1979

Edmondson, J. Howard: 1925–1971; Governor of Oklahoma, 1959–1963; Democratic Senator from Oklahoma, 1963–1965

Eisenhower, Dwight D.: 1890–1969; President of the United States, 1953–1961

Ellender, Allen J.: 1890–1972; Democratic Senator from Louisiana, 1937–1972

Elliot, J. Robert: b. 1910; judge, U.S. District Court, Middle District of Georgia, appointed 1962

Ellis, Frank B.: 1907–1969; Director, Office of Civil Defense and Mobilization, March 1961–February 1962; judge, U.S. District Court, Eastern District of Louisiana, April 1962–1965

Elman, Philip (Phil): b. 1918; Assistant to the Solicitor General, 1946–1961; member, Federal Trade Commission, 1961–1970

English, John: 1926?–1987; chairman, Nassau County (New York) Democratic Committee, 1958–1969

Ervin, Samuel J. (Sam): 1896–1985; Democratic Senator from North Carolina, 1954–1975

Estes, Billie Sol: b. 1925; Texas businessman involved in Democratic party affairs; member, National Cotton Advisory Committee, Department of Agriculture, July 1961–April 1962

Evans, Rowland, Jr. (Rowly): b. 1921; reporter, Associated Press, 1945–1955; staff member, *New York Herald Tribune*, 1955–1963; syndicated columnist, 1963–present

Farmer, James: b. 1920; national director, Congress of Racial Equality, February 1961–March 1966

Fitzgerald, Desmond (Des): 1910–1967; CIA officer and Deputy Director of Central Intelligence

Foley, Eugene P. (Gene): b. 1928; Deputy Assistant Secretary of Commerce, 1961–1962; Administrator, Small Business Administration, 1963–1965; Assistant Secretary of Commerce, 1965–1966

Folliard, Edward T. (Eddie): 1899–1976; staff writer and White House correspondent, *The Washington Post* and *Times Herald*, 1923–1976

Forrestal, Michael V. (Mike): b. 1927; Presidential Assistant for Far Eastern Affairs, January 1962–July 1964

Fortas, Abraham (Abe): 1910–1982; confidant and adviser to Lyndon Johnson; Associate Justice, U.S. Supreme Court, 1965–1969

Frankfurter, Felix: 1882–1965; Associate Justice, U.S. Supreme Court, 1939–1962

Freeman, Orville L.: b. 1918; Democratic Governor of Minnesota, 1954–1960; Secretary of Agriculture, January 1961–January 1969

Freund, Paul A.: b. 1908; professor, Harvard Law School, 1940–1976; professor emeritus since 1976

Friendly, Alfred H. (Al): 1911–1983; managing editor, *The Washington Post*, 1955–1966; associate editor and London correspondent, *The Washington Post*, 1966–1971

Fulbright, J. William: b. 1905; Democratic Senator from Arkansas, 1945–1975

Gallion, MacDonald: b. 1913; Attorney General of Alabama, 1959–1965, 1967–1971

Gewin, Walter: 1908–1981; judge, U.S. Court of Appeals, 5th Circuit, 1961–1977

Gilpatric, Roswell L. (Ros): b. 1906; Deputy Secretary of Defense, January 1961–January 1964

Glenn, John H., Jr.: b. 1921; astronaut; the first American to orbit the earth, February 20, 1962; Democratic Senator from Ohio, 1975–present

Goldberg, Arthur J.: b. 1908; Secretary of Labor, January 1961–October 1962; Associate Justice, U.S. Supreme Court, October 1962–July 1965

Goldwater, Barry M.: b. 1909; Republican Senator from Arizona, 1953–1965, 1969–1986; Republican candidate for President, 1964

Goodman, Andrew: one of three young civil rights workers reported missing on June 21, 1964, in Philadelphia, Mississippi. His body was found on August 4, 1964.

Goodwin, Richard N. (Dick): b. 1931; Assistant Special Counsel to the President, January 1961–November 1961; Deputy Assistant Secretary of State for Inter-American Affairs, November 1961–July 1962; Director, International Peace Corps Secretariat, December 1962–January 1964

Gordon, Lincoln: b. 1913; Ambassador to Brazil, August 1961–January 1966

Goulart, João: 1918–1976; President of Brazil, 1961–1964

Graham, Philip L. (Phil): 1915–1963; publisher, *The Washington Post*, 1946–1963; chairman of the board, *Newsweek*, 1961–1963

Greenberg, Jack: b. 1924; director-counsel, NAACP (National Association for the Advancement of Colored People) Legal Defense and Educational Fund, 1961–1984

Gregory, Dick: b. 1932; black comedian and social activist

Gromyko, Andrei A.: b. 1909; Soviet Foreign Minister, 1957–1985

Grove, Brandon H.: b. 1929; career Foreign Service officer, 1958–1961; Staff Assistant to the Under Secretary of State, 1961–1962; Special Assistant to the Deputy Under Secretary of State for Administration, 1962–1963; assistant to the American Ambassador to India, 1963–1965

Gullion, Edmund A. (Ed): b. 1913; career Foreign Service officer; Deputy Director, U.S. Disarmament Administration, 1961; Ambassador to the Republic of the Congo, 1961

Guthman, Edwin O. (Ed): b. 1919; Special Assistant for Public Information, Justice Department, 1961–1964; press secretary for Senator Robert F. Kennedy, January–May 1965

Hackett, David L. (Dave): Special Assistant to the U.S. Attorney General, 1961–1963

Halberstam, David: b. 1934; author; journalist; foreign correspondent, *The New York Times*, 1961–1967

Halleck, Charles H. (Charlie): b. 1900; Republican Representative from Indiana, 1935–1969; House Minority Leader, 1959–1965

Hamilton, Fowler (Milo): 1911–1984; Administrator, Agency for International Development (AID), September 1961–November 1962

Hanes, Arthur: Mayor of Birmingham, Alabama, 1961–1963

Hansberry, Lorraine: 1930–1965; playwright; first black woman to have a play produced on Broadway, *A Raisin in the Sun*

Harkins, Paul D.: b. 1904; commander, United States Military Assistance Command, Vietnam, January 1962–June 1964

Harriman, W. Averell: 1891–1986; Ambassador at Large, January 1961–November 1961; Assistant Secretary of State for Far Eastern Affairs, November 1961–March 1963; Under Secretary of State for Political Affairs, March 1963–February 1965

Harris, Oren: b. 1903; Democratic Representative from Arkansas, 1941–1966

Hastie, William H.: 1904–1976; judge, U.S. Court of Appeals, 3rd Circuit, 1949–1971; first black federal judge

Haya de la Torre, Victor Raul: candidate in the 1962 Peruvian presidential election

Heller, Walter W.: 1915–1987; Chairman, Council of Economic Advisers, January 1961–November 1964

Hemingway, Ernest M.: 1899–1961; American author

Hemingway, Mary W.: 1908–1986; wife of Ernest Hemingway

Herter, Christian A.: 1895–1966; Under Secretary of State, 1957–1959; Secretary of State, 1959–1961. Herter was named chief planner and negotiator on foreign trade by President Kennedy in November 1962.

Higgins, Marguerite (Maggie): 1920–1966; diplomatic correspondent for the *New York Herald Tribune*, 1958–1966

Hill, Lister: 1894–1984; Democratic Senator from Alabama, 1938–1969

Hilsman, Roger: b. 1919; Director, Bureau of Intelligence and Research, State Department, February 1961–May 1963; Under Secretary of State for Political Affairs, May 1963–February 1964

Hodges, Luther H.: 1898–1974; Democratic Governor of North Carolina, 1954–1960; Secretary of Commerce, January 1961–December 1964

Hoffa, James R.: b. 1913; presumed dead 1975; president, Teamsters Union, 1957–1971; target of numerous criminal investigations by the Kennedy Justice Department

Holeman, Frank: b. 1920; reporter, Washington bureau, New York *Daily News*, 1942–1943, 1946–1965; confidential assistant to the executive editor, New York *Daily News*, 1965–1968

Holland, Spessard L.: 1892–1971; Democratic Senator from Florida, 1946–1970

Hollings, Ernest F. (Fritz): b. 1922; Governor of South Carolina, 1959–1963; Kennedy appointee to the Advisory Commission on Intergovernmental Relations, 1962; Democratic Senator from South Carolina, 1966–present

Hood, James A.: b. 1942; desegregated the University of Alabama with Vivian Malone in 1956 but withdrew shortly thereafter; received B.A. at Wayne State University in 1969

Hoover, J. Edgar: 1895–1972; Director, FBI, 1924–1972

Hosono, Gunji: Japanese businessman and Kennedy friend

Houphouet–Boigny, Felix: b. 1905; President of the Republic of the Ivory Coast, 1960–present

Humphrey, George M.: 1890–1970; industrialist; Secretary of the Treasury, 1953–1957

Humphrey, Hubert H.: 1911–1978; Democratic Senator from Minnesota, 1949–1964, 1971–1978; Senate Majority Whip, 1961–1964; Vice President of the United States, January 1965–January 1969; Democratic candidate for President, 1968

Hundley, William G. (Bill): b. 1925; Special Assistant to the Attorney General, Organized Crime and Racketeering Section, Criminal Division, Justice Department, 1958–1961, 1963–1966

Jackson, Henry M. (Scoop): 1912–1983; Democratic Senator from Washington, 1953–1983

Jackson, Shelby: 1903–1972; superintendent, Louisiana State Board of Education, 1948–1964

Jagan, Cheddi B.: b. 1918; Prime Minister of British Guiana, 1961–1964

Jenkins, Walter: b. 1918; Johnson aide; White House Special Assistant, November 1963–October 1964

Johnson, Haynes: b. 1931; author; city reporter, night city editor, national correspondent, *The Washington Star*, 1957–1969; national correspondent, assistant managing editor, columnist, *The Washington Post*, 1969–present

Johnson, U. Alexis: b. 1908; Ambassador to Thailand, February 1958–April 1961; Deputy Under Secretary of State for Political Affairs, April 1961–July 1964, September 1965–July 1966

Johnston, Olin D.: 1896–1965; Democratic Senator from South Carolina, 1945–1965

Jones, Clarence: counsel for the Gandhi Society; lawyer and aide for Martin Luther King, Jr.

Jordan, William J. (Bill): b. 1923; journalist, Washington bureau, *The New York Times*, 1958–1961; member, Policy Planning Council, State Department, 1961–1962; Special Assistant to the Under Secretary for Political Affairs, State Department, 1962–1965

Kastenmeier, Robert W.: b. 1924; Democratic Representative from Wisconsin, 1959–present

Katzenbach, Nicholas deBelleville (Nick): b. 1922; Assistant U.S. Attorney General, January 1961–April 1962; Deputy U.S. Attorney General, April 1962–September 1964

Keating, Kenneth: 1900–1975; Republican Senator from New York, 1958–1965

Kennan, George F.: b. 1904; Ambassador to Yugoslavia, May 1961–July 1963; foreign affairs expert on Soviet-American relations

Kennedy, Edward M.: b. 1932; Democratic Senator from Massachusetts, 1963–present; Senate Majority Whip, 1969–1971

Kennedy, Ethel Skakel: b. 1928; married Robert F. Kennedy, 1950

Kennedy, Joseph P., Sr. (Joe): 1888–1969; father of John F. and Robert F. Kennedy; businessman and diplomat; first Chairman of the Securities and Exchange Commission, 1934–1935; Chairman, Maritime Commission, 1936–1937; Ambassador to Great Britain, 1937–1940

Keogh, Eugene J. (Gene): b. 1907; Democratic Representative from New York, 1937–1967

Kerner, Otto: 1908–1976; Democratic Governor of Illinois, 1961–1968

Kerr, Clark: b. 1911; President, University of California, 1958–1967

Kerr, Robert S.: 1896–1963; Democratic Senator from Oklahoma, 1949–1963

Khrushchev, Nikita S.: 1894–1971; Premier of the Soviet Union, 1958–1964

Killian, James R.: b. 1904; chairman, President's Foreign Intelligence Advisory Board, 1961–1968

Kilpatrick, Carroll: 1913–1984; staff writer, White House correspondent, *The Washington Post*

King, Coretta Scott: b. 1927; wife of Martin Luther King, Jr.; American civil rights leader

King, Reverend Dr. Martin Luther, Jr.: 1929–1968; president, Southern Christian Leadership Conference, 1957–1968

Kohler, Foy D.: b. 1908; Assistant Secretary of State for European Affairs, January 1959–July 1962; Ambassador to the Soviet Union, July 1962–September 1966

Korth, Fred: b. 1909; Secretary of the Navy, January 1962–October 1963

Krishna Menon, Vengalil Krishnan: 1897–1974; Indian politician; President, Indian League, 1947–1974; Indian representative at United Nations, 1952–1960; member, Indian Parliament, 1953–1957, 1957–1967, 1969–1974; Minister of Defense under Nehru

Krock, Arthur: 1886–1974; Washington columnist, *The New York Times*, 1952–1967

Kuchel, Thomas H.: b. 1910; Republican Senator from California, 1953–1969

Lambert, William (Bill): b. 1920; reporter, *Portland Oregonian*, 1950?–1959; consultant, Office of Education, HEW, 1962; correspondent, Los Angeles bureau, *Time*, 1962; investigative reporter and staff writer, *Life*, 1963–1972. In 1957, William Lambert and Wallace Turner won the Pulitzer Prize for their series of investigative reports on organized crime and the Teamsters in the Pacific Northwest.

Lansdale, General Edward G.: b. 1908; Air Force officer; head of the U.S. Military Mission to Vietnam, 1954; served as chief of the CIA's Saigon station for domestic affairs; adviser to Premier Ngo Dinh Diem

Lawford, Patricia Kennedy (Pat): b. 1924; married actor Peter Lawford; sister of John F. and Robert F. Kennedy

Lawrence, David L.: 1889–1966; Democratic Governor of Pennsylvania, 1959–1963

Lawrence, William H.: b. 1916; Radio and television news reporter; correspondent, *The New York Times*, 1943–1961

Lehman, Herbert H.: 1878–1963; Governor of New York, 1932–1943; Democratic Senator from New York, 1949–1957; adviser to reform-oriented New York Committee for Democratic Voters, January 1959–November 1961

LeMay, Curtis E.: b. 1906; Air Force Chief of Staff, June 1961–January 1965

Lemnitzer, General Lyman L.: b. 1899; Chairman, Joint Chiefs of Staff, October 1960–July 1962; Supreme Allied Commander, Europe, January 1963–June 1969

Levison, Stanley D.: 1912–1979; New York lawyer; adviser to Martin Luther King, Jr.

Lewis, Fulton, Jr.: 1903–1966; author of the "Washington Report" column; nightly news radio commentator on Mutual Broadcasting network

Lewis, John: b. 1940; Chairman, Student Nonviolent Coordinating Committee (SNCC, generally pronounced "snick")

Libonati, Roland V.: b. 1900; Democratic Representative from Illinois, 1957–1965

Lincoln, Evelyn N.: secretary to John F. Kennedy

Lindsay, John V.: b. 1921; Republican Representative from New York, 1959–1965

Lingo, Albert J. (Al): Alabama State Public Safety Director, 1963–1965

Lippmann, Walter: 1889–1974; journalist, essayist, and editor

Lodge, George: b. 1927; Assistant Secretary of Labor for International Affairs, 1958–1961; Republican candidate for Senator from Massachusetts, 1962

Long, Russell B.: b. 1918; Democratic Senator from Louisiana, 1949–present; Senate Majority Whip, 1965–1969

Lovett, Robert A. (Bob): b. 1895; investment banker

Luce, Henry R.: 1898–1967; editor in chief, *Time* and Time, Inc., 1923–1964

Luns, Joseph M.A.H.: b. 1911; Dutch politician and diplomat; Co-Minister for Foreign Affairs, The Hague, 1952–1956; Minister for Foreign Affairs, The Hague, 1952–1971; President, NATO Council, 1958–1959; Secretary-General, NATO, 1971–1983

Lynne, Seybourn H.: b. 1907; chief judge, U.S. District Court, Northern District of Alabama, 1953–1973

MacArthur, Douglas: 1880–1964; American general

Macmillan, Harold: 1894–1986; Prime Minister of Great Britain, 1957–1963

Maguire, Richard (Dick): b. 1914; White House staff member, 1961–1962; treasurer, Democratic National Committee, 1962–1968

Mahoney, William P., Jr.: b. 1916; U.S. Ambassador to Ghana, 1962–1965

Malone, Vivian: b. 1942; desegregated the University of Alabama with James Hood in 1956; graduated, 1965; worked for the Civil Rights Division, Justice Department

Mann, Floyd: Alabama State Public Safety Director, 1959–1963, 1968–1970

Mann, Thomas C. (Tom): b. 1912; Assistant Secretary of State for Inter-American Affairs, July 1960–March 1961; Ambassador to Mexico, March 1961–December 1963

Mansfield, Michael J. (Mike): b. 1903; Democratic Senator from Montana, 1953–1957; Senate Majority Leader, 1961–1977

March, Fredric: 1897–1975; American actor

Marshall, Burke: b. 1922; Assistant Attorney General, Civil Rights Division, Justice Department, February 1961–December 1964

Marshall, Thurgood: b. 1908; director-counsel, NAACP (National Association for the Advancement of Colored People) Legal Defense and Educational Fund, 1940–1961; judge, U.S. Court of Appeals, 2nd Circuit, 1961–1965; U.S. Solicitor General, 1965–1967; Associate Justice, U.S. Supreme Court, 1967–present

Martin, Edward M. (Ed): b. 1908; Assistant Secretary of State for Economic Affairs, August 1960–May 1962; Assistant Secretary of State for Inter-American Affairs, May 1962–December 1963

Martin, Louis E. (Louie): b. 1912; journalist; John F. Kennedy campaign staff, 1960; adviser to President Kennedy on the recruitment of blacks through his post with the Democratic National Committee

McCarthy, Eugene J. (Gene): b. 1916; Democratic Senator from Minnesota, 1959–1971

McCarthy, Joseph R.: 1908–1957; Republican Senator from Wisconsin, 1947–1957; chairman of the Senate permanent investigations subcommittee (Government Operations Committee)

McClellan, John L.: 1896–1977; Democratic Representative from Arkansas, 1935–1939; Democratic Senator from Arkansas, 1943–1977

McCone, John A.: b. 1902; Deputy to the Secretary of Defense, 1948–1950; Under Secretary of the Air Force, 1950–1951; Chairman, Atomic Energy Commission, 1958–1961; Director of Central Intelligence, CIA, November 1961–April 1965

McCulloch, William M. (Bill): 1901–1980; Republican Representative from Ohio, 1947–1973

McDonald, David J. (Dave): 1902–1979; president, United Steelworkers of America, 1952–1965

McHugh, General Godfrey T.: b. 1911; Air Force aide to John F. Kennedy, 1961–1963

McNamara, Robert S. (Bob): b. 1916; Secretary of Defense, January 1961–February 1968

McShane, James J. P. (Jim): 1916–1968; police officer; investigator, Senate Labor Rackets Committee, 1957–1960; Chief U.S. Marshal, 1961–1966?. McShane also escorted James Meredith to the University of Mississippi.

Meany, George: 1894–1980; president, AFL-CIO, 1955–1979

Menshikov, Mikhail A.: 1903?–1976; Soviet Ambassador to the United States, 1958–1962

Meredith, James H.: b. 1933; civil rights activist; the first black student to enter the University of Mississippi

Mikoyan, Anastas I.: 1895–1978; Soviet Deputy Premier, 1946–1964

Minow, Newton M. (Newt): b. 1926; Chairman, Federal Communications Commission, March 1961–June 1963

Mitchell, Clarence: 1911–1984; director, Washington bureau, National Association for the Advancement of Colored People, 1950–1978

Mollenhoff, Clark: b. 1921; journalist, Washington bureau, Cowles Publications, 1950–1969

Monroney, A. S. Michael (Mike): 1902–1980; Democratic Senator from Oklahoma, 1951–1969

Moscoso (Mora Rodriguez), (Jose) Teodoro: b. 1910; Ambassador to Venezuela, March–November 1961; Coordinator, Alliance for Progress, November 1961–May 1964

Moses, Robert P. (Bob): b. 1935; field secretary, Mississippi Student Nonviolent Coordinating Committee (SNCC), 1961–1965; director, Mississippi Council of Federated Organizations, 1962–1965; director, Mississippi Freedom Summer Project, 1964

Moss, Annie Lee: black teletype operator in the Signal Corps who was examined by Joseph McCarthy and Roy Cohn before the Senate Investigations Subcommittee about alleged Communist associations.

Moyers, Bill D.: b. 1934; White House Special Assistant, November 1963–June 1965; White House Press Secretary, July 1965–December 1966

Murphy, Charles S.: 1909–1983; Under Secretary of Agriculture, 1960–1965; Chairman, Civil Aeronautics Board, 1965–1968

Murphy, Robert: 1894–1978; Foreign Service officer; Deputy Under Secretary of State for Political Affairs

Murrow, Edward R. (Ed): 1908–1965; journalist, radio and television news broadcaster; Director, U.S. Information Agency, March 1961–January 1964

Nash, Diane: b. 1938; a student at Fisk University in Nashville, an early civil rights activist and head of the central committee of the Nashville Student Movement in the 1960s

Nehru, Jawaharlal: 1889–1964; first Prime Minister of independent India, 1947–1964

Nichols, Louis B.: b. 1906; assistant director of FBI, 1941–1951; assistant to the director of FBI, 1951–1957; executive vice president of Schenley Industries, Inc., 1957–1968

Nitze, Paul H.: b. 1907; Assistant Secretary of Defense for International Security Affairs, January 1961–October 1963; Secretary of the Navy, November 1963–June 1967. Nitze headed a task force on Cuba.

Nixon, Richard M.: b. 1913; Vice President of the United States, 1953–1961; Republican candidate for President, 1960; President of the United States, 1969–1974

Nkrumah, Kwame: 1909–1972; first President of Ghana, 1960–1966

Nolting, Frederick B., Jr.: b. 1911; Ambassador to South Vietnam, March 1961–August 1963

Norstad, Lauris: b. 1907; Supreme Commander, Allied Forces, Europe, April 1956–January 1963

Oberdorfer, Louis F. (Lou): b. 1919; Assistant Attorney General, Tax Division, Justice Department, 1961–1965

O'Boyle, Patrick A., Cardinal: b. 1896; Archbishop of Washington, 1948–1973; appointed Cardinal by Pope Paul VI, 1967

O'Brien, Lawrence E. (Larry): b. 1917; director of John F. Kennedy's Senate campaigns in 1952 and 1958, and the 1960 presidential campaign; Special Assistant to the President for Congressional Relations and Personnel, January 1961–August 1965

O'Connell, Daniel P. (Dan): 1887–1977; longtime head of Albany, New York, Democratic organization

O'Donnell, Kenneth P.: b. 1924; Special Assistant to the President, 1961–1965

Oehmann, Andrew F. (Andy): b. 1910; Executive Assistant to the U.S. Attorney General, 1961–1964

Onassis, Jacqueline Lee Bouvier Kennedy (Jackie): b. 1929; First Lady, January 1961–November 1963

Orrick, William H., Jr. (Bill): b. 1915; Assistant Attorney General, Civil Division, Justice Department, January 1961–June 1962; Deputy Secretary of

State for Administration, June 1962–May 1963; Assistant Attorney General, Antitrust Division, Justice Department, May 1963–April 1965

Parker, William H.: 1902–1966; Chief of Police, Los Angeles, California, 1950–1966

Patterson, John M.: b. 1921; Democratic Governor of Alabama, 1959–1963

Patton, James G. (Jim): 1902–1985; president, National Farmers Union, 1940–1966

Pincus, Walter H.: b. 1932; staff consultant to a Senate Foreign Relations Committee subcommittee investigating foreign government lobbying, 1962–1963

Pope, Allen L.: b. 1929?; CIA pilot captured in Indonesia in 1958 and condemned to death in 1960; released by Sukarno in 1962

Porter, Sylvia F.: b. 1913; financial columnist, editor, and author

Posner, William (Bill): 1915–1977; chairman, Monroe County (New York) Democratic Committee, June 1955–June 1961

Potter, Philip (Phil): b. 1907; reporter, *Baltimore Sun*; chief, New Delhi bureau, *Baltimore Sun*, 1961–1963; chief, Washington bureau, *Baltimore Sun*, 1964–1972; chief, London bureau, *Baltimore Sun*, 1972–1974

Powell, Adam Clayton, Jr.: 1908–1972; Democratic Representative from New York, 1945–1967, 1969

Powers, Francis Gary: 1929–1977; Central Intelligence Agency operative, 1956–1962. Powers was shot down during a U-2 espionage overflight of the Soviet Union on May 1, 1960.

Prendergast, Michael H. (Mike): b. 1913; chairman, New York State Democratic Committee

Randolph, A. Philip: 1889–1979; president, Brotherhood of Sleeping Car Porters, 1929–1968. Randolph worked with Bayard Rustin to organize the 1963 March on Washington for Jobs and Freedom.

Rauh, Joseph L., Jr. (Joe): b. 1911; lawyer active in liberal Democratic politics and civil rights activist; vice-chairman, Americans for Democratic Action, 1952–1955, 1957–1959; chief public spokesman for the ADA during the early 1960s; general counsel, Leadership Conference on Civil Rights, 1964–present

Rayburn, Samuel T. (Sam): 1882–1961; Democratic Representative from Texas, 1913–1961; Speaker of the House, 1940–1947, 1949–1953, 1955–1961

Reedy, George E., Jr.: b. 1917; Special Assistant to the Vice President, 1961; White House Press Secretary, March 1964–July 1965; White House Special Assistant, 1965–1966

Reis, Harold F.: b. 1916; First Assistant, Office of Legal Counsel, Justice Department, 1960–1964; Executive Assistant to the U.S. Attorney General, 1964–1967

Reston, James B. (Scotty): b. 1909; chief, Washington bureau, *The New York Times*, 1953–1964; associate editor, *The New York Times*, 1964–1968; executive editor, News and Sunday Departments, *The New York Times*, 1968–1969

Reuther, Walter P.: 1907–1970; president, United Automobile Workers, 1946–1970

Ribicoff, Abraham A. (Abe): b. 1910; Democratic Governor of Connecticut, 1952–1960; Secretary of Health, Education, and Welfare, January 1961–July 1962; Democratic Senator from Connecticut, 1963–1980

Rickover, Hyman G.: 1900–1986; Admiral; Director of Nuclear Propulsion, Naval Bureau of Ships, 1953–1981. Rickover championed the development of a nuclear Navy.

Roberts, Chalmers M.: b. 1910; chief diplomatic correspondent, *The Washington Post*, 1953–1971

Rockefeller, Nelson A.: 1908–1979; Republican Governor of New York, 1959–1973; Vice President of the United States, December 1974–January 1977

Rogers, William P. (Bill): b. 1913; U.S. Attorney General, 1957–1961

Rometsch, Ellie: one of the so-called party girls involved in the Bobby Baker scandal

Romney, George: b. 1907; chairman of the board and president, American Motors Corporation, 1954–1962; Republican Governor of Michigan, 1963–1969

Roosevelt, Eleanor R.: 1884–1962; First Lady, 1933–1945; delegate to the United Nations, 1945, 1949–1952, 1961–1962; Chairman, U.N. Commission on Human Rights, 1946–1951

Roosevelt, Franklin D., Jr.: b. 1914; one of several founders of ADA (Americans for Democratic Action), 1947; Liberal Representative from New York, 1949–1955; Under Secretary of Commerce, March 1963–May 1965

Roosevelt, Franklin D., Sr.: 1882–1945; 32nd U.S. President, 1933–1945

Rose, Frank A.: b. 1920; president, University of Alabama, 1958–1968

Rosenthal, Jacob (Jack): b. 1935; Assistant Director of Public Information, Justice Department, 1961–1964; Special Assistant to the U.S. Attorney General, 1964–1966

Rowe, James H., Jr. (Jim): b. 1909. A close friend and chief adviser to Lyndon Johnson for many years, Rowe served the Roosevelt administration as a member of several New Deal agencies and as secretary and assistant to President Roosevelt. He was Assistant U.S. Attorney General from 1941 to 1943 and counsel to the Democratic Policy Committee in 1956.

Rubirosa, Porfirio: 1909?–1965; Dominican-born diplomat

Rusk, Dean: b. 1909; Secretary of State, January 1961–January 1969

Russell, Richard B.: 1897–1971; Democratic Senator from Georgia, 1933–1971

Rustin, Bayard: 1910–1987; civil rights leader and close adviser to Martin Luther King, Jr.

Salinger, Pierre E. (George): b. 1925; press secretary for the 1960 Kennedy presidential campaign; White House Press Secretary, January 1961–March 1964

Saltonstall, Leverett: 1892–1979; Republican Senator from Massachusetts, 1944–1967

Sanford, James (Terry): b. 1917; Democratic Governor of North Carolina, 1961–1965

Sayre, Francis: b. 1915; member, President's Committee on Equal Employment Opportunity, 1961–1965; dean, Washington National Cathedral, 1951–1978

Schreiber, Walter R.: b. 1907; member, Tariff Commission, 1953–1964

Schwartz, Abba P.: b. 1916; Administrator, Bureau of Security and Consular Affairs, State Department, 1962–1965

Schwerner, Michael: one of three young civil rights workers reported missing on June 21, 1964, in Philadelphia, Mississippi. His body was found on August 4, 1964.

Scranton, William W.: b. 1917; Republican Representative from Pennsylvania, 1961–1963; Governor of Pennsylvania, 1963–1967

Segal, Bernard G. (Bernie): b. 1907; chairman, American Bar Association Standing Committee on the Federal Judiciary, 1956–1962; co-chairman, Lawyers Committee for Civil Rights Under Law, 1963–1965; president, American Bar Association, 1969–1970

Seigenthaler, John: b. 1927; journalist; Administrative Assistant to the U.S. Attorney General, 1961–1962

Sheridan, Walter J.: b. 1925; Special Assistant to the U.S. Attorney General, 1961–1964

Shriver, R. Sargent (Sarge): b. 1915; Director, Peace Corps, March 1961–February 1964; married Kennedy sister Eunice

Silberling, Edwyn (Ed): b. 1924; Special Assistant to the Attorney General, Organized Crime and Racketeering Section, Criminal Division, Justice Department, 1961–1963

Smathers, George A.: b. 1913; Democratic Senator from Florida, 1951–1969

Smith, Benjamin A.: b. 1916; Democratic Senator from Massachusetts, 1960–1962

Smith, Howard W.: 1883–1976; Democratic Representative from Virginia, 1931–1967

Smith, Jerome: b. 1939?; president, New Orleans chapter, Congress of Racial Equality

Smith, Reverend Kelly Miller: in the 1960s, president of the Nashville Christian Leadership Conference, the local affiliate of the Southern Christian Leadership Conference

Smith, Stephen E. (Steve): b. 1927; administrative assistant and presidential adviser; married Jean Kennedy

Sorensen, Theodore C. (Ted): b. 1928; John F. Kennedy's closest aide throughout his political career; Special Counsel to the President, January 1961–January 1964

Souvanna Phouma: 1901–1984; Laotian politician, headed coalition government established in 1962

Spaeth, Carl B.: b. 1907; dean and professor, Stanford Law School, 1946–1972; professor emeritus since 1972

Sparkman, John J.: b. 1899; Democratic Senator from Alabama, 1946–1979

Steele, John C.: b. 1917; chief, Washington bureau, Time-Life, Inc., 1958–1969

Stennis, John C.: b. 1901; Democratic Senator from Mississippi, 1947–present

Stevenson, Adlai E.: 1900–1965; Governor of Illinois, 1949–1953; Democratic candidate for President, 1952, 1956; Ambassador to the United Nations, January 1961–July 1965

Sukarno, Achmed: 1901–1970; President of Indonesia, 1949–1967

Sylvester, Arthur: b. 1901; Assistant Secretary of Defense for Public Affairs, January 1961–January 1967

Symington, William Stuart (Stu): b. 1901; Democratic Senator from Missouri, 1953–1977

Szulc, Tad: b. 1926; correspondent, Washington bureau, *The New York Times*, 1961–1965

Taft, William Howard: 1857–1930; jurist and 27th U.S. President, 1909–1913

Talmadge, Herman E.: b. 1913; Democratic Senator from Georgia, 1957–1981

Taylor, Hobart, Jr.: 1920–1981; Special Counsel, President's Committee on Equal Employment Opportunity, 1961–1962; Executive Vice President, President's Committee on Equal Employment, 1962–1965; Special Assistant and Associate Counsel to Lyndon Johnson, 1963–1965; Director, Export-Import Bank, 1965–1968

Taylor, Maxwell D.: 1901–1987; military representative of the President, July 1961–October 1961; Chairman, Joint Chiefs of Staff, October 1962–June 1964

Terris, Bruce J.: b. 1933; Assistant to Solicitor General, 1958–1965; co-chairman, National Conference on Law and Poverty, 1965; assistant director, National Crime Commission, 1965–1967

Thomas, Norman: 1884–1968; American Socialist leader; Socialist candidate for President, 1928–1948

Thompson, Llewellyn E., Jr. (Tommy): 1904–1972; Ambassador to the Soviet Union, April 1957–August 1962, January 1967–January 1969; Ambassador at Large and Special Adviser on Soviet Affairs to the Secretary of State, August 1962–October 1966

Tito, Josip Broz: 1892–1980; first President of the Republic of Yugoslavia, 1953–1980

Touré, Sékou: 1922–1984; President of Guinea, 1958–1984

Trammel, Seymore: b. 1920; lawyer; Wallace campaign adviser, 1968, 1970, 1972; Director of State Finances for Alabama, 1963–1968

Troutman, Robert B., Jr. (Bob): b. 1918; Kennedy family friend and adviser; John Kennedy's personal liaison to the 1960 Democratic convention in Los Angeles; campaign director for the southern states, 1960; presidential aide, 1961–1963

Trujillo Molina, Rafael Leonidas: 1891–1961; President of the Dominican Republic, 1930–1938, 1942–1952. Trujillo retained dictatorial authority until his assassination in May 1961.

Tucker, William H., Jr. (Bill): b. 1923; member, Interstate Commerce Commission, 1961–1967; Chairman, Interstate Commerce Commission, 1967

Tuttle, Elbert Parr: b. 1897; judge, U.S. Court of Appeals, 5th Circuit, 1954–1961; chief judge, 1961–1967

Udall, Stewart Lee: b. 1920; Democratic Representative from Arizona, 1954–1961; Secretary of the Interior, 1961–1969

Valachi, Joseph M.: 1904?–1971; member of the Genovese organized crime family who testified before the Senate Rackets Committee

Vance, Cyrus R. (Cy): b. 1917; General Counsel, Department of Defense, January 1961–June 1962; Secretary of the Army, July 1962–January 1964

Vandiver, S. Ernest: b. 1918; Democratic Governor of Georgia, 1959–1963

Wagner, Robert F., Jr.: b. 1910; Mayor of New York, 1954–1965; Ambassador to Spain, 1968–1969

Walker, Edwin A.: b. 1909; Major General, U.S. Army, 1957–1961

Wallace, George C.: b. 1919. Wallace was elected Governor of Alabama four times (1962, 1970, 1974, and 1982) and ran unsuccessfully for the presidency of the United States in 1968, 1972, and 1976.

Walsh, Lawrence E.: b. 1912; lawyer; Deputy U.S. Attorney General, 1957–1960

Warren, Earl: 1891–1974; Chief Justice, U.S. Supreme Court, September 1953–June 1969

Webb, James E.: b. 1906; director, National Aeronautics and Space Administration, February 1961–October 1968

Welsh, Matthew E.: b. 1912; Democratic Governor of Indiana, 1961–1965

West, Elmer G.: b. 1914; judge, U.S. District Court, Eastern District of Louisiana, 1961–1967

Wheeler, Earle G.: 1908–1975; Staff Director, Office of the Joint Chiefs of Staff, 1960–1962; Army Chief of Staff, October 1962–July 1964; Chairman, Joint Chiefs of Staff, July 1964–July 1970

White, Byron R.: b. 1917; Deputy U.S. Attorney General, January 1961–April 1962; Associate Justice, U.S. Supreme Court, 1962–present; John F. Kennedy's first Supreme Court nominee

Wilkins, Roy: 1901–1981; executive secretary, National Association for the Advancement of Colored People (NAACP), 1955–1977

Williams, Enrico: one-time head engineer and general manager of the biggest mining company in Cuba; Cuban rebel who participated in the Bay of Pigs

Williams, G. ("Soapy") Mennen: 1911–1988; Democratic Governor of Michigan, 1949–1961; Assistant Secretary of State for African Affairs, February 1961–March 1966

Williams, John Bell: 1918–1983; Democratic Representative from Mississippi, 1947–1968

Willis, Edwin E.: 1904–1972; Democratic Representative from Louisiana, 1949–1969

Wilson, Donald M.: b. 1925; reporter, *Life* magazine, 1949–1953; chief Far Eastern correspondent, *Life,* 1953–1956; chief Washington correspondent, 1956–1960; Deputy Director, U.S. Information Agency, 1961–1965; general manager, Time-Life International, 1965–1968

Wine, James W. (Jim): b. 1918; assistant general-secretary, National Council of Churches, 1950–1960; Ambassador to Luxembourg, 1961–1962; Ambassador to the Ivory Coast, 1962–1967; Special Assistant to the Secretary of State for Refugee and Migration Affairs, 1967–1968

Wirtz, W. Willard (Bill): b. 1912; Under Secretary of Labor, January 1961–September 1962; Secretary of Labor, September 1962–January 1969

Wofford, Harris L., Jr.: b. 1926; civil rights adviser to the 1960 Kennedy presidential campaign; Special Assistant to the President for Civil Rights, 1961–1962; Peace Corps Special Representative for Africa, Director of the Peace Corps Ethiopia Program, 1962–1964; Associate Director, Peace Corps, 1964–1966

Woodward, Robert F.: b. 1908; Foreign Service officer; Ambassador to Costa Rica, 1954–1958; Ambassador to Uruguay, 1958–1961; Ambassador to Chile, 1961; Assistant Secretary of State for Inter-American Affairs, 1961–1962; Ambassador to Spain, 1962–1965

Wright, J. Skelly: b. 1911; judge, U.S. District Court, 1949–1962; judge, U.S. Court of Appeals, District of Columbia Circuit, appointed 1962

Yarmolinsky, Adam: b. 1922; Special Assistant to the Secretary of Defense, January 1961–September 1965

Yates, Sidney R.: b. 1909; Democratic Congressman from Illinois, 1949–1963, 1965–present

THE KENNEDY PRESIDENCY: A CHRONOLOGY

1960

January 3: Senator John Fitzgerald Kennedy announces his candidacy for the Democratic presidential nomination.

February 1: Four black college students stage a sit-in at a Woolworth lunch counter, initiating a wave of similar protests.

April 21: Congress approves a voting rights act to prevent intimidation of black voters in the South.

July 13: Kennedy wins the Democratic presidential nomination. Lyndon Johnson is selected as his running mate.

1961

January 3: U.S. breaks diplomatic relations with Cuba.

January 20: John F. Kennedy is inaugurated as the thirty-fifth President of the United States.

January 31: The House votes to expand the Rules Committee from twelve members to fifteen.

March 1: By executive order, Kennedy creates the Peace Corps.

March 13: Kennedy proposes the Alliance for Progress, a U.S.-Latin American social and economic development project.

March 21: Kennedy and British Prime Minister Harold Macmillan meet at Key West.

March 23: Kennedy calls for an end to Communist involvement in Laos.

April 12: Soviet cosmonaut Yuri Gagarin becomes the first man to orbit the earth.

April 17–20: Cuban exiles undertake U.S.-sponsored Bay of Pigs invasion.

May 5: Commander Alan Shephard, Jr., makes the first U.S. manned suborbital space flight.

May 14: Violence erupts against Freedom Riders in Anniston, Alabama.

May 21: Freedom Riders are attacked at Montgomery, Alabama, bus terminal. Presidential aide John Seigenthaler is knocked unconscious. Robert Kennedy orders federal marshals to the scene.

May 22: Martin Luther King, Jr., addresses a mass rally at Ralph Abernathy's First Baptist Church in Montgomery while an angry mob surrounds the church and threatens those inside in a violent confrontation.

May 31: President Kennedy travels to Paris to confer with President Charles de Gaulle.

June 3–4: Kennedy and Khrushchev meet for a two-day summit in Geneva.

June 30: Kennedy signs the Housing Act of 1961.

September 16: U.S. announces its support for U.N. military action in Katanga.

October 1: Kennedy receives a request from South Vietnam for a bilateral defense treaty with the U.S.

October 27: Russian and American tanks face down one another in a tense confrontation at the Berlin border.

November 3: Maxwell Taylor returns from Vietnam and reports that U.S. aid can bring victory.

November 26: The State Department undergoes a high-level reorganization. George Ball replaces Chester Bowles as Under Secretary of State.

December 15–17: Kennedy conducts a good-will tour of Colombia, Puerto Rico, and Venezuela.

1962

January 6: U.S. resumes diplomatic ties with the Dominican Republic.

February 20: Astronaut John Glenn becomes the first American to orbit the earth: He circles three times in his Mercury space capsule.

March 13: Kennedy calls for increased allocations for foreign aid in fiscal year 1963.

March 14: The 17-nation U.N. disarmament conference opens in Geneva.

March 26: In *Baker* v. *Carr,* the Supreme Court holds that the federal judiciary has the constitutional authority to scrutinize the apportionment of seats in state legislatures.

April 10–13: Steel companies announce a hike in steel prices and then rescind it after vigorous protest from the Kennedy administration.

May 15: In response to renewed fighting, the U.S. sends naval and ground forces to Laos to support anti-Communist troops.

October 1: James Meredith becomes the first black student to enroll at the University of Mississippi after a night of violence resulting in two deaths and scores of injuries. Federal troops are needed to quell rioting and compel compliance with court orders to admit Meredith.

October 16: Kennedy convenes the Executive Committee of the National Security Council (ExComm) to discuss photographic evidence of Russian missile bases in Cuba.

October 22: Kennedy announces the existence of Soviet missile bases in Cuba and imposes a naval quarantine on the island. Soviet ships sail toward the blockade.

October 28: Kennedy and Khrushchev reach agreement to end the Cuban missile crisis.

November 6: Midterm elections: the Democrats retain majorities in both houses of Congress (gaining four seats in the Senate and losing six in the House); the Republicans win gubernatorial races in Pennsylvania, Ohio, and Michigan; Richard Nixon loses the California gubernatorial race to Edmund G. Brown; and Edward Kennedy is elected to the Senate.

November 20: By executive order, President Kennedy bars racial discrimination in federally funded housing.

November 20: The U.S. naval blockade of Cuba is lifted.

December 24: Cuba releases 1,113 prisoners from the 1961 Bay of Pigs invasion in exchange for shipments of medical supplies.

December 31: The joint U.S.-Great Britain Skybolt missile project is canceled.

1963

March 21: A reduction in U.S. foreign aid programs is recommended by investigative panel chaired by General Lucius Clay.

April 12–May 10: A series of civil rights demonstrations, police assaults, and riots in Birmingham, Alabama, culminates in an agreement to integrate business facilities.

May 12: Federal troops are dispatched to Fort McClellan, outside of Birmingham, when renewed rioting occurs.

June 10: Kennedy delivers American University policy address.

June 11: Over the protest of Governor George Wallace, two black students enroll at the University of Alabama.

June 11: Kennedy delivers a major civil rights address in a nationally televised appearance.

June 19: Kennedy submits a comprehensive civil rights bill to Congress.

June 26: Kennedy, visiting Berlin at the outset of a European tour, delivers his *"Ich bin ein Berliner"* address.

July 18–19: U.S. suspends relations with Peru following a military coup.

August 2: U.S. cuts off economic aid to Haiti.

August 5: U.S., Great Britain, and the Soviet Union sign a partial nuclear test ban treaty halting atmospheric, underwater, and outer-space testing.

August 23: More than 250,000 people participate in the civil rights March on Washington.

September 24: The Senate ratifies the partial nuclear test ban treaty.

September 25: U.S. suspends diplomatic relations with the Dominican Republic after a successful military coup against President Juan Bosch.

November 1: South Vietnamese President Diem is assassinated in a successful military coup.

November 22: President John F. Kennedy is assassinated in Dallas, Texas.

INDEX

ABOUT THE EDITORS

From 1961 to 1965, EDWIN GUTHMAN was Robert Kennedy's Special Assistant for Public Information in the Department of Justice, and Kennedy's first senatorial Press Secretary. Guthman's career in journalism began in 1941, when he became a reporter for the *Seattle Star*. After World War II, during which he was awarded the Purple Heart and the Silver Star, Guthman returned to the *Star*. In 1947 he joined the *Seattle Times* as a general-assignment reporter specializing in political and investigative journalism. Edwin Guthman won the Pulitzer Prize for national reporting in 1950. From 1965 to 1977 he was national editor of the *Los Angeles Times* and, from 1977 to 1987, editor of the *Philadelphia Inquirer*. He is the author of *We Band of Brothers* (1971), a memoir of Robert Kennedy, and is currently the Gannett Foundation Distinguished Professor of Journalism, University of Southern California.

JEFFREY SHULMAN received his doctorate in English literature from the University of Wisconsin, Madison, in 1980. He teaches in the department of English at Georgetown University. In 1984, he became managing editor of University Publications of America. In 1986, with John Moscato, he founded Twenty-First Century Books, of which he is currently president.